Solutions and Suggestions to Accompany

Logic and Rational Thought

Frank R. Harrison III

University of Georgia

West Publishing Company
St. Paul   New York   Los Angeles   San Francisco

99 98 97 96 95 94 93 92   8 7 6 5 4 3 2 1 0

ISBN 0–314–82965–2

Hello ---

Logic **and** **Rational** **Thought** is offered as a tool to help present an exceptionally good course in logic--formal, informal, or a combination of both. Of course, the success of any course ultimately rests with you, the instructor. The best of books cannot replace the enthusiasm that an instructor has for the subject being taught, skill at communicating that subject, concern for the student learning the material, and a wide scope of interests and knowledge that can be continually drawn on for timely examples. I have kept such qualities in mind while writing this book. Hopefully, then, **Logic** **and** **Rational** **Thought** will enhance your personal style of teaching logic. I should like to know your reactions to this book as you use it, as well as the opinions of your students. Now, several comments about this manual.

"A strange thing happened on the way to the --- " printers! Originally I had placed solutions to all odd numbered exercises in the back of the text. When the editor saw, in print, these 196 pages, he feared that this would make the book too long. Indeed, the text would have been over 730 pages. So, some of the solutions to the odd numbered exercises have been moved from the back of **Logic** **and** **Rational** **Thought** to **Solutions** **and** **Suggestions**. Since this manual was already typed and paged, these odd numbered exercises were not slipped in with the even numbered answers. Rather they are attached as "Part Two," while "Part One" contains answers to the even numbered exercises.

Notations such as **'1.3.A.'** appear in **Solutions** **and** **Suggestions**. The first entry indicates the specific chapter in which the exercises are found. The second entry designates the section of that chapter. The capital letter, if there is one, indicates the group of exercises in that section.

For some exercises the students are to supply personal answers. **1.1.A.** is an example. These exercises are often good "ice breakers" in a class. Students can respond, present some reasons for their position, and be encouraged by the instructor and their peers.

Other than truth tables, it is often the case that more than one "correct answer" (e.g., proofs showing the validity of a particular argument interpreted deductively) can be provided. Those answers in the back of the text and in this manual are, therefore, **guides**. For instance, the suggested proofs are often not the shortest possible nor the most elegant. However, they do follow the conventions and strategies developed in the text. Indeed, a bit of competition can be introduced into the work of students by encouraging them to construct proofs different from those found in the textbook. In analyzing exercises dealing with fallacies, I have suggested the fallacy, or fallacies, that seems the most blatant in an argument. Students may find others. When they do, it is well to make them explain their reasons for claiming that such-and-such is a fallacy.

When considering fallacies, it is important for students to understand that everything that looks like a fallacy is not one. First, assuming a particular error--say ambiguity--it might not appear in an argument. Hence, by definition, that error cannot be a fallacy in that context. Second, there are appropriate uses of, for example, appeals to authority. What is appropriate needs to be distinguised from what is fallacious. Third, students need to realize that they can commit a fallacy by accepting a fallacious argument when they are in a position to detect the fallacy but do not. The demands of rationality fall on both the presenter and receiver of what is said, and not only in arguments.

Using **Logic and Rational Thought**, you will find it extremely flexible. For instance, each chapter not only provides opportunities for further development of the topics introduced there, but also the chance to raise new, related issues. Chapters 1 and 13-15 are good examples.

In Chapter 1 the concepts of description, explanation, and argument could be discussed further, especially stressing that how a passage functions is dictated by the context in which it is used. You might wish to point out that there are types of non-deductive arguments other than inductive ones. Analogical arguments are good examples to introduce here. The importance of backgrounds, world views, gestalts, or whatever term you might prefer, is also an interesting topic to consider especially in treating the non-formal aspects of logic. In discussing the differences between sentences and statements, the concepts token and type can be introduced. Here you can also explain that some sentences are used to mention statements. And how logic and rational thought are useful in the everyday and professional life of the student cannot be stressed too much, nor too many examples of justifications of the usefulness of logic given. Students want a reply to "Why bother with logic and rational thought, anyway?" And they should be given one.

Chapters 13-15 also provide a number of possible topics to introduce in your discussions. Chapter 13 presents various openings into discussions concerning different views of how to understand what language is and how it functions. And while I have used Carnapian terminology, I do not wish to defend the philosophical underpinnings of Positivism historically associated with this terminology. One topic you might want to develop more fully in these chapters is _rational thought_. This can be done in relation to the grasp of logic that students have gained to this point in their studies. In discussing the concept _rational thought_ and fallacies, I typically find it important to amplify and argue for the thesis that if there is no universally agreed upon "correct" answer or solution to a particular question or problem, it does not follow that the question or problem is "subjective" in the sense that anyone's views are as good as anyone else's. The successful practice of rational thought demands many of the qualities that a connoisseur of anything must develop. Students, all too often trained to think in terms of "true/false" and "black/white," often find this point difficult to grasp.

There are, besides **Solutions and Suggestions**, two other auxiliary works that can be helpful to you. The first of these is a collection of new exercises, along with their answers, for each chapter of **Logic and Rational Thought**. These were prepared by Professor Eric Kraemer of the University of Wisconsin, La Crosse. Professor Kraemer has done an excellent job, and his material should be most helpful in supplying further exercises for students and creating quizzes and examinations. Second, I have customized "The LogicWorks" software (Philosophy Documentation Center) for use with the text. For the most part, the even numbered exercises of each chapter have been included. I have also retained some of the exercises used by Professor Rob Brady, author of "The LogicWorks." With "The Logic-Works" you can now send your students to a computer for practice with any chapter in **Logic and Rational Thought**. I find the computer an enticement to lure the student into practicing more. At first I was skeptical about using the computer for drill in logic. Now I am a "believer."

I wish to extend my special thanks in the preparation of **Solutions and Suggestions** to Messers Frank Scarpace and Mike Thompson of **Image Processing Software, Inc.**, located in Madison, Wisconsin. This company developed and distributes "<u>TURBOFONTS</u>," the software I used to type all of the logical notation both in the text and this manual. Frank and Mike are extremely helpful and courteous, willing to spend large amounts of time with their customers.

Although **Solutions and Suggestions** has been proofread many times, there are no doubt errors in it. If you find one, please let me know what and where it is. I shall correct it for any future printing. Of course, I should also appreciate your doing the same with any error you find in **Logic and Rational Thought**.

I hope that you and your students enjoy **Logic and Rational Thought**, and that it helps to make the mastery of logic easier and more profitable for all concerned.

Most cordially ---

Athens, Georgia

CONTENTS

```
************
**************

**** PART ONE ****

***************
*************
```

ANSWERS FOR EVEN NUMBERED EXERCISES

1.1.A.

The students are to supply their own views here. A good deal of "debate" can be generated in a class discussion revolving around this question. Even though much of such a discussion might be misguided, logically wrong, or simply naive, this is an opportunity for a class to come together and develop some excitement about logic.

1.1.B.

Here is an occasion to encourage the students to speak up, to voice their views, and to come to know one another somewhat better. The instructor can use this as a opportunity to gently point out, where legitimate, the wrong paths in logic any student might be taking. It is better still for the instructor to have other students point out flaws in presentations. The instructor might wish to begin introducing distinctions such as the form of an argument and the content of that argument, and the distinctions drawn between accepting positions as if true to see what follows from them and attempting to ascertain the truth of those positions.

1.2.

2.

   1) The Russian government is totally atheistic.

   2) **Any government that is totally atheistic is corrupt.**   [added premise]

   3) So, the Russian government is obviously corrupt.

4.

    1)   Men wearing glasses are perceived to be more intelligent and affluent than men who don't.

    2)   <u>Young men who appear intelligent and affluent are more impressive than those who don't appear that way</u>. [added premise]

    3)   <u>Young men should do what they can to impress their superiors</u>. [added premise]

    4)   Thus, young men should wear glasses in order to impress their superiors.

6.

    1)   Pursuing a professional degree provides one with specialized training for a specific job.

    2)   Pursuing a professional degree does not provide one with broad views, cultural appreciation, and moral values.

    3)   <u>A business degree is a professional degree</u>. [added premise]

    4)   Amy is pursuing a business degree.

    5)   Hence, while Amy's business will provide her with specialized training for a specific job, nonetheless it will not provide her with broad views, ultural appreciation, and moral values.

8.

    1)   Every time there is excessive greed, corruption and a general loss of the old virtues of the Republic, the dollar falls and the market collapses.

    2)   <u>Currently there is a great deal of greed, corruption and a general loss of the old virtues of this Republic</u>. [added premise]

    3)   Accordingly, the recent fall of the dollar and the collapse of the stock market could've been predicted.

10.

    1) To pass analytic chemistry, a person has to work very hard and be well prepared.

    2) **Dottie is taking analytic chemistry.** [added premise]

    3) Consequently, Dottie has to work very hard and be well prepared.

12.

    1) The probability is very high that anyone with the retrovirous <u>HTLV-3</u> will develop <u>AIDS</u>.

    2) Chuch has the retrovirous <u>HTLV-3</u>.

    3) Subsequently, Chuch will probably develop <u>AIDS</u>.

14.

    1) Family income is a measurement of the well-being of the national economy as a whole.

    2) The majority of families have a higher income than they did four years ago.

    3) Thus, the national economy, as a whole, is better now that it was four years ago.

1.3.A.

2. <u>Description</u>

4. <u>Argument</u>

    1) If I'm determined to do well in this assignment, I ought to study.

    2) If I ought to study, I can't go out tonight.

    3) I'm determined to so well in this assignment.

4) Consequently, I can't go out tonight.

6. Explanation

8. Argument

   1) Louis will be here today or he'll be here tomorrow.

   2) Louis hasn't come today.

   3) So, Louis will be here tomorrow.

10. Argument

   1) Tomorrow there is going to be heavy snow or rain.

   2) Tomorrow is Friday.

   3) If there is heavy snow or rain, I don't go to class.

   4) If it is Friday, I don't go to class.

   5) Hence. I'm not going to class tomorrow.

12. Explanation

14. Argument

   1) Any satisfactory system of physical explanation must be able to explain phenomena at the level of sub-atomic "particles" and phenomena at great astronomical distances.

   2) Newtonian mechanics can explain neither phenomena at the level of subatomic "particles" nor phenomena at great astronomical distances.

   3) Therefore, Newtonian mechanics isn't a satisfactory system of physical explanation.

1.3.B.

Having the students go to newspapers, magazines, journals, and the like for examples serves several ends. One of these is to show that logic **is applicable** outside of the classroom.

1.3.C.

Here is another opportunity for the student to stand before his peers, to defend some position, and for the instructor to encourage the students in their work.

1.4.

1. Deductively valid

2. Deductively invalid; inductively weak

3. Deductively invalid; inductively weak

4. Deductively valid

5. Deductively invalid; inductively weak

6. Deductively valid

7. Deductively invalid; inductively weak

8. Deductively invalid; inductively weak

9. Deductively valid

10. Deductively valid

11. Deductively invalid; inductively weak

12. Deductively invalid; inductively weak

13. Deductively valid

14. Deductively invalid; inductively strong

15. Deductively invalid; inductively strong

CHAPTER 2

2.3.

2.   ∿W

4.   ∿P

6.   V

8.   ∿I

10. ∿P

12. Q

14. S

2.4.

2.   O · B

4.   J · D

6.   P · ∿T

8.   A · V

10. L · ∿A

12. P · R

14. T · G

2.5.

2.   R ∨ ∿M

4.   M △ D

6.   ∿P ∨ ∿K

8.   M ∨ R

10. E △ ∿S

12. E ∨ ∿T

14. A △ ∿S

2.6.

2.   ∿M ∨ ∿G

4.   ∿(M ∨ G)

6.   C · ∿(R ∨ A)

8.   (K · A) △ S

10. (∿M · P) △ A

12. D ∨ (∿P · ∿M)

14. ∿{∿T · ∿[∿(E ∨ C) ∨ ∿(S ∨ Q)]}

2.7.

2.

A	B	∿A	∿B	∿A · ∿B
1	1	0	0	0
1	0	0	1	0
0	1	1	0	0
0	0	1	1	1

4.

A	B	∿A	∿B	∿A v ∿B
1	1	0	0	0
1	0	0	1	1
0	1	1	0	1
0	0	1	1	1

6.

A	B	∿A	∿A ∨ B	∿(∿A ∨ B)
1	1	0	1	0
1	0	0	0	1
0	1	1	1	0
0	0	1	1	0

8.

A	C	B	A · C	∿(A · C)	∿(A · C) Δ B
1	1	1	1	0	1
1	1	0	1	0	0
1	0	1	0	1	0
1	0	0	0	1	1
0	1	1	0	1	0
0	1	0	0	1	1
0	0	1	0	1	0
0	0	0	0	1	1

10.

C	B	A	D	∼B	∼A	C ∨ ∼B	∼A ∨ D	(C∨∼B) · (∼A∨D)
1	1	1	1	0	0	1	1	1
1	1	1	0	0	0	1	0	0
1	1	0	1	0	1	1	1	1
1	1	0	0	0	1	1	1	1
1	0	1	1	1	0	1	1	1
1	0	1	0	1	0	1	0	0
1	0	0	1	1	1	1	1	1
1	0	0	0	1	1	1	1	1
0	1	1	1	0	0	0	1	0
0	1	1	0	0	0	0	0	0
0	1	0	1	0	1	0	1	0
0	1	0	0	0	1	0	1	0
0	0	1	1	1	0	1	1	1
0	0	1	0	1	0	1	0	0
0	0	0	1	1	1	1	1	1
0	0	0	0	1	1	1	1	1

2.8.A.

2.   B ⊃ N

4.   C ⊃ D

6.   (C ∨ D) ⊃ (C ⊃ A)

8.   ∼(M ∨ Y) ⊃ T

10. (A Δ N) ⊃ S

12. (P ⊃ K) · (K ⊃ ∼F)

14. (D ∨ ∼A) ⊃ [∼H ⊃∼(C ∨ I)]

2.8.B.

2.

B	N	B ⊃ N
1	1	1
1	0	0
0	1	1
0	0	1

4.

C	D	C ⊃ D
1	1	1
1	0	0
0	1	1
0	0	1

6.

C	D	A	C ∨ D	C ⊃ A	(C ∨ D) ⊃ (C ⊃ A)
1	1	1	1	1	1
1	1	0	1	0	0
1	0	1	1	1	1
1	0	0	1	0	0
0	1	1	1	1	1
0	1	0	1	1	1
0	0	1	0	1	1
0	0	0	0	1	1

8.

M	Y	T	M ∨ Y	∿(M ∨ Y)	∿(M ∨ Y) ⊃ T
1	1	1	1	0	1
1	1	0	1	0	1
1	0	1	1	0	1
1	0	0	1	0	1
0	1	1	1	0	1
0	1	0	1	0	1
0	0	1	0	1	1
0	0	0	0	1	0

10.

A	N	S	A △ N	(A △ N) ⊃ S
1	1	1	0	1
1	1	0	0	1
1	0	1	1	1
1	0	0	1	0
0	1	1	1	1
0	1	0	1	0
0	0	1	0	1
0	0	0	0	1

12.

P	K	F	∿F	P ⊃ K	K ⊃ ∿F	(P ⊃ K) • (K ⊃ ∿F)
1	1	1	0	1	0	0
1	1	0	1	1	1	1
1	0	1	0	0	1	0
1	0	0	1	0	1	0
0	1	1	0	1	0	0
0	1	0	1	1	1	1
0	0	1	0	1	1	1
0	0	0	1	1	1	1

14.

D	A	H	C	I	~A	~H	D ∨ ~A	C ∨ I	~(C ∨ I) → con't
1	1	1	1	1	0	0	1	1	0
1	1	1	1	0	0	0	1	1	0
1	1	1	0	1	0	0	1	1	0
1	1	1	0	0	0	0	1	0	1
1	1	0	1	1	0	1	1	1	0
1	1	0	1	0	0	1	1	1	0
1	1	0	0	1	0	1	1	1	0
1	1	0	0	0	0	1	1	0	1
1	0	1	1	1	1	0	1	1	0
1	0	1	1	0	1	0	1	1	0
1	0	1	0	1	1	0	1	1	0
1	0	1	0	0	1	0	1	0	1
1	0	0	1	1	1	1	1	1	0
1	0	0	1	0	1	1	1	1	0
1	0	0	0	1	1	1	1	1	0
1	0	0	0	0	1	1	1	0	1
0	1	1	1	1	0	0	0	1	0
0	1	1	1	0	0	0	0	1	0
0	1	1	0	1	0	0	0	1	0
0	1	1	0	0	0	0	0	0	1
0	1	0	1	1	0	1	0	1	0
0	1	0	1	0	0	1	0	1	0
0	1	0	0	1	0	1	0	1	0
0	1	0	0	0	0	1	0	0	1
0	0	1	1	1	1	0	1	1	0
0	0	1	1	0	1	0	1	1	0
0	0	1	0	1	1	0	1	1	0
0	0	1	0	0	1	0	1	0	1
0	0	0	1	1	1	1	1	1	0
0	0	0	1	0	1	1	1	1	0
0	0	0	0	1	1	1	1	1	0
0	0	0	0	0	1	1	1	0	1

con't →

~H ⊃ ~(C ∨ I)	(D ∨ ~ A) ⊃ [~ H ⊃ ~(C ∨ I)]
1	1
1	1
1	1
1	1
0	0
0	0
0	0
1	1
1	1
1	1
1	1
1	1
0	0
0	0
0	0
1	1
1	1
1	1
1	1
1	1
0	0
0	0
0	0
1	1
1	1
1	1
1	1
1	1
0	0
0	0
0	0
1	1

2.9.A.

2. O ≡ ∿B

4. F ⊃ (S ≡ A)

6. R ≡ (∿M ∨ ∿J)

8. [(G ≡ P) · (P ≡ S)] ⊃ (G ≡ S)

10. R ≡ [C · ∿(T ∨ P)]

12. (W ⊃ P) ≡ (∿B · ∿A)

14. (A · I) ≡ [(P · S) ⊃ (A · ∿B)]

2.9.B.

2.

O	B	∿B	O ≡ ∿B
1	1	0	0
1	0	1	1
0	1	0	1
0	0	1	0

4.

F	S	A	S ≡ A	F ⊃ (S ≡ A)
1	1	1	1	1
1	1	0	0	0
1	0	1	0	0
1	0	0	1	1
0	1	1	1	1
0	1	0	0	1
0	0	1	0	1
0	0	0	1	1

6.

R	M	J	∿M	∿J	∿M ∨ ∿J	R ≡ (∿M ∨ ∿J)
1	1	1	0	0	0	0
1	1	0	0	1	1	1
1	0	1	1	0	1	1
1	0	0	1	1	1	1
0	1	1	0	0	0	1
0	1	0	0	1	1	0
0	0	1	1	0	1	0
0	0	0	1	1	1	0

8.

G	P	S	G ≡ P	P ≡ S	G ≡ S	(G≡P) · (P≡S) —con't
1	1	1	1	1	1	1
1	1	0	1	0	0	0
1	0	1	0	0	1	0
1	0	0	0	1	0	0
0	1	1	0	1	0	0
0	1	0	0	0	1	0
0	0	1	1	0	0	0
0	0	0	1	1	1	1

continued →	[(G ≡ P) · (P ≡ S)] ⊃ (G ≡ S)
	1
	1
	1
	1
	1
	1
	1

16

10.

R	C	T	P	T ∨ P	∿(T∨P)	C · ∿(T∨P)	R ≡ [C· ∿(T∨P)]
1	1	1	1	1	0	0	0
1	1	1	0	1	0	0	0
1	1	0	1	1	0	0	0
1	1	0	0	0	1	1	1
1	0	1	1	1	0	0	0
1	0	1	0	1	0	0	0
1	0	0	1	1	0	0	0
1	0	0	0	0	1	0	0
0	1	1	1	1	0	0	1
0	1	1	0	1	0	0	1
0	1	0	1	1	0	0	1
0	1	0	0	0	1	1	0
0	0	1	1	1	0	0	1
0	0	1	0	1	0	0	1
0	0	0	1	1	0	0	1
0	0	0	0	0	1	0	1

12.

W	P	B	A	∿B	∿A	W ⊃ P	∿B · ∿A	(W⊃P) ≡ (∿B· ∿A)
1	1	1	1	0	0	1	0	0
1	1	1	0	0	1	1	0	0
1	1	0	1	1	0	1	0	0
1	1	0	0	1	1	1	1	1
1	0	1	1	0	0	0	0	1
1	0	1	0	0	1	0	0	1
1	0	0	1	1	0	0	0	1
1	0	0	0	1	1	0	1	0
0	1	1	1	0	0	1	0	0
0	1	1	0	0	1	1	0	0
0	1	0	1	1	0	1	0	0
0	1	0	0	1	1	1	1	1
0	0	1	1	0	0	1	0	0
0	0	1	0	0	1	1	0	0
0	0	0	1	1	0	1	0	0
0	0	0	0	1	1	1	1	1

14.

A	I	P	S	B	$\sim$B	A · I	P · S	A · $\sim$B →con't
1	1	1	1	1	0	1	1	0
1	1	1	1	0	1	1	1	1
1	1	1	0	1	0	1	0	0
1	1	1	0	0	1	1	0	1
1	1	0	1	1	0	1	0	0
1	1	0	1	0	1	1	0	1
1	1	0	0	1	0	1	0	0
1	1	0	0	0	1	1	0	1
1	0	1	1	1	0	0	1	0
1	0	1	1	0	1	0	1	1
1	0	1	0	1	0	0	0	0
1	0	1	0	0	1	0	0	1
1	0	0	1	1	0	0	0	0
1	0	0	1	0	1	0	0	1
1	0	0	0	1	0	0	0	0
1	0	0	0	0	1	0	0	1
0	1	1	1	1	0	0	1	0
0	1	1	1	0	1	0	1	0
0	1	1	0	1	0	0	0	0
0	1	1	0	0	1	0	0	0
0	1	0	1	1	0	0	0	0
0	1	0	1	0	1	0	0	0
0	1	0	0	1	0	0	0	0
0	1	0	0	0	1	0	0	0
0	0	1	1	1	0	0	1	0
0	0	1	1	0	1	0	1	0
0	0	1	0	1	0	0	0	0
0	0	1	0	0	1	0	0	0
0	0	0	1	1	0	0	0	0
0	0	0	1	0	1	0	0	0
0	0	0	0	1	0	0	0	0
0	0	0	0	0	1	0	0	0

	(P• S) ⊃ (A• ∿B)	(A• I) ≡ [(P• S) ⊃ (A• ∿B)]
	0	0
	1	1
	1	1
	1	1
	1	1
	1	1
	1	1
	1	1
	0	1
	1	0
	1	0
	1	0
	1	0
	1	0
	1	0
	0	1
	0	1
	1	0
	1	0
	1	0
	1	0
	1	0
	1	0
	0	1
	0	1
	1	0
	1	0
	1	0
	1	0
	1	0
	1	0

CHAPTER 3

3.1.

2.

∿	O	·	N
0	1	0	1
0	1	0	0
1	0	1	1
1	0	0	0
		⇑	

4.

G	∨	D
1	1	1
1	1	0
0	1	1
0	0	0
	⇑	

6.

O	⊃	(R	⊃	O)
1	1	1	1	1
1	1	0	1	1
0	1	1	0	0
0	1	0	1	0
	⇑			

8.

(V	⊃	S)	·	(∿	W	⊃	∿	S)
1	1	1	1	0	1	1	0	1
1	1	1	0	1	0	0	0	1
1	0	0	0	0	1	1	1	0
1	0	0	0	1	0	1	1	0
0	1	1	1	0	1	1	0	1
0	1	1	0	1	0	0	0	1
0	1	0	1	1	0	1	1	0
0	1	0	1	1	0	1	1	0
			⇑					

10.

```
(I · H)  Δ  (I · D)
───────────────────
1 1 1    0   1 1 1
1 1 1    1   1 0 0
1 0 0    1   1 1 1
1 0 0    0   1 0 0
0 0 1    0   0 0 1
0 0 1    0   0 0 0
0 0 0    0   0 0 1
0 0 0    0   0 0 0
         ⇑
```

12.

```
K ⊃ (∿ N Δ W)
─────────────
1 1  0 1 1 1
1 0  0 1 0 0
1 0  1 0 0 1
1 1  1 0 1 0
0 1  0 1 1 1
0 1  0 1 0 0
0 1  1 0 0 1
0 1  1 0 1 0
   ⇑
```

14.

```
{[(F ⊃ O) · (T ⊃ ∿ R)] · ∿(∿ R · O)} ⊃ (∿ F ∨ ∿ T)
────────────────────────────────────────────────────
 1 1 1  0   1 0 0 1    0 1 0 1 0 1   1   0 1 0 0 1
 1 1 1  1   1 1 1 0    0 0 1 0 1 1   1   0 1 0 0 1
 1 1 1  1   0 1 0 1    1 1 0 1 0 1   1   0 1 1 1 0
 1 1 1  1   0 1 1 0    0 0 1 0 1 1   1   0 1 1 1 0
 1 0 0  0   1 0 0 1    0 1 0 1 0 0   1   0 1 0 0 1
 1 0 0  0   1 1 1 0    0 1 1 0 0 0   1   0 1 0 0 1
 1 0 0  0   0 1 0 1    0 1 0 1 0 0   1   0 1 1 1 0
 1 0 0  0   0 1 1 0    0 1 1 0 0 0   1   0 1 1 1 0
 0 1 1  0   1 0 0 1    0 1 0 1 0 1   1   1 0 1 0 1
 0 1 1  1   1 1 1 0    0 0 1 0 1 1   1   1 0 1 0 1
 0 1 1  1   0 1 0 1    1 1 0 1 0 1   1   1 0 1 1 0
 0 1 1  1   0 1 1 0    0 0 1 0 1 1   1   1 0 1 1 0
 0 1 0  0   1 0 0 1    0 1 0 1 0 0   1   1 0 1 0 1
 0 1 0  1   1 1 1 0    1 1 1 0 0 0   1   1 0 1 0 1
 0 1 0  1   0 1 0 1    1 1 0 1 0 0   1   1 0 1 1 0
 0 1 0  1   0 1 1 0    1 1 1 0 0 0   1   1 0 1 1 0
                                     ⇑
```

3.2.

2.

```
∿(S V ∿ S)
```

```
0  1  1  0  1
0  0  1  1  0
   ⇑
```
CONTRADICTION

4.

```
L ⊃ ∿ ∿ I
```

```
1  1  1  0  1
1  0  0  1  0
0  1  1  0  1
0  1  0  1  0
   ⇑
```
CONTINGENT

6.

```
(S ∨ P) · (∿ P · ∿ S)
```

```
1  1  1   0   0  1  0  0  1
1  1  0   0   1  0  0  0  1
0  1  1   0   0  1  0  1  0
0  0  0   0   1  0  1  1  0
          ⇑
```
CONTRADICTION

8.

```
[(V · B) Δ ∿ C] ⊃ [∿ C · (B ∨ V)]
```

```
1  1  1   1  0  1   0   0  1  0   1  1  1
1  1  1   0  1  0   1   1  0  1   1  1  1
1  0  0   0  0  1   1   0  1  0   0  1  1
1  0  0   1  1  0   1   1  0  1   0  1  1
0  0  1   0  0  1   1   0  1  0   1  1  0
0  0  1   1  1  0   1   1  0  1   1  1  0
0  0  0   0  0  1   1   0  1  0   0  0  0
0  0  0   1  1  0   0   1  0  0   0  0  0
                    ⇑
```
CONTINGENT

22

10.

```
[(S ⊃ M)  •  (M ⊃ R)]  •  (S  •  ∼ R)

  1 1 1   1   1 1 1      0    1 0 0 1
  1 1 1   0   1 0 0      0    1 1 1 0
  1 0 0   0   0 1 1      0    1 0 0 1
  1 0 0   0   0 1 0      0    1 1 1 0
  0 1 1   1   1 1 1      0    0 0 0 1
  0 1 1   0   1 0 0      0    0 0 1 0
  0 1 0   1   0 1 1      0    0 0 0 1
  0 1 0   1   0 1 0      0    0 0 1 0
                         ⇑
              CONTRADICTION
```

12.

```
∼(W •  E)  ∨  (S ∨ N)

 0 1 1 1   1   1 1 1
 0 1 1 1   1   1 1 0
 0 1 1 1   1   0 1 1
 0 1 1 1   0   0 0 0
 1 1 0 0   1   1 1 1
 1 1 0 0   1   1 1 0
 1 1 0 0   1   0 1 1
 1 1 0 0   1   0 0 0
 1 0 0 1   1   1 1 1
 1 0 0 1   1   1 1 0
 1 0 0 1   1   0 1 1
 1 0 0 1   1   0 0 0
 1 0 0 0   1   1 1 1
 1 0 0 0   1   1 1 0
 1 0 0 0   1   0 1 1
 1 0 0 0   1   0 0 0
           ⇑
     CONTINGENT
```

14.

$(F \cdot T) \supset \{[(\sim F \supset K) \cdot (\sim T \supset N)] \vee (N \cdot K)\}$

```
(F · T) ⊃ {[(~ F ⊃ K)  ·  (~ T ⊃ N)] ∨ (N · K)}
──────────────────────────────────────────────────────
1 1 1   1    0 1 1 1   1   0 1 1 1    1   1 1 1
1 1 1   1    0 1 1 1   1   0 1 1 0    1   0 0 1
1 1 1   1    0 1 1 0   1   0 1 1 1    1   1 0 0
1 1 1   1    0 1 1 0   1   0 1 1 0    1   0 0 0
1 0 0   1    0 1 1 1   1   1 0 1 1    1   1 1 1
1 0 0   1    0 1 1 1   0   1 0 0 0    0   0 0 1
1 0 0   1    0 1 1 0   1   1 0 1 1    1   1 0 0
1 0 0   1    0 1 1 0   0   1 0 0 0    0   0 0 0
0 0 1   1    1 0 1 1   1   0 1 1 1    1   1 1 1
0 0 1   1    1 0 1 1   1   0 1 1 0    1   0 0 1
0 0 1   1    1 0 0 0   0   0 1 1 1    0   1 0 0
0 0 1   1    1 0 0 0   0   0 1 1 0    0   0 0 0
0 0 0   1    1 0 1 1   1   1 0 1 1    1   1 1 1
0 0 0   1    1 0 1 1   0   1 0 0 0    0   0 0 1
0 0 0   1    1 0 0 0   0   1 0 1 1    0   1 0 0
0 0 0   1    1 0 0 0   0   1 0 0 0    0   0 0 0
            ⇑
        TAUTOLOGY
```

3.3.

2.   /∴ R
  1) R ⊃ I   Pr
  2) I   Pr

$[(R \supset I) \cdot I] \supset R$

```
[(R ⊃ I)  ·  I] ⊃ R
──────────────────────
1 1 1   1 1   1 1
1 0 0   0 0   1 1
0 1 1   1 1   0 0
0 1 0   0 0   1 0
            ⇑
   CONTINGENT/INVALID
```

24

4.   /∴ C
  1)   ∿C ⊃ ∿F   Pr
  2)   F   Pr

  [(∿ C ⊃ ∿ F) • F] ⊃ C
  ─────────────────────────
    0 1 1 0 1 1 1 1 1
    0 1 1 1 0 0 0 1 1
    1 0 0 0 1 0 1 1 0
    1 0 1 1 0 0 0 1 0
                    ⇑
         TAUTOLOGY/VALID

6.   /∴ O • D
  1)   O ∨ (U • D)   Pr
  2)   ∿U   Pr

  {[O ∨ (U • D)] • ∿ U} ⊃ (O • D)
  ─────────────────────────────────────
    1 1 1 1 1   0 0 1 1 1 1 1
    1 1 1 0 0   0 0 1 1 1 0 0
    1 1 0 0 1   1 1 0 1 1 1 1
    1 1 0 0 0   1 1 0 0 1 0 0
    0 1 1 1 1   0 0 1 1 0 0 1
    0 0 1 0 0   0 0 1 1 0 0 0
    0 0 0 0 1   0 1 0 1 0 0 1
    0 0 0 0 0   0 1 0 1 0 0 0
                         ⇑
              CONTINGENT/INVALID

8.   /∴ D ⊃ W
  1)   D • (L ⊃ W)   Pr

  [D • (L ⊃ W)] ⊃ (D ⊃ W)
  ─────────────────────────────
    1 1 1 1 1   1 1 1 1
    1 0 1 0 0   1 1 0 0
    1 1 0 1 1   1 1 1 1
    1 1 0 1 0   0 1 0 0
    0 0 1 1 1   1 0 1 1
    0 0 1 0 0   1 0 1 0
    0 0 0 1 1   1 0 1 1
    0 0 0 1 0   1 0 1 0
                 ⇑
      CONTINGENT/INVALID

25

10.   /∴ ~I · S
   1)   I ⊃ (S ⊃ R)   Pr
   2)   ~R   Pr

{[I ⊃ (S ⊃ R)] · ~ R} ⊃ (~ I · S)
―――――――――――――――――――――――――――――――――
   1 1   1 1 1   0 0 1   1   0 1 0 1
   1 0   1 0 0   0 1 0   1   0 1 0 1
   1 1   0 1 1   0 0 1   1   0 1 0 0
   1 1   0 1 0   1 1 0   0   0 1 0 0
   0 1   1 1 1   0 0 1   1   1 0 1 1
   0 1   1 0 0   1 1 0   1   1 0 1 1
   0 1   0 1 1   0 0 1   1   1 0 0 0
   0 1   0 1 0   1 1 0   0   1 0 0 0
                             ⇑
                   CONTINGENT/INVALID

12.   /∴ N
   1)   S ∨ P   Pr
   2)   S ∨ N   Pr
   3)   ~P   Pr

{[(S ∨ P) · (S ∨ N)] · ~ P} ⊃ N
―――――――――――――――――――――――――――――――
   1 1 1   1   1 1 1   0 0 1   1 1
   1 1 1   1   1 1 0   0 0 1   1 0
   1 1 0   1   1 1 1   1 1 0   1 1
   1 1 0   1   1 1 0   1 1 0   0 0
   0 1 1   1   0 1 1   0 0 1   1 1
   0 1 1   0   0 0 0   0 0 1   1 0
   0 0 0   0   0 1 1   0 1 0   1 1
   0 0 0   0   0 0 0   0 1 0   1 0
                               ⇑
                     CONTINGENT/INVALID

14.   /∴ P
  1)   P ∨ (N · S)   Pr
  2)   S ∨ ∿N   Pr

  {[P ∨ (N · S)] · (S ∨ ∿ N)} ⊃ P
  ─────────────────────────────────
    1 1   1 1 1   1   1 1 0 1   1 1
    1 1   1 0 0   0   0 0 0 1   1 1
    1 1   0 0 1   1   1 1 1 0   1 1
    1 1   0 0 0   1   0 1 1 0   1 1
    0 1   1 1 1   1   1 1 0 1   0 0
    0 0   1 0 0   0   0 0 0 1   1 0
    0 0   0 0 1   0   1 1 1 0   1 0
    0 0   0 0 0   0   0 1 1 0   1 0
                                ⇑
                    CONTINGENT/INVALID

16.   /∴ C
  1)   A ⊃ (R ≡ C)   Pr
  2)   ∿R ⊃ A   Pr
  3)   ∿A   Pr

  ({[A ⊃ (R ≡ C)] · (∿ R ⊃ A)} · ∿ A) ⊃ C
  ──
    1 1   1 1 1   1   0 1 1 1   0 0 1   1 1
    1 0   1 0 0   0   0 1 1 1   0 0 1   1 0
    1 0   0 0 1   0   1 0 1 1   0 0 1   1 1
    1 1   0 1 0   1   1 0 1 1   0 0 1   1 0
    0 1   1 1 1   1   0 1 1 0   1 1 0   1 1
    0 1   1 0 0   1   0 1 1 0   1 1 0   0 0
    0 1   0 0 1   0   1 0 0 0   0 1 0   1 1
    0 1   0 1 0   0   1 0 0 0   0 1 0   1 0
                                      ⇑
                    CONTINGENT/INVALID

27

18. /∴ D

1) (D ⊃ F) • (C ⊃ P)   Pr
2) ~(F • P)   Pr
3) C   Pr

(	{	[	(	D	⊃	F	)	•	(	C	⊃	P	)	]	•	~	(	F	•	P	)	}	•	C	)	⊃	D
				1	1	1		1		1	1	1			0	0		1	1	1			0	1		1	1
				1	1	1		0		1	0	0			0	1		1	0	0			0	1		1	1
				1	1	1		1		0	1	1			0	0		1	1	1			0	0		1	1
				1	1	1		1		0	1	0			1	1		1	0	0			0	0		1	1
				1	0	0		0		1	1	1			0	1		0	0	1			0	1		1	1
				1	0	0		0		1	0	0			0	1		0	0	0			0	1		1	1
				1	0	0		0		0	1	1			0	1		0	0	1			0	0		1	1
				1	0	0		0		0	1	0			0	1		0	0	0			0	0		1	1
				0	1	1		1		1	1	1			0	0		1	1	1			0	1		1	0
				0	1	1		0		1	0	0			0	1		1	0	0			0	1		1	0
				0	1	1		1		0	1	1			0	0		1	1	1			0	0		1	0
				0	1	1		1		0	1	0			1	1		1	0	0			0	0		1	0
				0	1	0		1		1	1	1			1	1		0	0	1			1	1		0	0
				0	1	0		0		1	0	0			0	1		0	0	0			0	1		1	0
				0	1	0		1		0	1	1			1	1		0	0	1			0	0		1	0
				0	1	0		1		0	1	0			1	1		0	0	0			0	0		1	0

⇑
CONTINGENT/INVALID

28

20.   /∴ ∿M
   1)   (A ⊃ M) · (S ⊃ C)   Pr
   2)   ∿(∿A · ∿S)   Pr
   3)   ∿C   Pr

```
({[(A ⊃ M) · (S ⊃ C)] · ∿(∿ A · ∿ S)} · ∿ C) ⊃ ∿ M
─────────────────────────────────────────────────────
    1 1 1  1  1 1 1   1 1 0 1 0 0 1   0 0 1   1 0 1
    1 1 1  0  1 0 0   0 1 0 1 0 0 1   0 1 0   1 0 1
    1 1 1  1  0 1 1   1 1 0 1 0 1 0   0 0 1   1 0 1
    1 1 1  1  0 1 0   1 1 0 1 0 1 0   1 1 0   0 0 1
    1 0 0  0  1 1 1   0 1 0 1 0 0 1   0 0 1   1 1 0
    1 0 0  0  1 0 0   0 1 0 1 0 0 1   0 1 0   1 1 0
    1 0 0  0  0 1 1   0 1 0 1 0 1 0   0 0 1   1 1 0
    1 0 0  0  0 1 0   0 1 0 1 0 1 0   0 1 0   1 1 0
    0 1 1  1  1 1 1   1 1 1 0 0 0 1   0 0 1   1 0 1
    0 1 1  0  1 0 0   0 1 1 0 0 0 1   0 1 0   1 0 1
    0 1 1  1  0 1 1   0 0 1 0 1 1 0   0 0 1   1 0 1
    0 1 1  1  0 1 0   0 0 1 0 1 1 0   0 1 0   1 0 1
    0 1 0  1  1 1 1   1 1 1 0 0 0 1   0 0 1   1 1 0
    0 1 0  0  1 0 0   0 1 1 0 0 0 1   0 1 0   1 1 0
    0 1 0  1  0 1 1   0 0 1 0 1 1 0   0 0 1   1 1 0
    0 1 0  1  0 1 0   0 0 1 0 1 1 0   0 1 0   1 1 0
                                               ⇑
                              CONTINGENT/INVALID
```

3.4.

2.   /∴ ∿E
   1)   E ⊃ C   Pr
   2)   C   Pr

```
[(E ⊃ C) · C] · ∿ ∿ E
─────────────────────────
   1 1 1   1 1   1 1 0 1
   1 0 0   0 0   0 1 0 1
   0 1 1   1 1   0 0 1 0
   0 1 0   0 0   0 0 1 0
                 ⇑
      CONTINGENT/INVALID
```

4.   /∴ ∿E
1)   ∿B   Pr
2)   E ⊃ ∿B   Pr

[∿ B • (E ⊃ ∿ B)] • ∿ ∿ E
─────────────────────────
  0 1 0 1 0 0 1   0 1 0 1
  0 1 0 0 1 0 1   0 0 1 0
  1 0 1 1 1 1 0   1 1 0 1
  1 0 1 0 1 1 0   0 0 1 0
                    ⇑
       CONTINGENT/INVALID

6.   /∴ ∿F ∨ G
1)   F ≡ G   Pr
2)   ∿G   Pr

[(F ≡ G) • ∿ G] • ∿(∿ F ∨ G)
─────────────────────────────
   1 1 1   0 0 1   0 0 0 1 1 1
   1 0 0   0 1 0   0 1 0 1 0 0
   0 0 1   0 0 1   0 0 1 0 1 1
   0 1 0   1 1 0   0 0 1 0 1 0
                  ⇑
       CONTRADICTION/VALID

8.   /∴ C ⊃ S
1)   C ⊃ ∿F   Pr
2)   ∿F ∨ S   Pr

[(C ⊃ ∿ F) • (∿ F ∨ S)] • ∿(C ⊃ S)
─────────────────────────────────────
   1 0 0 1 0 0 1 1 1   0 0 1 1 1
   1 0 0 1 0 0 1 0 0   0 1 1 0 0
   1 1 1 0 1 1 0 1 1   0 0 1 1 1
   1 1 1 0 1 1 0 1 0   1 1 1 0 0
   0 1 0 1 1 0 1 1 1   0 0 0 1 1
   0 1 0 1 0 0 1 0 0   0 0 0 1 0
   0 1 1 0 1 1 0 1 1   0 0 0 1 1
   0 1 1 0 1 1 0 1 0   0 0 0 1 0
                          ⇑
            CONTINGENT/INVALID

10.   /∴ C ∨ G
   1)   (C · P) ∨ G   Pr
   2)   ∿P   Pr

{[(C · P) ∨ G] · ∿ P} · ∿(C ∨ G)
─────────────────────────────────────
    1 1 1   1 1   0 0 1   0 0 1 1 1
    1 1 1   1 0   0 0 1   0 0 1 1 0
    1 0 0   1 1   1 1 0   0 0 1 1 1
    1 0 0   0 0   0 1 0   0 0 1 1 0
    0 0 1   1 1   0 0 1   0 0 0 1 1
    0 0 1   0 0   0 0 1   0 1 0 0 0
    0 0 0   1 1   1 1 0   0 0 0 1 1
    0 0 0   0 0   0 1 0   0 1 0 0 0
                          ⇑
              CONTRADICTION/VALID

12.   /∴ ∿(P ∨ I)
   1)   P ⊃ (R · I)   Pr
   2)   ∿R   Pr

{[P ⊃ (R · I)] · ∿ R} · ∿ ∿(P ∨ I)
───
    1 1   1 1 1   0 0 1   0 1 0 1 1 1
    1 0   1 0 0   0 0 1   0 1 0 1 1 0
    1 0   0 0 1   0 1 0   0 1 0 1 1 1
    1 0   0 0 0   0 1 0   0 1 0 1 1 0
    0 1   1 1 1   0 0 1   0 1 0 0 1 1
    0 1   1 0 0   0 0 1   0 0 1 0 0 0
    0 1   0 0 1   1 1 0   1 1 0 0 1 1
    0 1   0 0 0   1 1 0   0 0 1 0 0 0
                          ⇑
              CONTINGENT/INALID

31

14.   /∴ M ∨ ∿I
  1)   (I · W) ∨ M   Pr
  2)   ∿(W ∨ I)   Pr

{[(I · W) ∨ M] · ∿(W ∨ I)} · ∿(M ∨ ∿ I)

```
   1 1 1  1 1  0 0 1 1 1   0 0 1 1 0 1
   1 1 1  1 0  0 0 1 1 1   0 1 0 0 0 1
   1 0 0  1 1  0 0 0 1 1   0 0 1 1 0 1
   1 0 0  0 0  0 0 0 1 1   0 1 0 0 0 1
   0 0 1  1 1  0 0 1 1 0   0 0 1 1 1 0
   0 0 1  0 0  0 0 1 1 0   0 0 0 1 1 0
   0 0 0  1 1  1 1 0 0 0   0 0 1 1 1 0
   0 0 0  0 0  0 1 0 0 0   0 0 0 1 1 0
                            ⇑
```

CONTRADICTION/VALID

16.   /∴ ∿(G ∨ B)
  1)   W ⊃ (B ⊃ G)   Pr
  2)   ∿(B ∨ ∿W)   Pr

{[W ⊃ (B ⊃ G)] · ∿(B ∨ ∿ W)} · ∿ ∿(G ∨ B)

```
   1 1  1 1 1   0 0 1 1 0 1   0 1 0 1 1 1
   1 0  1 0 0   0 0 1 1 0 1   0 1 0 0 1 1
   1 1  0 1 1   1 1 0 0 0 1   1 1 0 1 1 0
   1 1  0 1 0   1 1 0 0 0 1   1 0 1 0 0 0
   0 1  1 1 1   0 0 1 1 1 0   0 1 0 1 1 1
   0 1  1 0 0   0 0 1 1 1 0   0 1 0 0 1 1
   0 1  0 1 1   0 0 0 1 1 0   0 1 0 1 1 0
   0 1  0 1 0   0 0 0 1 1 0   0 0 1 0 0 0
                              ⇑
```

CONTINGENT/INVALID

18.

/∴ W ⊃ (H · I)

1) ∿(H ∨ I) ⊃ (∿P ⊃ ∿W)   Pr

[∿(H ∨ I) ⊃ (∿ P ⊃ ∿ W)] · ∿[W ⊃ (H · I)]

0	1	1	1	1	0	1	1	0	1	0	0	1	1	1	1	1
0	1	1	1	1	0	1	1	1	0	0	0	0	1	1	1	1
0	1	1	1	1	1	0	0	0	1	0	0	1	1	1	1	1
0	1	1	1	1	1	0	1	1	0	0	0	0	1	1	1	1
0	1	1	0	1	0	1	1	0	1	1	1	1	0	1	0	0
0	1	1	0	1	0	1	1	1	0	0	0	0	1	1	0	0
0	1	1	0	1	1	0	0	0	1	1	1	1	0	1	0	0
0	1	1	0	1	1	0	1	1	0	0	0	0	1	1	0	0
0	0	1	1	1	0	1	1	0	1	1	1	1	0	0	0	1
0	0	1	1	1	0	1	1	1	0	0	0	0	1	0	0	1
0	0	1	1	1	1	0	0	0	1	1	1	1	0	0	0	1
0	0	1	1	1	1	0	1	1	0	0	0	0	1	0	0	1
1	0	0	0	1	0	1	1	0	1	1	1	1	0	0	0	0
1	0	0	0	1	0	1	1	1	0	0	0	0	1	0	0	0
1	0	0	0	0	1	0	0	0	1	0	1	1	0	0	0	0
1	0	0	0	1	1	0	1	1	0	0	0	0	1	0	0	0

⇑

CONTINGENT/INVALID

20.   /∴ ∿(I · R)
  1)   I ≡ F   Pr
  2)   F Δ P   Pr
  3)   ∿P   Pr

```
{ [ ( I ≡ F ) · ( F Δ P ) ] · ∿ P } · ∿ ∿ ( I · R )
─────────────────────────────────────────────────────
     1 1 1   0   1 0 1     0 0 1   0 1 0 1 1 1
     1 1 1   0   1 0 1     0 0 1   0 0 1 1 0 0
     1 1 1   1   1 1 0     1 1 0   1 1 0 1 1 1
     1 1 1   1   1 1 0     1 1 0   0 0 1 1 0 0
     1 0 0   0   0 1 1     0 0 1   0 1 0 1 1 1
     1 0 0   0   0 1 1     0 0 1   0 0 1 1 0 0
     1 0 0   0   0 0 0     0 1 0   0 1 0 1 1 1
     1 0 0   0   0 0 0     0 1 0   0 0 1 1 0 0
     0 0 1   0   1 0 1     0 0 1   0 0 1 0 0 1
     0 0 1   0   1 0 1     0 0 1   0 0 1 0 0 0
     0 0 1   0   1 1 0     0 1 0   0 0 1 0 0 1
     0 0 1   0   1 1 0     0 1 0   0 0 1 0 0 0
     0 1 0   1   0 1 1     0 0 1   0 0 1 0 0 1
     0 1 0   1   0 1 1     0 0 1   0 0 1 0 0 0
     0 1 0   0   0 0 0     0 1 0   0 0 1 0 0 1
     0 1 0   0   0 0 0     0 1 0   0 0 1 0 0 0
                            ⇑
            CONTINGENT/INVALID
```

3.5.

2.   /∴ B ⊃ A   /∴ 1 ⊃ 0   = 0
  1)   A   1   = 1

                                   Truth-Value Assignment

                                          A = 1
                                          B = 0

                                       INVALID

4.   /∴ B   /∴ 0   = 0
   1)   (A ⊃ B) ∨ A   (0 ⊃ 0) ∨ 0   = 1

                                                   Truth-Value Assignment

                                                          A = 0
                                                          B = 0

                                                          INVALID

6.   /∴ A ⊃ C   /∴ 1 ⊃ 0   = 0
   1)   A ∨ (B • C)   1 ∨ (0 • 0)   = 1
   2)   B ≡ C   0 ≡ 0   = 1

                                                   Truth-Value Assignment

                                                          A = 1
                                                          B = 0
                                                          C = 0

                                                          INVALID

8.   /∴ A △ B   /∴ 1 △ 1   = 0
   1)   (A • B) ≡ C   (1 • 1) ≡ 1   = 1
   2)   ∿D ⊃ ∿C   ∿1 ⊃ ∿1   = 1
   3)   B ∨ A   1 ∨ 1   = 1

                                                   Truth-Value Assignment

                                                          A = 1
                                                          B = 1
                                                          C = 1
                                                          D = 1

                                                          INVALID

10.   /∴ C ∨ B   /∴ 0 ∨ 0   = 0
   1)   (A ≡ B) ⊃ [C ∨ (A · B)]   (1 ≡ 0) ⊃ [0 ∨ (1 · 0)] = 1
   2)   (A ⊃ C) · (C ⊃ B)   X (1 ⊃ 0) · (0 ⊃ 0)   = 0
   3)   (B ⊃ C) · (C ⊃ A)   (0 ⊃ 0) · (0 ⊃ 1)   = 1

                                           Truth-Value Assignment

                                                   A = 1
                                                   B = 0
                                                   C = 0

                                                   VALID

12.   /∴ C Δ B   /∴ 1 Δ 1   = 0
   1)   ∿[(B · ∿C) · ∿A]   ∿[(1 · ∿1) · ∿1]   = 1
   2)   ∿(A · ∿B)   ∿(1 · ∿1)   = 1
   3)   ∿(∿C · ∿B)   ∿(1 · ∿1)   = 1

                                           Truth-Value Assignment

                                                   A = 1
                                                   B = 1
                                                   C = 1

                                                   INVALID

14.   /∴ A Δ B   /∴ 1 Δ 1   = 0
   1)   (A ≡ B) · (B ≡ C)   (1 ≡ 1) · (1 ≡ 1)   = 1
   2)   ∿C ⊃ ∿D   ∿1 ⊃ ∿1   = 1
   3)   A ∨ D   1 ∨ 1   = 1

                                           Truth-Value Assignment

                                                   A = 1
                                                   B = 1
                                                   C = 1
                                                   D = 1

                                                   INVALID

16.   /∴ A · (C · B)   /∴ 1 · (0 · 0)   = 0
  1)   (D ∨ B) ⊃ C   (0 ∨ 0) ⊃ 0   = 1
  2)   A △ B   1 △ 0   = 1
  3)   (C ∨ B) ⊃ D   (0 ∨ 0) ⊃ 0   = 1
  4)   D ⊃ (B · ∿D)   0 ⊃ (0 ⊃ ∿0)   = 1

                          Truth-Value Assignment

                                   A = 1
                                   B = 0
                                   C = 0
                                   D = 0

                              INVALID

18. /∴ (C ⊃ B) ∨ ∿(B ∨ C)   /∴ (1 ⊃ 0) ∨ ∿(0 ∨ 1)   = 0
  1)   (A ⊃ B) ⊃ (C ⊃ B)   (1 ⊃ 0) ⊃ (1 ⊃ 0)   = 1
  2)   (D ⊃ C) ⊃ ∿(B ∨ C) X   (1 ≡ 1) ⊃ ∿(0 ∨ 1)   = 0

                          Truth-Value Assignment

                                   A = 1
                                   B = 0
                                   C = 1
                                   D = 1

                               VALID

20.   /∴ C ∨ ∿E   /∴ 0 ∨ 1   = 0
  1)   A ⊃ (B ⊃ C)   1 ⊃ (0 ⊃ 0)   = 0
  2)   ∿D ⊃ (E ⊃ ∿C)   ∿1 ⊃ (1 ⊃ ∿0)   = 1
  3)   ∿(A · D) ⊃ ∿(B ∨ E)   ∿(1 · 1) ⊃ ∿(0 ∨ 0)   = 1
  4)   E ∨ B   1 ∨ 0   = 1

                          Truth-Value Assignment

                                   A = 1
                                   B = 0
                                   C = 0
                                   D = 1
                                   E = 1

                              INVALID

37

3.6.

2. /∴ C
1) A Pr
2) A ⊃ C Pr

A · (A ⊃ C)
_____
```
1 1   1 1 1
1 0   1 0 0
0 0   0 1 1
0 0   0 1 0
    ⇑
```
CONTINGENT/CONSISTENT

[A · (A ⊃ C)] ⊃ C
_____
```
1 1   1 1 1     1 1
1 0   1 0 0     1 0
0 0   0 1 1     1 1
0 0   0 1 0     1 0
              ⇑
```
    TAUTOLOGY/VALID

4. /∴ J
1) J ∨ (B · ∿J) Pr

J ∨ (B · ∿ J)
_____
```
1 1   1 0 0 1
1 1   0 0 0 1
0 1   1 1 1 0
0 0   0 0 1 0
  ⇑
```
CONTINGENT/CONSISTENT

[J ∨ (B · ∿ J)] ⊃ J

1	1	1	0	0	1	1	1
1	1	0	0	0	1	1	1
0	1	1	1	1	0	0	0
0	0	0	0	1	0	1	0

⇑
CONTINGENT/INVALID

6.   /∴ W ⊃ ∿A
  1)   W ⊃ L   Pr
  2)   (L ⊃ ∿A) · W   Pr

(W ⊃ L) · [(L ⊃ ∿ A) · W]

1	1	1	0	1	0	0	1	0	1	
1	1	1	1	1	1	1	0	1	1	
1	0	0	0	0	1	0	1	1	1	
1	0	0	0	0	1	1	0	1	1	
0	1	1	0	1	0	0	1	0	0	
0	1	1	0	1	1	1	0	0	0	
0	1	0	0	0	1	0	1	0	0	
0	1	0	0	0	1	1	0	0	0	

⇑
CONTINGENT/CONSISTENT

{(W ⊃ L) · [(L ⊃ ∿ A) · W]} ⊃ (W ⊃ ∿ A)

1	1	1	0	1	0	0	1	0	1	1	1	0	0	1
1	1	1	1	1	1	1	0	1	1	1	₅ 1	1	0	
1	0	0	0	0	1	0	1	1	1	1	1	0	0	1
1	0	0	0	0	1	1	0	1	1	1	1	1	1	0
0	1	1	0	1	0	0	1	0	0	1	0	1	0	1
0	1	1	0	1	1	1	0	0	0	1	0	1	1	0
0	1	0	0	0	1	0	1	0	0	1	0	1	0	1
0	1	0	0	0	1	1	0	0	0	1	0	1	1	0

⇑
TAUTOLOGY/VALID

8.   /∴ W ∨ ∿A
  1)   S ∨ W   Pr
  2)   ∿(∿W ⊃ S)   Pr

(S ∨ W) • ∿(∿ W ⊃ S)
_____

  1 1 1   0 0 0 1 1 1
  1 1 0   0 0 1 0 1 1
  0 1 1   0 0 0 1 1 0
  0 0 0   0 1 1 0 0 0
           ⇑
CONTRADITION/INCONSISTENT

[(S ∨ W) • ∿(∿ W ⊃ S)] ⊃ (W ∨ ∿ A)
_____

  1 1 1   0 0 0 1 1 1   1   1 1 0 1
  1 1 1   0 0 0 1 1 1   1   1 1 1 0
  1 1 0   0 0 1 0 1 1   1   0 0 0 1
  1 1 0   0 0 1 0 1 1   1   0 1 1 0
  0 1 1   0 0 0 1 1 0   1   1 1 0 1
  0 1 1   0 0 0 1 1 0   1   1 1 1 0
  0 0 0   0 1 1 0 0 0   1   0 0 0 1
  0 0 0   0 1 1 0 0 0   1   0 1 1 0
                                ⇑
                      TAUTOLOGY/VALID

10.   /∴ ∿M
  1)   (S Δ P) • P   Pr
  2)   S ≡ ∿M   Pr

[(S Δ P) • P] • (S ≡ ∿ M)
_____

  1 0 1   0 1   0   1 0 0 1
  1 0 1   0 1   0   1 1 1 0
  1 1 0   0 0   0   1 0 0 1
  1 1 0   0 0   0   1 1 1 0
  0 1 1   1 1   1   0 1 0 1
  0 1 1   1 1   0   0 0 1 0
  0 0 0   0 0   0   0 1 0 1
  0 0 0   0 0   0   0 0 1 0
                 ⇑
      CONTINGENT/CONSISTENT

40

{[(S △ P) • P] • (S ≡ ∿ M)} ⊃ ∿ M

{	[	(S	△	P)	•	P]	•	(S	≡	∿	M)	}	⊃	∿	M
		1	0	1	0	1	0	1	0	0	1		1	0	1
		1	0	1	0	1	0	1	1	1	0		1	1	0
		1	1	0	0	0	0	1	0	0	1		1	0	1
		1	1	0	0	0	0	1	1	1	0		1	1	0
		0	1	1	1	1	1	0	1	0	1		0	0	1
		0	1	1	1	1	0	0	0	1	0		1	1	0
		0	0	0	0	0	0	0	1	0	1		1	0	1
		0	0	0	0	0	0	0	0	1	0		1	1	0

⇑
CONTINGENT/INVALID

12.   /∴ J • R

1)   ∿(C ∨ ∿J)   Pr
2)   C ∨ R   Pr
3)   C   Pr

[∿(C ∨ ∿ J) • (C ∨ R)] • C

[	∿	(C	∨	∿	J)	•	(C	∨	R)]	•	C
	0	1	1	0	1	0	1	1	1	0	1
	0	1	1	0	1	0	1	1	0	0	1
	0	1	1	1	0	0	1	1	1	0	1
	0	1	1	1	0	0	1	1	0	0	1
	1	0	0	0	1	1	0	1	1	0	0
	1	0	0	0	1	0	0	0	0	0	0
	0	0	1	1	0	0	0	1	1	0	0
	0	0	1	1	0	0	0	0	0	0	0

⇑
CONTRADICTION/INCONSISTENT

{[∿(C ∨ ∿ J) • (C ∨ R)] • C} ⊃ (J • R)

{	[	∿	(C	∨	∿	J)	•	(C	∨	R)]	•	C}	⊃	(J	•	R)
		0	1	1	0	1	0	1	1	1	0	1	1	1	1	1
		0	1	1	0	1	0	1	1	0	0	1	1	1	0	0
		0	1	1	1	0	0	1	1	1	0	1	1	0	0	1
		0	1	1	1	0	0	1	1	0	0	1	1	0	0	0
		1	0	0	0	1	1	0	1	1	0	0	1	1	1	1
		1	0	0	0	1	0	0	0	0	0	0	1	1	0	0
		0	0	1	1	0	0	0	1	1	0	0	1	0	0	1
		0	0	1	1	0	0	0	0	0	0	0	1	0	0	0

⇑
TAUTOLOGY/VALID

41

14.   /∴ M ≡ L
   1)   L ⊃ (G ⊃ M)   Pr
   2)   G   Pr
   3)   M ⊃ (G · L)   Pr

{ [L ⊃ (G ⊃ M)] · G } · [M ⊃ (G · L)]
_____

   1 1   1 1 1   1 1   1   1 1   1 1 1
   1 0   1 0 0   0 1   0   0 1   1 1 1
   1 1   0 1 1   0 0   0   1 0   0 0 1
   1 1   0 1 0   0 0   0   0 1   0 0 1
   0 1   1 1 1   1 1   0   1 0   1 0 0
   0 1   1 0 0   1 1   1   0 1   1 0 0
   0 1   0 1 1   0 0   0   1 0   0 0 0
   0 1   0 1 0   0 0   0   0 1   0 0 0
                         ⇑
              CONTINGENT/CONSISTENT

({ { [L ⊃ (G ⊃ M)] · G] } · [M ⊃ (G · L)]) ⊃ (M ≡ L)
_____

   1 1   1 1 1   1 1   1   1 1   1 1 1   1   1 1 1
   1 0   1 0 0   0 1   0   0 1   1 1 1   1   0 0 1
   1 1   0 1 1   0 0   0   1 0   0 0 1   1   1 1 1
   1 1   0 1 0   0 0   0   0 1   0 0 1   1   0 0 1
   0 1   1 1 1   1 1   0   1 0   1 0 0   1   1 0 0
   0 1   1 0 0   1 1   1   0 1   1 0 0   1   0 1 0
   0 1   0 1 1   0 0   0   1 0   0 0 0   1   1 0 0
   0 1   0 1 0   0 0   0   0 1   0 0 0   1   0 1 0
                                             ⇑
                               TAUTOLOGY/VALID

42

16.   /∴ ~(~B · C)

   1)   ~K ≡ B   Pr
   2)   K ⊃ ~A   Pr
   3)   C Δ ~A   Pr

[(~ K ≡ B) · (K ⊃ ~A)] · (C Δ ~ A)
──
   0 1 0 1   0   1 0 0 1   0   1 1 0 1
   0 1 0 1   0   1 0 0 1   0   0 0 0 1
   0 1 0 1   0   1 1 1 0   0   1 0 1 0
   0 1 0 1   0   1 1 1 0   0   0 1 1 0
   0 1 1 0   0   1 0 0 1   0   1 1 0 1
   0 1 1 0   0   1 0 0 1   0   0 0 0 1
   0 1 1 0   1   1 1 1 0   0   1 0 1 0
   0 1 1 0   1   1 1 1 0   1   0 1 1 0
   1 0 1 1   1   0 1 0 1   1   1 1 0 1
   1 0 1 1   1   0 1 0 1   0   0 0 0 1
   1 0 1 1   1   0 1 1 0   0   1 0 1 0
   1 0 1 1   1   0 1 1 0   1   0 1 1 0
   1 0 0 0   0   0 1 0 1   0   1 1 0 1
   1 0 0 0   0   0 1 0 1   0   0 0 0 1
   1 0 0 0   0   0 1 1 0   1   1 0 1 0
   1 0 0 0   0   0 1 1 0   0   0 1 1 0
                           ⇑
              CONTINGENT/CONSISTENT

{ [(~ K ≡ B) · (K ⊃ ~A)] · (C Δ ~ A) } ⊃ ~(~ B · C)
──
   0 1 0 1   0   1 0 0 1   0   1 1 0 1   1 1 0 1 0 1
   0 1 0 1   0   1 0 0 1   0   0 0 0 1   1 1 0 1 0 0
   0 1 0 1   0   1 1 1 0   0   1 0 1 0   1 1 0 1 0 1
   0 1 0 1   0   1 1 1 0   0   0 1 1 0   1 1 0 1 0 0
   0 1 1 0   0   1 0 0 1   0   1 1 0 1   1 0 1 0 1 1
   0 1 1 0   0   1 0 0 1   0   0 0 0 1   1 1 1 0 0 0
   0 1 1 0   1   1 1 1 0   0   1 0 1 0   1 0 1 0 1 1
   0 1 1 0   1   1 1 1 0   1   0 1 1 0   1 1 1 0 0 0
   1 0 1 1   1   0 1 0 1   1   1 1 0 1   1 1 0 1 0 1
   1 0 1 1   1   0 1 0 1   0   0 0 0 1   1 1 0 1 0 0
   1 0 1 1   1   0 1 1 0   0   1 0 1 0   1 1 0 1 0 1
   1 0 1 1   1   0 1 1 0   1   0 1 1 0   1 1 0 1 0 0
   1 0 0 0   0   0 1 0 1   0   1 1 0 1   1 0 1 0 1 1
   1 0 0 0   0   0 1 0 1   0   0 0 0 1   1 1 1 0 0 0
   1 0 0 0   0   0 1 1 0   0   1 0 0 0   1 0 1 0 1 1
   1 0 0 0   0   0 1 1 0   0   0 1 1 0   1 1 1 0 0 0
                                           ⇑
                              TAUTOLOGY/VALID

18.   /∴ T · (U ⊃ Q)

1) A ⊃ Q   Pr
2) A · ∿U   Pr
3) T ⊃ ∿(A ⊃ ∿U)   Pr
4) Q ⊃ U   Pr

{[(A ⊃ Q) · (A · ∿ U)] · [T ⊃ ∿(A ⊃ ∿ U)]} · (Q ⊃ U)

A ⊃ Q	·	A · ∿ U	·	T ⊃ ∿ (A ⊃ ∿ U)	·	Q ⊃ U
1 1 1	0	1 0 0 1	0	1 1 1 1 0 0 1	0	1 1 1
1 1 1	0	1 0 0 1	0	0 1 1 1 0 0 1	0	1 1 1
1 1 1	1	1 1 1 0	0	1 0 0 1 1 1 0	0	1 0 0
1 1 1	1	1 1 1 0	1	0 1 0 1 1 1 0	0	1 0 0
1 0 0	0	1 0 0 1	0	1 1 1 1 0 0 1	0	0 1 1
1 0 0	0	1 0 0 1	0	0 1 1 1 0 0 1	0	0 1 1
1 0 0	0	1 1 1 0	0	1 0 0 1 1 1 0	0	0 1 0
1 0 0	0	1 1 1 0	0	0 1 0 1 1 1 0	0	0 1 0
0 1 1	0	0 0 0 1	0	1 0 0 0 1 0 1	0	1 1 1
0 1 1	0	0 0 0 1	0	0 1 0 0 1 0 1	0	1 1 1
0 1 1	0	0 0 1 0	0	1 0 0 0 1 1 0	0	1 0 0
0 1 1	0	0 0 1 0	0	0 1 0 0 1 1 0	0	1 0 0
0 1 0	0	0 0 0 1	0	1 0 0 0 1 0 1	0	0 1 1
0 1 0	0	0 0 0 1	0	0 1 0 0 1 0 1	0	0 1 1
0 1 0	0	0 0 1 0	0	1 0 0 0 1 1 0	0	0 1 0
0 1 0	0	0 0 1 0	0	0 1 0 0 1 1 0	0	0 1 0

⇑
CONTRADICTION/INCONSISTENT

```
(([[(A⊃Q)• (A •  ∿U)]• [T ⊃ ∿(A ⊃ ∿U)]}• (Q ⊃ U))  ⊃  [T • (U⊃Q)]
```

```
111 0 1 0 01  0 1 1 1 1 0 01   0 1 1 1   1 1 1 111
111 0 1 0 01  0 0 1 1 1 0 01   0 1 1 1   1 0 0 111
111 1 1 1 10  0 1 0 0 1 1 10   0 1 0 0   1 1 1 011
111 1 1 1 10  1 0 1 0 1 1 10   0 1 0 0   1 0 0 011
100 0 1 0 01  0 1 1 1 1 0 01   0 0 1 1   1 1 0 100
100 0 1 0 01  0 0 1 1 1 0 01   0 0 1 1   1 0 0 100
100 0 1 1 10  0 1 0 0 1 1 10   0 0 1 0   1 1 1 010
100 0 1 1 10  0 0 1 0 1 1 10   0 0 1 0   1 0 0 010
011 0 0 0 01  0 1 0 0 0 1 01   0 1 1 1   1 1 1 111
011 0 0 0 01  0 0 1 0 0 1 01   0 1 1 1   1 0 0 111
011 0 0 0 10  0 1 0 0 0 1 10   0 1 0 0   1 1 1 011
011 0 0 0 10  0 0 1 0 0 1 10   0 1 0 0   1 0 0 011
010 0 0 0 01  0 1 0 0 0 1 01   0 0 1 1   1 1 0 100
010 0 0 0 01  0 0 1 0 0 1 01   0 0 1 1   1 0 0 100
010 0 0 0 10  0 1 0 0 0 1 10   0 0 1 0   1 1 1 010
010 0 0 0 10  0 0 1 0 0 1 10   0 0 1 0   1 0 0 010
                                         ⇑
                                  TAUTOLOGY/VALID
```

20.

$/\therefore \sim(R \cdot \sim W) \supset D$

1) $[(R \cdot B) \cdot (H \vee W)] \supset D$ Pr

```
[(R ·  B) ·  (H ∨ W)] ⊃ D
─────────────────────────
 1 1 1  1   1 1 1   1 1
 1 1 1  1   1 1 1   0 0
 1 1 1  1   1 1 0   1 1
 1 1 1  1   1 1 0   0 0
 1 1 1  1   0 1 1   1 1
 1 1 1  1   0 1 1   0 0
 1 1 1  0   0 0 0   1 1
 1 1 1  0   0 0 0   1 0
 1 0 0  0   1 1 1   1 1
 1 0 0  0   1 1 1   1 0
 1 0 0  0   1 1 0   1 1
 1 0 0  0   1 1 0   1 0
 1 0 0  0   0 1 1   1 1
 1 0 0  0   0 1 1   1 0
 1 0 0  0   0 0 0   1 1
 1 0 0  0   0 0 0   1 0
 0 0 1  0   1 1 1   1 1
 0 0 1  0   1 1 1   1 0
 0 0 1  0   1 1 0   1 1
 0 0 1  0   1 1 0   1 0
 0 0 1  0   0 1 1   1 1
 0 0 1  0   0 1 1   1 0
 0 0 1  0   0 0 0   1 1
 0 0 1  0   0 0 0   1 0
 0 0 0  0   1 1 1   1 1
 0 0 0  0   1 1 1   1 0
 0 0 0  0   1 1 0   1 1
 0 0 0  0   1 1 0   1 0
 0 0 0  0   0 1 1   1 1
 0 0 0  0   0 1 1   1 0
 0 0 0  0   0 0 0   1 1
 0 0 0  0   0 0 0   1 0
                     ⇑
```

CONTINGENT/CONSISTENT

46

```
{[(R · B) ·  (H ∨ W)]  ⊃ D}  ⊃  [∿(R ·  ∿ W)  ⊃ D]

  1 1 1   1   1 1 1    1 1   1    1 1 0 0 1   1 1
  1 1 1   1   1 1 1    0 0   1    1 1 0 0 1   0 0
  1 1 1   1   1 1 0    1 1   1    0 1 1 1 0   1 1
  1 1 1   1   1 1 0    0 0   1    0 1 1 1 0   1 0
  1 1 1   1   0 1 1    1 1   1    1 1 0 0 1   1 1
  1 1 1   1   0 1 1    0 0   1    1 1 0 0 1   0 0
  1 1 1   0   0 0 0    1 1   1    0 1 1 1 0   1 1
  1 1 1   0   0 0 0    1 0   1    0 1 1 1 0   1 0
  1 0 0   0   1 1 1    1 1   1    1 1 0 0 1   1 1
  1 0 0   0   1 1 1    1 0   0    1 1 0 0 1   0 0
  1 0 0   0   1 1 0    1 1   1    0 1 1 1 0   1 1
  1 0 0   0   1 1 0    1 0   1    0 1 1 1 0   1 0
  1 0 0   0   0 1 1    1 1   1    1 1 0 0 1   1 1
  1 0 0   0   0 1 1    1 0   0    1 1 0 0 1   0 0
  1 0 0   0   0 0 0    1 1   1    0 1 1 1 0   1 1
  1 0 0   0   0 0 0    1 0   1    0 1 1 1 0   1 0
  0 0 1   0   1 1 1    1 1   1    1 0 0 0 1   1 1
  0 0 1   0   1 1 1    1 0   0    1 0 0 0 1   0 0
  0 0 1   0   1 1 0    1 1   1    1 0 0 1 0   1 1
  0 0 1   0   1 1 0    1 0   0    1 0 0 1 0   0 0
  0 0 1   0   0 1 1    1 1   1    1 0 0 0 1   1 1
  0 0 1   0   0 1 1    1 0   0    1 0 0 0 1   0 0
  0 0 1   0   0 0 0    1 1   1    1 0 0 1 0   1 1
  0 0 1   0   0 0 0    1 0   0    1 0 0 1 0   0 0
  0 0 0   0   1 1 1    1 1   1    1 0 0 0 1   1 1
  0 0 0   0   1 1 1    1 0   0    1 0 0 0 1   0 0
  0 0 0   0   1 1 0    1 1   1    1 0 0 1 0   1 1
  0 0 0   0   1 1 0    1 0   0    1 0 0 1 0   0 0
  0 0 0   0   0 1 1    1 1   1    1 0 0 0 1   1 1
  0 0 0   0   0 1 1    1 0   0    1 0 0 0 1   0 0
  0 0 0   0   0 0 0    1 1   1    1 0 0 1 0   1 1
  0 0 0   0   0 0 0    1 0   0    1 0 0 1 0   0 0
                              ⇑
                  CONTINGENT/INVALID
```

47

3.7.

2.

    a)   ∿(M · R)
    b)   ∿M ∨ ∿R

∿(M · R) ≡ (∿ M ∨ ∿ R)

```
0 1 1 1   1   0 1 0 0 1
1 1 0 0   1   0 1 1 1 0
1 0 0 1   1   1 0 1 0 1
1 0 0 0   1   1 0 1 1 0
          ⇑
```
TAUTOLOGY/LOGICALLY EQUIVALENT

4.

    a)   ∿(H ∨ G)
    b)   ∿G · ∿H

∿(H ∨ G) ≡ (∿ G · ∿ H)

```
0 1 1 1   1   0 1 0 0 1
0 1 1 0   1   1 0 0 0 1
0 0 1 1   1   0 1 0 1 0
1 0 1 0   1   1 0 1 1 0
          ⇑
```
TAUTOLOGY/LOGICALLY EQUIVALENT

6.

    a)   P · A
    b)   ∿(∿P · ∿A)

(P · A) ≡ ∿(∿ P · ∿ A)

```
1 1 1   1 1 0 1 0 0 1
1 0 0   0 1 0 1 0 1 0
0 0 1   0 1 1 0 0 0 1
0 0 0   1 0 1 0 1 1 0
        ⇑
```
CONTINGENT/NOT LOGICALLY EQUIVALENT

8.

    a)   B ∨ C
    b)   ∿(∿B ∨ ∿C)

   (B ∨ C) ≡ ∿(∿ B ∨ ∿ C)
   _____

    1 1 1   1 1 0 1 0 0 1
    1 1 0   0 0 0 1 1 1 0
    0 1 1   0 0 1 0 1 0 1
    0 0 0   1 0 1 0 1 1 0
            ⇑
   CONTINGENT/NOT LOGICALLY EQUIVALENT

10.

    a)   (S ∨ B) · ∿(S · B)
    b)   (∿B ⊃ S) · (∿S · ∿B)

   [(S ∨ B) · ∿(S · B)] ≡ [(∿ B ⊃ S) · (∿ S · ∿ B)]
   _____

    1 1 1   0 0 1 1 1   1   0 1 0 1   0   0 1 0 0 1
    1 1 0   1 1 1 0 0   0   1 0 1 1   0   0 1 0 1 0
    0 1 1   1 1 0 0 1   1   0 1 1 0   0   1 0 0 0 1
    0 0 0   0 1 0 0 0   1   1 0 0 0   0   1 0 1 1 0
                         ⇑
            CONTINGENT/NOT LOGICALLY EQUIVALENT

12.

    a)   S ⊃ (B · P)
    b)   S ⊃ (B ⊃ P)

   [S ⊃ (B · P)] ≡ [S ⊃ (B ⊃ P)]
   _____

    1 1   1 1 1   1   1 1   1 1 1
    1 0   1 0 0   1   1 0   1 0 0
    1 0   0 0 1   0   1 1   0 1 1
    1 0   0 0 0   0   1 1   0 1 0
    0 1   1 1 1   1   0 1   1 1 1
    0 1   1 0 0   1   0 1   1 0 0
    0 1   0 0 1   1   0 1   0 1 1
    0 1   0 0 0   1   0 1   0 1 0
                   ⇑
        CONTINGENT/NOT LOGICALLY EQUIVALENT

14.

a) (F ∨ ∿D) • (E ∨ ∿D)
b) ∿D ∨ (F • E)

[(F ∨ ∿ D) • (E ∨ ∿ D)] ≡ [∿ D ∨ (F • E)]

1	1	0	1	1	1	1	0	1	1	0	1	1	1	1
1	1	0	1	0	0	0	0	1	1	0	1	0	1	0	0
1	1	1	0	1	1	1	1	0	1	1	0	1	1	1	1
1	1	1	0	1	0	1	1	0	1	1	0	1	1	0	0
0	0	0	1	0	1	1	0	1	1	0	1	0	0	0	1
0	0	0	1	0	0	0	0	1	1	0	1	0	0	0	0
0	1	1	0	1	1	1	1	0	1	1	0	1	0	0	1
0	1	1	0	1	0	1	1	0	1	1	0	1	0	0	0

⇑
TAUTOLOGY/LOGICALLY EQUIVALENT

16.

a) (D ⊃ A) • (D ⊃ F)
b) D ⊃ (A • F)

[(D ⊃ A) • (D ⊃ F)] ≡ [D ⊃ (A • F)]

1	1	1	1	1	1	1	1	1	1	1	1	1
1	1	1	0	1	0	0	1	1	0	1	0	0
1	0	0	0	1	1	1	1	1	0	0	0	1
1	0	0	0	1	0	0	1	1	0	0	0	0
0	1	1	1	0	1	1	1	0	1	1	1	1
0	1	1	1	0	1	0	1	0	1	1	0	0
0	1	0	1	0	1	1	1	0	1	0	0	1
0	1	0	1	0	1	0	1	0	1	0	0	0

⇑
TAUTOLOGY/LOGICALLY EQUIVALENT

18.

a) B ∨ [M · (T ∨ S)]
b) (T ∨ S) · (M ∨ B)

{B ∨ [M · (T ∨ S)]} ≡ [(T ∨ S) · (M ∨ B)]

{B	∨	[M	·	(T	∨	S)]}	≡	[(T	∨	S)	·	(M	∨	B)]
1	1	1	1	1	1	1	1	1	1	1	1	1	1	1
1	1	1	1	1	1	0	1	1	1	0	1	1	1	1
1	1	1	1	0	1	1	1	0	1	1	1	1	1	1
1	1	1	0	0	0	0	0	0	0	0	0	1	1	1
1	1	0	0	1	1	1	1	1	1	1	1	0	1	1
1	1	0	0	1	1	0	1	1	1	0	1	0	1	1
1	1	0	0	0	1	1	1	0	1	1	1	0	1	1
1	1	0	0	0	0	0	0	0	0	0	0	0	1	1
0	1	1	1	1	1	1	1	1	1	1	1	1	1	0
0	1	1	1	1	1	0	1	1	1	0	1	1	1	0
0	1	1	1	0	1	1	1	0	1	1	1	1	1	0
0	0	1	0	0	0	0	1	0	0	0	0	1	1	0
0	0	0	0	1	1	1	1	1	1	1	0	0	0	0
0	0	0	0	1	1	0	1	1	1	0	0	0	0	0
0	0	0	0	0	1	1	1	0	1	1	0	0	0	0
0	0	0	0	0	0	0	1	0	0	0	0	0	0	0

⇑

CONTINGENT/NOT LOGICALLY EQUIVALENT

51

20.
a)   (B ∨ W) ∨ ~(T ∨ S)
b)   [T ⊃ (W · B)] · [S ⊃ (B · W)]

```
[(B ∨ W) ∨ ~(T ∨ S)] ≡ {[T ⊃ (W · B)] · [S ⊃ (B · W)]}
───────────────────────────────────────────────────────────
   1 1 1   1 0 1 1 1   1   1 1   1 1 1   1   1 1   1 1 1
   1 1 1   1 0 1 1 0   1   1 1   1 1 1   1   0 1   1 1 1
   1 1 1   1 0 0 1 1   1   0 1   1 1 1   1   1 1   1 1 1
   1 1 1   1 1 0 0 0   1   0 1   1 1 1   1   0 1   1 1 1
   1 1 0   1 0 1 1 1   0   1 0   0 0 1   0   1 0   1 0 0
   1 1 0   1 0 1 1 0   0   1 0   0 0 1   0   0 1   1 0 0
   1 1 0   1 0 0 1 1   0   0 1   0 0 1   0   1 0   1 0 0
   1 1 0   1 1 0 0 0   1   0 1   0 0 1   1   0 1   1 0 0
   0 1 1   1 0 1 1 1   0   1 0   1 0 0   0   1 0   0 0 1
   0 1 1   1 0 1 1 0   0   1 0   1 0 0   0   0 1   0 0 1
   0 1 1   1 0 0 1 1   0   0 1   1 0 0   0   1 0   0 0 1
   0 1 1   1 1 0 0 0   1   0 1   1 0 0   1   0 1   0 0 1
   0 0 0   0 0 1 1 1   1   1 0   0 0 0   0   1 0   0 0 0
   0 0 0   0 0 1 1 0   1   1 0   0 0 0   0   0 1   0 0 0
   0 0 0   0 0 0 1 1   1   0 1   0 0 0   0   1 0   0 0 0
   0 0 0   1 1 0 0 0   1   0 1   0 0 0   1   0 1   0 0 0
                       ⇑
```
CONTINGENT/NOT LOGICALLY EQUIVALENT

52

4.1.B.

2.   /∴ F
    1)   ⋏D   Pr
    2)   F ∨ D ⌡   Pr
    3)   ⋏F   AP

    4) F   D   2, ID
       X   X   VALID

4.   /∴ ⋏C
    1)   C ≡ O ⌡   Pr
    2)   O   Pr
    3)   ⋏⋏C ⌡   AP
    4)   C   3, DN

    5) C   ⋏C   1, ME
    6) O   ⋏O   1, ME
                X   INVALID

6.   /∴ ⋏S
    1)   S ≡ P ⌡   Pr
    2)   ⋏P   Pr
    3)   ⋏⋏S ⌡   AP
    4)   S   3, DN

    5) S   ⋏S   1, ME
    6) P   ⋏P   1, ME
       X   X   VALID

8.   /∴ F · N
    1)   ⋏(⋏P ∨ ⋏F) ⌡   Pr
    2)   N   Pr
    3)   ⋏(F · N) ⌡   AP
    4)   ⋏⋏P ⌡   1, DID
    5)   ⋏⋏F ⌡   1, DID
    6)   P   4, DN
             |

7)   F   5, DN

8) ∿F   ∿N   3, DC
     X   X   VALID

10.   /∴ F ≡ R
   1)   P ≡ F ↲   Pr
   2)   ∿P △ R ↲   Pr
   3)   ∿(F ≡ R) ↲   AP

   4)   F   R   3, DME
   5)   ∿R   ∿F   3, DME

   6) P ∿P   P ∿P 1, ME
   7) F ∿F   F ∿F 1, ME
         X   X

   8)∿P   R   ∿P   R   2, ED
   9)∿R   ∿∿P ↲ ∿R   ∿∿P ↲ 2, ED
   10)X   P   X   P   9, DN
           X   X   VALID

12.   /∴ (R · ∿U) · V
   1)   R △ U ↲   Pr
   2)   ∿(U ∨ ∿V) ↲   Pr
   3)   ∿[(R · ∿U) · V] ↲   AP
   4)   ∿U   2, DID
   5)   ∿∿V ↲   2, DID
   6)   V   5, DN

   7)   R   U   1, ED
   8)   ∿U   ∿R   1, ED
               X

   9) ∿(R · ∿U) ↲   ∿V   3, DC

   10) ∿R   ∿∿U ↲   9, DC
   11) X   U   10, DN
           X   VALID

54

14.   /∴ W ∨ C
 1)   ~(D • ~W) ↓   Pr
 2)   ~(~C • E) ↓   Pr
 3)   D ∨ E ↓   Pr
 4)   ~(W ∨ C) ↓   AP
 5)   ~W   4, DID
 6)   ~C   4, DID

 7) ~~C ↓   ~E   2, DC
 8)   C   7, DN
      X
 9)   ~D   ~~W ↓   1, DC
10)   W   9, DN
               X
11) D   E   3, ID
    X   X   VALID

16.   /∴ ~I ≡ R
 1)   ~(A • I) • R ↓   Pr
 2)   (~I ⊃ A) ∨ ~R ↓   Pr
 3)   ~(~I ≡ R) ↓   AP
 4)   ~(A • I)   1, C
 5)   R   1, C

 6)   ~A   ~I   4, DC

 7)~I ⊃ A ↓   ~R   ~I ⊃ A ↓   ~R   2, ID
              X   X

 8)~~I ↓   A   ~~I ↓   A   7, MI
 9) I   X   I   8, DN
                  X
10)   ~I   R   3, DME
11)   ~R   ~~I ↓   3, DME
12)   X   I   11, DN
                            X   VALID

55

18.   /∴ (A · B) Δ L
   1)   L ≡ B ↲   Pr
   2)   (B ⊃ L) ⊃ A ↲   Pr
   3)   B   Pr
   4)   ∿[(A · B) Δ L] ↲   AP

   5)   L   ∿L   1, ME
   6)   B   ∿B   1, ME
                          X

   7) ∿(B ⊃ L) ↲   A   2, MI
   8)   B   7, DMI
   9)   ∿L   7, DMI

10) A·B ↲   ∿(A·B) ↲   A·B ↲   ∿(A·B) ↲   4, DED
11) L   ∿L   L   ∿L   4, DED
12) A   A   10, C
13) B   B   10, C
14)   ∿A   ∿B   ∿A   ∿B   10, DC
            X   X   X   INVALID

20.   /∴ S ∨ W
   1)   M ⊃ ∿(S ∨ W) ↲   Pr
   2)   W ⊃ (M ⊃ S) ↲   Pr
   3)   ∿(W ∨ ∿M) ↲   Pr
   4)   ∿(S ∨ W) ↲   Pr
   5)   ∿W   3, DID
   6)   ∿∿M ↲   3, DID
   7)   M   6, DN
   8)   ∿S   4, DID
   9)   ∿W   4, DID

10)   ∿M   ∿(S ∨ W) ↲   1, MI
11)   X   ∿S   10, DC
12)   ∿W   10, DC

56

13)   /∿W   M ⊃ S ↓\   2, MI

14)   ∿M   S   13, MI
                   X   X   INVALID

4.2.

2.   /∴ ∿(R ∨ ∿F)
   1)   R ∨ F ↓   Pr
   2)   ∿F ∨ ∿R ↓   Pr

   3)   R   F   1 ID

   4) ∿F   ∿R   ∿F   ∿R   2 ID
           X   X   CONSISTENT

4.   /∴ ∿I ⊃ ∿R
   1)   ∿(R · I) ↓   Pr
   2)   R ⊃ I ↓   Pr

   3)   ∿R   ∿I   1, DC

   4) ∿R   I ∿R   I   2, MI
              X   CONSISTENT

6.   /∴ D ∨ F
   1)   F ≡ D ↓   Pr
   2)   ∿(D ∨ F) ↓   Pr
   3)   ∿D   2, DMI
   4)   ∿F   2, DMI

   5)   F   ∿F   1, ME
   6)   D   ∿D   1, ME
         X   CONSISTENT

57

8.   ∴ S ⊃ (D ≡ F)
   1)   S ⊃ (F ⊃ D) ✓   Pr
   2)   D ⊃ (S ⊃ F) ✓   Pr

   3)   ~S   F ⊃ D ✓   1, MI

   4)   ~F   D   3, MI

 5)~D S ⊃ F ✓ ~D S ⊃ F ✓ ~D S ⊃ F ✓   2, MI
                                  X
 6)   ~S   F   ~S   F   ~S   F   5, MI
                   X

                                          CONSISTENT

10.   ∴ D ⊃ (~T · C)
   1)   ~T   Pr
   2)   [(C · D) ∨ ~T] · D ✓ Pr
   3)   ~(C · ~T) ✓   Pr
   4)   (C · D) ∨ ~T ✓   2, C
   5)   D   2, C

   6)   ~C   ~~T ✓   3, DC
   7)   T   6, DN

 8) C · D ✓   ~T   C · D ✓   ~T   4, ID
 9)   C   C   X   8, C
 10)   D   D   8, C
       X
                                      CONSISTENT

12.   ∴ B · (L ∨ C)
   1)   (B ⊃ ~C) · B ✓   Pr
   2)   B ⊃ L   Pr
   3)   (~C ⊃ R) · ~R ✓   Pr
   4)   B ⊃ ~C ✓   1, C
   5)   B   1, C
   6)   ~C ⊃ R ✓   3, C

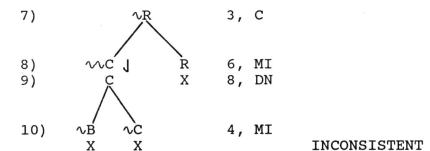

7)   ∿R   3, C

8)   ∿∿C ⌡   R   6, MI
9)   C   X   8, DN

10)   ∿B   ∿C   4, MI
         X   X   INCONSISTENT

Note that the inconsistency in #12 is generated from only the first and third premises.

14.   /∴ T

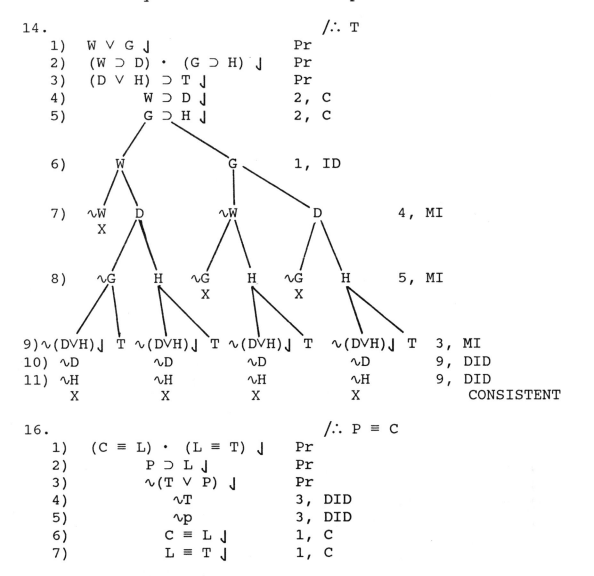

1)   W ∨ G ⌡   Pr
2)   (W ⊃ D) • (G ⊃ H) ⌡   Pr
3)   (D ∨ H) ⊃ T ⌡   Pr
4)   W ⊃ D ⌡   2, C
5)   G ⊃ H ⌡   2, C

6)   W   G   1, ID

7)   ∿W   D   ∿W   D   4, MI
      X

8)   ∿G   H ∿G   H ∿G   H   5, MI
                  X   X

9)∿(D∨H)⌡ T ∿(D∨H)⌡ T ∿(D∨H)⌡ T ∿(D∨H)⌡ T   3, MI
10) ∿D   ∿D   ∿D   ∿D   9, DID
11) ∿H   ∿H   ∿H   ∿H   9, DID
     X   X   X   X   CONSISTENT

16.   /∴ P ≡ C

1)   (C ≡ L) • (L ≡ T) ⌡   Pr
2)   P ⊃ L ⌡   Pr
3)   ∿(T ∨ P) ⌡   Pr
4)   ∿T   3, DID
5)   ∿p   3, DID
6)   C ≡ L ⌡   1, C
7)   L ≡ T ⌡   1, C

59

```
8)        ∿P              L           2, MI
         /  \            /  \
9)      C    ∿C         C    ∿C       6, ME
10)     L    ∿L         L    ∿L       6, ME
                              X
       /\   /\          /\
11)L ∿L L ∿L          L  ∿L           7, ME
12)T ∿T T ∿T           T   ∿T          7, ME
   X  X X                X    X
```
                                              CONSISTENT

18.   /∴ P ⊃ R
  1)   (D △ P) ≡ R ↙   Pr
  2)   ∿P ⊃ (R △ D) ↙   Pr

```
3)        D △ P ↙      ∿(D △ P) ↙      1, ME
4)          R             ∿R           1, ME
          /   \          /  \
5)      D       P                      3, ED
6)      ∿P      ∿D                     3, ED
7)                      D    ∿D        3, DED
8)                      P    ∿P        3, DED
```

```
9)∿∿P↙ R△D↙ ∿∿P↙ R△D↙ ∿∿P↙ R△D↙ ∿∿P↙ R△D↙  2, MI
10)  P        P        P        P            9, DN
     X                          X
11)    R  D      R  D      R  D     R   D     9, ED
12)  ∿D  ∿R    ∿D  ∿R    ∿D  ∿R   ∿D  ∿R      9, ED
     X         X         X         X    X
```
                                          CONSISTENT

20.   /∴ ∿(H △ G)
  1)   (G · ∿C) ⊃ (K ∨ C) ↙   Pr
  2)   K ⊃ ∿(H ∨ L) ↙   Pr
  3)   ∿C ∨ ∿(L ∨ H) ↙   Pr
  4)   ∿(∿G ∨ ∿L) ↙   Pr
  5)   ∿∿G ↙   4, DID
  6)   ∿∿L ↙   4, DID

                    60

7)   G   5, DN
8)   L   6, DN

9)   ~(G · ~C) ↲   K ∨ C ↲   1, MI

10)   ~G ~~C ↲   9, DC
11)   X   C   10, DN
12)   K   C   9, ID

13) ~C ~(L∨H)↲ ~C ~(L∨H)↲ ~C ~(L∨H)↲   3, ID
14) X   ~L   ~L   X   ~L   13, DID
15)   ~H   ~H   ~H   13, DID
         X   X   X

16)   ~K ~(H ∨ L) ↲   2, MI
17)   X   ~H   16, DID
18)   ~L   16, DID
                X

                                 INCONSISTENT

4.3.

2-a.
   1)   I ∨ (H ⊃ G) ↲   ———

   2) I   H ⊃ G   1, ID

   3)   ~H   G   2, MI

2-b.
   1) ~[I ∨ (H ⊃ G)] ↲   ———
   2)   ~I   1, DID
   3)   ~(H ⊃ G) ↲   1, DID
   4)   H   3, DMI

61

5) $\curlywedge$G   3, DMI

Since #2 is neither a contradiction nor a
tautology, it is CONTINGENT.

4-a.
  1) G $\lor$ ($\curlywedge$G $\cdot$ W) $\downarrow$ ——

  2) G $\curlywedge$G $\cdot$ W $\downarrow$ 1, ID
  3) $\curlywedge$G   2, C
  4)   W   2, C

4-b.
  1) $\curlywedge$[G $\lor$ ($\curlywedge$G $\lor$ W)] $\downarrow$ ——
  2) $\curlywedge$G   1, DID
  3) $\curlywedge$($\curlywedge$G $\cdot$ W) $\downarrow$ 1, DID

  4) $\curlywedge\curlywedge$G $\downarrow$ $\curlywedge$W   3, DC
  5)   G
         X

Since #4 is neither a contradiction nor a
tautology, it is CONTINGENT.

6-a.
  1) (M $\cdot$ L) $\supset$ (S $\lor$ $\curlywedge$L) $\downarrow$ ——

  2) $\curlywedge$(M $\cdot$ L) $\downarrow$ S $\lor$ $\curlywedge$L $\downarrow$ 1, MI

  3) $\curlywedge$M $\curlywedge$L   2, DC
  4)   S $\curlywedge$L   2, ID

6-b.
  1) $\curlywedge$[(M $\cdot$ L) $\supset$ (S $\lor$ $\curlywedge$L)] $\downarrow$ ——
  2)   M $\cdot$ L $\downarrow$ 1, DMI
  3) $\curlywedge$(S $\lor$ $\curlywedge$L) $\downarrow$ 1, DMI
  4)   M   2, C
  5)   L   2, C
  6) $\curlywedge$S   3, DID

7)   ∿S ↓   3, DID
8)   L   7, DN

Since #6 is neither a contradiction nor a tautology, it is CONTINGENT.

8-a.

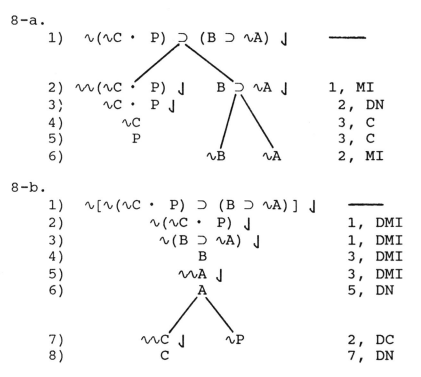

1) ~(~C · P) ⊃ (B ⊃ ~A) ↓   ——

2) ∿(~C · P) ↓   B ⊃ ~A ↓   1, MI
3)   ~C · P ↓   2, DN
4)   ~C   3, C
5)   P   3, C
6)   ~B   ~A   2, MI

8-b.

1) ~[~(~C · P) ⊃ (B ⊃ ~A)] ↓   ——
2)   ~(~C · P) ↓   1, DMI
3)   ~(B ⊃ ~A) ↓   1, DMI
4)   B   3, DMI
5)   ∿A ↓   3, DMI
6)   A   5, DN

7)   ∿C ↓   ~P   2, DC
8)   C   7, DN

Since #8 is neither a contradiction nor a tautology, it is CONTINGENT.

10-a.

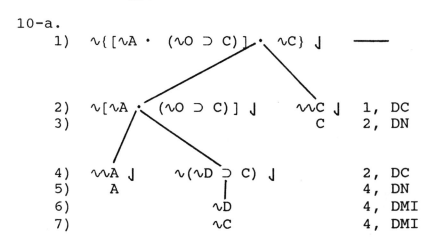

1) ~{[~A · (~O ⊃ C)] · ~C} ↓   ——

2) ~[~A · (~O ⊃ C)] ↓   ∿C ↓   1, DC
3)   C   2, DN

4) ∿A ↓   ~(~D ⊃ C) ↓   2, DC
5)   A   4, DN
6)   ~D   4, DMI
7)   ~C   4, DMI

63

10-b.
```
1)  ~~{[~A • (~O ⊃ C)] • ~C} ✓      ———
2)  [~A • (~O ⊃ C)] • ~C ✓          1, DN
3)      ~A • (~O ⊃ C) ✓             2, C
4)            ~C                     2, C
5)            ~A                     3, C
6)         ~O ⊃ C ✓                 3, C

7)      ~~O ✓        C               6, MI
8)        O          X               7, DN
```

Since #10 is neither a contradiction nor a tautology, it is CONTINGENT.

12.
```
1)  (C ⊃ B) ≡ (~B • C) ✓            ———

2)   C ⊃ B ✓     ~(C ⊃ B) ✓         1, ME
3)  ~B • C ✓     ~(~B • C) ✓         1, ME
4)    ~B                             3, C
5)     C                             3, C

6) ~C     B                          2, MI
7)  X     X                  C        2, DMI
8)                          ~B        2, DMI

9)                   ~~B ✓    ~C      3, DC
                      B       X       9, DN
                      X
```
                                    CONTRADICTION
14.
```
1)  ~(P V D) Δ ~(~D ⊃ P) ✓          ———

2) ~(P V D) ✓     ~(~D ⊃ P) ✓       1, ED
3)~~(~D ⊃ P) ✓   ~~(P V D) ✓        1, ED
4)     ~P                            2, DID
5)     ~D                            2, DID
6)  ~D ⊃ P ✓                        3, DN
      /\           |
```
```
64
```

7) ~~D ✓   P   6, MI
8)   D   X   7, DN
9)   X   ~D   2, DMI
10)   ~P   2, DMI
11)   P ∨ D ✓   3, DN

12)   P   D   11, ID
               X   X   CONTRADICTORY

16-a.
1)   ~(C ∨ S) ∆ ~(C ⊃ ~D) ✓   ———

2) ~(C ∨ S) ✓   ~(C ⊃ ~D) ✓   1, ED
3) ~~(C ⊃ ~D) ✓   ~~(C ∨ S) ✓   1, ED
4)   ~C   2, DID
5)   ~S   2, DID
6)   C ⊃ ~D ✓   3, DN

7) ~C   ~D   6, MI
8)   C   2, DMI
9)   ~~D ✓   2, DMI
10)   D   9, DN
11)   C ∨ S ✓   3, DN

12)   C   S   11, ID

16-b.
1)   ~[~(C ∨ S) ∆ ~(C ⊃ ~D)] ✓   ———

2) ~(C ∨ S) ✓   ~~(C ∨ S) ✓   1, DED
3) ~(C ⊃ ~D) ✓   ~~(C ⊃ ~D) ✓ 1, DED
4)   ~C   2, DID
5)   ~S   2, DID
6)   C   3, DMI
7)   ~~D ✓   3, DMI
8)   D   7, DN
9)   X   C ∨ S ✓   2, DN
10)   C ⊃ ~D ✓   3, DN

65

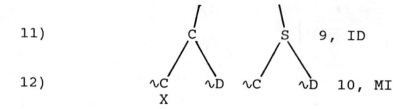

11)   C   S   9, ID

12)   ∿C   ∿D   ∿C   ∿D   10, MI
      X

Since #16 is neither a contradiction nor a tautology, it is CONTINGENT.

18.

1)   (D ≡ S) △ (∿S ≡ D) ↓   ———

2)   D ≡ S ↓   ∿S ≡ D ↓   1, ED
3) ∿(∿S ≡ D) ↓ ∿(D ≡ S) ↓   1, ED

4)   D   ∿D   2, ME
5)   S   ∿S   2, ME

6) ∿S   ∿∿S ↓   ∿S   ∿∿S ↓   3, DME
7)   D   ∿D   D   ∿D   3, DME
8)   X   S   X   S   6, DN
       X   X

9)   ∿S   ∿∿S ↓   2, ME
10)   D   ∿D   2, ME
11)   S   9, DN

12)   D   ∿D   D   ∿D   3, DME
13)   S   ∿S   S   ∿S   3, DME
       X   X   X   X

                           CONTRADICTION

20-a.

1)   [L ≡ ∿(A ∨ T)] △ [(L • M) ≡ ∿A] ↓   ———

2)   L ≡ ∿(A ∨ T) ↓   (L • M) ≡ ∿A ↓   1, ED
3)   ∿[(L • M) ≡ ∿A] ↓ ∿[L ≡ ∿(A ∨ T)] ↓   1, ED

66

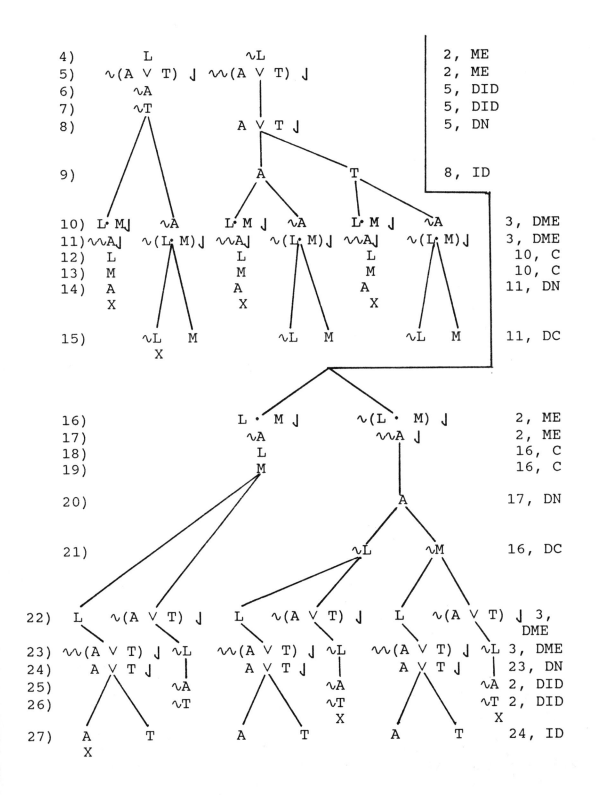

20-b.

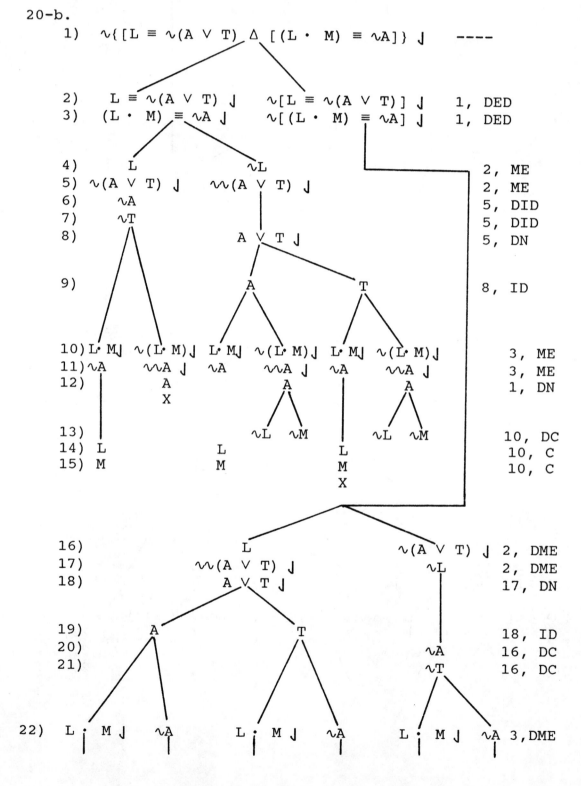

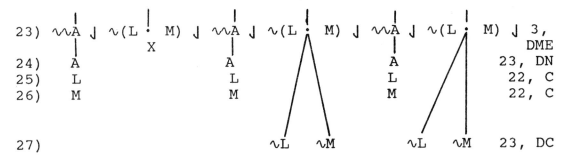

23) ∿∿A ⌡ ∿(L ∙ M) ⌡ ∿∿A ⌡ ∿(L ∙ M) ⌡ ∿∿A ⌡ ∿(L ∙ M) ⌡ 3,
                X   DME
24) A   A   A   23, DN
25) L   L   L   22, C
26) M   M   M   22, C

27)   ∿L   ∿M   ∿L   ∿M   23, DC

Since #20 is neither a contradiction nor a
tautology, it is CONTINGENT.

4.4.

2.
    a)   G ∨ ∿B
    b)   B ⊃ G

    1)   ∿[(G ∨ ∿B) ≡ (B ⊃ G)] ⌡   ----

    2) G ∨ ∿B ⌡   B ⊃ G ⌡   1, DME
    3) ∿(B ⊃ G) ⌡   ∿(G ∨ ∿B) ⌡ 1, DME
    4)   B   3, DMI
    5)   ∿G   3, DMI

    6) G   ∿B   2, ID
    7) X   X   ∿G   3, DID
    8)   ∿∿B ⌡   3, DID
    9)   B   8, DN

    10)   ∿B   G   2, MI
                    X   X   LOGICALLY EQUIVALENT

4.
    a)   C Δ T
    b)   ∿C ⊃ T

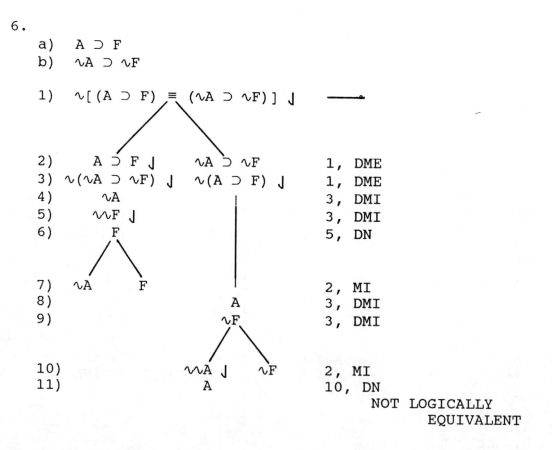

2)   C △ T ↓   ∿C ⊃ T ↓   1, DME
3) ∿(∿C ⊃ T) ↓   ∿(C △ T) ↓   1, DME
4)   ∿C   3, DMI
5)   ∿T   3, DMI

6)   C   T   2, ED
7   ∿T   ∿C   2, ED
8)   X   X   ∿∿C ↓   T   2, MI
9)   C   8, DN

10)   C ∿C C ∿C   3, DED
11)   T ∿T T ∿T   3, DED
                       X   X

                              NOT LOGICALLY
                              EQUIVALENT

6.

a)   A ⊃ F
b)   ∿A ⊃ ∿F

1)   ∿[(A ⊃ F) ≡ (∿A ⊃ ∿F)] ↓   ————•

2)   A ⊃ F ↓   ∿A ⊃ ∿F   1, DME
3) ∿(∿A ⊃ ∿F) ↓   ∿(A ⊃ F) ↓   1, DME
4)   ∿A   3, DMI
5)   ∿∿F ↓   3, DMI
6)   F   5, DN

7)   ∿A   F   2, MI
8)   A   3, DMI
9)   ∿F   3, DMI

10)   ∿∿A ↓   ∿F   2, MI
11)   A   10, DN

                              NOT LOGICALLY
                              EQUIVALENT

70

8.
   a)   ∿(A ∨ M)
   b)   ∿M ∨ ∿A

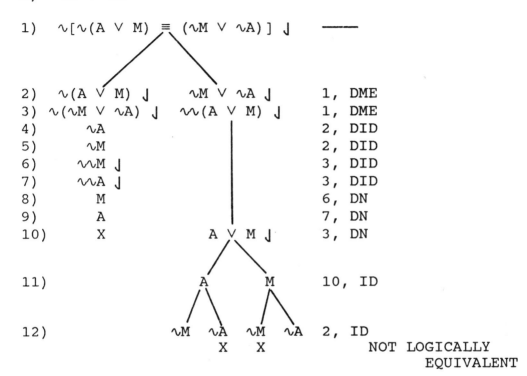

   1)   ∿[∿(A ∨ M) ≡ (∿M ∨ ∿A)] ↲   ————

   2)   ∿(A ∨ M) ↲   ∿M ∨ ∿A ↲   1, DME
   3) ∿(∿M ∨ ∿A) ↲   ∿∿(A ∨ M) ↲   1, DME
   4)   ∿A   2, DID
   5)   ∿M   2, DID
   6)   ∿∿M ↲   3, DID
   7)   ∿∿A ↲   3, DID
   8)   M   6, DN
   9)   A   7, DN
   10)   X   A ∨ M ↲   3, DN

   11)   A   M   10, ID

   12)   ∿M   ∿A   ∿M   ∿A   2, ID
                    X   X
                                        NOT LOGICALLY
                                        EQUIVALENT

10.
   a)   H ⊃ (V ≡ R)
   b)   (H · V) ⊃ R

   1)   ∿{[H ⊃ (V ≡ R)] ≡ [(H · V) ≡ R]} ↲   ————

   2)   H ⊃ (V ≡ R) ↲   (H · V) ⊃ R ↲   1, DME
   3) ∿[(H · V) ⊃ R] ↲ ∿[H ⊃ (V ≡ R)] ↲   1, DME
   4)   H · V ↲   3, DMI
   5)   ∿R   3, DMI
   6)   H   4, C
   7)   V   4, C

   8)   ∿H   V ≡ R ↲   2, MI
         X

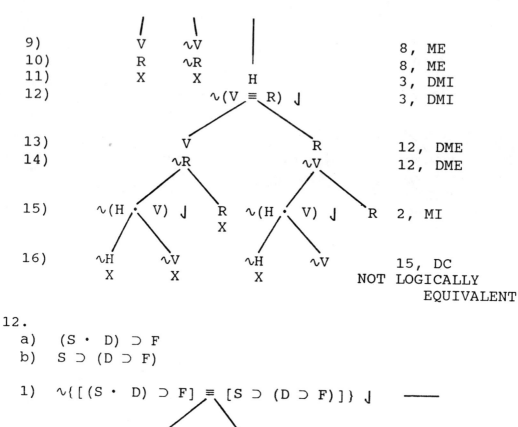

9)	V	~V		8, ME
10)	R	~R		8, ME
11)	X	X	H	3, DMI
12)		~(V ≡ R) J		3, DMI

13) V   R   12, DME
14) ~R   ~V   12, DME

15) ~(H • V) J   R   ~(H • V) J   R   2, MI
                 X

16) ~H   ~V   ~H   ~V   15, DC
     X   X   X   NOT LOGICALLY
                                  EQUIVALENT

12.
  a) (S · D) ⊃ F
  b) S ⊃ (D ⊃ F)

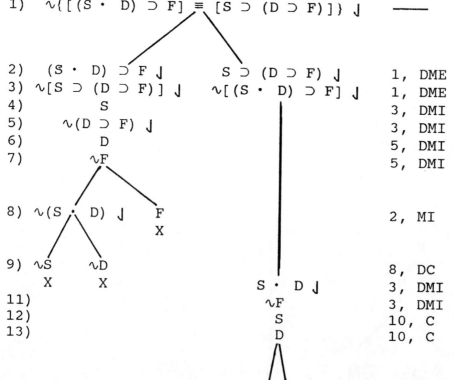

1) ~{[(S · D) ⊃ F] ≡ [S ⊃ (D ⊃ F)]} J   ——

2)	(S · D) ⊃ F J	S ⊃ (D ⊃ F) J	1, DME
3)	~[S ⊃ (D ⊃ F)] J	~[(S · D) ⊃ F] J	1, DME
4)	S		3, DMI
5)	~(D ⊃ F) J		3, DMI
6)	D		5, DMI
7)	~F		5, DMI

8) ~(S · D) J   F   2, MI
                X

9) ~S   ~D   8, DC
    X   X
                   S · D J   3, DMI
11)   ~F   3, DMI
12)   S   10, C
13)   D   10, C

14) ∿S   D ⊃ F ⌡   2, MI
     X

15)   ∿D   F   14, MI
           X   X   LOGICALLY
                       EQUIVALENT

14.
  a) R · (S ∨ B)
  b) (R · S) ∨ (R · B)

  1) ∿{[R · (S ∨ B)] ≡ [(R · S) ∨ (R · B)]} ⌡   ----

  2) R · (S ∨ B) ⌡   (R · S) ∨ (R · B) ⌡   1, DME
  3) ∿[(R · S) ∨ (R · B) ⌡ ∿[R · (S ∨ B)] ⌡   1, DME
  4)   R   2, C
  5)   S ∨ B ⌡   2, C
  6)   ∿(R · S) ⌡   3, DID
  7)   ∿(R · B) ⌡   3, DID

  8)   ∿R   ∿S   6, DC
       X

  9)   ∿R   ∿B   7, DC
          X

  10)   S   B   5, ID
  11)   X   X ∿R   ∿(S ∨ B) ⌡ 3, DC
  12)   ∿S   11, DID
  13)   ∿B   11, DID

  14)   R · S ⌡   R · B ⌡   R · S ⌡   R · B ⌡ 2,
         | | | | ID
  15)   R   R   R   R   14, C
  16)   S   B   S   B   14, C
         X   X   X   X
                                LOGICALLY
                                EQUIVALENT

73

16.
   a)   (P ∨ A) · (M ∨ C)
   b)   (C · M) ∨ (A · P)

1)   ∿{[(P ∨ A) · (M ∨ C)] ≡ [(C · M) ∨ (A · P)]} ↲   ----

2)   (P ∨ A) · (M ∨ C) ↲   (C · M) ∨ (A · P) ↲   1, DME
3)   ∿[(C · M) ∨ (A · P)] ↲   ∿[(P ∨ A) · (M ∨ C)] ↲   1, DME
4)   P ∨ A ↲   2, C
5)   M ∨ C ↲   2, C
6)   ∿(C · M) ↲   3, DID
7)   ∿(A · P) ↲   3, DID

8)   P   A   4, ID

9)   ∿A   ∿P   ∿A   ∿P   7, DC
              X   X

11) ∿C ∿M   ∿C ∿M   6, DC

12)   ∿(P ∨ A) ↲   ∿(M ∨ C) ↲ 3, DC

13)   ∿P   ∿M 12, DID
14)   ∿A   ∿C 12, DID

15)   C·M ↲   A·P ↲   C·M ↲   A·P ↲ 2, ID
16)   C   A   C   A   15, C
17)   M   P   M   P   15, C
                   X   X
                         NOT LOGICALLY
                         EQUIVALENT

18.
   a)   (G · O) ∨ (E · F)
   b)   [(O · G) ∨ E] · F

74

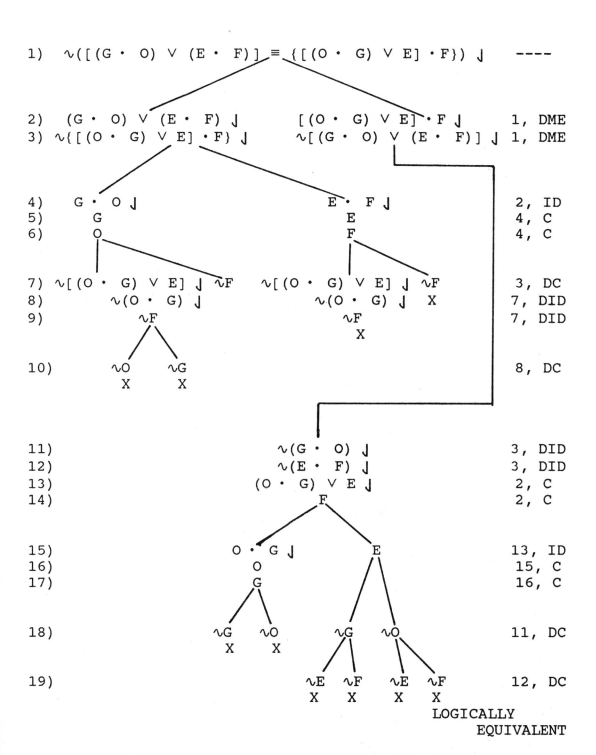

1) ~([[(G • O) ∨ (E • F)] ≡ {[(O • G) ∨ E] • F}) ⌡   ----

2) (G • O) ∨ (E • F) ⌡   [(O • G) ∨ E] • F ⌡   1, DME
3) ~{[(O • G) ∨ E] • F} ⌡   ~[(G • O) ∨ (E • F)] ⌡   1, DME

4)   G • O ⌡   E • F ⌡   2, ID
5)   G   E   4, C
6)   O   F   4, C

7) ~[(O • G) ∨ E] ⌡ ~F   ~[(O • G) ∨ E] ⌡ ~F   3, DC
8)   ~(O • G) ⌡   ~(O • G) ⌡   X   7, DID
9)   ~F   ~F   7, DID
                                         X

10)   ~O   ~G   8, DC
         X   X

11)   ~(G • O) ⌡   3, DID
12)   ~(E • F) ⌡   3, DID
13)   (O • G) ∨ E ⌡   2, C
14)   F   2, C

15)   O • G ⌡   E   13, ID
16)   O   15, C
17)   G   16, C

18)   ~G   ~O   ~G   ~O   11, DC
                   X   X

19)   ~E ~F ~E ~F   12, DC
                               X   X   X   X
                                          LOGICALLY
                                          EQUIVALENT

75

20.

a) $(R \equiv A) \supset G$
b) $G \lor {\sim}(A \mathbin{\triangle} {\sim}R)$

1) ${\sim}\{[(R \equiv A) \supset G] \equiv [G \lor {\sim}(A \mathbin{\triangle} {\sim}R)]\}$ ⌡   ----

2) $(R \equiv A) \supset G$ ⌡ $G \lor {\sim}(A \mathbin{\triangle} {\sim}R)$ ⌡   1, DME
3) ${\sim}[G \lor {\sim}(A \mathbin{\triangle} {\sim}R)]$ ⌡ ${\sim}[(R \equiv A) \supset G]$ ⌡   1, DME
4) ${\sim}G$ 3, DID
5) ${\sim}{\sim}(A \mathbin{\triangle} {\sim}R)$ ⌡   3, DID
6) $A \mathbin{\triangle} {\sim}R$ ⌡   5, DN

7) ${\sim}(R \equiv A)$ ⌡   G   2, MI
                        X

8) R   A   7, DME
9) ${\sim}A$ ${\sim}R$ 7, DME

10) A ${\sim}R$ A ${\sim}R$ 6, ED
11) ${\sim}{\sim}R$⌡ ${\sim}A$ ${\sim}{\sim}R$⌡ ${\sim}A$ 6, ED
12) R   X   R   X   11, DN
13) X   X $R \equiv A$ ⌡   3, DMI
14) ${\sim}G$ 3, DMI

15)   R ${\sim}R$ 13, ME
16)   A ${\sim}A$ 13, ME

17)   G ${\sim}(A \mathbin{\triangle} {\sim}R)$ ⌡   G ${\sim}(A \mathbin{\triangle} {\sim}R)$ ⌡   2, ID
            X   X

18)   A ${\sim}A$ A ${\sim}A$ 7, DED
19) ${\sim}R$ ${\sim}{\sim}R$ ⌡ ${\sim}R$ ${\sim}{\sim}R$ ⌡ 17, DED
20)   X   R   X   R   19, DN
                         X   X

LOGICALLY
EQUIVALENT

5.1.

2.   /∴ C
  1)   (A ⊃ B) Δ C   Pr
  2)   ∿(A ⊃ B)   Pr

                                      /∴ ∿[C ⊃ (D ⊃ B)]
  1)   [(A ∨ B) ⊃ ∿(C ∨ D)] Δ ∿[C ⊃ (D ⊃ B)]   Pr
  2)   ∿[(A ∨ B) ⊃ ∿(C ∨ D)]   Pr

4.   /∴ C ⊃ A
  1)   (A ≡ B) ⊃ C   Pr
  2)   B ≡ A   Pr

                              /∴ ∿[C ⊃ (D ⊃ B)] ⊃ (A ∨ B)
  1)   [(A ∨ B) ≡ ∿(C ∨ D)] ⊃ ∿[C ⊃ (D ⊃ B)]   Pr
  2)   ∿(C ∨ D) ≡ (A ∨ B)   Pr

6.   /∴ (A • ∿C) ⊃ ∿B
  1)   A ⊃ (B ⊃ C)   Pr

                    /∴ {(A ∨ B) • ∿∿[C ⊃ (D ⊃ B)]} ⊃ ∿∿(C ∨ D)
  1)   (A ∨ B) ⊃ {∿(C ∨ D) ⊃ ∿[C ⊃ (D ⊃ B)]}   Pr

8.   /∴ ∿C • ∿A
  1)   A ⊃ (B • B)   Pr
  2)   (B • ∿B) ⊃ C   Pr

                              /∴ ∿∿[C ⊃ (D ⊃ B)] • ∿(A ∨ B)
  1)   (A ∨ B) ⊃ [∿(C ∨ D) • ∿(C ∨ D)]   Pr
  2)   [∿(C ∨ D) • ∿∿(C ∨ D)] ⊃ ∿[C ⊃ (D ⊃ B)]   Pr

10.   /∴ (∿A • B) • C
  1)   ∿A • (B • C)   Pr

                  /∴ [∿(A ∨ B) • ∿(C ∨ D)] • ∿[C ⊃ (D ⊃ B)]
  1)   ∿(A ∨ B) • {∿(C ∨ D) • ∿[C ⊃ (D ⊃ B)]}   Pr

5.2.A.

2.
    1)   Pr
    2)   1, Com
    3)   /∴ 2, Simp

4.
    1)   Pr
    2)   Pr
    3)   2, Com
    4)   3, Simp
    5)   /∴ 4, 1, Conj

6.
    1)   Pr
    2)   1, Simp
    3)   1, Com
    4)   3, Simp
    5)   2, Simp
    6)   2, Com
    7)   6, Simp
    8)   4, 7, Conj
    9)   /∴ 8, 5, Conj

8.
    1)   Pr
    2)   Pr
    3)   1, Simp
    4)   1, Com
    5)   4, Simp
    6)   5, Simp
    7)   5, Com
    8)   7, Simp
    9)   2, Com
   10) 9, Simp
   11) 8, 3, Conj
   12) 10, 6, Conj
   13) /∴ 11, 12, Conj

10.
    1)   Pr
    2)   1, Simp
    3)   1, Com
    4)   3, Simp

```
 5)   2, Simp
 6)   2, Com
 7)   6, Simp
 8)   7, Com
 9)   8, Simp
10)   4, Simp
11)   4, Com
12)  11, Simp
13)  12, Com
14)  13, Simp
15)  10, 5, Conj
16)  14, 9, Conj
17)  /∴ 16, 15, Conj
```

5.2.B.

```
2.                    /∴ B
    1)  A · B      Pr
    2)  B · A      1, Com
    3)  /∴ B       2, Simp

4.                    /∴ A · B
    1)  A            Pr
    2)  B            Pr
    3)  /∴ A · B  1, 2, Conj

6.                              /∴ A ∨ B
    1)  (A ∨ B) · (C ∨ D)    Pr
    2)  /∴ A ∨ B             1, Simp

8.                              /∴ ∿(B · ∿A)
    1)  ∿(A · ∿B) · ∿(B · ∿A)    Pr
    2)  ∿(B · ∿A) · ∿(A · ∿B)    1, Com
    3)  /∴ ∿(B · ∿A)             2, Simp

10.                 /∴ ∿(B · ∿C) · [∿(C · ∿D) · ∿(∿A · ∿B)]
    1)  ∿(∿A · ∿B) · ∿(B · ∿C)    Pr
    2)  ∿(C · ∿D)                 Pr
    3)  ∿(∿A · ∿B)                1, Simp
    4)  ∿(B · ∿C) · ∿(∿A · ∿B)    1, Com
    5)  ∿(B · ∿C)                 4, Simp
```

6) $\sim$(C $\cdot$ $\sim$D) $\cdot$ $\sim$($\sim$A $\cdot$ $\sim$B)   2, 3, Conj
7) /$\therefore$ $\sim$(B $\cdot$ $\sim$C) $\cdot$ [$\sim$(C $\cdot$ $\sim$D) $\cdot$ $\sim$($\sim$A $\cdot$ $\sim$B)] 5, 6, Conj

5.2.C.

2.   /$\therefore$ D
   1) T $\cdot$ D   Pr
   2) D $\cdot$ T   1, Com
   3) /$\therefore$ D   2, Simp

4.   /$\therefore$ C $\cdot$ S
   1) C $\cdot$ (S $\cdot$ R)   Pr
   2) C   1, Simp
   3) (S $\cdot$ R) $\cdot$ C   1, Com
   4) S $\cdot$ R   3, Simp
   5) S   4, Simp
   6) /$\therefore$ C $\cdot$ S   2, 5, Conj

6.   /$\therefore$ R $\cdot$ G
   1) R $\cdot$ [N $\cdot$ (G $\cdot$ P)]   Pr
   2) R   1, Simp
   3) [N $\cdot$ (G $\cdot$ P)] $\cdot$ R   1, Com
   4) N $\cdot$ (G $\cdot$ P)   3, Simp
   5) (G $\cdot$ P) $\cdot$ N   4, Com
   6) G $\cdot$ P   5, Simp
   7) G   6, Simp
   8) /$\therefore$ R $\cdot$ G   2, 7, Conj

8.   /$\therefore$ (I $\supset$ E) $\cdot$ (P $\supset$ S)
   1) (I $\supset$ E) $\cdot$ (E $\supset$ N)   Pr
   2) (N $\supset$ P) $\cdot$ (P $\supset$ S)   Pr
   3) I $\supset$ E   1, Simp
   4) (P $\supset$ S) $\cdot$ (N $\supset$ P)   2, Com
   5) P $\supset$ S   4, Simp
   6) /$\therefore$ (I $\supset$ E) $\cdot$ (P $\supset$ S) 3, 5, Conj

10.   /$\therefore$ [S $\cdot$ (T $\vee$ A)] $\cdot$ [L $\cdot$ (D $\vee$ P)]
   1) [(T $\vee$ A) $\cdot$ (D $\vee$ P)] $\cdot$ (L $\cdot$ S)   Pr
   2) (T $\vee$ A) $\cdot$ (D $\vee$ P)   1, Simp
   3) T $\vee$ A   2, Simp

4)	(D ∨ P) • (T ∨ A)	2, Com
5)	D ∨ P	4, Simp
6)	(L • S) • [(T ∨ A) • (D ∨ P)]	1, Com
7)	L • S	6, Simp
8)	L	7, Simp
9)	S • L	7, Com
10)	S	9, Si^{a}p
11)	S • (T ∨ A)	10, 3, Conj
12)	L • (D ∨ P)	8, 5, Conj
13)	/∴ [S • (T ∨ A)] • [L • (D ∨ P)]	11, 12, Conj

5.3.A.

2.
1)	Pr	
2)	1, Com	
3)	2, Simp	
4)	/∴ 3, Add	

4.
1)	Pr	
2)	Pr	
3)	Pr	
4)	2, Com	
5)	4, 1, DS	
6)	3, Add	
7)	6, Com	
8)	/∴ 5, 7, Conj	

6.
1)	Pr	
2)	Pr	
3)	1, Simp	
4)	1, Com	
5)	4, Simp	
6)	2, Simp	
7)	2, Com	
8)	7, Simp	
9)	3, Com	
10)	9, 6, DS	
11)	8, 5, DS	
12)	/∴ 11, 10, Conj	

8.
```
1)   Pr
2)   Pr
3)   Pr
4)   Pr
5)   1, Simp
6)   1, Conj
7)   6, Simp
8)   2, 5, DS
9)   8, Com
10)  9, 4, DS
11)  10, Add
12)  11, Com
13)  3, Com
14)  13, 7, DS
15)  14, Com
16)  15, 4, DS
17)  /∴ 12, 16, Conj
```

10.
```
1)   Pr
2)   Pr
3)   1, Simp
4)   1, Com
5)   4, Simp
6)   5, Simp
7)   5, Com
8)   7, Simp
9)   2, Simp
10)  2, Com
11)  10, Simp
12)  9, Com
13)  12, 8, DS
14)  3, Com
15)  14, 6, DS
16)  13, 15, DS
17)  11, Com
18)  17, 15, DS
19)  18, Com
20)  19, 6, DS
21)  20, 16, Conj
22)  /∴ 21, Add
```

5.3.B.

2.   /∴ B
   1)   ∿A   Pr
   2)   A ∨ B   Pr
   3)   /∴ B   2, 1, DS

4.   /∴ C ∨ B
   1)   A ∨ B   Pr
   2)   ∿A   Pr
   3)   B   1, 2, DS
   4)   B ∨ C   3, Add
   5)   /∴ C ∨ B 4, Com

6.   /∴ (A · C) ∨ D
   1)   A · ∿B   Pr
   2)   C ∨ B   Pr
   3)   A   1, Simp
   4)   ∿B · A   1, Com
   5)   ∿B   4, Simp
   6)   B ∨ C   2, Com
   7)   C   6, 5, DS
   8)   A · C   3, 7, Conj
   9)   /∴ (A · C) ∨ D 8, Add

8.   /∴ (C ∨ A) · (B ∨ D)
   1)   (D · C) ∨ (A · B)   Pr
   2)   ∿(A · B)   Pr
   3)   (A · B) ∨ (D · C)   1, Com
   4)   D · C   3, 2, DS
   5)   D   4, Simp
   6)   D ∨ B   5, Add
   7)   B ∨ D   6, Com
   8)   C · D   4, Com
   9)   C   8, Simp
   10) C ∨ A   9, Add
   11) /∴ (C ∨ A) · (B ∨ D) 10 7, Conj

10.   /∴ [(B · ∿A) ∨ E] · [(C · ∿D) ∨ F]
   1)   (B ∨ A) · ∿A   Pr
   2)   (D ∨ C) · ∿D   Pr
   3)   B ∨ A   1, Simp

4)	∿A · (B ∨ A)	1, Com
5)	∿A	4, Simp
6)	A ∨ B	3, Com
7)	B	6, 5, DS
8)	B · ∿A	7, 5, Conj
9)	(B · ∿A) ∨ E	8, Add
10)	D ∨ C	2, Simp
11)	∿D · (D ∨ C)	2, Com
12)	∿D	11, Simp
13)	C	10, 12, DS
14)	C · ∿D	13, 12, Conj
15)	(C · ∿D) ∨ F	14, Add
16)	/∴ [(B · ∿A) ∨ E] · [(C · ∿D) ∨ F]	9, 15, Conj

5.3.C.

2.   /∴ P

1)	∿A · (P ∨ A)	Pr
2)	∿A	1, Simp
3)	(P ∨ A) · ∿A	1, Com
4)	P ∨ A	3, Simp
5)	A ∨ P	4, Com
6)	/∴ P	5, 2, DS

4.   /∴ (P ∨ A) · ∿S

1)	∿E ∨ (P · A)	Pr
2)	∿S · ∿∿E	Pr
3)	∿S	2, Simp
4)	∿∿E · ∿S	2, Com
5)	∿∿E	4, Simp
6)	P · A	1, 5, DS
7)	P	6, Simp
8)	P ∨ A	7, Add
9)	/∴ (P ∨ A) · ∿S	8, 3, Conj

6.   /∴ (I ∨ C) · (S ∨ T)

1)	(R ∨ I) · (L ∨ T)	Pr
2)	∿R · ∿L	Pr
3)	R ∨ I	1, Simp
4)	∿R	2, Simp

```
 5)  I                        3, 4, DS
 6)  I ∨ C                     5, Add
 7)  (L ∨ T) · (R ∨ I)        1, Com
 8)  L ∨ T                     7, Simp
 9)  ∿L · ∿R                   2, Com
10)  ∿L                        9, Simp
11)  T                         8, 10, DS
12)  T ∨ S                     11, Add
13)  S ∨ T                     12, Com
14)  /∴ (I ∨ C) · (S ∨ T)     6, 13, Conj
```

8.   /∴P
```
 1)  ∿(M ≡ S) · [∿A ∨ (M ≡ S)]      Pr
 2)  A ∨ ∿(∿L · S)                   Pr
 3)  P ∨ (∿L · S)                    Pr
 4)  ∿(M ≡ S)                        1, Simp
 5)  [∿A ∨ (M ≡ S)] · ∿(M ≡ S)      1, Com
 6)  ∿A ∨ (M ≡ S)                    5, Simp
 7)  (M ≡ S) ∨ ∿A                    6, Com
 8)  ∿A                              7, 4, DS
 9)  ∿(∿L · S)                       2, 8, DS
10)  (∿L · S) ∨ P                    3, Com
11)  /∴ P                            10, 9, DS
```

10.   /∴ (∿S ⊃ I) · (∿I ∨ ∿L)
```
 1)  ∿U ∨ (U ⊃ S)                     Pr
 2)  (S · ∿L) ∨ U                     Pr
 3)  ∿(U ⊃ S) · (∿S ⊃ I)             Pr
 4)  (U ⊃ S) ∨ ∿U                     1, Com
 5)  ∿(U ⊃ S)                         3, Simp
 6)  ∿U                               4, 5, DS
 7)  U ∨ (S · ∿L)                     2, Com
 8)  S · ∿L                           7, 6, DS
 9)  ∿L · S                           8, Com
10)  ∿L                               9, Simp
11)  ∿L ∨ ∿I                          10, Add
12)  ∿I ∨ ∿L                          11, Com
13)  (∿S ⊃ I) · ∿(U ⊃ S)             3, Com
14)  ∿S ⊃ I                           13, Simp
15)  /∴ (∿S ⊃ I) · (∿I ∨ ∿L)  14, 12, Conj
```

5.4.B.

2.
```
   1)  Pr
   2)  Pr
   3)  /∴ 1, 2, MT
```

4.
```
   1)  Pr
   2)  Pr
   3)  1, Simp
   4)  1, Com
   5)  4, Simp
   6)  5, 2, MT
   7)  /∴ 3, 6, MT
```

6.
```
   1)  Pr
   2)  Pr
   3)  Pr
   4)  Pr
   5)  Pr
   6)  4, 2, MP
   7)  3, 6, MT
   8)  1, 7, MP
   9)  5, 8, MP
  10)  /∴ 9, 8, Conj
```

8.
```
   1)  Pr
   2)  Pr
   3)  Pr
   4)  3, Simp
   5)  3, Com
   6)  5, Simp
   7)  4, Add
   8)  7, Com
   9)  2, 8, MP
  10)  1, 9, MP
  11)  10, 6, MP
  12)  11, 4, Conj
  13)  6, 9, Conj
  14)  /∴ 13, 12, Conj
```

10.
    1) Pr
    2) Pr
    3) Pr
    4) Pr
    5) Pr
    6) 3, Simp
    7) 3, Com
    8) 7, Simp
    9) 4, 5, MP
    10) 9, Simp
    11) 9, Com
    12) 11, Simp
    13) 8, 10, MT
    14) 6, 13, MT
    15) 2, Com
    16) 15, 14, DS
    17) 1, 16, MP
    18) /∴ 17, 12, MT

5.4.C.

2.   /∴ C
    1) A ∨ B   Pr
    2) (B ⊃ C) • ∿A   Pr
    3) ∿A • (B ⊃ C)   2, Com
    4) ∿A   3, Simp
    6) B   1, 4, DS
    7) B ⊃ C   2, Simp
    8) /∴ C   7, 6, MP

4.   /∴ ∿B • ∿A
    1) ∿(B ∨ C) ∨ A   Pr
    2) ∿A   Pr
    3) (D ∨ E) ⊃ (B ∨ C)   Pr
    4) ∿B ∨ (D ∨ E)   Pr
    5) A ∨ ∿(B ∨ C)   1, Com
    6) ∿(B ∨ C)   5, 2, DS
    7) ∿(D ∨ E)   3, 6, MT

8) (D ∨ E) ∨ ∿B   4, Com
9) ∿B   8, 7, DS
10) /∴ ∿B • ∿A   9, 2, Conj

6.   /∴ (∿A • ∿B) • (C • D)
1) (B ⊃ A) • (∿B ⊃ C)   Pr
2) (C ⊃ D) • ∿A.   Pr
3) B ⊃ A   1, Simp
4) ∿A • (C ⊃ D)   2, Com
5) ∿A   4, Simp
6) ∿B   3, 5 MT
7) ∿A • ∿B   5, 6, Conj
8) (∿B ⊃ C) • (B ⊃ A)   1, Com
9) ∿B ⊃ C   8, Simp
10) C   9, 6, MP
11) C ⊃ D   2, Simp
12) D   11, 10, MP
13) C • D   10, 12, Conj
14) /∴ (∿A • ∿B) • (C • D)   7, 13, Conj

8.   /∴ F ∨ E
1) (A ⊃ B) • (C ⊃ D)   Pr
2) A • ∿D   Pr
3) (∿C • B) ⊃ (E ∨ D)   Pr
4) A ⊃ B   1, Simp
5) A   2, Simp
6) B   4, 5 MP
7) (C ⊃ D) • (A ⊃ B)   1, Com
8) C ⊃ D   7, Simp
9) ∿D • A   2, Com
10) ∿D   9, Simp
11) ∿C   8, 10, MT
12) ∿C • B   11, 6, Conj
13) E ∨ D   3, 12, MP
14) D ∨ E   13, Com
15) E   14, 10, DS
16) E ∨ F   15, Add
17) /∴ F ∨ E   16, Com

10.   /∴ A • D
1) (A ∨ B) • (C ∨ D)   Pr
2) (B ⊃ E) • (C ⊃ F)   Pr
3) [(∿E • ∿F) ∨ G] • ∿G   Pr

88

4)	A ∨ B	1, Simp
5)	B ∨ A	4, Com
6)	B ⊃ E	2, Simp
7)	(~E · ~F) ∨ G	3, Simp
8)	G ∨ (~E · ~F)	7, Com
9)	~G · [(~E · ~F) ∨ G]	3, Com
10)	~G	9, Simp
11)	~E · ~F	8, 10, DS
12)	~E	11, Simp
13)	~B	6, 12, MT
14)	A	5, 13, DS
15)	(C ∨ D) · (A ∨ B)	1, Com
16)	C ∨ D	15, Simp
17)	(C ⊃ F) · (B ⊃ E)	2, Com
18)	C ⊃ F	17, Simp
19)	~F · ~E	11, Com
20)	~F	19, Simp
21)	~C	18, 20, DS
22)	D	16, 21, DS
23)	/∴ A · D	14, 22, Conj

5.4.D.

2.   /∴ ~~F

1)	~F ⊃ ~E	Pr
2)	~E ⊃ ~A	Pr
3)	~~A	Pr
4)	~~E	2, 3, MT
5)	/∴ ~~F	1, 4, MT

4.   /∴ C · S

1)	C · ~R	Pr
2)	E ⊃ R	Pr
3)	(C · ~E) ⊃ S	Pr
4)	C	1, Simp
5)	~R · C	1, Com
6)	~R	5, Simp
7)	~E	2, 6, MT

```
    8)   C · ∿E              4, 7, Conj
    9)   S                   3, 8, MP
   10)  /∴ C · S             4, 9, Conj

6.                             /∴ H · ∿C
    1)   (C ⊃ I) · (I ⊃ S)     Pr
    2)   ∿S ∨ R                Pr
    3)   ∿S ⊃ H                Pr
    4)   ∿R                    Pr
    5)   R ∨ ∿S                2, Com
    6)   ∿S                    5, 4, DS
    7)   H                     3, 6, MP
    8)   C ⊃ I                 1, Simp
    9)   (I ⊃ S) · (C ⊃ I)     1, Com
   10)   I ⊃ S                 9, Simp
   11)   ∿I                    10, 6, MT
   12)   ∿C                    8, 11, MT
   13)  /∴ H · ∿C              7, 12, Conj

8.                             /∴ (B · ∿R) ∨ (B · R)
    1)   (S ∨ R) · ∿C          Pr
    2)   I ⊃ C                 Pr
    3)   (S · ∿I) ⊃ B          Pr
    4)   R ⊃ C                 Pr
    5)   ∿C · (S ∨ R)          1, Com
    6)   ∿C                    5, Simp
    7)   ∿I                    2, 6 MT
    8)   S ∨ R                 1, Simp
    9)   R ∨ S                 8, Com
   10)   ∿R                    4, 6, MT
   11)   S                     9, 10, DS
   12)   S · ∿I                11, 7, Conj
   13)   B                     3, 12, MP
   14)   B · ∿R                13, 10, Conj
   15)  /∴ (B · ∿R) ∨ (B · R)  14, Add

10.                            /∴ [(T · L) · (S · B)] · M
    1)   T ⊃ M                 Pr
    2)   ∿(M Δ A)              Pr
    3)   (S ∨ R) ⊃ B           Pr
    4)   S ⊃ (L · ∿∿A)         Pr
    5)   (T ∨ ∿A) ∨ (M Δ A)    Pr
    6)   S                     Pr
```

7)	S ∨ R	6, Add
8)	B	3, 7, MP
9)	(M Δ A) ∨ (T ∨ ∿A)	5, Com
10)	T ∨ ∿A	9, 2, DS
11)	∿A ∨ T	10, Com
12)	L · ∿∿A	4, 6, MP
13)	L	12, Simp
14)	∿∿A · L	12, Com
15)	∿∿A	14, Simp
16)	T	11, 15, DS
17)	M	1, 16, MP
18)	T · L	16, 13, Conj
19)	S · B	6, 8, Conj
20)	(T · L) · (S · B)	18, 19, Conj
21)	/∴ [(T · L) · (S · B)] · M	20, 17, Conj

5.5.B.

2.
1)	Pr
2)	Pr
3)	Pr
4)	1, 3, 2, CD

4.
1)	Pr
2)	Pr
3)	2, Simp
4)	2, Com
5)	4, Simp
6)	5, 3, 1, CD
7)	6, Add
8)	/∴ 7, Com

6.
1)	Pr
2)	Pr
3)	Pr
4)	Pr
5)	Pr
6)	1, 5, DS
7)	3, 5, MP

```
    8)   4, 2, HS
    9)   8, 7, 6, CD
   10)  /∴ 9, Com

8.
    1)  Pr
    2)  Pr
    3)  1, Simp
    4)  1, Com
    5)  4, Simp
    6)  2, Simp
    7)  2, Com
    8)  7, Simp
    9)  3, 5, HS
   10)  6, 9, 8, CD
   11) /∴ 10, Com

10.
    1)  Pr
    2)  Pr
    3)  Pr
    4)  Pr
    5)  3, Simp
    6)  3, Com
    7)  6, Simp
    8)  7, Simp
    9)  7, Com
   10)  9, Simp
   11)  4, Simp
   12)  4, Com
   13)  12, Simp
   14)  2, 10, MP
   15)  14, Simp
   16)  14, Com
   17)  16, Simp
   18)  1, 15, MP
   19)  18, 11, 5, CD
   20)  8, 17, Conj
   21)  13, 20, MP
   22) /∴ 19, 21, Conj
```

5.5.C.

2.   /∴ A ⊃ D
   1)   A ⊃ B   Pr
   2)   B ⊃ C   Pr
   3)   C ⊃ D   Pr
   4)   A ⊃ C   1, 2, HS
   5)   /∴ A ⊃ D 4, 3, HS

4.   /∴ B ⊃ E
   1)   A ∨ (B ⊃ C)   Pr
   2)   (C ⊃ E) • ∿A   Pr
   3)   ∿A • (C ⊃ E)   2, Com
   4)   ∿A   3, Simp
   5)   B ⊃ C   1, 4, DS
   6)   C ⊃ E   2, Simp
   7)   /∴ B ⊃ E   5, 6, HS

6.   /∴ E ∨ F
   1)   (A ⊃ B) • (C ⊃ D)   Pr
   2)   A ∨ C   Pr
   3)   (D ⊃ F) • (B ⊃ E)   Pr
   4)   A ⊃ B   1, Simp
   5)   (B ⊃ E) • (D ⊃ F)   3, Com
   6)   B ⊃ E   5, Simp
   7)   A ⊃ E   4, 6, HS
   8)   (C ⊃ D) • (A ⊃ B)   1, Com
   9)   C ⊃ D   8, Simp
   10) D ⊃ F   3, Simp
   11) C ⊃ F   9, 10, HS
   12) /∴ E ∨ F   7, 11, 2, CD

8./∴ {[C ∨ (∿E ∨ ∿F)] • [∿(∿G • ∿H) ∨ I]} ∨ [C • ∿(∿G •
                                                        ∿H)]
   1)   [• (A • B) ⊃ C] • [D ⊃ (∿E ∨ ∿F)]   Pr
   2)   [∿(A • B) ∨ D] • [E ∨ ∿(∿A • ∿B)]   Pr
   3)   [E ⊃ ∿(∿G • ∿H)] • [∿(∿A • ∿S) ⊃ I]   Pr
   4)   ∿(A • B) ⊃ C   1, Simp
   5)   [D ⊃ (∿E ∨ ∿F)] • [• (A • B) ⊃ C]   1, Com
   6)   D ⊃ (∿E ∨ ∿F)   5, Simp
   7)   ∿(A • B) ∨ D   2, Simp

93

8)   C ∨ (~E ∨ ~F)   4, 6, 7, CD
9)   E ⊃ ~(~G · ~H)   3, Simp
10) [~(~A · ~S) ⊃ I] · [E ⊃ ~(~G · ~H)]   3 Com
11) ~(~A · ~S) ⊃ I   10, Simp
12) [E ∨ ~(~A · ~B)] · [~(A · B) ∨ D]   2, Com
13) E ∨ ~(~A · ~B)   12, Simp
14) ~(~G · ~H) ∨ I   9, 11, 13, CD
15) [C ∨ (~E ∨ ~F)] · [~(~G · ~H) ∨ I]   8, 14, Conj
16) /∴ {[C ∨ (~E ∨ ~F)] · [~(~G · ~H) ∨ I]} ∨ [C · ~(~G ·
                                            ~H)] 15, Add

10.   /∴ H ∨ F
1)   (A ∨ ~B) ⊃ (C ∨ D)   Pr
2)   [~E ⊃ (C ⊃ F)] · [~G ⊃ (D ⊃ H)]   Pr
3)   [E ⊃ (H ∨ I)] · [G ⊃ (I ∨ J)]   Pr
4)   ~(H ∨ I) · ~(I ∨ J)   Pr
5)   (I ∨ J) ∨ [(H ∨ I) ∨ (A ∨ ~B)]   Pr
6)   E ⊃ (H ∨ I)   3, Simp
7)   ~(H ∨ I)   4, Simp
8)   ~E   6, 7, MT
9)   ~E ⊃ (C ⊃ F)   2, Simp
10) C ⊃ F   9, 8, MP
11) [G ⊃ (I ∨ J)] · [E ⊃ (H ∨ I)]   3, Com
12) G ⊃ (I ∨ J)   11, Simp
13) ~(I ∨ J) · ~(H ∨ I)   4, Com
14) ~(I ∨ J)   13, Simp
15) ~G   12, 14, MT
16) [~G ⊃ (D ⊃ H)] · [~E ⊃ (C ⊃ F)]   2, Com
17) ~G ⊃ (D ⊃ H)   16, Simp
18) D ⊃ H   17, 15, MP
19) (H ∨ I) ∨ (A ∨ ~B)   5, 14, DS
20) A ∨ ~B   19, 7, DS
21) C ∨ D   1, 20, MP
22) F ∨ H   10, 18, 21, CD
23) /∴ H ∨ F   22, Com

5.5.D.

2.   /∴ T ∨ B
  1) (C ∨ E) ⊃ T   Pr
  2) (G ⊃ C) • (S ⊃ E)   Pr
  3) S ∨ G   Pr
  4) G ⊃ C   2, Simp
  5) (S ⊃ E) • (G ⊃ C)   2, Com
  6) S ⊃ E   5, Simp
  7) E ∨ C   6, 4, 3, CD
  8) C ∨ E   7, Com
  9) T   1, 8, MP
  10) /∴ T ∨ B   9, Add

4.   /∴ H ∨ A
  1) (K ∨ C) • (K ⊃ T)   Pr
  2) (T ⊃ A) • (C ⊃ H)   Pr
  3) (K ⊃ T) • (K ∨ C)   1, Com
  4) K ⊃ T   3, Simp
  5) T ⊃ A   2, Simp
  6) K ⊃ A   4, 5, HS
  7) (C ⊃ H) • (T ⊃ A)   2, Com
  8) C ⊃ H   7, Simp
  9) K ∨ C   1, Simp
  10) A ∨ H   6, 8, 9, CD
  11) /∴ H ∨ A   10, Com

6.   /∴ P ∨ R
  1) ∿C ⊃ (E ⊃ P)   Pr
  2) C ⊃ U   Pr
  3) ∿C ⊃ (∿I ⊃ R)   Pr
  4) ∿U • (∿I ∨ E)   Pr
  5) ∿U   4, Simp
  6) ∿C   2, 5, MT
  7) ∿I ⊃ R   3, 6, MP
  8) E ⊃ P   1, 6, MP
  9) (∿I ∨ E) • ∿U   4, Com
  10) ∿I ∨ E   9, Simp
  11) R ∨ P   7, 8, 10, CD
  12) /∴ P ∨ R   11, Com

8.   /∴ (I · A) ∨ (E ∨ M)
   1) (C ∨ I) ∨ A   Pr
   2) ∿A · (U ⊃ M)   Pr
   3) (C ⊃ U) · (I ⊃ E)   Pr
   4) C ⊃ U   3, Simp
   5) (U ⊃ M) · ∿A   2, Com
   6) U ⊃ M   5, Simp
   7) C ⊃ M   4, 6, HS
   8) (I ⊃ E) · (C ⊃ U)   3, Com
   9) I ⊃ E   8, Simp
  10) A ∨ (C ∨ I)   1, Com
  11) ∿A   2, Simp
  12) C ∨ I   10, 11, DS
  13) M ∨ E   7, 9, 12, CD
  14) E ∨ M   13, Com
  15) (E ∨ M) ∨ (I · A)   14, Add
  16) /∴ (I · A) ∨ (E ∨ M)   15, Com

10.   /∴ (H · L) ∨ (H ∨ L)
   1) E ⊃ (W ⊃ H)   Pr
   2) (E ∨ ∿M) · (∿M ⊃ I)   Pr
   3) ∿I · (I ⊃ L)   Pr
   4) ∿∿M ⊃ (I ∨ W)   Pr
   5) (I ⊃ L) · ∿I   3, Com
   6) I ⊃ L   5, Simp
   7) (∿M ⊃ I) · (E ∨ ∿M)   2, Com
   8) ∿M ⊃ I   7, Simp
   9) ∿I   3, Simp
  10) ∿∿M   8, 9, MT
  11) E ∨ ∿M   2, Simp
  12) ∿M ∨ E   11, Com
  13) E   12, 10, DS
  14) W ⊃ H   1, 13, MP
  15) I ∨ W   4, 10, MP
  16) L ∨ H   6, 14, 15, CD
  17) H ∨ L   16, Com
  18) (H ∨ L) ∨ (H · L)   17, Add
  19) /∴ (H · L) ∨ (H ∨ L)   18, Com

CHAPTER 6

6.1.A.

2.
- 1) Pr
- 2) 1, Com
- 3) 2, Com
- 4) /∴ 3, Assoc

4.
- 1) Pr
- 2) 1, Com
- 3) 2, Com
- 4) 3, Assoc
- 5) 4, Assoc
- 6) 5, Com
- 7) 6, Assoc
- 8) /∴ 7, Assoc

6.
- 1) Pr
- 2) 1, Assoc
- 3) 2, Assoc
- 4) 3, Com
- 5) 4, Assoc
- 6) 5, Com
- 7) 6, Assoc
- 8) 7, Com
- 9) /∴ 8, Com

8.
- 1) Pr
- 2) Pr
- 3) Pr
- 4) Pr
- 5) Pr
- 6) 2, Assoc
- 7) 6, Com
- 8) 7, Com
- 9) 8, 1, HS
- 10) 5, Com
- 11) 3, 10, HS
- 12) 9, 11, MP

```
13) 12, Com
14) 13, Assoc
15) /∴ 14, 4, DS
```

10.
```
1)  Pr
2)  Pr
3)  Pr
4)  Pr
5)  Pr
6)  2, Simp
7)  6, Assoc
8)  7, Com
9)  1, 8, DS
10) 3, Assoc
11) 10, Com
12) 11, Assoc
13) 4, Com
14) 13, Assoc
15) 5, Simp
16) 14, 15, DS
17) 12, 16, DS
18) 9, 17, MP
19) 5, Com
20) 19, Simp
21) 2, Com
22) 21, Simp
23) 18, 20, 22, CD
24) /∴ 23, Com
```

6.1.B.

2.   /∴ (C ∨ B) ∨ (D ∨ A)
```
1)  (A ∨ B) ∨ (C ∨ D)         Pr
2)  (C ∨ D) ∨ (A ∨ B)         1, Com
3)  C ∨ [D ∨ (A ∨ B)]         2, Assoc
4)  C ∨ [(D ∨ A) ∨ B]         3, Assoc
5)  C ∨ [B ∨ (D ∨ A)]         4, Com
6)  /∴ (C ∨ B) ∨ (D ∨ A)      5, Assoc
```

4.   /∴ {C ∨ [C · (B · A)]} ∨ D
   1) [(A · B) · C] ∨ (D ∨ C)   Pr
   2) [(A · B) · C] ∨ (C ∨ D)   1, Com
   3) {[(A · B) · C] ∨ C} ∨ D   2, Assoc
   4) {C ∨ [(A · B) · C]} ∨ D   3, Com
   5) {C ∨ [C ∨ (A · B)]} ∨ D   4, Com
   6) /∴ {C ∨ [C ∨ (B · A)]} ∨ D   5, Com

6.   /∴ D ≡ E
   1) (A Δ B) ⊃ C   Pr
   2) (D ⊃ C) ⊃ (E ≡ D)   Pr
   3) D ⊃ (B Δ A)   Pr
   4) (B Δ A) ⊃ C   1, Com
   5) D ⊃ C   3, 4, HS
   6) E ≡ D   2, 5, MP
   7) /∴ D ≡ E   6, Com

8.   /∴ G ∨ H
   1) (A ∨ B) ⊃ (D ∨ C)   Pr
   2) E · [E ⊃ (C ⊃ G)]   Pr
   3) (B ∨ A) ⊃ (D ⊃ H)   Pr
   4) (F ∨ E) ⊃ (A ∨ B)   Pr
   5) E   2, Simp
   6) [E ⊃ (C ⊃ G)] · E   2, Com
   7) E ⊃ (C ⊃ G)   6, Simp
   8) C ⊃ G   7, 5 MP
   9) E ∨ F   5, Add
   10) F ∨ E   9, Com
   11) A ∨ B   4, 10, MP
   12) B ∨ A   11, Com
   13) D ⊃ H   3, 12, MP
   14) D ∨ C   1, 11, MP
   15) H ∨ G   13, 8, 14, CD
   16) /∴ G ∨ H   15, Com

10.   /∴ H ∨ (C ∨ D)
   1) [(H · G) · E] ⊃ C   Pr
   2) A ⊃ [(G · H) · E]   Pr
   3) (B ⊃ D) · {[F ∨ (I ∨ B)] ∨ (G ∨ A)}   Pr
   4) ∿(I ∨ F) · ∿G   Pr
   5) [(G · H) · E] ⊃ C   1, Com
   6) A ⊃ C   2, 5 HS
   7) B ⊃ D   3, Simp

99

```
 8)  {[F ∨ (I ∨ B)] ∨ (G ∨ A)} · (B ⊃ D)     3, Com
 9)  [F ∨ (I ∨ B)] ∨ (G ∨ A)                  8, Simp
10)  [(F ∨ I) ∨ B] ∨ (G ∨ A)                  9, Assoc
11)  [(I ∨ F) ∨ B] ∨ (G ∨ A)                 10, Com
12)  (I ∨ F) ∨ [B ∨ (G ∨ A)]                 11, Assoc
13)  ∿(I ∨ F)                                  4, Simp
14)  B ∨ (G ∨ A)                             12, 13, DS
15)  (G ∨ A) ∨ B                             14, Com
16)  G ∨ (A ∨ B)                             15, Assoc
17)  ∿G · ∿(I ∨ F)                             4, Com
18)  ∿G                                       17, Simp
19)  A ∨ B                                    16, 18, DS
20)  C ∨ D                                    6, 7, 19, CD
21)  (C ∨ D) ∨ H                             20, Add
22)  /∴ H ∨ (C ∨ D)                           21, Com
```

6.1.C.

2.   /∴ R ∨ A
```
 1)  ∿(P △ A)           Pr
 2)  M ∨ (A △ P)        Pr
 3)  M ⊃ R              Pr
 4)  (A △ P) ∨ M        2, Com
 5)  ∿(A △ P)           1, Com
 6)  M                  4, 5, DS
 7)  R                  3, 6, MP
 8)  /∴ R ∨ A           7, Add
```

4.   /∴ G ∨ P
```
 1)  (W ≡ D) ⊃ G        Pr
 2)  (S ⊃ G) ⊃ P        Pr
 3)  S ⊃ (D ≡ W)        Pr
 4)  (D ≡ W) ⊃ G        1, Com
 5)  S ⊃ G              3, 4, HS
 6)  P                  2, 5, MP
 7)  P ∨ G              6, Add
 8)  /∴ G ∨ P           7, Com
```

6. /∴ G

1) (C ∨ D) ∨ (L ∨ T)   Pr
2) (L ∨ C) ⊃ G   Pr
3) ∿(T ∨ D)   Pr
4) (L ∨ T) ∨ (C ∨ D)   1, Com
5) (L ∨ T) ∨ (D ∨ C)   4, Com
6) L ∨ [T ∨ (D ∨ C)]   5, Assoc
7) L ∨ [(T ∨ D) ∨ C]   6, Assoc
8) [(T ∨ D) ∨ C] ∨ L   7, Com
9) (T ∨ D) ∨ (C ∨ L)   8, Assoc
10) C ∨ L   9, 3, DS
11) L ∨ C   10, Com
12) /∴ G   2, 11, MP

8. /∴ U ∨ E

1) ∿(I Δ P)   Pr
2) (P Δ I) ∨ (R ⊃ I)   Pr
3) ∿P • (I ⊃ U)   Pr
4) (R ⊃ U) ⊃ [P ∨ (C ⊃ E)]   Pr
5) (C ∨ P) ∨ R   Pr
6) ∿(P Δ I)   1, Com
7) R ⊃ I   2, 6 DS
8) (I ⊃ U) • ∿P   3, Com
9) I ⊃ U   8, Simp
10) R ⊃ U   7, 9, HS
11) P ∨ (C ⊃ E)   4, 10, MP
12) ∿P   3, Simp
13) C ⊃ E   11, 12, DS
14) (P ∨ C) ∨ R   5, Com
15) P ∨ (C ∨ R)   14, Assoc
16) C ∨ R   15, 12, DS
17) R ∨ C   16, Com
18) /∴ U ∨ E   10, 13, 17, CD

10. /∴ (S ∨ D) ∨ F

1) I ⊃ [(D ∨ O) ∨ U]   Pr
2) U ⊃ (I • D)   Pr
3) ∿O • (T • I)   Pr
4) (T ∨ I) ⊃ (D ⊃ S)   Pr
5) (D • I) ⊃ F   Pr
6) ∿O   3, Simp
7) (T • I) • ∿O   3, Com
8) T • I   7, Simp

101

9)	T	8, Simp
10)	I · T	8, Com
11)	I	10, Simp
12)	T ∨ I	9, Add
13)	D ⊃ S	4, 12, MP
14)	(D ∨ O) ∨ U	1, 11, MP
15)	(O ∨ D) ∨ U	14, Com
16)	O ∨ (D ∨ U)	15, Assoc
17)	D ∨ U	16, 6, DS
18)	U ⊃ (D · I)	2, Com
19)	U ⊃ F	18, 5, HS
20)	S ∨ F	13, 19, 17, CD
21)	(S ∨ F) ∨ D	20, Add
22)	S ∨ (F ∨ D)	21, Assoc
23)	S ∨ (D ∨ F)	22, Com
24)	/∴ (S ∨ D) ∨ F	23, Assoc

6.2.A.

2.
```
1)  Pr
2)  Pr
3)  Pr
4)  3 DN
5)  1, 4, MT
6)  /∴ 2, 5, DS
```

4.
```
1)  Pr
2)  Pr
3)  2, DN
4)  1, 3, MT
5)  4, DN
6)  5, Add
7)  /∴ 6, Com
```

6.
```
1)  Pr
2)  Pr
3)  Pr
4)  3, Simp
```

```
   5)  1, 4, MT
   6)  5, DN
   7)  3, Com
   8)  7, Simp
   9)  8, Com
  10)  9, 4, DS
  11)  2, 10, MP
  12)  11, Trans
  13)  /∴ 6, 12, HS
```

8.
```
   1)  Pr
   2)  Pr
   3)  Pr
   4)  Pr
   5)  4, Simp
   6)  2, 5, MT
   7)  6, DN
   8)  4, Com
   9)  8, Simp
  10)  1, 9, MP
  11)  10, Trans
  12)  3, Com
  13)  12, Assoc
  14)  13, 5, DS
  15)  /∴ 7, 11, 14, CD
```

10.
```
   1)  Pr
   2)  Pr
   3)  Pr
   4)  Pr
   5)  Pr
   6)  1, Assoc
   7)  6, Assoc
   8)  7, Com
   9)  8, Assoc
  10)  9, 2, DS
  11)  10, DN
  12)  3, 11, MT
  13)  12, DN
  14)  2, Com
  15)  4, 14, DS
  16)  13, 15, HS
  17)  16, DN
  18)  5, 18, MT
```

```
19)  18, DN
20)  19, Trans
21)  /∴ 16, 20, HS
```

6.2.B.

2.   /∴ A ⊃ C
```
  1)  (A ⊃ B) • (∿C ⊃ ∿B)     Pr
  2)  A ⊃ B                    1, Simp
  3)  (∿C ⊃ ∿B) • (A ⊃ B)      1, Com
  4)  ∿C ⊃ ∿B                  3, Simp
  5)  B ⊃ C                    4, Trans
  6)  /∴ A ⊃ C                 2, 5, HS
```

4.   /∴ B ⊃ D
```
  1)  ∿A ⊃ ∿B                  Pr
  2)  C ⊃ (∿D ⊃ ∿A)            Pr
  3)  ∿C ⊃ ∿E                  Pr
  4)  E                        Pr
  5)  B ⊃ A                    1, Trans
  6)  E ⊃ C                    3, Trans
  7)  C                        6, 4, MP
  8)  ∿D ⊃ ∿A                  2, 7, MP
  9)  A ⊃ D                    8, Trans
 10)  /∴ B ⊃ D                 5, 9, HS
```

6.   /∴ D ∨ E
```
  1)  (B ∨ A) ⊃ C              Pr
  2)  A                        Pr
  3)  ∿(B ⊃ D) ⊃ ∿A            Pr
  4)  C ⊃ (A ⊃ E)              Pr
  5)  A ∨ B                    2, Add
  6)  B ∨ A                    5, Com
  7)  C                        1, 6, MP
  8)  A ⊃ E                    4, 7, MP
  9)  A ⊃ (B ⊃ D)              3, Trans
 10)  B ⊃ D                    9, 2, MP
 11)  /∴ D ∨ E                 10, 8, 6, CD
```

Following is a proof of #6 that does not use the third premise:

$$/\therefore D \lor E$$

1)	(B ∨ A) ⊃ C	Pr
2)	A	Pr
3)	∿(B ⊃ D) ⊃ ∿A	Pr
4)	C ⊃ (A ⊃ E)	Pr
5)	A ∨ B	2, Add
6)	B ∨ A	5, Com
7)	C	1, 6, MP
8)	A ⊃ E	4, 7, MP
9)	E	8, 2, MP
10)	E ∨ D	9, Add
11)	/∴ D ∨ E	10, Com

8. $$/\therefore F \supset H$$

1)	B ⊃ ∿[(A ∨ C) ∨D]	Pr
2)	A · (∿B ⊃ C)	Pr
3)	(A · C) ⊃ (∿G ⊃ ∿F)	Pr
4)	G ⊃ H	Pr
5)	A	2, Simp
6)	A ∨ (C ∨ D)	5, Add
7)	(A ∨ C) ∨ D	6, Assoc
8)	∿∿[(A ∨ C) ∨ D]	7, DN
9)	∿B	1, 8, MT
10)	(∿B ⊃ C) · A	2, Com
11)	∿B ⊃ C	10, Simp
12)	C	11, 9 MP
13)	A · C	5, 12, Conj
14)	∿G ⊃ ∿F	3, 13, MP
15)	F ⊃ G	14, Trans
16)	/∴ F ⊃ H	15, 4, HS

10. $$/\therefore A \lor C$$

1)	(∿B ⊃ ∿E) · (∿E ⊃ ∿A)	Pr
2)	∿(A ∨ C) ⊃ ∿(C ⊃ B)	Pr
3)	∿A ⊃ ∿D	Pr
4)	(∿D ⊃ ∿F) · (∿F ⊃ ∿C)	Pr
5)	∿D ⊃ ∿F	4, Simp
6)	(∿F ⊃ ∿C) · (∿D ⊃ ∿F)	4, Com
7)	∿F ⊃ ∿C	6, Simp
8)	∿D ⊃ ∿C	5, 7, HS

9) ⌐A ⊃ ⌐C   3, 8, HS
10) (⌐E ⊃ ⌐A) · (⌐B ⊃ ⌐E)   1, Com
11) ⌐E ⊃ ⌐A   10, Simp
12) ⌐E ⊃ ⌐C   11, 9, HS
13) ⌐B ⊃ ⌐E   1, Simp
14) ⌐B ⊃ ⌐C   13, 12, HS
15) C ⊃ B   14, Trans
16) (C ⊃ B) ⊃ (A ∨ C)   2, Trans
17) /∴ A ∨ C   16, 15, MP

6.2.C.

2.   /∴ C ⊃ ⌐E
  1) (C ⊃ D) · (E ⊃ ⌐D)   Pr
  2) C ⊃ D   1, Simp
  3) (E ⊃ ⌐D) · (C ⊃ D)   1, Com
  4) E ⊃ ⌐D   3, Simp
  5) ⌐⌐D ⊃ ⌐E   4, Trans
  6) D ⊃ ⌐E   5, DN
  7) /∴ C ⊃ ⌐E   2, 6, HS

4.   /∴ L ⊃ F
  1) D · ⌐B   Pr
  2) R ⊃ F   Pr
  3) (⌐R ⊃ ⌐L) ∨ ⌐(D ∨ B)   Pr
  4) ⌐(D ∨ B) ∨ (⌐R ⊃ ⌐L)   3, Com
  5) D   1, Simp
  6) D ∨ B   5, Add
  7) ⌐⌐(D ∨ B)   6, DN
  8) ⌐R ⊃ ⌐L   4, 7, DS
  9) L ⊃ R   8, Trans
  10) /∴ L ⊃ F   9, 2, HS

6.   /∴ S ∨ E
  1) B ⊃ (⌐S ⊃ I)   Pr
  2) B · [D ∨ (⌐B ∨ ⌐I)]   Pr
  3) ⌐(⌐E ⊃ ⌐D) ⊃ ⌐B   Pr
  4) B   2, Simp
  5) ⌐S ⊃ I   1, 4, MP
  6) ⌐I ⊃ ⌐⌐S   5, Trans

7)	~I ⊃ S	6, DN
8)	B ⊃ (~E ⊃ ~D)	3, Trans
9)	~E ⊃ ~D	8, 4, MP
10)	D ⊃ E	9, Trans
11)	[D ∨ (~B ∨ ~I)] · B	2, Com
12)	D ∨ (~B ∨ ~I)	11, Simp
13)	(~B ∨ ~I) ∨ D	12, Com
14)	~B ∨ (~I ∨ D)	13, Assoc
15)	~~B	4, DN
16)	~I ∨ D	14, 15, DS
17)	/∴ S ∨ E	7, 10, 16, CD

8.   /∴ (~L ∨ ~P) · (~S ∨ ~L)

1)	(L ⊃ ~W) · (C ⊃ ~P)	Pr
2)	(S ⊃ ~C) · (W ∨ C)	Pr
3)	L ⊃ ~W	1, Simp
4)	~~W ⊃ ~L	3, Trans
5)	W ⊃ ~L	4, DN
6)	(C ⊃ ~P) · (L ⊃ ~W)	1, Com
7)	C ⊃ ~P	6, Simp
8)	(W ∨ C) · (S ⊃ ~C)	2, Com
9)	W ∨ C	8, Simp
10)	~L ∨ ~P	5, 7, 9, CD
11)	S ⊃ ~C	2, Simp
12)	~~C ⊃ ~S	11, Trans
13)	C ⊃ ~S	12, DN
14)	~L ∨ ~S	5, 13, 9, CD
15)	~S ∨ ~L	14, Com
16)	/∴ (~L ∨ ~P) · (~S ∨ ~L)	10, 15, Conj

10.   /∴ ~I ∨ (F ⊃ ~~K)

1)	~(~K ⊃ ~F) ⊃ ~J	Pr
2)	F ⊃ (B ∨ U)	Pr
3)	~(~I ∨ ~J)	Pr
4)	(U ∨ B) ⊃ ~I	Pr
5)	~I ∨ [(~J ∨ F) ∨ J]	Pr
6)	(B ∨ U) ⊃ ~I	4, Com
7)	F ⊃ ~I	2, 6, HS
8)	J ⊃ (~K ⊃ ~F)	1, Trans
9)	J ⊃ (F ⊃ K)	8, Trans
10)	J ⊃ (F ⊃ ~~K)	9, DN
11)	~I ∨ [~J ∨ (F ∨ J)]	5, Assoc

12) $(\sim I \lor \sim J) \lor (F \lor J)$ 11, Assoc
13) $F \lor J$ 12, 3, DS
14) $/\therefore \sim I \lor (F \supset \sim K)$ 7, 10, 13, CD

6.3.A.

2.
   1)   Pr
   2)   Pr
   3)   2, Add
   4)   3, Com
   5)   4, DeM
   6) $/\therefore$ 1, 5, DS

4.
   1)   Pr
   2)   Pr
   3)   1, Com
   4)   3, Dist
   5)   4, Simp
   6)   4, Com
   7)   6, Simp
   8)   7, Com
   9)   8, 2, DS
   10) $/\therefore$ 5, 9, Conj

6.
   1)   Pr
   2)   Pr
   3)   2, Simp
   4)   2, Com
   5)   4, Simp
   6)   5, 3, DS
   7)   6, 3, Conj
   8)   7, DeM
   9)   1, 8, MP
   10)   9, Add
   11)   10, DN
   12)   11, DeM
   13)   12, DN
   14) $/\therefore$ 3, 13, Conj

8.

   1)   Pr
   2)   1, Dist
   3)   2, Dist
   4)   3, Com
   5)   4, Simp
   6)   5, Com
   7)   6, Dist
   8)   7, Dist
   9)   8, Com
 10) 9, Com
 11) 10, Simp
 12) 11, Dist
 13) 12, Simp
 14) 13, Assoc
 15) 14, DeM
 16) /∴ 15, Com

10.

   1)   Pr
   2)   Pr
   3)   Pr
   4)   Pr
   5)   3, Simp
   6)   5, Trans
   7)   4, Trans
   8)   7, DN
   9)   2, Assoc
 10) 9, Com
 11) 3, Com
 12) 11, Simp
 13) 1, Com
 14) 13, Simp
 15) 12, 14, MT
 16) 1, Simp
 17) 16, DeM
 18) 17, Com
 19) 18, 15, DS
 20) 19, Add
 21) 20, DeM
 22) 10, 21, DS
 23) 22, Com
 24) /∴ 6, 8, 23, CD

6.3.B.

2.   /∴ ∿(C · A)
   1) ∿A ∨ (B ∨ ∿C)   Pr
   2) ∿B   Pr
   3) (B ∨ ∿C) ∨ ∿A   1, Com
   4) B ∨ (∿C ∨ ∿A)   3, Assoc
   5) ∿C ∨ ∿A   4, 2, DS
   6) /∴ ∿(C · A)   5, DeM

4.   /∴ ∿[(A · B) · (E · D)]
   1) ∿A ∨ [∿B ∨ (C · ∿D)]   Pr
   2) (∿A ∨ ∿B) ∨ (C · ∿D)   1, Assoc
   3) (∿A ∨ ∿B) ∨ (∿D · C)   2, Com
   4) [(∿A ∨ ∿B) ∨ ∿D] · [(∿A ∨ ∿B) ∨ C]   3, Dist
   5) (∿A ∨ ∿B) ∨ ∿D   4, Simp
   6) [(∿A ∨ ∿B) ∨ ∿D] ∨ ∿E   5, Add
   7) (∿A ∨ ∿B) ∨ (∿D ∨ ∿E)   6, Assoc
   8) (∿A ∨ ∿B) ∨ (∿E ∨ ∿D)   7, Com
   9) ∿(A · B) ∨ (∿E ∨ ∿D)   8, DeM
  10) ∿(A · B) ∨ ∿(E · D)   9, DeM
  11) /∴ ∿[(A · B) · (E · D)] 10, DeM

6.   /∴ ∿(A · ∿C) · ∿(B · ∿C)
   1) (∿A · ∿B) ∨ (C · D)   Pr
   2) [(∿A · ∿B) ∨ C] · [(∿A · ∿B) ∨ D]   1, Dist
   3) (∿A · ∿B) ∨ C   2, Simp
   4) C ∨ (∿A · ∿B)   3, Com
   5) (C ∨ ∿A) · (C ∨ ∿B)   4, Dist
   6) (∿A ∨ C) · (C ∨ ∿B)   5, Com
   7) (∿A ∨ C) · (∿B ∨ C)   6, Com
   8) (∿A ∨ ∿∿C) · (∿B ∨ C)   7, DN
   9) (∿A ∨ ∿∿C) · (∿B ∨ ∿∿C)   8, DN
  10) ∿(A · ∿C) · (∿B ∨ ∿∿C)   9, DeM
  11) /∴ ∿(A · ∿C) · ∿(B · ∿C) 10, DeM

8.   /∴ ∿(C · D)
   1) (C ⊃ ∿A) · (D ⊃ ∿B)   Pr
   2) (A · E) ∨ (E · B)   Pr
   3) C ⊃ ∿A   1, Simp
   4) ∿∿A ⊃ ∿C   3, Trans
   5) A ⊃ ∿C   4, DN

110

6)	(D ⊃ ∿B) · (C ⊃ ∿A)	1, Com
7)	D ⊃ ∿B	6, Simp
8)	∿∿B ⊃ ∿D	7, Trans
9)	B ⊃ ∿D	8, DN
10)	(E · A) ∨ (E · B)	2, Com
11)	E · (A ∨ B)	10, Dist
12)	(A ∨ B) · E	11, Com
13)	A ∨ B	12, Simp
14)	∿C ∨ ∿D	5, 9, 13, CD
15)	/∴ ∿(C · D)	14, DeM

10.   /∴ ∿(∿G · ∿E)

1)	(∿A · D) ∨ (B ⊃ G)	Pr
2)	∿(∿E ⊃ ∿C) ⊃ (∿D · ∿A)	Pr
3)	(A · B) ∨ (C · A)	Pr
4)	(A · B) ∨ (A · C)	3, Com
5)	A · (B ∨ C)	4, Dist
6)	A	5, Simp
7)	A ∨ D	6, Add
8)	D ∨ A	7, Com
9)	∿∿(D ∨ A)	8, DN
10)	∿(∿D · ∿A)	9, DeM
11)	∿∿(∿E ⊃ ∿C)	2, 10, MT
12)	∿E ⊃ ∿C	11, DN
13)	C ⊃ E	12, Trans
14)	A ∨ ∿D	6, Add
15)	∿∿(A ∨ ∿D)	14, DN
16)	∿(∿A · ∿∿D)	15, DeM
17)	∿(∿A · D)	16, DN
18)	B ⊃ G	1, 17, DS
19)	(B ∨ C) · A	5, Cọm
20)	B ∨ C	19, Simp
21)	G ∨ E	18, 13, 20, CD
22)	∿∿(G ∨ E)	21, DN
23)	/∴ ∿(∿G · ∿E)	22, DeM

6.3.C.

2.   /∴ ∿E ∨ S
   1)   C   Pr
   2)   ∿(E · C) ∨ S   Pr
   3)   (∿E ∨ ∿C) ∨ S   2, DeM
   4)   (∿C ∨ ∿E) ∨ S   3, Com
   5)   ∿C ∨ (∿E ∨ S)   4, Assoc
   6)   ∿∿C   1, DN
   7)   /∴ ∿E ∨ S   5, 6, DS

4.   /∴ ∿(∿P ∨ ∿A)
   1)   (P · O) ∨ (F · P)   Pr
   2)   ∿A ⊃ ∿(O ∨ F)   Pr
   3)   (P · O) ∨ (P · F)   1, Com
   4)   P · (O ∨ F)   3, Dist
   5)   P   4, Simp
   6)   (O ∨ F) · P   4, Com
   7)   O ∨ F   6, Simp
   8)   ∿∿(O ∨ F)   7, DN
   9)   ∿∿A   2, 8, MT
   10) A   9, DN
   11) P · A   5, 10 Conj
   12) ∿∿(P · A)   11, DN
   13) /∴ ∿(∿P ∨ ∿A) 12, DeM

6.   /∴ G ∨ I
   1)   (B ∨ I) ⊃ ∿(A ∨ U) Pr
   2)   I ∨ (G ∨ B)   Pr
   3)   A ∨ (F · U)   Pr
   4)   A ∨ (U · F)   3, Com
   5)   (A ∨ U) · (A ∨ F) 4, Dist
   6)   A ∨ U   5, Simp
   7)   ∿∿(A ∨ U)   6, DN
   8)   ∿(B ∨ I)   1, 7, MT
   9)   ∿B · ∿I   8, DeM
   10) (I ∨ G) ∨ B   2, Assoc
   11) B ∨ (I ∨ G)   10, Com
   12) ∿B   9, Simp
   13) I ∨ G   11, 12, DS
   14) /∴ G ∨ I   13, Com

8.   /∴ T
   1) ~(~T · ~C) ∨ ~(W ∨ S)   Pr
   2) ~C · S   Pr
   3) ~(W ∨ S) ∨ ~(~T · ~C)   1, Com
   4) S · ~C   2, Com
   5) S   4, Simp
   6) S ∨ W   5, Add
   7) W ∨ S   6, Com
   8) ~~(W ∨ S)   7, DN
   9) ~(~T · ~C)   3, 8, DS
   10) ~~(T ∨ C)   9, DeM
   11) T ∨ C   10, DN
   12) C ∨ T   11, Com
   13) ~C   2, Simp
   14) /∴ T   12, 13, DS

10.   /∴ (S · A) ∨ (E · S)
   1) S ⊃ {A ∨ [~(R ∨ P) ∨ (E · D)]}   Pr
   2) (S · P) ∨ (R · S)   Pr
   3) (S · P) ∨ (S · R)   2, Com
   4) S · (P ∨ R)   3, Dist
   5) S   4, Simp
   6) A ∨ [~(R ∨ P) ∨ (E · D)]   1, 5, MP
   7) [~(R ∨ P) ∨ (E · D)] ∨ A   6, Com
   8) ~(R ∨ P) ∨ [(E · D) ∨ A]   7, Assoc
   9) (P ∨ R) · S   4, Com
   10) P ∨ R   9, Simp
   11) R ∨ P   10, Com
   12) ~~(R ∨ P)   11, DN
   13) (E · D) ∨ A   8, 12, DS
   14) A ∨ (E · D)   13, Com
   15) (A ∨ E) · (A ∨ D)   14, Dist
   16) A ∨ E   15, Simp
   17) S · (A ∨ E)   5, 16, Conj
   18) (S · A) ∨ (S · E)   17, Dist
   19) /∴ (S · A) ∨ (E · S)   18, Com

6.4.A.

2.
   1)   Pr
   2)   Pr
   3)   1, Impl
   4)   3, Dist
   5)   4, Simp
   6)   5, Com
   7)   /∴ 6,2, DS

4.
   1)   Pr
   2)   Pr
   3)   1, DeM
   4)   3, Com
   5)   4, Dist
   6)   5, Com
   7)   6, Simp
   8)   7, Com
   9)   8, Impl
  10) /∴ 9, 2, HS

6.
   1)   Pr
   2)   Pr
   3)   2, Simp
   4)   2, Com
   5)   4, Simp
   6)   1, DeM
   7)   6, DN
   8)   7, Impl
   9)   3, DeM
  10) 9, DN
  11) 10, Impl
  12) 5, Impl
  13) 12, DN
  14) /∴ 8, 11, 13, CD

8.
   1)   Pr
   2)   Pr
   3)   Pr
   4)   2, Simp
   5)   2, Com

```
 6)  5, Simp
 7)  1, Com
 8)  7, Exp
 9)  3, Com
10)  9, Impl
11)  8, 10, HS
12)  4, Impl
13)  6, Impl
14)  13, DN
15)  11, 12, 14, CD
16)  15, DN
17)  /∴ 16, DeM
```

10.
```
 1)  Pr
 2)  Pr
 3)  1, Impl
 4)  3, Impl
 5)  4, DN
 6)  5, DeM
 7)  6, DN
 8)  7, Dist
 9)  8, Com
10)  9, Simp
11)  10, Com
12)  11, Dist
13)  12, Simp
14)  13, Com
15)  14, Impl
16)  2, Impl
17)  16, Dist
18)  17, Com
19)  18, Simp
20)  19, Impl
21)  /∴ 15, 20. HS
```

6.4.B.

2.   /∴ B ⊃ [C ⊃ (A ⊃ D)]
```
 1)  A ⊃ [B ⊃ (C ⊃ D)]        Pr
 2)  (A · B) ⊃ (C ⊃ D)        1, Exp
 3)  (B · A) ⊃ (C ⊃ D)        2, Com
```

```
4)  B ⊃ [A ⊃ (C ⊃ D)        3, Exp
5)  B ⊃ [(A • C) ⊃ D]       4, Exp
6)  B ⊃ [(C • A) ⊃ D]       5, Com
7)  /∴ B ⊃ [C ⊃ (A ⊃ D)] 6, Exp
```

4.   /∴ A ⊃ (∿D ⊃ ∿B)
```
1)  A ⊃ (B ⊃ C)       Pr
2)  ∿(C • ∿D)         Pr
3)  (A • B) ⊃ C       1, Exp
4)  ∿C ∨ ∿∿D          2, DeM
5)  ∿C ∨ D            4, DN
6)  C ⊃ D             5, Impl
7)  (A • B) ⊃ D       3, 6, HS
8)  A ⊃ (B ⊃ D)       7, Exp
9)  /∴  A ⊃ (∿D ⊃ ∿B)  8, Trans
```

6.   /∴ (B ⊃ ∿D) ⊃ ∿A
```
1)  A ⊃ (B • C)       Pr
2)  A ⊃ (C • D)       Pr
3)  ∿A ∨ (B • C)      1, Impl
4)  (∿A ∨ B) • (∿A ∨ C)  3 Dist
5)  ∿A ∨ B            4, Simp
6)  ∿A ∨ (C • D)      2, Impl
7)  ∿A ∨ (D • C)      6, Com
8)  (∿A ∨ D) • (∿A ∨ C)  7, Dist
9)  ∿A ∨ D            8, Simp
10) (∿A ∨ B) • (∿A ∨ D)  5, 9, Conj
11) ∿A ∨ (B • D)      10, Dist
12) A ⊃ (B • D)       11, Impl
13) ∿(B • D) ⊃ ∿A     12, Trans
14) (∿B ∨ ∿D) ⊃ ∿A   13, DeM
15) /∴ (B ⊃ ∿D) ⊃ ∿A   14, Impl
```

8.   /∴ A ⊃ (B • D)
```
1)  A ⊃ (C • B)           Pr
2)  (C • D) ∨ (∿A • C)    Pr
3)  ∿A ∨ (C • B)          1, Impl
4)  ∿A ∨ (B • C)          3, Com
5)  (∿A ∨ B) • (∿A ∨ C)   4, Dist
6)  ∿A ∨ B                5, Simp
7)  (C • D) ∨ (C • ∿A)    2, Com
8)  C • (D ∨ ∿A)          7, Dist
9)  (D ∨ ∿A) • C          8, Com
```

116

10) D ∨ ~A   9, Simp
11) ~A ∨ D   10, Com
12) (~A ∨ B) · (~A ∨ D)   6, 11, Conj
13) ~A ∨ (B · D)   12, Dist
14) /∴ A ⊃ (B · D)   13, Impl

10.   /∴ A ⊃ ~C

1) (A · B) ⊃ [C ⊃ (D · E)]   Pr
2) ~(B ⊃ E)   Pr
3) ~(~B ∨ E)   2, Impl
4) ~~B · ~E   3, DeM
5) B · ~E   4, DN
6) (B · A) ⊃ [C ⊃ (D · E)]   1, Com
7) B ⊃ {A ⊃ [C ⊃ (D · E)]}   6, Exp
8) B   5, Simp
9) A ⊃ [C ⊃ (D · E)]   7, 8, MP
10) (A · C) ⊃ (D · E)   9, exp
11) ~E · B   5, Com
12) ~E   11, Simp
13) ~E ∨ ~D   12, Add
14) ~D ∨ ~E   13, Com
15) ~(D · E)   14, DeM
16) ~(A · C)   10, 15, MT
17) ~A ∨ ~C   16, DeM
18) /∴ A ⊃ ~C   17, Impl

6.4.C.

2.   /∴ ~D ⊃ K

1) ~(~D ∨ ~C) ∨ K   Pr
2) ~~(D · C) ∨ K   1, DeM
3) (D · C) ∨ K   2, DN
4) K ∨ (D · C)   3, Com
5) (K ∨ D) · (K ∨ C)   4, Dist
6) K ∨ D   5, Simp
7) D ∨ K   6, Com
8) ~~D ∨ K   7, DN
9) /∴ ~D ⊃ K   8, Impl

117

4.   /∴ I ⊃ E
 1)   I ⊃ [A ⊃ (K ⊃ E)]   Pr
 2)   A · K   Pr
 3)   (I · A) ⊃ (K ⊃ E)   1, Exp
 4)   (A · I) ⊃ (K ⊃ E)   3, Com
 5)   A ⊃ [I ⊃ (K ⊃ E)]   4, Exp
 6)   A   2, Simp
 7)   I ⊃ (K ⊃ E)   5, 6, MP
 8)   (I · K) ⊃ E   7, Exp
 9)   (K · I) ⊃ E   8, Com
10)   K ⊃ (I ⊃ E)   9, Exp
11)   K · A   2, Com
12)   K   11, Simp
13)   /∴ I ⊃ E   10, 12, MP

Following are two proofs for #6. The construc-
tion of the first, and longer, of these is guided
by the strategies developed in the text. The
second is more "intuitive," relying on only the
second premise of the argument and a critical use
of Addition. Such examples are instructive to
point out to the student. They show that while
following strategiges will usually lead to a
proof, nonetheless it might not be the most ef-
ficient or exciting of proofs.

6-a.   /∴ (P · S) ⊃ K
 1)   [I ⊃ (S · M)] · [P ⊃ (S ⊃ I)]   Pr
 2)   S ⊃ (K · M)   Pr
 3)   ∿S ∨ (K · M)   2, Impl
 4)   (∿S ∨ K) · (∿S ∨ M)   3, Dist
 5)   ∿S ∨ K   4, Simp
 6)   I ⊃ (S · M)   1, Simp
 7)   ∿I ∨ (S · M)   6, Impl
 8)   (∿I ∨ S) · (∿I ∨ M)   7, Dist
 9)   ∿I ∨ S   8, Simp
10)   [P ⊃ (S ⊃ I)] · [I ⊃ (S · M)]   1, Com
11)   P ⊃ (S ⊃ I)   1, Simp
12)   (P · S) ⊃ I   11, Exp
13)   I ⊃ S   9, Impl
14)   (P · S) ⊃ S   12, 13, HS
15)   S ⊃ K   5, Impl
16)   /∴ (P · S) ⊃ K   14, 15, HS

118

6-b.   /∴ (P · S) ⊃ K
   1) [I ⊃ (S · M)] · [P ⊃ (S ⊃ I)]   Pr
   2) S ⊃ (K · M)   Pr
   3) ∿S ∨ (K · M)   2, Impl
   4) (∿S ∨ K) · (∿S ∨ M)   3, Dist
   5) ∿S ∨ K   4, Simp
   6) (∿S ∨ K) ∨ ∿P   5, Add
   7) ∿P ∨ (∿S ∨ K)   6, Com
   8) P ⊃ (∿S ∨ K)   7, Impl
   9) P ⊃ (S ⊃ K)   8, Impl
   10) /∴ (P · S) ⊃ K   9, Exp

8.   /∴ W ⊃ [(∿J ∨ ∿E) · (J ∨ E)]
   1) (W · E) ⊃ ∿J   Pr
   2) (W · ∿J) ⊃ (E · ∿R)   Pr
   3) ∿(W · ∿J) ∨ (E · ∿R)   2, Impl
   4) [∿(W · ∿J) ∨ E] · [∿(W · ∿J) ∨ ∿R]   3, Dist
   5) ∿(W · ∿J) ∨ E   4, Simp
   6) (∿W ∨ ∿∿J) ∨ E   5, DeM
   7) (∿W ∨ J) ∨ E   6, DN
   8) ∿W ∨ (J ∨ E)   7, Assoc
   9) ∿(W · E) ∨ ∿J   1, Impl
   10) (∿W ∨ ∿E) ∨ ∿J   9, DeM
   11) ∿W ∨ (∿E ∨ ∿J)   10, Assoc
   12) ∿W ∨ (∿J ∨ ∿E)   11, Com
   13) [∿W ∨ (∿J ∨ ∿E)] · [∿W ∨ (J ∨ E)]   12, 8, Conj
   14) ∿W ∨ [(∿J ∨ ∿E) · (J ∨ E)]   13, Dist
   15) /∴ W ⊃ [(∿J ∨ ∿E) · (J ∨ E)]   14, Impl

10.   /∴ (K · S) ⊃ (∿I · F)
   1) S ⊃ [(I · K) ∨ (A · F)]   Pr
   2) ∿(K · I)   Pr
   3) ∿S ∨ [(I · K) ∨ (A · F)]   1, Impl
   4) [∿S ∨ (I · K)] ∨ (A · F)   3, Assoc
   5) [(I · K) ∨ ∿S] ∨ (A · F)   4, Com
   6) (I · K) ∨ [∿S ∨ (A · F)]   5, Assoc
   7) ∿(I · K)   2, Com
   8) ∿S ∨ (A · F)   6, 7, DS
   9) ∿S ∨ (F · A)   8, Com
   10) (∿S ∨ F) · (∿S ∨ A)   9, Dist
   11) ∿S ∨ F   10, Simp
   12) (∿S ∨ F) ∨ ∿K   11, Add
   13) ∿K ∨ (∿S ∨ F)   12, Com

14) (∿K ∨ ∿S) ∨ F   13, Assoc
15) ∿(K · S) ∨ F   14, DeM
16) ∿K ∨ ∿I   2, DeM
17) (∿K ∨ ∿I) ∨ ∿S   16, Add
18) ∿K ∨ (∿I ∨ ∿S)   17, Assoc
19) ∿K ∨ (∿S ∨ ∿I)   18, Com
20) (∿K ∨ ∿S) ∨ ∿I   19, Assoc
21) ∿(K · S) ∨ ∿I   20, DeM
22) [∿(K · S) ∨ ∿I] · [∿(K · S) ∨ F]   21, 15, Conj
23) ∿(K · S) ∨ (∿I · S)   22, Dist
24) /∴ (K · S) ⊃ (∿I · S)   23, Impl

6.5.A.

2.
   1)   Pr
   2)   1, Equiv
   3)   2, Impl
   4)   3, Impl
   5)   4, DN
   6)   5, Com
   7)   6, Com
   8) /∴ 7, Equiv

4.
   1)   Pr
   2)   Pr
   3)   1, Simp
   4)   1, Com
   5)   4, Simp
   6)   5, Impl
   7)   3, Impl
   8)   6, 7, Conj
   9)   8, Dist
   10) 9, Equiv
   11) 10, Impl
   12) /∴ 11, 2, HS

6.
   1)   Pr
   2)   Pr
   3)   2, Simp

    4) 2, Com
    5) 4, Simp
    6) 3, Trans
    7) 6, DN
    8) 5, 7, HS
    9) 8, Impl
    10) 9, DN
    11) 1, Dist
    12) 11, Simp
    13) 10, 12 Conj
    14) /∴ 13, Equiv

8.
    1) Pr
    2) Pr
    3) Pr
    4) 1, Com
    5) 4, Dist
    6) 5, Simp
    7) 6, Com
    8) 7, 2, DS
    9) 3, Trans
    10) 9, Exp
    11) 10, 2, MT
    12) 8, DN
    13) 12, DeM
    14) 11, 13, Conj
    15) 14, DeM
    16) /∴ 15, Equiv

10.
    1) Pr
    2) Pr
    3) Pr
    4) 1, Exp
    5) 4, Com
    6) 2, 5, HS
    7) 6, Impl
    8) 7, Taut
    9) 3, Dist
    10) 9, Simp
    11) 10, Com
    12) 11, Com
    13) 12, Dist
    14) 13, Simp
    15) 14, Com
    16) 15, 8, DS

17) 16, Add
18) 17, Com
19) /∴ 18, Impl

6.5.B.

2.   /∴ A Δ B
   1) ~(A ≡ B)   Pr
   2) ~[(A · B) ∨ (~A · ~B)]   1, Equiv
   3) ~(A · B) · ~(~A · ~B)   2, DeM
   4) (~A ∨ ~B) · ~(~A · ~B)   3, DeM
   5) (~A ∨ ~B) · ~~(A ∨ B)   4, DeM
   6) (~A ∨ ~B) · A ∨ B)   5, DN
   7) (A ∨ B) · (~A ∨ ~B)   6, Com
   8) /∴ A Δ B   7, Equiv

4.   /∴ A ∨ D
   1) ~A ⊃ B   Pr
   2) B ⊃ (~C ⊃ A)   Pr
   3) ~D ⊃ ~C   Pr
   4) ~A ⊃ (~C ⊃ A)   1, 2 HS
   5) ~A ⊃ (~A ⊃ ~~C)   4, Trans
   6) ~A ⊃ (~A ⊃ C)   5, DN
   7) (~A · ~A) ⊃ C   6, Exp
   8) ~A ⊃ C   7, Taut
   9) C ⊃ D   3, Trans
   10) ~A ⊃ D   8, 9, HS
   11) ~~A ∨ D   10, Impl
   12) /∴ A ∨ D   11, DN

6.   /∴ A ⊃ (B Δ C)
   1) ~(A · B) ⊃ C   Pr
   2) ~B   Pr
   3) ~~(A · B) ∨ C   1, Impl
   4) (A · B) ∨ C   3, DN
   5) C ∨ (A · B)   4, Com
   6) C ∨ (B · A)   5, Com
   7) (C ∨ B) · (C ∨ A) 6, Dist
   8) C ∨ B   7, Simp
   9) B ∨ C   8, Com

122

10) (B ∨ C) ∨ ~A   9, Add
11) ~A ∨ (B ∨ C)   10, Com
12) ~B ∨ (~C ∨ ~A)   2, Add
13) (~B ∨ ~C) ∨ ~A   12, Assoc
14) ~A ∨ (~B ∨ ~C)   13, Com
15) [~A ∨ (B ∨ C)] · [~A ∨ (~B ∨ ~C)]   11, 14, Conj
16) ~A ∨ [(B ∨ C) · (~B ∨ ~C)]   15, Dist
17) ~A ∨ (B Δ C)   16, Equiv
18) /∴ A ⊃ (B Δ C)   17, Impl

8.   /∴ A Δ B

1) ~(A ≡ ~B) ⊃ C   Pr
2) A ⊃ (C ⊃ ~D)   Pr
3) ~(~A ∨ ~D)   Pr
4) (A · C) ⊃ ~D   2, Exp
5) (C · A) ⊃ ~D   4, Com
6) C ⊃ (A ⊃ ~D)   5, Exp
7) ~(A ⊃ ~D)   3, Impl
8) ~C   6, 7, MT
9) ~~(A ≡ ~B)   1, 8, MT
10) A ≡ ~B   9, DN
11) (A ⊃ ~B) · (~B ⊃ A)   10, Equiv
12) (~A ∨ ~B) · (~B ⊃ A)   11, Impl
13) (~A ∨ ~B) ∨ (~~B ∨ A)   12, Impl
14) (~A ∨ ~B) · (B ∨ A)   13, DN
15) (~A ∨ ~B) · (A ∨ B)   14, Com
16) (A ∨ B) · (~A ∨ ~B)   15, Com
17) /∴ A Δ B   16, Equiv

10.   /∴ C ≡ B

1) A ⊃ ~(B · ~C)   Pr
2) ~[~(B ∨ D) · C]   Pr
3) A · ~D   Pr
4) A   3, Simp
5) ~(B · ~C)   1, 4, MP
6) ~B ∨ ~~C   5, DeM
7) ~B ∨ C   6, DN
8) B ⊃ C   7, Impl
9) ~~(B ∨ D) ∨ ~C   2, DeM
10) (B ∨ D) ∨ ~C   9, DN
11) (D ∨ B) ∨ ~C   10, Com
12) D ∨ (B) ∨ ~C   11, Assoc
13) ~D · A   3, Com

```
14)  ⌐D                     13, Simp
15)  B ∨ ⌐C                 12, 14, DS
16)  ⌐C ∨ B                 15, Com
17)  C ⊃ B                  16, Impl
18)  (C ⊃ B) · (B ⊃ C)      17, 8, Conj
19)  /∴ C ≡ B               18, Equiv
```

6.5.C.

```
2.                                    /∴ C ≡ A
    1)  C Δ ⌐A                        Pr
    2)  (C ∨ ⌐A) · (⌐C ∨ ⌐⌐A)         1 Equiv
    3)  (C ∨ ⌐A) · (⌐C ∨ A)           2 DN
    4)  (C ∨ ⌐A) · (C ⊃ A)            3 Impl
    5)  (⌐A ∨ C) · (C ⊃ A)            4 Com
    6)  (A ⊃ C) · (C ⊃ A)             5 Impl
    7)  (C ⊃ A) · (A ⊃ C)             6 Com
    8)  /∴ C ≡ A                      7 Equiv

4.                                    /∴ ⌐(E Δ U)
    1)  U ≡ E                         Pr
    2)  (U · E) ∨ (⌐U · ⌐E)           1, Equiv
    3)  ⌐⌐[(U · E) ∨ (⌐U · ⌐E)]       2, DN
    4)  ⌐[⌐(U · E) · ⌐(⌐U · ⌐E)]      3, DeM
    5)  ⌐[(⌐U ∨ ⌐E) · ⌐(⌐U · ⌐E)]     4, DeM
    6)  ⌐[(⌐U ∨ ⌐E) · (⌐⌐(U ∨ E)]     5, DeM
    7)  ⌐[(⌐U ∨ ⌐E) · (U ∨ E)]        6, DN
    8)  ⌐[(U ∨ E) · (⌐U ∨ ⌐E)]        7, Com
    9)  ⌐(U Δ E)                      8, Equiv
   10)  /∴ ⌐(E Δ U)                   9, Com

6.                                    /∴ ⌐P · (E ∨ D)
    1)  P ⊃ (W · C)                   Pr
    2)  W Δ C                         Pr
    3)  (W ⊃ E) · (C ⊃ D)             Pr
    4)  (W ∨ C) · (⌐W ∨ ⌐C)           2, Equiv
    5)  (⌐W ∨ ⌐C) · (W ∨ C)           4, Com
    6)  ⌐W ∨ ⌐C                       5, Simp
    7)  ⌐(W · C)                      6, DeM
```

8)	∿P	1, 7, MT
9)	W ⊃ E	3, Simp
10)	(C ⊃ D) • (W ⊃ E)	3, Com
11)	C ⊃ D	10, Simp
12)	W ∨ C	4, Simp
13)	E ∨ D	9, 11, 12, CD
14)	/∴ ∿P • (E ∨ D)	8, 13, Conj

8.   /∴ E ⊃ ∿J

1)	E ⊃ L	Pr
2)	∿(∿F ⊃ ∿E) ⊃ ∿L	Pr
3)	∿(J • F) ∨ ∿J	Pr
4)	L ⊃ (∿F ⊃ ∿E)	2, Trans
5)	L ⊃ (E ⊃ F)	4, Trans
6)	E ⊃ (E ⊃ F)	1, 5, HS
7)	(E • E) ⊃ F	6, Exp
8)	E ⊃ F	7, Taut
9)	(J • F) ⊃ ∿J	3, Impl
10)	(F • J) ⊃ ∿J	9, Com
11)	F ⊃ (J ⊃ ∿J)	10, Exp
12)	E ⊃ (J ⊃ ∿J)	8, 11, HS
13)	E ⊃ (∿J ∨ ∿J)	12, Impl
14)	/∴ E ⊃ ∿J	13, Taut

10.   /∴ A • F

1)	(L ≡ ∿P) • (P Δ D)	Pr
2)	(L ≡ D) ⊃ (∿C • R)	Pr
3)	(A ∨ C) • (∿R ∨ F)	Pr
4)	L ≡ ∿P	1, Simp
5)	(P Δ D) • (L ≡ ∿P)	1, Com
6)	P Δ D	5, Simp
7)	(L ⊃ ∿P) • (∿P ⊃ L)	4, Equiv
8)	(P ∨ D) • (∿P ∨ ∿D)	6, Equiv
9)	L ⊃ ∿P	7, Simp
10)	P ∨ D	8, Simp
11)	∿∿P ∨ D	10, DN
12)	∿P ⊃ D	11, Impl
13)	L ⊃ D	9, 12, HS
14)	(∿P ⊃ L) • (L ⊃ ∿P)	7, Com
15)	(∿P ∨ ∿D) • (P ∨ D)	8, Com
16)	∿P ∨ ∿D	15, Simp
17)	∿D ∨ ∿P	16, Com
18)	D ⊃ ∿P	17, Impl

19) ∿P ⊃ L	14, Simp
20) D ⊃ L	18, 19, HS
21) (L ⊃ D) · (D ⊃ L)	13, 20, Conj
22) L ≡ D	21, Equiv
23) ∿C · R	2, 22, MP
24) A ∨ C	3, Simp
25) C ∨ A	24, Com
26) ∿C	23, Simp
27) A	25, 26, DS
28) (∿R ∨ F) · (A ∨ C)	3, Com
29) ∿R ∨ F	28, Simp
30) R · ∿C	23, Com
31) R	30, Simp
32) ∿∿R	31, DN
33) F	29, 32, DS
34) /∴ A · F	27, 33, Conj

CHAPTER 7

7.1.A.

12.   /∴ ∿(V · B)
   1) (C ⊃ B) ⊃ ∿V   Pr
   2) ∿∿V ⊃ ∿(C ⊃ B) 1, Trans
   3) V ⊃ ∿(C ⊃ B)   2, DN
   4) ∿V ∨ ∿(C ⊃ B)   3, Impl
   5) ∿V ∨ ∿(∿C ∨ B) 4, Impl
   6) ∿V ∨ (∿∿C · ∿B) 5, DeM
   7) ∿V ∨ (C · ∿B)   6, DN
   8) ∿V ∨ (∿B · C)   7, Com
   9) (∿V ∨ ∿B) · (∿V ∨ C) 8, Dist
  10) ∿V ∨ ∿B   9, Simp
  11) /∴ ∿(V · B)   10, DeM

15.   /∴ P ⊃ (G ⊃ B)
   1) [(P ∨ M) · (G ∨ L)] ⊃ B   Pr
   2) ∿[(P ∨ M) · (G ∨ L)] ∨ B   1, Impl
   3) [∿(P ∨ M) ∨ ∿(G ∨ L)] ∨ B 2, DeM
   4) [(∿P · ∿M) ∨ ∿(G ∨ L)] ∨ B 3, Dem
   5) [(∿P · ∿M) ∨ (∿G · ∿L)] ∨ B 4, DeM
   6) B ∨ [(∿P · ∿M) ∨ (∿G · ∿L)] 5, Com
   7) [B ∨ (∿P · ∿M)] ∨ (∿G · ∿L) 6, Assoc
8) {[B ∨ (∿P · ∿M)] ∨ ∿G} · {[B ∨ (∿P · ∿M)] ∨ ∿L} 7, Dist
   9) [B ∨ (∿P · ∿M)] ∨ ∿G   8, Simp
  10) ∿G ∨ [B ∨ (∿P · ∿M)]   9, Com
  11) (∿G ∨ B) ∨ (∿P · ∿M)   10, Assoc
  12) [(∿G ∨ B) ∨ ∿P] · [(∿G ∨ B) ∨ ∿M] 11, Dist
  13) (∿G ∨ B) ∨ ∿P   12, Simp
  14) ∿P ∨ (∿G ∨ B)   13, Com
  15) P ⊃ (∿G ∨ B)   14, Impl
  16) /∴ P ⊃ (G ⊃ B)   15, Impl

19.   /∴ (D ⊃ S) · (P ⊃ H)
   1) D ⊃ (M · S)   Pr
   2) P ⊃ (H · L)   Pr
   3) ∿D ∨ (M · S)   1, Impl
   4) ∿D ∨ (S · M)   3, Com
   5) (∿D ∨ S) · (∿D ∨ M) 4, Dist

```
6)   ⋁D ∨ S              5, Simp
7)   D ⊃ S              6, Impl
8)   ⋁P ∨ (H · L)       2, Impl
9)   (⋁P ∨ H) · (⋁P ∨ L)   8, Dist
10)  ⋁P ∨ H             9, Simp
11)  P ⊃ H              10, Impl
12) /∴ (D ⊃ S) · (P ⊃ H)   7, 11, Conj
```

7.1.B.(710)

```
2.                            /∴ A ⊃ (⋁B ∨ D)
     1)   A ⊃ (B ⊃ C)      Pr
     2)   (B · C) ⊃ D      Pr
  →3)   A                  CP, /∴ ⋁B ∨ D
  →4)   B                  CP, /∴ D
     5)   B ⊃ C            1, 3, MP
     6)   C                5, 4, MP
     7)   B · C            4, 6, Conj
     8)   D                2, 7, MP

     9)   B ⊃ D            4-8, CP
     10)  ⋁B ∨ D           9, Impl

     11) /∴ A ⊃ (⋁B ∨ D)   3-10   CP
```

```
4.                                        /∴ B ⊃ (D ⊃ A)
     1)   ⋁A ⊃ [⋁(B ∨ C) ∨ ⋁(D ∨ E)]    Pr
  →2)   B                               CP, /∴ D ⊃ A
  →3)   D                               CP, /∴ A
     4)   B ∨ C                          2, Add
     5)   D ∨ E                          3, Add
     6)   (B ∨ C) · (D ∨ E)             4, 5, Conj
     7)   ⋁⋁[(B ∨ C) · (D ∨ E)]         6, DN
     8)   ⋁[⋁(B ∨ C) ∨ ⋁(D ∨ E)]        7, DeM
     9)   ⋁⋁A                            1, 8, MT
     10)  A                              9, DN

     11) D ⊃ A                           3-10, CP

     12) /∴ B ⊃ (D ⊃ A)                  2-11, CP
```

6.   /∴ A ⊃ (C ∨ E)

   1)   (~A · B) ∨ (D · C)   Pr
┌→2)   A   CP, /∴ C ∨ E
│ 3)   A ∨ ~B   2, Add
│ 4)   ~~(A ∨ ~B)   3, DN
│ 5)   ~(~A · ~~B)   4, DeM
│ 6)   ~(~A · B)   5, DN
│ 7)   D · C   1, 6, DS
│ 8)   C · D   7, Com
│ 9)   C   8, Simp
│ 10) C ∨ E   9, Add
└─
  11) /∴ A ⊃ (C ∨ E)   2-10, CP

8.   /∴ A ⊃ ~[(D · B) ∨ ~E]

   1)   A ⊃ [~D ∨ (~B · C)]   Pr
   2)   A ⊃ (E · F)   Pr
┌→3)   A   CP /∴ ~[(D · B) ∨ ~E]
│ 4)   ~D ∨ (~B · C)   1, 3 MP
│ 5)   (~D ∨ ~B) · (~D ∨ C)   4, Dist
│ 6)   ~D ∨ ~B   5, Simp
│ 7)   ~(D · B)   6, DeM
│ 8)   E · F   2, 3, MP
│ 9)   E   8, Simp
│ 10) ~~E   9, DN
│ 11) ~(D · B) · ~~E   7, 10, Conj
│ 12) ~[(D · B) ∨ ~E]   11, DeM
└─
  13) /∴ A ⊃ ~{(D · B) ∨ ~E] 3-12, CP

10.   /∴ A ⊃(C ⊃ E)

   1)   (~A · B) ∨ [(A · ~C) ∨ (D · E)]   Pr
┌─→2) A   CP, /∴ C ⊃ E
│┌→3) C   CP, /∴ E
││ 4) A ∨ ~B   2, Add
││ 5) ~~A ∨ ~B   4, DN
││ 6) ~(~A · B)   5, DeM
││ 7) (A · ~C) ∨ (D · E)   1, 6, DS
││ 8) C ∨ ~A   3, Add
││ 9) ~A ∨ C   8, Com
││ 10) ~A ∨ ~~C   9, DN
││ 11) ~(A · ~C)   10, DeM
││ 12) D · E   7, 11, DS

13)	E · D	12, Com
14)	E	13, Simp
15)	C ⊃ E	3-13, CP
16)	/∴ A⊃ (C ⊃ E)	2-15, CP

7.1.C.

2.   /∴ ∿E ⊃ [∿R · (∿B ⊃ ∿E)]

1)	[(E ⊃ B) ⊃ R] ⊃ E	Pr
→2)	∿E	CP, /∴ ∿R · (∿B ⊃ ∿E)
3)	∿[(E ⊃ B) ⊃ R]	1, 2, MT
4)	∿[∿(E ⊃ B) ∨ R]	3, Impl
5)	∿∿(E ⊃ B) · ∿R	4, DeM
6)	(E ⊃ N) · ∿R	5, DN
7)	∿R · (E ⊃ B)	6, Com
8)	∿R · (∿B ⊃ ∿E)	7, Trans
9)	/∴ ∿E · [∿R · (∿B ⊃ ∿E)]	2-8, CP

4.   /∴ P ⊃ (C ∨ D)

1)	(∿P · V) ∨ (C · S)	Pr
2)	(V · D) ∨ [(C · ∿S) ∨ C]	Pr
→3)	P	CP, /∴ C ∨ D
4)	P ∨ ∿V	3, Add
5)	∿∿(p ∨ ∿V)	4, DN
6)	∿(∿P · ∿∿V)	5, DeM
7)	∿(∿P · V)	6, DN
8)	C · S	1, 7, DS
9)	C	8, Simp
10)	C ∨ D	9, Add
11)	P ⊃ (C ∨ D)	3-10, CP

6.   /∴ I ∨ P

1)	∿(D · ∿P)	Pr
2)	∿W ⊃ (∿I ⊃ F)	Pr
3)	∿W	Pr

4)	∿(F · ∿D)	Pr
5)	∿I ⊃ F	2, 3, MP
6)	∿F ∨ ∿∿D	4, DeM
7)	∿D ∨ ∿∿P	1, DeM
→8)	∿I	CP, /∴ P
9)	F	5, 8, MP
10)	∿∿F	9, DN
11)	∿∿D	6, 10, DS
12)	∿∿P	7, 11, DS
13)	P	12, DN

14)	∿I ⊃ P	5-13, CP
15)	∿∿I ∨ P	14, Impl
16)	/∴ I ∨ P	15, DN

8. /∴ N ⊃ [A ⊃ (P ⊃ G)]

1)	[(∿G · P) · A] ⊃ ∿N	Pr
→2)	N	CP, /∴ A ⊃ (P ⊃ G)
→3)	A	CP, /∴ P ⊃ G
→4)	P	CP, /∴ G
5)	∿∿N	2, DN
6)	∿[(∿G · P) · A]	1, 5, MT
7)	∿(∿G · P) ∨ ∿A	6, DeM
8)	∿A ∨ ∿(∿G · P)	7, Com
9)	∿∿A	3, DN
10)	∿(∿G · P)	8, 9, DS
11)	∿∿G ∨ ∿P	10, DeM
12)	G ∨ ∿P	11, DN
13)	∿P ∨ G	12, Com
14)	∿∿P	4, DN
15)	G	13, 14, DS

16)	P ⊃ G	4-15, CP

17)	A ⊃ (P ⊃ G)	3-16, C

18)	/∴ N ⊃ [A ⊃ (P ⊃ G)]	2-17, CP

10. /∴ S ∨ ∿A

1)	P ⊃ (M ≡ C)	Pr
2)	∿(M · A) · P	Pr
3)	(S ∨ ∿P) ∨ C	Pr
4)	P · ∿(M · A)	2, Com

5)	P	4, Simp
6)	M ≡ C	1, 5, MP
7)	(M ⊃ C) • (C ⊃ M)	6, Equiv
8)	(C ⊃ M) • (M ⊃ C)	7, Com
9)	C ⊃ M	8, Simp
10)	(~P ∨ S) ∨ C	3, Com
11)	~P ∨ (S ∨ C)	10, Assoc
12)	~~P	5, DN
13)	S ∨ C	11, 12, DS
14)	~(M • A)	2, Simp
15)	~M ∨ ~A	14, DeM
→16)	~S	CP, /∴ ~A
17)	C	13, 16, DS
18)	M	9, 17, MP
19)	~~M	18, DN
20	~A	15, 19, DS
21)	~S ⊃ ~A	16-20, CP
22)	~~S ∨ ~A	21, Impl
23)	/∴ S ∨ ~A	22, DN

7.2.A.

2.

		/∴ ~(C • B)	
1)	(A ⊃ B) ⊃ ~C	Pr
→2)	~~(C • B)	Pr
3)	C • B	2, DN
4)	C	3, Simp
5)	~~C	4, DN
6)	~(A ⊃ B)	1, 5, MT
7)	~(~A ∨ B)	6, Impl
8)	~~A • ~B	7, DeM
9)	B • C	3, Com
10)	B	9, Simp
11)	~B • ~~A	8, Com
12)	~B	11, Simp
13)	B • ~B	10, 12, Conj
14)	~(C • B)	2-13, IP

4. $/\therefore$ D ⊃ C

1) A ⊃ [(B · C) ∨ ∿D]   Pr
2) A   Pr
3) (B · C) ∨ ∿D   1, 2, MP
→4) ∿(D ⊃ C)   IP
5) ∿(∿D ∨ C)   4, Impl
6) ∿∿D · ∿C   5, DeM
7) ∿C · ∿∿D   6, Com
8) ∿C   7, Simp
9) ∿C ∨ ∿B   8, Add
10) ∿B ∨ ∿C   9, Com
11) ∿(B · C)   10, DeM
12) ∿D   3, 11, DS
13) ∿∿D   6, Simp
14) ∿D · ∿∿D   12, 13, Conj

15) $/\therefore$ D ⊃ C   4-14, IP

6. $/\therefore$ E ∨ C

1) (A ⊃ B) ⊃ C   Pr
2) (A ⊃ D) · (∿B ⊃ ∿D)   Pr
3) A ⊃ D   2, Simp
4) (∿B ⊃ ∿D) · (A ⊃ D)   2, Com
5) ∿B ⊃ ∿D   4, Simp
6) D ⊃ B   5, Trans
7) A ⊃ B   6, 3, HS
→8) ∿(E ∨ C)   IP
9) ∿E · ∿C   8, DeM
10) ∿C · ∿E   9, Com
11) ∿C   10, Simp
12) ∿(A ⊃ B)   1, 11, MT
13) (A ⊃ B) · ∿(A ⊃ B)   12, 7, Conj

14) $/\therefore$ E ∨ C   3-13, IP

8. $/\therefore$ C ∨ E

1) (A ⊃ B) · (B ⊃ C)   Pr
2) D ∨ A   Pr
3) D ⊃ E   Pr
4) A ⊃ B   1 Simp
5) (B ⊃ C) · (A ⊃ B)   1 Com
6) B ⊃ C   5 Simp

133

```
 ┌→7)    ∿(C ∨  E)              IP
 │  8)    ∿C ·  ∿E              8, DeM
 │  9)    ∿E ·  ∿C              8, Com
 │ 10)    ∿E                    9, Simp
 │ 11)    ∿D                    3, 10, MT
 │ 12)    A                     2, 11, DS
 │ 13)    B                     4, 13, MP
 │ 14)    C                     6, 13, MP
 │ 15)    ∿C                    8, Simp
 │ 16)    C ·  ∿C              14, 15, Conj
 └──────────────────────────────────────
   17)  /∴ C ∨ E               7-16, IP
```

10.   /∴ F ∨ C

```
   1)    (A △ B) ⊃ C           Pr
   2)    ∿D · (D ∨ A)          Pr
   3)    (A · B) ⊃ D           Pr
   4)    ∿D                     2, Simp
   5)    (D ∨ A) ·  ∿D         2, Com
   6)    D ∨ A                  5, Simp
   7)    A                      6, 4, DS
   8)    A ∨ B                  7, Add
   9)    ∿(A · B)              3, 4, MT
  10)    ∿A ∨ ∿B               9, DeM
  11)    (A ∨ B) · (∿A ∨ ∿B)  8, 10, Conj
  12)    A △ B                 11, Equiv
┌→13)    ∿(F ∨ C)             IP
│ 14)    ∿F · ∿C              13, DeM
│ 15)    ∿C · ∿F              14, Com
│ 16)    ∿C                   15, Simp
│ 17)    ∿(A △ B)             1, 7, MT
│ 18)    (A △ B) · ∿(A △ B)   17, 8, Conj
└──────────────────────────────────────
  19)  /∴ F ∨ C               4-18, IP
```

7.2.B.

2.   /∴ ∿N

```
   1)    (N · F) ⊃ I           Pr
   2)    ∿I · F                Pr
```

134

3)	∿I	2, Simp
4)	F · ∿I	2, Com
5)	F	4, Simp
6)	∿(N · F)	1, 3, MT
7)	∿N ∨ ∿F	6, DeM
→8)	∿∿N	IP
9)	N	8, DN
10)	N · F	9, 5, Conj
11)	I	1, 7, MP
12)	I · ∿I	11, 3, Conj
13)	∿N	3–10, IP

4.   /∴ L △ ∿I

1)	P ∨ [(∿L · W) ∨ (I · M)^{6}	Pr
2)	∿P · (∿I · ∿L)	Pr
3)	∿P	2, Simp
4)	(∿I · ∿L) · ∿P	2, Com
5)	∿I · ∿L	4, Simp
→6)	∿(L △ ∿I)	IP
7)	∿[(L · ∿∿I) ∨ (∿I · ∿L)]	6, Equiv
8)	∿(L · ∿∿I) · ∿(∿I · ∿L)	7, DeM
9)	∿(∿I · ∿L) · ∿(L · ∿∿I)	8, Com
10)	∿(∿I · ∿L)	9, Simp
11)	(∿I · ∿L) · ∿(∿I · ∿L)	5, 10, Conj
12) /∴ L △ ∿I		6–11, IP

6.   /∴ S ∨ A

1)	[(D ≡ C) ⊃ A] · [∿(C ≡ D) ⊃ S]	Pr
2)	(D ≡ C) ⊃ A	1, Simp
3)	[∿(C ≡ D) ⊃ S] · [(D ≡ C) ⊃ A]	1, Com
4)	∿(C ≡ D) ⊃ S	3, Simp
→5)	∿(S ∨ A)	IP
6)	∿S · ∿A	5, DeM
7)	∿A · ∿S	6, Com
8)	∿A	7, Simp
9)	∿(D ≡ C)	2, 8, MT
10)	∿S	6, Simp
11)	∿∿(C ≡ D)	4, 10, MT

135

12)	~~(D ≡ C)	11, Com
13)	~(D ≡ C) • ~~(D ≡ C)	9, 12, Conj
14)	/∴ S ∨ A	2-13, IP

8.   /∴ E • I

1)	M ⊃ (C ⊃ Q)	Pr
2)	Q ⊃ ~(C • M)	Pr
3)	(M • C) ∨ (I • E)	Pr
4)	(I • E) ∨ (M • C)	3, Com
→5)	~(E • I)	IP
6)	~(I • E)	5, Com
7)	M • C	4, 6, DS
8)	M	7, Simp
9)	C • M	7, Com
10)	C	9, Simp
11)	C ⊃ Q	1, 8, MP
12)	Q	11, 10, MP
13)	~(C • M)	2, 12, MP
14)	~C ∨ ~M	13, DeM
15)	~~C	10, DN
16)	~M	14, 15, DS
17)	M • ~M	8, 16, Conj
18)	/∴ E • I	5-17, IP

10.   /∴ (T • L) ⊃ R

1)	~(T • ~R) ∨ (C • T)	Pr
2)	C ⊃ (T • ~L)	Pr
→3)	~[(T • L) ⊃ R]	IP
4)	~[~(T • L) ∨ R]	3, Impl
5)	~~(T ∨ L) • ~R	4, DeM
6)	(T • L) • ~R	5, DN
7)	T • L	6, Simp
8)	T	7, Simp
9)	~R • (T • L)	6, Com
10)	~R	9, Simp
11)	T • ~R	8, 10, Conj
12)	~~(T • ~R)	11, DN
13)	C • T	1, 12, DS
14)	C	13, Simp
15)	T • ~L	2, 14, MP
16)	L • T	7, Com

136

```
            17)  L                              16, Simp
            18)  ∿L · T                         15, Com
            19)  ∿L                             18, Simp
            20)  L · ∿L                         17, 19 Conj

            21)  /∴ (T · L) ⊃ R                 3-20, IP


7.2.C.


2.                                        /∴ ∿A ⊃ [∿C · (∿B ⊃ ∿A)]
        1)   [(A ⊃ B) ⊃ C] ⊃ A        Pr
    →2)   ∿A                            CP, /∴ ∿C · (∿B ⊃ ∿A)
  ┌→3)    ∿[∿C · (∿B ⊃ ∿A)]            IP
  │   4)   ∿[(A ⊃ B) ⊃ C]               1, 2, MT
  │   5)   ∿[∿C ⊃ ∿(A ⊃ B)]            4, Trans
  │   6)   ∿[∿C ⊃ ∿(∿B ⊃ ∿A)]         5, Trans
  │   7)   ∿[∿∿C ∨ ∿(∿B ⊃ ∿A)]        6, Impl
  │   8)   ∿∿[∿C · (∿B ⊃ ∿A)]          7, DeM
  │   9)   ∿C · (∿B ⊃ ∿A)              8, DN
  │  10)   [∿C · (∿B ⊃ ∿A)] · ∿[∿C · (∿B ⊃ ∿A)]  9, 3, Conj

       11)  ∿C · (∿B ⊃ ∿A)             3-10, IP

       12)  /∴ ∿A ⊃ [∿C · (∿B ⊃ ∿A)]   2-11, CP

4.                                        /∴ (A · B) ⊃ C
        1)   ∿A ∨ [∿B ∨ (C · D)]       Pr
    →2)   A · B                          CP, /∴ C
  ┌→3)    ∿C                             IP
  │   4)   (∿A ∨ ∿B) ∨ (C · D)          1, Assoc
  │   5)   ∿(A · B) ∨ (C · D)           4, DeM
  │   6)   ∿∿(A · B)                     2, DN
  │   7)   C · D                         5, 6, DS
  │   8)   C                             7, Simp
  │   9)   C · ∿C                        8, 3, Conj

       10)  C                            3-9, IP

       11)  /∴ (A · B) ⊃ C              2-10, CP


                        137
```

6.   /∴ A ⊃ (C ∨ E)

```
    1)   (~A · B) ∨ (C · D)              Pr
    2)   (B · E) ∨ [(C · ~D) ∨ C]        Pr
→3)   A                              CP, /∴ C ∨ E
 →4)   ~(C ∨ E)                       IP
    5)   A ∨ ~B                          3, Add
    6)   ~~(A ∨ ~B)                      5, DN
    7)   ~(~A · ~~B)                     6, DeM
    8)   ~(~A · B)                       7, DN
    9)   C · D                           1, 8, DS
   10)   C                               9, Simp
   11)   ~C · ~E                         4, DeM
   12)   ~C                              11, Simp
   13)   C · ~C                          10, 12, Conj
   14)   C ∨ E                           4-13 IP
   15)   /∴ A ⊃ (C ∨ E)                  3-14, CP
```

8.   /∴ B ⊃ (C · D)

```
    1)   (A · B) ⊃ (C · A)              Pr
    2)   (~B · A) ∨ (D · A)             Pr
→3)   B                              CP, /∴ C · D
 →4)   ~(C · D)                       IP
    5)   B ∨ ~A                          3, Add
    6)   ~~(B ∨ ~A)                      5, DN
    7)   ~(~B · ~~A)                     6, DeM
    8)   ~(~B · A)                       7, DN
    9)   D · A                           2, 8, DS
   10)   A · D                           9, Com
   11)   A                               10, Simp
   12)   A · B                           11, 3, Conj
   13)   C · A                           1, 12, MP
   14)   C                               13, Simp
   15)   D                               9, Simp
   16)   C · D                           14, 15, Conj
   17)   (C · D) · ~(C · D)              16, 4, Conj
   18)   C · D                           4-17, IP
   19)   /∴ B ⊃ (C · D)                  3-18, CP
```

10.   /∴ ~(~E • B)

```
    1)   (A ⊃ B) ⊃ (C • D)      Pr
    2)   D ⊃ (C • E)            Pr
→   3)   B                      CP, /∴ E
→   4)   ~E                     IP
    5)   B ∨ ~A                 3, Add
    6)   ~A ∨ B                 5, Com
    7)   A ⊃ B                  6, Impl
    8)   C • D                  1, 7, MP
    9)   D • C                  8, Com
    10)  D                      9, Simp
    11)  ~E ∨ ~C                4, Add
    12)  ~C ∨ ~E                11, Com
    13)  ~(C • E)               12, DeM
    14)  ~D                     2, 13, MT
    15)  D • ~D                 10, 14, Conj

    16)  E                      4-15, IP

    17)  B ⊃ E                  3-16, CP
    18)  ~B ∨ E                 17, Impl
    19)  E ∨ ~B                 18, Com
    20)  ~~(E ∨ ~B)             19, DN
    21)  ~(~E • ~~B)            20, DeM
    22)  /∴ ~(~E • B)           21, DN
```

7.2.D.

2.   /∴ S ⊃ D

```
    1)   [(~S ∨ B) ∨ D] • ~B    Pr
    2)   (~S ∨ B) ∨ D           1, Simp
    3)   ~B • [(~S ∨ B) ∨ D]    1, Com
    4)   ~B                     4, Simp
    5)   ~S ∨ (B ∨ D)           2, Assoc
→   6)   S                      CP, /∴ D
→   7)   ~D                     IP
    8)   ~~S                    6, DN
    9)   B ∨ D                  5, 8, DS
    10)  ~B • ~D                4, 7, Conj
```

	11)	᷒(B ∨ D)	10, DeM
	12)	(B ∨ D) • ᷒(B ∨ D)	8, 11, Conj
	13)	D	3-12, IP
	14)	/∴ S ⊃ D	2-13, CP

4.   /∴ ᷒T ∨ ᷒(᷒S • P)

   1)   (E ∨ ᷒P) ∨ ᷒T   Pr
   2)   (E ⊃ ᷒S) • S   Pr
   3)   E ⊃ ᷒S   2, Simp
   4)   S • (E ⊃ ᷒S)   2, Com
   5)   S   4, Simp
   6)   ᷒᷒S   5, DN
   7)   ᷒E   3, 6, MT
→8)   T   CP, /∴ ᷒(᷒S • P)
→9)   ᷒᷒(᷒S • P)   IP
   10)   ᷒S • P   9, DN
   11)   ᷒S   10, Simp
   12)   S • ᷒S   5, 11, Conj
   13)   ᷒(᷒S • P)   9-12, IP
   14)   T ⊃ ᷒(᷒S • P)   8-13, CP
   15)   /∴ ᷒T ∨ ᷒(᷒S • P)   14, Impl

6.   /∴ ᷒C ⊃ (P ∨ E)

   1)   (᷒C • ᷒E) ⊃ A   Pr
   2)   ᷒(A ∨ S)   Pr
   3)   ᷒A • ᷒S   2, DeM
   4)   ᷒A   3, Simp
   5)   ᷒(᷒C • ᷒E)   1, 4, MT
   6)   ᷒᷒(C ∨ E)   5, DeM
   7)   C ∨ E   6, DN
→8)   ᷒C   CP, /∴ P ∨ E
→9)   ᷒(P ∨ E)   IP
   10)   E   7, 8, DS
   11)   ᷒P • ᷒E   9, DeM
   12)   ᷒E • ᷒P   11, Com
   13)   ᷒E   12, Simp
   14)   E • ᷒E   10, 13, Conj

```
    | 15)  P ∨ E                    9-14, IP

      16)  /∴ ∿C ⊃ (P ∨ E)    8-15, CP

8.                                    /∴ H ⊃ [G ⊃ (S ⊃ P)]
       1)  ∿{∿P • [S • (G • H)]}     Pr
       2)  ∿∿P ∨ ∿[S • (G • H)]      1, DeM
       3)  P ∨ ∿[S • (G • H)]        2, DN
       4)  P ∨ [∿S ∨ ∿(G • H)]       3, Dem
       5)  P ∨ [∿S ∨ (∿G ∨ ∿H)]      4, Dem
  ┌→6)  H • (G • S)                   CP, /∴ P
  │┌→7)  ∿P                          IP
  ││ 8)  ∿S ∨ (∿G ∨ ∿H)             5, 7, DS
  ││ 9)  (G • S) • H                 6, Com
  ││10)  G • S                       9, Simp
  ││11)  S • G                       10, Com
  ││12)  S                           11, Simp
  ││13)  ∿∿S                         12, DN
  ││14)  ∿G ∨ ∿H                     8, 13, DS
  ││15)  G                           10, Simp
  ││16)  ∿∿G                         15, DN
  ││17)  ∿H                          14, 16, DS
  ││18)  H                           6, Simp
  ││19)  H • ∿H                      18, 17, Conj
  │
  │ 20)  P                           7-19, IP

     21)  [H • (G • S )] ⊃ P         6-20, CP
     22)  H ⊃ [(G • S ) ⊃ P]         21, Exp
     23)  /∴ H ⊃ [G ⊃ (S ⊃ P)]       22, Exp

10.                                   /∴ ∿(A • ∿T)
      1)  ∿{F • ∿(A ≡ W)]            Pr
      2)  W Δ ∿T                     Pr
      3)  ∿[∿F • ∿(W • ∿T)]          Pr
      4)  ∿F ∨ ∿∿(A ≡ W)            1, DeM
      5)  ∿F ∨ (A ≡ W)              4, DN
      6)  ∿∿[F ∨ (W • ∿T)]          3, DeM
      7)  F 2 (W • ∿T)               6, DN
      8)  (W ∨ ∿T) • (∿W ∨ ∿∿T)     2, Equiv
      9)  (∿W ∨ ∿∿T) • (W ∨ ∿T)     8, Com
     10)  ∿W ∨ ∿∿T                   9, Simp
     11)  ∿W ∨ T                     10, DN
```

141

```
         12) T ∨ ∿W                    11, Com
    ┌→13) A                            CP, /∴ T
    ├→14) ∿T                           IP
    │   15) ∿W                         12, 14, DS
    │   16) ∿W ∨ T                     15, Add
    │   17) ∿∿(∿W ∨ T)                 16, DN
    │   18) ∿(∿∿W · ∿ T)               17, DeM
    │   19) ∿(W · ∿T)                  18, DN
    │   20) (W · ∿T) ∨ F               7, Com
    │   21) F                          20, 19, DS
    │   22) A ∨ W                      13, Add
    │   23) ∿W ∨ ∿A                    15, Add
    │   24) ∿A ∨ ∿W                    23, Com
    │   25) ∿(A · W)                   24, DeM
    │   26) ∿∿(A ∨ W)                  22, DN
    │   27) ∿(∿A · ∿W)                 26, DeM
    │   28) ∿(A · W) · ∿(∿A · ∿W)   25, 27, Conj
    │   29) ∿[(A · W) ∨ (∿A · ∿W)]  28, DeM
    │   30) ∿(A ≡ W)                   29, Equiv
    │   31) (A ≡ W) ∨ ∿F               5, Com
    │   32) ∿F                         31, 10, DS
    │   33) F · ∿F                     21, 32, Conj
    │                                ─────────────────
    │   34) T                          14-33, IP
    └
        35) A ⊃ T                      13-34, CP
        36) ∿A ∨ T                     35, Impl
        37) ∿∿(∿A ∨ T)                 36, DN
        38) ∿(∿∿A · ∿T)                37, DeM
        39) /∴ ∿(A · ∿T)               38, DN
```

7.3.A.

```
1.                         /∴ G ∨ ∿P
    1) G Δ E          Pr
    2) ∿(G · ∿E)      Pr
    3) ∿E ∨ G         Pr
    4) ∿G             pr
    5) (G ∨ E) · (∿G ∨ ∿E)  1, Equiv
```

6)   G ∨ E   5, Simp
7)   E ∨ G   6, Com
8)   G ∨ ⋁E   3, Com
9)   ⋁E   8, 4, DS
10) G   7, 9, DS
11) /∴ G ∨ ⋁P   11, Add

2.

1)   G △ E   Pr
2)   ⋁(G · ⋁E)   Pr
3)   ⋁E ∨ G   Pr
4)   ⋁G   pr
5)   (G ∨ E) · (⋁G ∨ ⋁E) 1, Equiv
6)   G ∨ E   5, Simp
7)   E   6, 4, DS
8)   G ∨ ⋁E   3, Com
9)   ⋁E   8, 4, DS
10) E · ⋁E   7, 9, Conj

7.3.B.

2)   /∴ B ∨ C
1)   A · (B ⊃ ⋁A)   Pr
2)   (C · B) ∨ (B · A)   Pr
3)   A   1, Simp
4)   (B · C) ∨ (B · A)   2, Com
5)   B · (C ∨ A)   4, Dist
6)   B   5, Simp
7)   (B ⊃ ⋁A) · A   1, Com
8)   B ⊃ ⋁A   7, Simp
9)   ⋁A   8, 6, MP
10) A · ⋁A   3, 9, Conj

4.   /∴ C ⊃ A
1)   A ∨ (B △ C)   Pr
2)   (⋁B · ⋁C) ∨ A   Pr
3)   ⋁A   Pr
4)   B △ C   1, 3, DS
5)   (B ∨ C) · (⋁B ∨ ⋁C)   4, Equiv
6)   B ∨ C   5, Simp

7) A ∨ (∿B · ∿C)   2, Com
8) ∿B · ∿C   7, 3, DS
9) ∿(B ∨ C)   8, DeM
10) (B ∨ C) · ∿(B ∨ C) 6, 9, Conj

6.   /∴ A ⊃ C
1) A ⊃ B   Pr
2) ∿B · ∿C   Pr
3) (A ≡ B) ⊃ C   Pr
4) ∿B   2, Simp
5) ∿B ∨ A   4, Add
6) B ⊃ A   5, Impl
7) (A ⊃ B) · (B ⊃ A)   1, 6, Conj
8) A ≡ B   7, Equiv
9) C   3, 8, MP
10) ∿C · ∿B   2, Com
11) ∿C   10, Simp
12) C · ∿C   9, 12, Conj

8.   /∴ B ⊃ (C ⊃ ∿A)
1) (A · C) ∨ (∿B · A)   Pr
2) A ≡ B   Pr
3) B ⊃ (C ⊃ ∿B)   Pr
4) (A · C) ∨ (A · ∿B)   1, Com
5) A · (C ∨ ∿B)   4, Dist
6) (A ⊃ B) · (B ⊃ A)   2, Equiv
7) A ⊃ B   6, Simp
8) A   5, Simp
9) B   7, 8, MP
10) C ⊃ ∿B   3, 9, MP
11) ∿∿B   9, DN
12) ∿C   10, 11, MT
13) (C ∨ ∿B) · A   5, Com
14) C ∨ ∿B   13, Simp
15) ∿B   14, 15, DS
16) B · ∿B   9, 15, Conj

10.   /∴ D ⊃ (B · C)
1) (A Δ B) ∨ (C · D)   Pr
2) (B · A) · ∿D   Pr
3) (C · D) ∨ (A Δ B)   1, Com
4) ∿D · (B · A)   2, Com
5) ∿D   4, Simp

6)	∿D ∨ ∿C	5, Add
7)	∿C ∨ ∿D	6, Com
8)	∿(C • D)	7, DeM
9)	A Δ B	3, 8, DS
10)	(A ∨ B) • (∿A ∨ ∿B)	9, Equiv
11)	(∿A ∨ ∿B) • (A ∨ B)	10, Com
12)	∿A ∨ ∿B	11, Simp
13)	B • A	2, Simp
14)	B	13, Simp
15)	A • B	13, Com
1ⁱ)	A	15, Simp
17)	∿∿A	16, DN
18)	∿B	12, 17, DS
19)	B • ∿B	14, 18, Conj

7.3.C.

2.   /∴ T

1)	T ∨ (E • T)	Pr
2)	∿(E ∨ T)	Pr
3)	∿E • ∿T	2, DeM
4)	∿T • ∿E	3, Com
5)	∿T	4, Simp
6)	E • T	1, 5, DS
7)	E	6, Simp
8)	∿E	3, Simp
9)	E • ∿E	7, 8, Conj

4.   /∴ A ⊃ M

1)	A ⊃ (∿M ⊃ ∿R)	Pr
2)	R	Pr
3)	A • ∿M	Pr
4)	A	3, Simp
5)	∿M ⊃ ∿R	1, 4, MP
6)	∿M • A	3, Com
7)	∿M	6, Simp
8)	∿R	5, 7, MP
9)	R • ∿R	2, 8, Conj

6.   /∴ D ≡ I

   1)   M ∨ (D Δ I)   Pr
   2)   ~M · ~(D ∨ I)   Pr
   3)   ~M   2, Simp
   4)   (D Δ I)   1, 3, DS
   5)   (D ∨ I) · (~D ∨ ~I)   4, Equiv
   6)   D ∨ I   5, Simp
   7)   ~(D ∨ I) · ~M   2, Com
   8)   ~(D ∨ I)   7, Simp
   9)   (D ∨ I) · ~(D ∨ I)   4, 8, Conj

8.   /∴ C · R

   1)   (M ⊃ R) ∨ (~I · C)   Pr
   2)   (I · M) · ~R   Pr
   3)   I · M   2, Simp
   4)   I   3, Simp
   5)   I ∨ ~C   4, Add
   6)   ~~(I ∨ ~C)   5, DN
   7)   ~(~I · ~~C)   6, DeM
   8)   ~(~I · C)   7, DN
   9)   (~I · C) ∨ (M ⊃ R)   1, Com
  10) M ⊃ R   9, 8, DS
  11) ~R · (I · M)   2, Com
  12) ~R   11, Simp
  13) ~M   10, 12, MT
  14) M · I   3, Com
  15) M   14, Simp
  16) M · ~M   15, 13, Conj

10.   /∴ E ⊃ P

   1)   (N ∨ W) ⊃ ~B   Pr
   2)   ~(E ∨ P) ⊃ W   Pr
   3)   (P ∨ W) ⊃ B   Pr
   4)   ~(E ∨ P) ∨ (N ∨ M)   Pr
   5)   ~N · ~M   Pr
   6)   (N ∨ M) ∨ ~(E ∨ P)   4, Com
   7)   ~(N ∨ M)   5, DeM
   8)   ~(E ∨ P)   6, 7, DS
   9)   W   2, 8, MP
  10) W ∨ N   9, Add
  11) N ∨ W   10, Com
  12) ~B   1, 11, MP
  13) W ∨ P   9, Add

```
14) P ∨ W                    13, Com
15) B                        3, 14, MP
16) B · ∿B                   15, 12, Conj
```

7.4.A.

2-a.

```
 ┌→1)   A ⊃ B       CP, /∴ ∿(B · C) ⊃ ∿(C · A)
 │┌→2)  C · A       CP, /∴ B · C
 ││ 3)  A · C       2, Com
 ││ 4)  A           3, Simp
 ││ 5)  B           1, 4, MP
 ││ 6)  C           2, Simp
 ││ 7)  B · C       5, 6, Conj
 │└──────────────────────────────
 │  8)  (C · A) ⊃ (B · C)   2-7, CP
 │  9)  ∿(B · C) ⊃ ∿(C · A) 8, Trans
 └──────────────────────────────
   10) (A ⊃ B) ⊃ [∿(B · C) ⊃ ∿(C · A)]   1-9, CP
```

2-b.

```
 ┌→1)   ∿{(A ⊃ B) ⊃ [∿(B · C) ⊃ ∿(C · A)]}      IP
 │ 2)   ∿{∿(A ⊃ B) ∨ [∿(B · C) ⊃ ∿(C · A)]}     1, Impl
 │ 3)   ∿∿(A ⊃ B) · ∿[∿(B · C) ⊃ ∿(C · A)]      2, DeM
 │ 4)   (A ⊃ B) · ∿[∿(B · C) ⊃ ∿(C · A)]        3, DN
 │ 5)   (A ⊃ B) · ∿[∿∿(B · C) ∨ ∿(C · A)]       4, Impl
 │ 6)   (A ⊃ B) · ∿∿[∿(B · C) · (C · A)]        5, DeM
 │ 7)   (A ⊃ B) · [∿(B · C) · (C · A)]          6, DN
 │ 8)   A ⊃ B                                   7, Simp
 │ 9)   [∿(B · C) · (C · A)] · (A ⊃ B)          7, Com
 │ 10)  ∿(B · C) · (C · A)                      9, Simp
 │ 11)  ∿(B · C)                                10, Simp
 │ 12)  ∿B ∨ ∿C                                 11, DeM
 │ 13)  ∿C ∨ ∿B                                 12, Com
 │ 14)  (C · A) · ∿(B · C)                       10, Com
 │ 15)  C · A                                    14, Simp
 │ 16)  A · C                                    15, Com
 │ 17)  A                                        16, Simp
 │ 18)  B                                        8, 17, MP
 │ 19)  C                                        15, Simp
```

147

20) $\sim\!\sim\!C$	19, DN
21) $\sim\!B$	13, 20, DS
22) $B \cdot \sim\!B$	18, 21, Conj

23) $(A \supset B) \supset [\sim(B \cdot C) \supset \sim(C \cdot A)]$ 1-22, IP

4-a.

→1) $(A \supset B) \supset A$ CP, /∴ A
2) $\sim(A \supset B) \vee A$ 1, Impl
3) $\sim(\sim\!A \vee B) \vee A$ 2, Impl
4) $(\sim\!\sim\!A \cdot \sim\!B) \vee A$ 3, DeM
5) $(A \cdot \sim\!B) \vee A$ 4, DN
6) $A \vee (A \cdot \sim\!B)$ 5, Com
7) $(A \vee A) \cdot (A \vee \sim\!B)$ 6, Dist
8) $A \vee A$ 7, Simp
9) A 8, Taut

10) $[(A \supset B) \supset A] \supset A$ 1-9, CP

4-b.

→1) $\sim\{[(A \supset B) \supset A] \supset A\}$ IP
2) $\sim\{\sim[(A \supset B) \supset A] \vee A\}$ 1, Impl
3) $\sim\!\sim\![(A \supset B) \supset A] \cdot \sim\!A$ 2, DeM
4) $[(A \supset B) \supset A] \cdot \sim\!A$ 3, DN
5) $(A \supset B) \supset A$ 4, Simp
6) $\sim\!A \cdot [(A \supset B) \supset A]$ 4, Com
7) $\sim\!A$ 6, Simp
8) $\sim\!A \vee B$ 7, Add
9) $A \supset B$ 8, Impl
10) A 5, 9, MP
11) $A \cdot \sim\!A$ 10, 7, Conj

12) $[(A \supset B) \supset A] \supset A$ 1-11, IP

6-a.

→1) $B \cdot A$ CP, /∴ $A \supset B$
2) B 1, Simp
3) $B \vee \sim\!A$ 2, Add
4) $\sim\!A \vee B$ 3, Com
5) $A \supset B$ 4, Impl

6) $(B \cdot A) \supset (A \supset B)$ 1-5, CP
7) $\sim(A \supset B) \supset \sim(B \cdot A)$ 6, Trans

```
    8)   ∿∿(A ⊃ B) ∨ ∿(B • A)  7, Impl
    9)   (A ⊃ B) ∨ ∿(B • A)     8, DN

6-b.
 ┌─→1)  ∿[(A ⊃ B) ∨ ∿(B • A)]       IP
 │   2)  ∿(A ⊃ B) • ∿∿(B • A)        1, DeM
 │   3)  ∿(A ⊃ B) • (B • A)          2, DN
 │   4)  ∿(A ⊃ B)                    3, Simp
 │   5)  ∿(∿A ∨ B)                   4, Impl
 │   6)  ∿∿A • ∿B                    5, DeM
 │   7)  ∿B • ∿∿A                    6, Com
 │   8)  ∿B                          7, Simp
 │   9)  (B • A) • ∿(A ⊃ B)          3, Com
 │  10)  B • A                       9, Simp
 │  11)  B                           10, Simp
 │  12)  B • ∿B                      11, 8, Conj
 └──────────────────────────────────

    13)  (A ⊃ B) ∨ ∿(B • A)         1-12, IP

8-a.
 ┌─→1)  (A ⊃ B)        CP, /∴ A ⊃ (A ⊃ B)
 │┌→2)  A              CP, /∴ A • B
 ││ 3)  B              1, 2, MP
 ││ 4)  A • B          2, 3, Conj
 │└─────────────────────────────────
 │  5)  A ⊃ (A • B)    2-4, CP
 └──────────────────────────────────

    6)   (A ⊃ B) ⊃ [A ⊃ (A • B)]  1-5, CP

8-b.
 ┌─→1)  ∿{(A ⊃ B) ⊃ [A ⊃ (A • B)]}      IP
 │   2)  ∿{∿(A ⊃ B) ∨ [A ⊃ (A • B)]}     1, Impl
 │   3)  ∿∿(A ⊃ B) • ∿[A ⊃ (A • B)]      2, DeM
 │   4)  ∿∿(A ⊃ B)                       3, Simp
 │   5)  A ⊃ B                           4, DN
 │   6)  ∿[A ⊃ (A • B)] • ∿∿(A ⊃ B)      3, Com
 │   7)  ∿[A ⊃ (A • B)]                  6, Simp
 │   8)  ∿[∿A ∨ (A • B)]                 7, Impl
 │   9)  ∿∿A • ∿(A • B)                  8, DeM
 │  10)  ∿∿A                             9, Simp
 │  11)  A                               10, DN
 │  12)  B                               5, 11, MP
 │  13)  ∿(A • B) • ∿∿A                  9, Com
```

149

14) ~(A · B)   13, Simp
15) ~A ∨ ~B   14, DeM
16) ~B   15, 10, DS
17) B · ~B   12, 16, Conj

18) (A ⊃ B) ⊃ [A ⊃ (A · B)]   1-17, IP

10-a.

→1)   A   CP, /∴ A ∨ (A · B)
  2)   A ∨ (A · B)   1, Add

  3)   A ⊃ [A ∨ (A · B)]   1 - 2, CP
→4)   A ∨ (A · B)   CP, /∴ A
  5)   (A ∨ A) · (A ∨ B)   4, Dist
  6)   A ∨ A   5, Simp
  7)   A   6, Taut

  8)   [A ∨ (A · B)] ⊃ A   4-7, CP
  9)   {A ⊃ [A ∨ (A· B)]} · {[A ∨ (A· B)] ⊃ A} 3, 8, Conj
 10)   A ≡ [A ∨ (A · B)]   9, Equiv

10-b.

→1)   ~{A ≡ [A ∨ (A · B)]}   IP
  2)   ~⇑{A · [A ∨ (A· B)]} ∨ {~A · ~[A ∨ (A · B)]}Ｏ 1, Equiv
  3)   ~{A · [A ∨ (A· B)]} · ~{~A · ~[A ∨ (A · B)]}   2, DeM
  4)   {~A ∨ ~[A ∨ (A· B)]} · ~{~A · ~[A ∨ (A· B)]} 3, DeM
  5)   {~A ∨ ~[A ∨ (A· B)]} · {~~A ∨ ~~[A ∨ (A· B)]} 4, DeM
  6)   {~A ∨ ~[A ∨ (A· B)]} · {A ∨ ~~[A ∨ (A· B)]}   5, DN
  7)   {~A ∨ ~[A ∨ (A· B)]} · {A ∨ [A ∨ (A· B)]}   6, DN
  8)   {~A ∨ [~A · ~(A· B)]} · {A ∨ [A ∨ (A· B)]}   7, DeM
  9)   {(~A∨~A) · [~A∨~(A· B)]} · {A∨[A ∨ (A· B)]}   8, Dist
 10)   {~A · [~A ∨ ~(A· B)]} · {A ∨ [A ∨ (A· B)]}   9, Taut
 11)   {~A · [~A ∨ ~(A· B)]} · {(A∨A) ∨ (A· B)]}   10, Assoc
 12)   {~A · [~A ∨ ~(A· B)]} · [A ∨ (A· B)]   11, Taut
 13)   {~A · [~A ∨ ~(A· B)]} · [(A ∨ A) · (A ∨ B)] 12, Dist
 14)   {~A · [~A ∨ ~(A · B)]} · [A · (A ∨ B)]   13, Taut
 15)   ~A · [~A ∨ ~(A · B)]   14, Simp
 16)   ~A   15, Simp
 17)   [A · (A ∨ B)] · {~A · [~A ∨ ~(A · B)]}   14, Com
 18)   A · (A ∨ B)   17, Simp

150

| 19) A | 18, Simp |
| 20) A • ∼A | 19, 16, Conj |

21) A ≡ [A ∨ (A • B)]   1-20, IP

7.4.B.

2-a.

∼(G • ∼T) ∨ ∼(∼I • ∼G)

→1)	G • ∼T	CP, /∴ ∼(∼I • ∼G)
2)	G	1 ,Simp
3)	G ∨ I	2, Add
4)	I ∨ G	3, Com
5)	∼∼(I ∨ G)	4, DN
6)	∼(∼I • ∼G)	5, Dem

7) (G • ∼T) ⊃ ∼(∼I • ∼G)   1-6, CP
8) ∼(G • ∼T) ∨ ∼(∼I • ∼G) 7, Impl

2-b.

→1)	∼[∼(G • ∼T) ∨ ∼(∼I • ∼G)]	IP
2)	∼∼[(G • ∼T) • (∼I • ∼G)]	1, DeM
3)	(G • ∼T) • (∼I • ∼G)	2, DN
4)	G • ∼T	3, Simp
5)	G	4, Simp
6)	(∼I • ∼G) • (G • ∼T)	3, Com
7)	∼I • ∼G	6 Simp
8)	∼G • ∼I	7, Com
9)	∼G	8, Simp
10)	G • ∼G	5, 9, Conj

11) ∼(G • ∼T) ∨ ∼(∼I • ∼G)   1-10, IP

4-a.

∼[∼(K ⊃ E) • E]

| →1) | ∼(K ⊃ E) | CP, /∴ ∼E |

```
    2)   ⸯ(ⸯK ∨ E)        1, Impl
    3)   ⸯⸯK • ⸯE          2, DeM
    4)   ⸯE • ⸯⸯK          3, Com
    5)   ⸯE               4, Simp

    6)   ⸯ(K ⊃ E) ⊃ ⸯE    1-5, CP
    7)   ⸯⸯ(K ⊃ E) ∨ ⸯE   6, Impl
    8)   ⸯ[ⸯ(K ⊃ E) • E] 7, DeM
```

4-b.
```
   →1)   ⸯⸯ[ⸯ(K ⊃ E) • E]    IP
    2)   ⸯ(K ⊃ E) • E        1, DN
    3)   ⸯ(K ⊃ E)            2, Simp
    4)   ⸯ(ⸯK ∨ E)           3, Impl
    5)   ⸯⸯK • ⸯE            4, DeM
    6)   ⸯE • ⸯⸯK            5, Com
    7)   ⸯE                  6, Simp
    8)   E • ⸯ(K ⊃ E)        2, Com
    9)   E                   8, Simp
    10)  E • ⸯE              9, 7, Conj

    11)  ⸯ[ⸯ(K ⊃ E) • E]     1-10, IP
```

6-a.
```
        [(C ⊃ O) • (B ⊃ V)] ⊃ [(C ∨ B) ⊃ (O ∨ V)]

   →1)   (C ⊃ O) • (B ⊃ V)     CP, /∴ (C ∨ B) ⊃ (O ∨ V)
   →2)   C ∨ B                  CP, /∴ O ∨ V
    3)   C ⊃ O                  1, Simp
    4)   (B ⊃ V) • (C ⊃ O)      1, Com
    5)   B ⊃ V                  4, Simp
    6)   O ∨ V                  3, 5, 2, CD

    7)   (C ∨ B) ⊃ (O ∨ V)      2-6, CP

    8)   [(C ⊃ O) • (B ⊃ V)] ⊃ [(C ∨ B) ⊃ (O ∨ V)]   1-7, CP
```

6-b.
```
   →1)   ⸯ{[(C ⊃ O) • (B ⊃ V)] ⊃ [(C ∨ B) ⊃ (O ∨ V)]} IP
    2)   ⸯ{ⸯ[(C ⊃ O) • (B ⊃ V)] ∨ [(C∨B) ⊃ (O∨V)]}    1, Impl
    3)   ⸯⸯ[(C ⊃ O) • (B ⊃ V)] • ⸯ[(C ∨ B) ⊃ (O ∨ V)] 2, DeM
    4)   ⸯⸯ[(C ⊃ O) • (B ⊃ V)]                         3, Simp
```

5) (C ⊃ O) · (B ⊃ V)   4, DN
6) ~[(C ∨ B) ⊃ (O ∨ V)] · ~~[(C ⊃ O) · (B ⊃ V)]   3, Com
7) ~[(C ∨ B) ⊃ (O ∨ V)]   6, Simp
8) ~[~(C ∨ B) ∨ (O ∨ V)]   7, Impl
9) ~~(C ∨ B) · ~(O ∨ V)   8, DeM
10) ~~(C ∨ B)   9, Simp
11) C ∨ B   10, DN
12) C ⊃ O   5, Simp
13) (B ⊃ V) · (C ⊃ O)   5, Com
14) B ⊃ V   13, Simp
15) O ∨ V   12, 14, 11, CD
16) ~(O ∨ V) · ~~(C ∨ B)   9, Com
17) ~(O ∨ V)   16, Simp
18) (O ∨ V) · ~(O ∨ V)   15, 17, Conj

19) [(C ⊃ O) · (B ⊃ V)] ⊃ [(C ∨ B) ⊃ (O ∨ V)] 1-18, IP

8-a.

$$~(F \equiv A) \lor (F \lor ~A)$$

→1) F ≡ A   CP, /∴ F Δ ~A
2) (F ⊃ A) · (A ⊃ F)   1, Equiv
3) (~F ∨ A) · (A ⊃ F)   2, Impl
4) (~F ∨ A) · (~A ∨ F)   3, Impl
5) (~A ∨ F) · (~F ∨ A)   4, Com
6) (F ∨ ~A) · (~F ∨ A)   5, Com
7) (F ∨ ~A) · (~F ∨ ~~A)   6, DN
8) F Δ ~A   7, Equiv

9) (F ≡ A) ⊃ (F Δ ~A)   1-8, CP

8-b.

→1) ~[~(F ≡ A) ∨ (F ∨ ~A)]   IP
2) ~~(F ≡ A) · ~(F ∨ ~A)   1, DeM
3) (F ≡ A) · ~(F ∨ ~A)   2, DN
4) F ≡ A   3, Simp
5) ~(F ∨ ~A) · (F ≡ A)   3, Com
6) ~(F ∨ ~A)   5, Simp
7) ~[(F ∨ ~A) · (~F ∨ ~~A)]   6 Equiv
8) ~[(F ∨ ~A) · (~F ∨ A)]   7, DN
9) ~[(~A ∨ F) · (~F ∨ A)]   8, Com
10) ~[(~F ∨ A) · (~A ∨ F)]   9, Com

11)	$\sim[(F \supset A) \cdot (\sim A \lor F)]$	10, Impl
12)	$\sim[(F \supset A) \cdot (A \supset F)]$	11, Impl
13)	$\sim(F \equiv A)$	12, Equiv
14)	$(F \equiv A) \cdot \sim(F \equiv A)$	4, 13, Conj
15)	$\sim(F \equiv A) \lor (F \triangle \sim A)$	1-14, IP

10-a.

$$(\{P \supset [(R \cdot H) \lor \sim F]\} \cdot P) \supset (\sim F \lor H)$$

→1)	$\{P \supset [(R \cdot H) \lor \sim F]\} \cdot P$	CP, $/\therefore \sim F \lor H$
→2)	F	CP, $/\therefore H$
3)	$P \supset [(R \cdot H) \lor \sim F]$	1, Simp
4)	$P \cdot \{P \supset [(R \cdot H) \lor \sim F]\}$	1, Com
5)	P	4, Simp
6)	$(R \cdot H) \lor \sim F$	3, 5, MP
7)	$\sim F \lor (R \cdot H)$	6, Com
8)	$\sim\sim F$	2, DN
9)	$R \cdot H$	7, 8, DS
10)	$H \cdot R$	9, Com
11)	H	11, Simp
12)	$F \supset H$	2-11, CP
13)	$\sim F \lor H$	12, Impl
14)	$(\{P \supset [(R \cdot H) \lor \sim F]\} \cdot P) \supset (\sim F \lor H)$	1-13, CP

10-b.

→1)	$\sim[(\{P \supset [(R \cdot H) \lor \sim F]\} \cdot P) \supset (\sim F \lor H)]$	IP
2)	$\sim[\sim(\{P \supset [(R \cdot H) \lor \sim F]\} \cdot P) \lor (\sim F \lor H)]$	1, Impl
3)	$\sim\sim(\{P \supset [(R \cdot H) \lor \sim F]\} \cdot P) \cdot \sim(\sim F \lor H)$	2, DeM
4)	$(\{P \supset [(R \cdot H) \lor \sim F]\} \cdot P) \cdot \sim(\sim F \lor H)$	3, DN
5)	$\{P \supset [(R \cdot H) \lor \sim F]\} \cdot P$	4, Simp
6)	$P \supset [(R \cdot H) \lor \sim F]$	5, Simp
7)	$P \cdot \{P \supset [(R \cdot H) \lor \sim F]\}$	5, Com
8)	P	7, Simp
9)	$(R \cdot H) \lor \sim F$	6, 8, MP
10)	$\sim F \lor (R \cdot H)$	9, Com
11)	$\sim F \lor (H \cdot R)$	10, Com
12)	$(\sim F \lor H) \cdot (\sim F \lor R)$	11, Dist
13)	$\sim F \lor H$	12, Simp
14)	$\sim(\sim F \lor H) \cdot \sim\sim(\{P \supset [(R \cdot H) \lor \sim F]\} \cdot P)$	4, Com

15) ~(~F ∨ H)		14, Simp
16) (~F ∨ H) · ~(~F ∨ H)		13, 15, Conj

17) ({P ⊃ [(R · H) ∨ ~F]} · P) ⊃ (~F ∨ H)   1-16, IP

7.5.A.

2.
```
┌→1)  ~[(A ⊃ B) ≡ (~A ∨ B)]                                IP
│  2)  ~[(~A ∨ B) ≡ (~A ∨ B)]                               1, Impl
│  3)  ~{[(~A ∨ B) · (~A ∨ B)] ∨ [~(~A ∨ B) ·. ~(~A ∨ B)]}
│                                                           2, Equiv
│  4)  ~{(~A ∨ B) ∨ [~(~A ∨ B) · ~(~A ∨ B)]}                3, Taut
│  5)  ~[(~A ∨ B) ∨ ~(~A ∨ B)]                              4, Taut
│  6)  ~(~A ∨ B) · ~~(~A ∨ B)                               5, DeM
```
7) (A ⊃ B) ≡ (~A ∨ B)   1-6, IP

4.
```
┌→1)  ~{[(A · B) ⊃ C] ≡ [A ⊃ (B ⊃ C)]}                      IP
│  2)  ~{[(A · B) ⊃ C] ≡ [(A · B) ⊃ C)]}                    1, Exp
│  3)  ~({[[(A · B) ⊃ C] · [(A · B) ⊃ C)]} ∨
│           {~[(A · B) ⊃ C] · ~[(A · B) ⊃ C)]})             2, Equiv
│  4)  ~([(A · B) ⊃ C)] ∨ {~[(A · B) ⊃ C] ·
│                   ~[(A · B) ⊃ C)]})                       3, Taut
│
│  5)  ~{[(A · B) ⊃ C)] ∨ ~[(A · B) ⊃ C]}                   4, Taut
│  6)  ~[(A · B) ⊃ C)] · ~~[(A · B) ⊃ C]                    5, DeM
```
7) [(A · B) ⊃ C] ≡ [A ⊃ (B ⊃ C)]   1-6, IP

6.
```
┌→1)  ~{[A · (B ∨ C)] ≡ [(A · B) ∨ (A · C)]}                IP
│  2)  ~{[A · (B ∨ C)] ≡ [(A · (B ∨ C)]}                    1, Dist
│  3)  ~({[A · (B ∨ C)] · [(A · (B ∨ C)]} ∨
│           {~[A · (B ∨ C)] · ~[(A · (B ∨ C)]})             2, Equiv
│  4)  ~([A · (B ∨ C)] ∨ {~[A · (B ∨ C)] ·
│                   ~[(A · (B ∨ C)]})                       3, Taut
│  5)  ~{[A · (B ∨ C)] ∨ ~[(A · (B ∨ C)]}                   4, Taut
│  6)  ~[A · (B ∨ C)] ∨ ~~[(A · (B ∨ C)]                    5, Taut
```

155

7)   [A · (B ∨ C)] ≡ [(A · B) ∨ (A · C)]   1-6, IP

8.

```
→1)   ~{(A ≡ B) ≡ [(A · B) ∨ (~A · ~B)]}        IP
 2)   ~[(A ≡ B) ≡ (A ≡ B)]                        1, Equiv
 3)   ~{[(A ≡ B) · (A ≡ B)] ∨ [~(A ≡ B) · ~(A ≡ B)]} 2,
                                                     Equiv
 4)   ~{(A ≡ B) ∨ [~(A ≡ B) · ~(A ≡ B)]}          3, Taut
 5)   ~[(A ≡ B) ∨ ~(A ≡ B)]                       4, Taut
 6)   ~(A ≡ B) ∨ ~~(A ≡ B)                        5, DeM
```

7)   (A ≡ B) ≡ [(A · B) ∨ (~A · ~B)]   1-6, IP

10.

```
→1)   ~{(A Δ B) ≡ [(A · ~B) ∨ (B · ~A)]}          IP
 2)   ~[(A Δ B) ≡ (A Δ B)]                         1, Equiv
 3)   ~{[(A Δ B) · (A Δ B)] ∨ [~(A Δ B) · ~(A Δ B)]} 2,
                                                      Equiv
 4)   ~{(A Δ B) ∨ [~(A Δ B) · ~(A Δ B)]}           3, Taut
 5)   ~[(A Δ B) ∨ ~(A Δ B)]                        4, Taut
 6)   ~(A Δ B) · ~~(A Δ B)                         5, DeM
```

7)   (A Δ B) ≡ [(A · ~B) ∨ (B · ~A)]   1-6, IP

7.5.B.

2.

  a)   (P · R) ⊃ S
  b)   P ⊃ ~(S ∨ ~R)

                          /∴ P ⊃ (S ∨ ~R)

```
1)   (P · R) ⊃ S        Pr
2)   P ⊃ (R ⊃ S)        1, Exp
3)   P ⊃ (~S ⊃ ~R)      2, Trans
4)   P ⊃ (~~S ∨ ~R)     3, Impl
5)   /∴ P ⊃ (S ∨ ~R)    4, DN
```

                              /∴ (P • R) ⊃ S
1)   P ⊃ (S ∨ ∿R)   Pr
2)   P ⊃ (∿S ⊃ ∿R)   1, Impl
3)   P ⊃ (R ⊃ S)   2, Trans
4)   /∴ (P • R) ⊃ S   3, Exp

4.

a)   G ⊃ (S • D)
b)   (G ⊃ S) • (G ⊃ D)

                              /∴ (G ⊃ S) • (G ⊃ D)
1)   G ⊃ (S • D)   Pr
2)   ∿G ∨ (S • D)   1, Impl
3)   (∿G ∨ S) • (∿G ∨ D)   2, Dist
4)   (G ⊃ S) • (∿G ∨ D)   3, Impl
5)   /∴ (G ⊃ S) • (G ⊃ D)   4, Impl

                              /∴ G ⊃ (S • D)
1)   (G ⊃ S) • (G ⊃ D)   Pr
2)   (∿G ∨ S) • (G ⊃ D)   1, Impl
3)   (∿G ∨ S) • (∿G ∨ D)   2, Impl
4)   ∿G ∨ (S • D)   3, Dist
5)   /∴ G ⊃ (S • D)   4, Impl

6.

a)   S ⊃ (P ∨ D)
b)   (S ⊃ P) ∨ (S ⊃ D)

                              /∴ (S ⊃ P) ∨ (S ⊃ D)
1)   S ⊃ (P ∨ D)   Pr
2)   ∿S ∨ (P ∨ D)   1, Impl
3)   (∿S ∨ P) ∨ D   2, Assoc
4)   [(∿S ∨ P) ∨D] ∨ ∿S   3, Add
5)   (∿S ∨ P) ∨ (D ∨ ∿S)   4, Assoc
6)   (∿S ∨ P) ∨ (∿S ∨ D)   5, Com
7)   (S ⊃ P) ∨ (∿S ∨ D)   6, Impl
8)   /∴ (S ⊃ P) ∨ (S ⊃ D)   7, Impl

                              /∴ S ⊃ (P ∨ D)
1)   (S ⊃ P) ∨ (S ⊃ D)   Pr
2)   (∿S ∨ P) ∨ (S ⊃ D)   1, Impl
3)   (∿S ∨ P) • (∿S ∨ D)   2, Impl

```
4)  [(∿S ∨ P) ∨ ∿S] ∨ D    3, Assoc
5)  [∿S ∨ (∿S ∨ P)] ∨ D    4, Com
6)  [(∿S ∨ ∿S) ∨ P] ∨ D    5, Assoc
7)  (∿S ∨ P) ∨ D           6, Taut
8)  ∿S ∨ (P ∨ D)           7, Assoc
9)  /∴ S ⊃ (P ∨ D)         8, Impl
```

8.

    a)   (B Δ R) Δ G

    b)   R Δ (∿B ≡ G)

```
                            /∴ R Δ (∿B ≡ G)
1)  (B Δ R) Δ G       Pr
2)  (R Δ B) Δ G       1 Com
3)  R Δ (B Δ G)       2 Assoc
4)  R Δ [(B ∨ G) • (∿B ∨ ∿G)]        3, Equiv
5)  R Δ [(∿∿B ∨ G) • (∿B ∨ ∿G)]      4, DN
6)  R Δ [(∿B ⊃ G) • (∿B ∨ ∿G)]       5, Impl
7)  R Δ [(∿B ⊃ G) • (∿G ∨ ∿B)]       6, Com
8)  R Δ [(∿B ⊃ G) • (G ⊃ ∿B)]        7, Impl
9)  /∴ R Δ (∿B ≡ G)                   8, Equiv
```

```
                            /∴ (B Δ R) Δ G
1)  R Δ (∿B ≡ G)       Pr
2)  R Δ [(∿B ⊃ G) • (G ⊃ ∿B)]        1, Equiv
3)  R Δ [(∿∿B ∨ G) • (G ⊃ ∿B)]       2, Impl
4)  R Δ [B ∨ G) • (G ⊃ ∿B)]          3, DN
5)  R Δ [B ∨ G) • (∿G ∨ ∿B)]         4, Impl
6)  R Δ [B ∨ G) • (∿B ∨ ∿G)]         5, Com
7)  R Δ (B Δ G)                       6, Equiv
8)  (R Δ B) Δ G                       7, Assoc
9)  /∴ (B Δ R) Δ G                    8, Com
```

10.

    a)   (S • A) ⊃ (H ∨ R)

    b)   (∿R • S) ⊃ (H ∨ ∿A)

```
                            /∴ (∿R • S) ⊃ (H ∨ ∿A)
1)  (S • A) ⊃ (H ∨ R)       Pr
2)  ∿(S • A) ∨ (H ∨ R)      1, Impl
3)  (∿S ∨ ∿A) ∨ (H ∨ R)     2, DeM
4)  (H ∨ R) ∨ (∿S ∨ ∿A)     3, Com
5)  [(H ∨ R) ∨ ∿S] ∨ ∿A     4, Assoc
```

158

```
6)  [H ∨ (R ∨ ∿S)] ∨ ∿A    5, Assoc
7)  [(R ∨ ∿S) ∨ H] ∨ ∿A    6, Com
8)  (R ∨ ∿S) ∨ (H ∨ ∿A)    7, Assoc
9)  ∿(R ∨ ∿S) ⊃ (H ∨ ∿A)     8, Impl
10) (∿R • ∿∿S) ⊃ (H ∨ ∿A)    9, DeM
11) /∴ (∿R • S) ⊃ (H ∨ ∿A)  10, DN


                              /∴ (S • A) ⊃ (H ∨ R)
1)  (∿R • S) ⊃ (H ∨ ∿A)      Pr
2)  ∿(∿R • S) ∨ (H ∨ ∿A)     1, Impl
3)  (∿∿R ∨ ∿S) ∨ (H ∨ ∿A)    2, DeM
4)  (R ∨ ∿S) ∨ (H ∨ ∿A)      3, DN
5)  (R ∨ ∿S) ∨ (∿A ∨ H)      4, Com
6)  [(R ∨ ∿S) ∨ ∿A] ∨ H      5, Assoc
7)  [R ∨ (∿S) ∨ ∿A)] ∨ H     6, Assoc
8)  [(∿S ∨ ∿A) ∨ R] ∨ H      7, Com
9)  (∿S ∨ ∿A) ∨ (R ∨ H)      8, Assoc
10) ∿(S • A) ∨ (R ∨ H)       9, DeM
11) ∿(S • A) ∨ (H ∨ R)      10, Com
12) /∴ (S • A) ⊃ (H ∨ R)    11, Impl
```

8.1.

This exercise provides an opportunity for students to apply the material mastered in this section to their own interests, in current events that are of interest to them, etc. The instructor might want students to present and share their examples in class.

8.2.

2.   All persons who are identical to John Venn are English logicians.

All V are L.

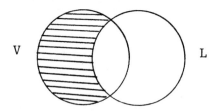

4.   Some students who are poor in their studies are not happy in their social life.

Some S are not H.

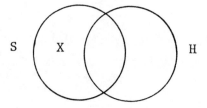

6. All persons who are friends in time of need are real friends.

All F are R.

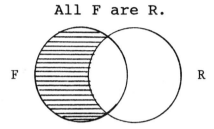

8. All persons who are identical to Henry Kissinger are persons who are Secretary of State under two presidents.

All K are S.

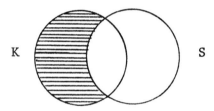

10. Some sincere professors are persons concerned about their students.

Some P are C.

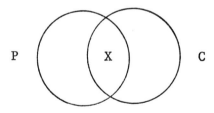

12. All groups identical to R. E. M. are groups that began in Athens, Georgia.

All R are A.

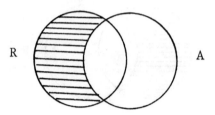

14. Some experiences of life are bitterly absurd.

Some E are A.

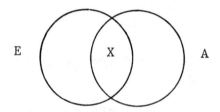

16. Some nosey people are lonely people.

Some N are L.

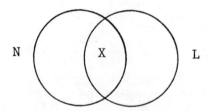

18. Some people are rewarded by society for no good
    reason.

    Some P are R.

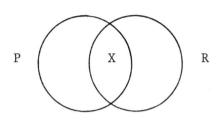

20. No moral persons are persons who can suffere real
    disgrace.

    No M are D.

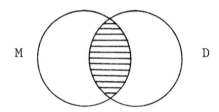

22. All persons who are identical to George Boole are
    persons who introduce the hyupothetical interpre-
    tation of categorical statements.

    All B are I.

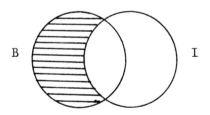

24. Some persons who are business majors are persons who want to make a great deal of money.

Some B are W.

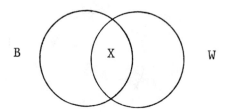

26. All students who pass are students who work hard.

All P are W.

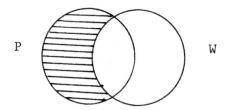

28. All months identical to Novenber, 1988, are months that are important for the Democrates.

All N are M.

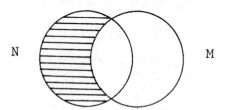

30. All events that are the reduction of nuclear armament
    are events that increase the cost of conventional
    national defense.

All R are I.

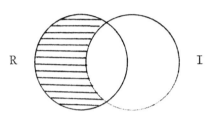

8.3.A.

2. Some Iraqis are persons who want war with Israel.

Some I are W.

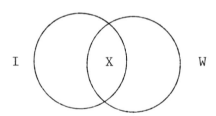

Assuming the traditional square of opposition, if
an **I** statement is assumed true, then the
following hold:

        A statements are undetermined
        E statements are false
        O statements are undetermined

Assuming the traditional square of opposition, if
an **I** statement is assumed false, then the
following hold:

        A statements are false
        E statements are true
        O statements are true

4. Some bureaucrates in local government are not
    competent decision makers.

    Some B are not D.

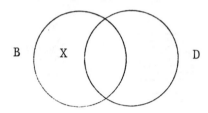

    Assuming the traditional square of opposition, if
    an <u>O</u> statement is assumed true, then the
    following hold:

    <u>A</u> statements are false
    <u>E</u> statements are undetermined
    <u>I</u> statements are undetermined

    Assuming the traditional square of opposition, if
    an <u>O</u> statement is assumed false, then the
    following hold:

    <u>A</u> statements are true
    <u>E</u> statements are false
    <u>I</u> statements are true

8.3.B.

2. No lazy persons are persons who achieve very much.

    No L are A.

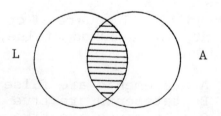

166

Assuming the Boolean square of opposition, if an **E** statement is assumed true, then the following hold:

> **A** statements are undetermined
> **I** statements are false
> **O** statements are undetermined

Assuming the Boolean square of opposition, if an **E** statement is assumed false, then the following hold:

> **A** statements are undetermined
> **I** statements are true
> **O** statements are undetermined

4.   Some cigarette smokers are not surviveres of lung cancer.

Some C are not S.

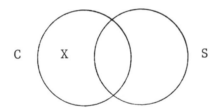

Assuming the Boolean square of opposition, if an **O** statement is assumed true, then the following hold:

> **A** statements are false
> **E** statements are undetermined
> **I** statements are undetermined

Assuming the Boolean square of opposition, if an **O** statement is assumed false, then the following hold:

> **A** statements are undetermined
> **E** statements are undetermined
> **I** statements are true

8.4.A.

2. Some chemical substances are things not in liquid form.

            Some S are not L.
                NONE

4. No chemical elements are things representative of ambiguous species of matter.

            No E are R.
            No R are E.

8.4.B.

2. All retroviruses that are identical to HTLV-3 are causal agents of AIDS.

            All R are A.
            No R are non-A.

4. Some AIDS cases now reported are cases that resulted from using contaminated needles in varous drug practices.

            Some A are N.
            Some A are not non-N.

8.4.C.(846)

2. Some start-up business are not things that remain privately controlled.

            Some B are not C.
            Some non-C are non-B.

4.   All treasury notes are things that can be used to
create   safe investments in a bear market.

All N are I.
All non-I are non-N.

8.4.D.

2.   /∴ No non-D are C
   1)   All C are D   Pr
   2)   All non-D are non-C 1, Contraposition
   3)   No non-D are C   2, Obversion

4.   /∴ Some non-H are C
   1)   Some C are not H   Pr
   2)   Some C are non-H   1, Obvewrsion
   3)   Some non-H are C   2, Conversion

CHAPTER 9

9.1.A.

2. No punk musicians are musicians who do jazz.
    No country singers in Nashville are musicians who do
        jazz.

    ───

    So, no country singers in Nashville are punk musicians.

                        No P are J
                        No C are J

                        ──────────

                        No C are P

                    EEE-2

4. All musicians into acid rock are non-punk players
    No Sixties rock stars are punk players.

    ───

    So, no Sixties rock stars are musicians into rock acid.

                        All A are non-P
                        No S are P

                        ──────────

                        No S are A

**This argument has four terms that must be reduced to
three:**

                        No A are P (obversion)
                        No S are P

                        ──────────

                        No S are A

No musicians into acid rock are punk players.
No Sixties rock stars are punk players.

───

So, no Sixties rock stars are musicians into rock acid.

                    EEE-2

6. All things creating inflationary pressures are
     potentially injurious to the stock market.
   No things that are controlled economic growth are
     potentially harmful to the stock market.

   So, some things that are controlled economic growth are
     not things that create inflationary pressures.

                 All P are I
                 No G are H
                 _____

                 Some G are not P

   **This argument has four terms that must be reduced to
   three by using 'injurious' = def. 'harmful':**

                 All P are H
                 No G are H
                 _____

                 Some G are not P

                    AEO-2

8. All junk stocks are things that are likely to have
     quick price fluctuations in an unstable market.
   Some blue chip stocks are things that are likely to
     have quick price fluctuations in an unstable market.

   So, some blue chip stocks are junk stocks.

                 All J are F
                 Some B are F
                 _____

                 Some B are J

                    AII-2

10. No Eigtheenth Century harpsichords are pitched on A-
      440.
    All Eighteenth Century harpsichords are baroque musical
      instruments.

    No baroque musical instruments are pitched on A-440.

```
                No H are P
                All H are I
                ----------
                No I are P

                   EAE-3
```

12. All psychedelic drugs are life treatening substances.
    All life threatening substances are harmful things.

So, some harmful things are psychedelic drugs.

```
                All D are S
                All S are H
                -----------
                Some H are D

                   AAI-4
```

14. No illegal drugs are safe things to use.
    All illegal drugs are expensive substances.

So, some expensive substances are not safe things to
    use.

```
                No D are U
                All D are E
                -----------
                Some E are not U

                   EAO-1
```

9.1.B.

Here is another opportunity for students to apply what they
are learning to topics of interest to them, and top share
their results in class.

9.2.A.

2. EEE-2

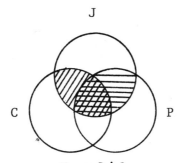

J

C   P

Invalid
under both interpretations

4. EEE-2

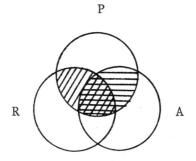

P

R   A

Invalid
under both interpretations

6. AEO-2

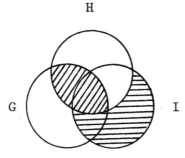

H

G   I

Invalid under Boolean interpretation

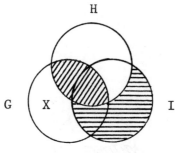

Valid if G's exist

8. AII-2

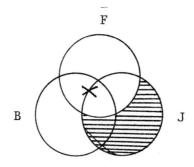

Invalid
under both interpretations

10. EAE-3

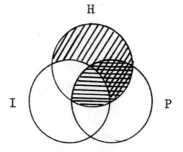

Invalid
under both interpretations

12. AAI-4

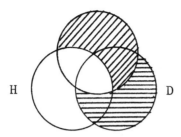

Invalid under Boolean Interpretation

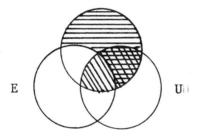

Valid if D's exist

14. EAO-3

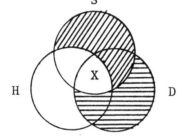

Invalid under Boolean interpretation

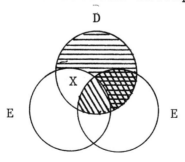

Valid if D's exist

2. No profootball players are college atheletes.
    Some scholars are college athletes.
    _____

    So, some scholars are not profootball players.

No P are A
Some S are A
_____

Some S are not P

EIO-2

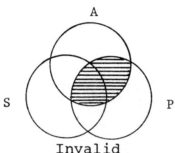

Invalid
under both interpretations

4. No persons who are big tax spenders are non-liberals.
    All persons who are identical to Senator Kennedy are
            liberals.
    _____

    So, all persons who are identical to Senator Kennedy
        are big tax spenders.

No S are non-L
All K are L
_____

All K are S

**This argument has four terms that must be reduced to
three:**

All S are L
All K are L
_____

All K are S

All persons who are big tax spenders are liberals.
All persons who are identical to Senator Kennedy are
      liberals.

_____

So, all persons who are identical to Senator Kennedy
    are big tax spenders.

AAA-2

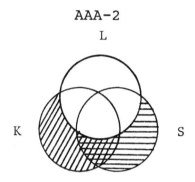

Invalid
under both interpretations

6. All politicians are persons who want to throw mud
     during an election year.
    All of today's candidates are politicians.

_____

So, some of the current candidates are persons who want
    to throw mud during an election year.

All P are W
All T are P

_____

Some C are W

**This argument has four terms that must be reduced to
three by using 'today's candidates' = def. 'current
candidates':**

All P are W
All C are P

_____

Some C are W

AAI-1

177

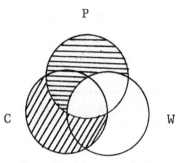

Invalid under Boolean interpretation

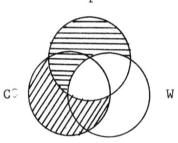

Valid if C's exist

8. All things understandable solely in terms of atoms in
    motion are explainable in classical mechanics.
    No discoveries in quantum physics are understandable
    solely in terms opf atoms in motion.

    _____

    So, some findings in quantum physics are not
    explainable in classical mechanics.

                    All U are E
                    No D are U

                    _____

                    Some F are not E

**This argument has four terms that must be reduced to
three by using 'discoveries' = def. 'findings':**

                    All U are E
                    No D are U

                    _____

                    Some D are not E

                    AEO-1

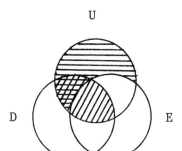

Invalid
under both interpretations

10. All sales of stock in one market and purchases of stock
    index futures in another market are forms of index
    arbitrage.
    Some forms of index arbitrage are permissible in a
    consistently strady market.
    _____
    Some permissible things in a consistnetly steady market
    are sales of stocks in one market and purchase of
    stock index futures in another market.

           All S are A
           Some A are P
           _____
           Some P are S

              AII-4

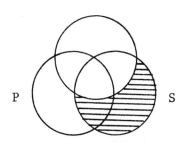

Invalid
under both interpretations

12. All examples of Norman architecture are things noted
    for their massive strength.
    All things that are identical to Durham Cathedral are
    examples of Norman architecture.
    _____

So, all things that are identical to Durham Cathedral
are things noted for their massive strength.

$$\begin{array}{l} \text{All N are S} \\ \text{All D are N} \\ \hline \text{All D are S} \end{array}$$

AAA-1

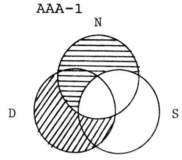

Valid under Boolean interpretation

14. Some ancient, but presently used, English cathedrals
are not Norman in origin.
No examples of Saxon ecclesiastical structures are
Norman in origin.

So, some examples of Saxon ecclesiastical structures
are not ancient, but presently used, English
cathedrals.

$$\begin{array}{l} \text{Some C are not N} \\ \text{No S are N} \\ \hline \text{Some S are not C} \end{array}$$

OEO-2

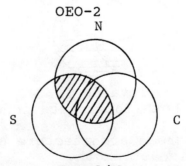

Invalid
under both interpretations

9.3.A.

Invalid Arguments in Group A of Section 1:

1. Exercise 2 is invalid, breaking Rule 4. Hence, the fallacy of exclusive premises appears in this argument.

2. Exercise 4 is invalid, breaking Rule 4. Hence, the fallacy of exclusive premises appears in this argument.

3. Exercise 6 is invalid under a Boolean interpretation, breaking Rule 5. Hence, the fallacy of existential import appears in this argument. However, if G is assumed to exist, 6 is valid.

4. Exercise 8 is invalid, breaking Rule 1. The middle term, F, is not distributed in the premises. Hence, the fallacy of undistributed middle appears in this argument.

5. Exercise 10 is invalid, breaking Rule 2. While B is distributed in the conclusion, it is not distributed in the minor premise. Hence, the fallacy of the illicit minor appears in this argument.

6. Exercise 12 is invalid under a Boolean interpretation, breaking Rule 5. Hence, the fallacy of existential import appears in this argument. However, if D is assumed to exist, 12 is valid.

7. Exercise 14 is invalid under a Boolean interpretation, breaking Rule 5. Hence, the fallacy of existential import appears in this argument. However, if D is assumed to exist, 14 is valid.

Invalid Arguments in Group B of Section 2:

1. Exercise 4 is invalid, breaking Rule 1. The middle term, L, is not distributed in the premises. So, the fallacy of undistributed middle appears in this argument.

2. Exercise 6 is invalid under a Boolean interpretation, breaking Rule 5. Hence, the fallacy of existential import appears in this argument. However, if C is assumed to exist, 6 valid.

3. Exercise 8 is invalid under a Boolean interpretation, breaking Rule 5. Hence, the fallacy of existential import appears in this argument. Exercise 8 also breaks Rule 2. While E is distributed in the conclusion, it is not distributed in the major premise. Hence, the fallacy of the illicit major also appears in this agrument.

4. Exercise 10 is invalid, breaking Rule 1. The middle term, A, is not distributed in the premises. Hence, the fallacy of undistributed middle appears in this argument.

5. Exercise 14 is invalid, breaking Rule 2. While C is distributed in the conclusion, it is not distributed in the major premise. Hence, the fallacy of the illicit major appears in this argument.

9.3.B.

2. No instances of hard rock music heard today are instances of things known during the Fifties.
Some instances of progressive jazz are not instances of things known during the Fifties.
_____
So, some instances of progressive jazz are not instances of hard rock music heard today.

No R are K
Some J are not K
_____

Some J are not R

EOO-2   Invalid

Rule broken: # 4. No valid syllogism can have
two negative premises. Hence, the fallacy of
exclusive premises appears in this argument.

4. No folk-singers are rock 'n roll musicians.
Some rock 'n roll musicians are guitarists.
_____

Some guitarists are folk-singers.

No F are R
Some R are G
_____

Some G are F

EII-4   Invalid

Rule broken: # 3. No valid syllogism can have a
negative premise and an affirmative conclusion.

6. All anabolic processes are organic growth processes.
Some metabolic processes are anabolic processes.
_____

So, some metabolic processes are organic growth
    processes.

All A are O
Some M are A
_____

Some M are O

AII-1   Valid

8. All persons who are non-conservative are persons who
    are non-fundamentalists.
All persons who are fundamentalists are persons who
    tend toward the Republican Party.
_____

So, some persons who tend toward the Republican Party
    are persons who are conservative.

```
All non-C are non-F
All  F  are R
_____

Some R are C
```

This argument has four terms that must be reduced to three:

```
All F are C (simple conversion)
All F are R
_____

Some R are C
```

All persons who are fundamentalists are persons who are
      conservative.
All persons who are fundamentalists are persons who
      tend toward the Republican Party.
_____

So, some persons who tend toward the Republican Party
      are persons who are conservative.

AAI-3   Invalid

Rule broken: #5.   Any syllogism having only
universal   premises   must   have   a   universal
conclusion to be valid under a Boolean interpretation.   Hence, the fallacy of existential
import appears in this argument.   However, if C
is assumed, the argument is valid under an
existential interpretation.

10. All things that are chlorine are things that are
       halogen.
    All things that are chlorine are things that are non-
       metallic Group VII B elements.
    _____

    All non-metallic Group VII B elements are things that
       are halogen.

```
All C are H
All C are E
_____

All E are H

AAA-3     Invalid
```

Rule broken: #2. While E is distributed in the conclusion, it is not distributed in the minor premise. Hence, the fallacy of the illicit minor appears in this argument.

12. All things that are salt are things that are a chief natural source of chlorine.
Some compounds that are sodium chloride are things that are salt.
_____

All compounds that are sodium chloride are things that are a chief natural source of chloride.

    All S are N
    Some C are S
    _____

    All C are N

    AIA-1   Invalid

Rule breoken: #2. While C is distributed in the conclusion, it is not distributed in the minor premise. Hence, the fallacy of the illicit minor appears in this argument.

14. All persons who are college students are persons who look forward to great personal success after graduation.
No persons who are college students are persons who expect to fail in life.
_____

So, some persons who anticipate great personal success after graduation are persons wwho are not expecting to fail in life.

    All C are L
    No C are E
    _____

    Some A are not E

This argument has four terms that must be reduced to three by using 'to anticipate' = def. 'to look forward to':

All persons who are college students are persons who
    look forward to great personal success after grad-
    uation.
No persons who are college students are persons who
    expect to fail in life.
_____

So, some persons who look forward to great personal
    success after graduation are persons who are not
    expecting to fail in life.

                All C are L
                No C are E
                _____

                Some L are not E

                AEO-3   Invalid

Rule broken: #5. Any syllogism having only universal
premises must have a universal conclusion to be valid
under a Boolean interpretation. Hence, the fallacy of
existential import appears in this argument. However,
if C is assumed, the argument is valid under an existential interpretation.

9.4.A.

2.   All victimless crimes are non-violent acts.
    _____

    So, some crimes are not violent acts.

    No victemless crimes are violent acts. (obversion)
                ...???...
    _____

    So, some crimes are not violent acts.

    No victemless crimes are violent acts.
    Some crimes are victemless crimes.
    _____

    So, some crimes are not violent acts.

```
                   No V are A
                   Some C are V
                   ─────────────────

                   Some C are not V

                        EIO-1    Valid
```

4. No bands using a great deal of metal are non-loud
    bands.
                    ...???...
    ───

    So, some rock 'n' roll bands are bands using a great
        deal of metal.

    All bands using a great deal of metal are loud
        bands. (obversion)
    Some rock 'n' roll bands are loud bands.
    ───

    So, some rock 'n' roll bands are bands using a great
        deal of metal.

```
                   All M are L
                   Some R are L
                   ─────────────

                   Some R are M

                        AII-2    Invalid
```

Rule broken: #1. The middle term, L, is not distributed in the premises. Hence, the fallacy of undistributed middle appears in this argument.

6.   ...???...
    All politicians are scoundrels.
    ─────────────────────────────────────

    So, some politicians are corrupt.

    All scoundrels are corrupt.
    All politicians are scoundrels.
    ─────────────────────────────────────

    So, some politicians are corrupt.

```
         All S are C
         All P are S
         ─────────────
         Some P are C

         AAI-1     Invalid
```

Rule broken: #5. Any syllogism having only universal premises must have a universal conclusion to be valid under a Boolean interpretation. Hence, the fallacy of existential import appears in this argument. However, if P is assumed, the argument is valid under an existential interpretation.

8.   ...???...
    Some politicians are not liars.
    ──────────────────────────────────

    Some politicians are honest.

Since the minor premise is negative while the conclusion is affirmative, in order not to break Rule 4, (a) the minor premise will have to be changed by obversion to an affirmative one or (b) the affirmative conclusion changed by obversion to a negative one.

8-a.   ....???...
        Some P are non-L   (Obversion)
        ──────────────────────────────

        Some P are H

    All non-liars are honest.
    Some politicians are non-liars.
    ──────────────────────────────────

    So, some politicians are honest.

```
              All non-L are H
              Some P are non-L
              ──────────────────

              Some P are H

              AII-1     Valid
```

8-b. ...???...
      Some P are not L
      _____

      Some P are not non-H

      All non-honest things are liars.
      Some politicians are not liars
      _____

      So, some politicians are not non-honest.
          (obversion)

                  All non-H are L
                  Some P are not L
                  _____

                  Some P are not non-H

                  AOO-2   Valid

10. Some Republicans are wealthy.
    Some fundamentalists are Republicans.
    _____

                    ...???...

    Some Republicans are wealthy.
    Some fundamentalists are Republicans.
    _____

    So, some fundamentalists are Republicans.

                    III-2   Invalid

    Rule broken: #1. The middle term, R, is not dis-
    tributed in the premises. Hence, the fallacy of
    undistributed middle appears in this argument.
    The conclusion might be 'So, some Republicans
    are fundamentalists'. The argument, however, is
    still invalid and for the same reason.

2. No students with a strong minor in marketing are
        students who are going to fail in sales.
    Some students majoring in the humanities are students
        with a strong minor in marketing.
    All students majoring in the humanities are students
        having a good grasp of communications skills.
    _____

    So, some students having a good grasp of communication
        skills are not going to fail in sales.

                      No M are S
                      Some H are M
                      All H are C
                      _____

                   Some C are not S

                         All H are C
                         Some H are M
                         No M are S
                         _____

                     Some C are not S

                         All H are C
                         Some H are M
                         _____

                      Some C are M

                   AEE-1   Valid

                      Some C are M
                      No M are S
                      _____

                   Some C are not S

                      IEO-4   Valid

    Since every enthymeme making up the sorities is
    valid, the sorites is valid.

4. No products conducive to a person's good health are
        products forbidden by the **FDA**.

No products to be avoided are products non-forbidden by
    the **FDA**.
All products dangerous to a person's well-being are
    products to be avoided.

So, all products dangerous to a person's well-being are
    products non-conducive to a person's good health.

```
            No C are F
            No A are non-F
            All D are A
            ────────────
            All D are non-C


            No F are C   (simple conversion)
            All A are F  (obversion)
            All D are A
            ────────────
            All D are non-C

            All F are non-C  (obversion)
            All A are F
            All D are A
            ────────────
            All D are non-C

                 All D are A
                 All A are F
                 All F are non-C
                 ──────────────
                 All D are non-C

                      All D are A
                      All A are F
                      ───────────
                      All D are F

                 AAA-4     Valid

                      All D are F
                      All F are non-C
                      ──────────────
                      All D are non-C

                 AAA-4     Valid
```

191

Since every enthymeme making up the sorities is
valid, the sorites is valid.

6. Some drugs sold on the street are cocaine products.
    All non-potentially fatal substances are non-cocaine
        products.
    All designer drugs are sold on the street.
    ──

    So, some designer drugs are not potentially fatal sub-
        stances.

                    Some S are C
                    All non-P are non-C
                    All D are S
                    ──────────────────

                    Some D are not P

                        All D are S
                        Some S are C
                        All non-P are non-C
                        ──────────────────

                        Some D are not P

                            All D are S
                            Some S are C
                            ──────────────

                            - - - -

No matter what the conclusion is, a syllogism
with these premises would be invalid because the
middle term, S, is not distributed at least once.
Hence, since at least one of the enthymemes
making up the sorities is invalid, the sorites
itself is invalid.

8. No simplistic compositions are complex in structure.
    No elegant baroque compositions of J. S. Bach are non-
        complex in structure.
    All non-ingenious works of Bach are non-elegant baroque
        compositions.
    All ingenious works of Bach are examples of baroque
        music.
    ──

    So, all examples of baroque music are non-simplistic
        compositions.

```
No S are C
No E are non-C
All non-I are non-E
All I are M
─────────────────
All M are non-S

     All I are M
     All non-I are non-E
     No E are non-C
     No S are C
     ─────────────────
     All M are non-S

          All I are M
          All non-I are non-E
          ─────────────────
               ...???...

          All I are M
          All E are I   (contraposition)
          ─────────────────
          All E are M

     AAA-1      Valid

          All E are M
          No E are non-C
          ─────────────────
               ...???...

          All E are M
          All E are C   (obversion)
          ─────────────────
          All C are M

     AAA-3      Invalid
```

Rule broken: #2. While C is distributed in the conclusion, it is not distriburted in the minor premise. Thus, the fallacy of the illicit minor appears in this argument. Hence, since at least one of the enthymemes making up the sorities is invalid, the sorites itself is invalid.

10. No social liberals are non-political activists.
    All political activists are engatged in political
       reforms.
    Some social liberals are financial moderates.
    All financial moderates are careful with the tax
       dollar.
    All persons who are non-interested in lowering the
       national deficit are non-careful with the tax
       dollar.
    _____

    So, all persons interested in lowering the national
       deficit are engaged in political reforms.

                        No L are non-A
                        All A are E
                        Some L are M
                        All M are C
                        All non-I are non-C
                        _____

                        All I are E

                        All non-I are non-C
                        All M are C
                        Some L are M
                        No L are non-A
                        All A are E
                        _____

                        All I are E

                        All C are I   (simple contraposition)
                        All M are C
                        Some L are M
                        All L are A   (obversion)
                        All A are E
                        _____

                        All I are E

                        All C are I
                        All M are C
                        _____

                        All M are I

                        AAA-1   Valid

```
      All M are I
      Some L are M
      ───────────────
      Some L are I

AII-1      Valid

      Some L are I
      All L are A
      ───────────────
      Some A are I

IAI-3      Valid

      Some A are I
      All A are E
      ───────────────
      All I are E

IAA-3      Invalid
```

Rule broken: #2. While I is distributed in the conclusion, it is not distributed in the major premise. Hence, the fallacy of the illicit major appears in this argument. Thus, since at least one of the enthymemes making up the sorities is invalid, the sorites itself is invalid.

CHAPTER 10

10.1.

2.   Pp ∨ Rp

4.   Sm ⊃ Bm

6.   (Sb · Pb) ⊃ (Cg · Pg)

8.   (Cj · Tj) ∨ Hj

10. (Rp ⊃ Pa) · Da

12. (Sa · Ca) · ∿Ra

14. (Sg · Kg) · Mg

16. [(Mh · Bh) · Ph] ⊃ Gh

18. (St · Wt) ≡ (Pm ∨ Dm)

20. (Wb · Tb) ⊃ (Cb ⊃ Fb)

22. Bt · [Wt ≡ (St · Ft)]

24. (Pe · We) Δ (Bh ⊃ Ch)

26. [(Ah · Rh) · Ph] Δ (Fh · Ih)

28. [(Bc · Mc) · Ac] Δ [(Hc · Ic) · Oc]

30. {[(Fj · Aj) · Oj] · Kj} ⊃ [(Af · Gf) · Sf]

10.2.

2.   (x)(Gx ⊃ ∿Dx)

4.   (x)(Ax ⊃ Dx)

6.   (x)(Ux ⊃ Cx)

8.   (∃x)[(∿Lx • Ax) • Rx]

10. (x)[(Bx • Ax) ⊃ ∿Sx]

12. (∃x)[(Fx • Px) • ∿Dx]

14. (∃x)[(Ex • Kx) • Rx]

16. (x)[Sx ⊃ (Cx ⊃ ∿Fx)]

18. (x){[Px • (Gx • ∿Tx)] ⊃ ∿Cx}

20. (x){[Mx • (Lx • Rx)] ⊃ Hx}

22. (x){[Ix • (Sx • Mx)] ⊃ ∿Tx}

24. (x){[(Rx ∨ Fx) • (Cx • Sx)] ⊃ ∿Vx}

26. (∃x){[Cx • (Ax ∨ Bx)] • (Tx ⊃ ∿Sx)}

28. (∃x)([[(Ox • Sx) • Px] ⊃ Cx} • ∿(Fx ∨ Bx))

30. (x){[Ax • (Cx • Rx)] ⊃ [DX ⊃ (Gx • Sx)]}

10.3.

2.   ∿(∃x)(Jx • Wx)

4.   (x)(Cx ≡ ∿Qx)

6.   Ws ∨ (x)(Px ⊃ ∿Wx)

8.   ∿(x)(Px ⊃ Rx) • (∃x)(Px • Rx)

10. (Pt ∨ Pi) ⊃ (x)(Ex ⊃ Hx)

12. (x)[(Px • Ex) ⊃ Rx]

14. (∃x)(Px • Rx) ⊃ (x)(Sx ⊃ Jx)

16. Cj ⊃ (∃x)[(Jx • Wx) • Vx)]

18. (x)[(Ax · Gx) ≡ ∿(Sx ∨ Hx)]

20. (x){[(Px · ∿Ix) ⊃ Mx] ≡ ∿∿Tx}

22. (∃x)(Mx · Cx) ⊃ (∃x)[(Ex · Cx) ∨ Ix]

24. (x)[Gx ⊃ (Hx ⊃ Mx)] Δ (∃x)(Gx · Hx) · (∿Vx · ∿Mx)]

26. (x){[Px · (Fx · Ax)] ⊃ ∿Ix} ≡ ∿(∃x)[(Px · Fx) · (Ax · Ix)]

28. [(∃x)(Gx · Dx) ∨ (∃x)(Gx · Cx)] ≡ (∃x)[(Dx ∨ Cx) · (Gx ∨ Lx)]

30. ∿(∃x){[Gx · (Px ∨ Mx)] · ∿[Ax ≡ ∿(Hx · Rx)]}

10.4.

2. (∃x)(∃y)Rxy

4. (x)(∃y)Cxy

6. ∿(∃x)(y)Axy

8. (∃x)(y)∿Rxy

10. (∃x)(∃y)∿Rxy

12. (x)(Nx ⊃ ∿Sax)

14. (x)(y)[(Ny · Sxy) ⊃ Nx]

16. (x)[Nx ⊃ (∃y)(Ny · Sxy)]

18. (x)[Hx ⊃ (∃y)(Ey · Mxy)]

20. (x)[(Sx · Px) ⊃ (∃y)(Iy · Exy)]

22. (x)[(Lx · Px) ⊃ ∿(∃y)(Fy · Kxy)]

24. (x){[Px · (∃y)(Py · Wxy)] ⊃ Wxx}

26. (x)(Px ⊃ (y)[[(Py · Fy) · Nxy] ⊃ (Gy · Fy)})

28. (x)(Ix ⊃[(∃y)[Py · (z)(Az ⊃ Fzy)] · Gxy})

30. (x)[(Fx · Ux) · (∃y)(By · ∿Axy)] ⊃ [(∃z)[Bz ·
                                          (Rz △ Mz)]

11.1.

2.   /∴ (∃x)∿Px
  1)   (x)(Ux ⊃ ∿Px)   Pr
  2)   (∃X)Dx ↲   Pr
  3)   ∿(∃x)∿Px ↲   AP
  4)   (x)∿∿Px   3, QD
  5)   Da   2, EI
  6)   ∿∿Pa ↲   4, UI
  7)   Pa   6, DN
  8) Da ⊃ ∿Pa ↲   1, UI

  9) ∿Da   ∿Pa   8, MI
      X   X   VALID

4.   /∴ (x)(Dx ⊃ Px)
  1)   (x)(Dx ⊃ Mx)   Pr
  2)   (x)(Mx ⊃ Px)   Pr
  3)   ∿(x)(Dx ⊃ Px) ↲ AP
  4)   (∃x)∿(Dx ⊃ Px) ↲3, QD
  5)   ∿(Da ⊃ Pa) ↲ 4, EI
  6)   Da   5, DMI
  7)   ∿Pa   5, DMI
  8)   Da ⊃ Ma ↲   1, UI
  9)   Ma ⊃ Pa ↲   2, UI

  10) ∿Da   Ma   8, MI
      X

  11)   ∿Ma Pa 9, MI
        X   X   VALID

6.   /∴ ∿Md
  1)   (x)(Ax ⊃ Cx)   Pr
  2)   (x)(Mx ⊃ Cx)   Pr
  3)   ∿Ad   Pr
  4)   ∿∿Md ↲   AP
  5)   Md   4, DN

6) Md ⊃ Cd ↓   2, UI

7) ∿Md   Cd   6, MI
     X   Ad ⊃ Cd ↓   1, UI

9)   ∿Ad   Cd   8, MI

                        INVALID

8.   /∴ (x)(Mx ⊃ Cx)
1)   (x)(Bx ⊃ Mx) ⊃ (x)(Mx ⊃ Cx) ↓   Pr
2)   (x)(Bx ⊃ Cx) • (x)(Cx ⊃ Mx) ↓   Pr
3)   ∿(x)(Mx ⊃ Cx) ↓   AP
4)   (∃x)∿(Mx ⊃ Cx) ↓   3, QD
5)   ∿(Ma ⊃ Ca) ↓   4, EI
6)   Ma   5, DMI
7)   ∿Ca   5, DMI

8) ∿(x)(Bx ⊃ Mx) ↓   (x)(Mx ⊃ Cx)   1, MI
9) (∃x)∿(Bx ⊃ Mx) ↓   8, QD
10)   ∿(Bb ⊃ Mb) ↓   9, EI
11)   Bb   10, DMI
12)   ∿Mb   10, DMI
13) (x)(Bx ⊃ Cx)   (x)(Bx ⊃ Cx)   2, C
14) (x)(Cx ⊃ Mx)   (x)(Cx ⊃ Mx)   2, C
15)   Bb ⊃ Cb ↓   13, UI
16)   Cb ⊃ Mb ↓   14, UI

17)   ∿Bb   Cb   15, MI
        X

18)   ∿Cb   Mb   16, MI
19)   X   X   Ma ⊃ Ca ↓   8, UI
20)   Ba ⊃ Ca   13, UI
21)   Ca ⊃ Ma   14, UI

22)   ∿Ma   Ca   19, MI
                           X   X   VALID

201

10.   /∴ (∃x)(Px • Lx)

```
1)   (x)[(Lx • Px) ⊃ (Ix ⊃ Sx)]        Pr
2)   (∃x)(Px • ∿Sx) ↓                    Pr
3)   (x)(Px ⊃ Ix)                        Pr
4)  ∿(∃x)(Px • Lx) ↓                     AP
5)   (x)∿(Px • Lx)                       4, QD
6)        Pa • ∿Sa ↓                     2, EI
7)            Pa                         6, C
8)           ∿Sa                         6, C
9)        Pa ⊃ Ia ↓                      3, UI


10)    ∿Pa          Ia                   9, MI
11)     X      ∿(Pa • La) ↓              5, UI


12)          ∿Pa          ∿La            11, DC
              X
13)          (La • Pa) ⊃ (Ia ⊃ Sa) ↓1, UI


14)      ∿(La • Pa) ↓      Ia ⊃ Sa ↓ 13, MI


15)    ∿La        ∿Pa                    14, DC
                   X
16)                    ∿Ia    Sa 14, MI
                        X      X         INVALID
```

12.   /∴ ∿(∃x)[Ax • ∿(Hx ⊃ Sx)]

```
1)  ∿(∃x)[(Hx • Ax) • Sx] ↓      Pr
2)   (x)[Ax ⊃ (Sx ⊃ Hx)]         Pr
3)  ∿∿(∃x)[Ax • ∿(Hx ⊃ Sx)] ↓   AP
4)   (x)∿[(Hx • Ax) • Sx]        1, QD
5)   (∃x)[Ax • ∿(Hx ⊃ Sx)] ↓     3, DN
6)        Aa • ∿(Ha ⊃ Sa) ↓      6, EI
7)      ∿[(Ha • Aa) • Sa] ↓      4, UI
8)           Aa                   6, C
9)       ∿(Ha ⊃ Sa) ↓            6, C
10)          Ha                   9, DMI
11)         ∿Sa                   9, DMI
12)     Aa ⊃ (Sa ⊃ Ha) ↓         2, UI
```

202

13) ∿Aa   Sa ⊃ Ha ✓   12, MI
        X

14)   ∿Sa   Ha   13, MI

15) ∿(Ha • Aa)✓ ∿Sa   ∿(Ha • Aa)✓ ∿Sa   7, DC

16) ∿Ha   ∿Aa   ∿Ha   ∿Aa   15, DC
     X   X   X   X

                                    INVALID

14.   /∴ (x)[(Fx • Dx) ⊃ (Px ∨ ∿Bx)]
  1)   (x){(Dx • Fx) ⊃ [∿Px ⊃ ∿(Sx ∨ Bx)]}   Pr
  2)   ∿(x)[(Fx • Dx) ⊃ (Px ∨ ∿Bx)] ✓   AP
  3)   (∃x)∿[(Fx • Dx) ⊃ (Px ∨ ∿Bx)] ✓   2, QD
  4)   ∿[(Fa • Da) ⊃ (Pa ∨ ∿Ba)] ✓   3, EI
  5)   Fa • Da ✓   4, DMI
  6)   ∿(Pa ∨ ∿Ba) ✓   4, DMI
  7)   ∿Pa   7, DID
  8)   ∿∿Ba ✓   7, DID
  9)   Ba   8, DN
 10)   Fa   5, C
 11)   Da   5, C
 12)   (Da • Fa) ⊃ [∿Pa ⊃ ∿(Sa ∨ Ba)] ✓   1, UI

 13)   ∿(Da • Fa) ✓   ∿Pa ⊃ ∿(Sa ∨ Ba) ✓   12, MI

 14) ∿Da   ∿Fa   13, DC
 15)   X   X   ∿∿Pa ✓   ∿(Sa ∨ Ba) ✓   13, MI
 16)   Pa   15, DN
 17)   X   ∿Sa   15, DID
 18)   ∿Ba   15, DID
                                  X

                                    VALID

16.   /∴ (x){[Px • (y)(Py ⊃ Fxy)] ⊃ ∿Px}
  1)   (x)(Px ⊃ ∿Fxx)   Pr
  2)   ∿(x){[Px • (y)(Py ⊃ Fxy)] ⊃ ∿Px} ✓   AP

```
3)   (∃x)∿{[Px • (y)(Py ⊃ Fxy)] ⊃ ∿Px}  ↲  2, QD
4)       ∿{[Pa • (y)(Py ⊃ Fay)] ⊃ ∿Pa}  ↲  3, EI
5)             Pa • (y)(Py ⊃ Fay) ↲          4, DMI
6)                   ∿∿Pa ↲                   4, DMI
7)                    Pa                       6, DN
8)                    Pa                       5, C
9)            (y)(Py ⊃ Fay)                    5, C
10)             Pa ⊃ Faa ↲                     9, UI
```

```
11)        ∿Pa          Faa                   10, MI
12)         X      Pa ⊃ ∿Faa ↲                1, UI
```

```
13)             ∿Pa        ∿∿Faa ↲            12, MI
14)              X          Faa               13, DN
                            X                        VALID
```

18.   /∴ (∃x)(Cx • Wsx)

```
1)   (x)[Sx ⊃ (∃x)(Cy • Exy)]      Pr
2)   Ss • (x)(Esx ⊃ Wsx) ↲         Pr
3)   ∿(∃x)(Cx • Wsx) ↲             AP
4)      (x)∿(Cx • Wsx)             3, QD
5)            Ss                   2, C
6)       (x)(Esx ⊃ Wsx)            2, C
7)    Sx ⊃ (∃x)(Cy • Exy) ↲        1, UI
```

```
8) ∿Ss         (∃y)(Cy • Esy) ↲   7, MI
9)  X             Ca • Esa ↲       8, EI
10)                 Ca             9, C
11)                 Esa            9, C
12)             Esa ⊃ Wsa ↲        6, UI
```

```
13)         ∿Esa        Wsa           12, MI
14)          X      ∿(Ca • Wsa) ↲ 4, UI
```

```
15)            ∿Ca         ∿Wsa   14, DC
                X            X             VALID
```

20.   /∴ (x)[(Nx • Ix) ⊃ (∃y)(Py • Cyx)]
   1)   (x){Px ⊃ (∃y)[(Ny • Iy) • Cxy]}   Pr
   2)   ∿(x)[(Nx • Ix) ⊃ (∃y)(Py • Cyx)] ↓ AP
   3)   (∃x)∿[(Nx • Ix) ⊃ (∃y)(Py • Cyx)] ↓   2, QD
   4)   ∿[(Na • Ia) ⊃ (∃y)(Py • Cya)] ↓   3, EI
   5)   Na • Ia ↓   4, DMI
   6)   ∿(∃y)(Py • Cya) ↓   4, DMI
   7)   Na   5, C
   8)   Ia   5, C
   9)   (y)∿(Py • Cya)   6, QD
   10)   ∿(Pb • Cba) ↓   9, UI
   11)   Pb ⊃ (∃y)[(Ny • Iy) • Cby] ↓   1, UI

   12) ∿Pb   (∃y)[(Ny • Iy) • Cby] ↓   11, MI
   13)   (Nc • Ic) • Cbc ↓   12, EI
   14)   Nc • Ic ↓   13, C
   15)   Cbc   13, C
   16)   Nc   14, C
   17)   Ic   14, C

   18) ∿Pb ∿Cba   ∿Pc   ∿Cba   10, DC
                                             VALID

11.2.A.

2.   /∴   Mb • Pb
   1)   Gb • Pb ↓   Pr
   2)   (x)(Gx ⊃ Mx)   Pr
   3)   Gb ⊃ Mb ↓   2, UI
   4)   Gb   1, C
   5)   Pb   1, C

   6)   ∿Gb   Mb   3, MI
         X   CONSISTENT

205

4.   /∴ (x)(Cx ⊃ Hx)
   1)   ∿(∃x)(Cx • ∿Hx) ↓   Pr
   2)   (x)(Hx ⊃ ∿Sx)   Pr
   3)   (x)∿(Cx • ∿Hx)   1, QD
   4)   Ha ⊃ ∿Sa ↓   2, UI
   5)   ∿(Ca • ∿Ha) ↓   3, UI

   6)   ∿Ha   ∿Sa   4, MI

   7) ∿Ca ∿∿Ha ↓ ∿Ca ∿∿Ha ↓   5, DC
   8)   Ha   Ha   7, DN
          X   CONSISTENT

6.   /∴ ∿(x)∿(Sx • ∿Hx)
   1)   ∿(x)(Hx ∨ Sx) ↓   Pr
   2)   (x)(∿Sx ⊃ Hx)   Pr
   3)   (∃x)∿(Hx ∨ Sx) ↓ 1, QD
   4)   ∿(Ha ∨ Sa) ↓   3, EI
   5)   ∿Ha   4, DID
   6)   ∿Sa   4, DID
   7)   ∿Sa ⊃ Ha ↓   2, UI

   8) ∿∿Sa ↓   Ha   7, MI
   9)   Sa   X   8, DN
        X   INCONSISTENT

8.   /∴ (∃x)(Dx • ∿Hx)
   1)   (x)[Dx ⊃ (∿Ux ⊃ Hx)]   Pr
   2)   (∃x)(Dx • ∿Ux) ↓   Pr
   3)   Da • ∿Ua ↓   2, EI
   4)   Da   3, C
   5)   ∿Ua   3, C
   6)   Da ⊃ (∿Ua ⊃ Ha) ↓   1, UI

   7) ∿Da   ∿Ua ⊃ Ha ↓   6, MI

   8)   ∿∿Ua ↓   Ha   7, MI
   9)   Ua   X   8, DN
           X   CONSISTENT

206

10.   /∴ ∿(x)(Sx ⊃ Ix)

  1) (x)[Sx ⊃ (Cx • Ix)]   Pr
  2) ∿(x)(Sx ⊃ Cx) ✓   Pr
  3) (∃x)∿(Sx ⊃ Cx) ✓   2, QD
  4)   ∿(Sa ⊃ Ca) ✓   3, EI
  5)   Sa   4, DMI
  6)   ∿Ca   4, DMI
  7)   Sa ⊃ (Ca • Ia) ✓   1, UI

  8) ∿Sa   Ca • Ia ✓   7, MI
  9)   X   Ca   8, C
 10)   Ia   8, C
                 X   INCONSISTENT

12.   /∴ (∃x)[(Px • Ix) • ∿Sx]

  1) (x)[Ix ⊃ (Px ⊃ Sx)]   Pr
  2) (∃x)[Ix • ∿(Sx ∨ ∿Px)] ✓   Pr
  3)   Ia • ∿(Sa ∨ ∿Pa) ✓   2, EI
  4)   Ia   3, C
  5)   ∿(Sa ∨ ∿Pa) ✓   3, C
  6)   ∿Sa   5, DID
  7)   ∿∿Pa ✓   5, DID
  8)   Pa   7, DN
  9)   Ia ⊃ (Pa ⊃ Sa) ✓   1, UI

 10) ∿Ia   Pa ⊃ Sa ✓   9, MI
      X

 11)   ∿Pa   Sa   10, MI
             X   X   INCONSISTENT

14.   /∴ (∃x)(Cx • ∿Dx)

  1) (x)(Cx ⊃ Dx)   Pr
  2) (x)[Dx ⊃ (Ix ⊃ Fx)]   Pr
  3) (x)[Cx ⊃ (Ix ∨ Dx)]   Pr
  4) (∃x)[Cx • ∿(Fx ∨ Dx)] ✓ Pr
  5)   Ca • ∿(Fa ∨ Da) ✓   4, EI
  6)   Ca   5, C
  7)   ∿(Fa ∨ Da) ✓   5, C
  8)   ∿Fa   7, DID
  9)   ∿Da   7, DID

10)   Ca ⊃ Da √   1, UI

11)   ∿Ca   Da   10, MI
      X   X   INCONSISTENT

16.   /∴ (∃y)[Vy · (x)(Sx ⊃ Cyx)]
1)   (∃x)Sx √   Pr
2)   (x){Sx ⊃ [Ex ⊃ (∃y)(Vy · Cyx)]}   Pr
3)   (x)(Sx ⊃ Ex)   Pr
4)   Sa   1, EI
5)   Sa ⊃ Ea √   3, UI

6)   ∿Sa   Ea   5, MI
7)   X   Sa ⊃ [Ea ⊃ (∃y)(Vy · Cya)] √   2, UI

8)   ∿Sa   Ea ⊃ (∃y)(Vy · Cya) √   7, MI
       X

9)   ∿Ea   (∃y)(Vy · Cya) √   8, MI
10)   X   Vb · Cba √   9, EI
11)   Vb   10, C
12)   Cba   10, C
13)   Sb ⊃ [Eb ⊃ (∃y)(Vy · Cyb)]   2, UI

Since #16 is nonterminating, it is CONSISTENT

18.   /∴(x)(Cx ⊃ Tx)
1)   (x){[Px · (∃y)(Py · Rxy)] ⊃ ∿Tx}   Pr
2)   (∃x){Cx · [PX · (∃y)(Py · Rxy)]} √   Pr
3)   Ca · [Pa · (∃y)(Py · Ray)]} √   2, EI
4)   Ca   3, C
5)   Pa · (∃y)(Py · Ray) √   3, C
6)   Pa   5, C
7)   (∃y)(Py · Ray) √   5, C
8)   Pb · Rab √   7, EI
9)   Pb   8, C
10)   Rab   8, C
11)   [Pa · (∃y)(Py · Ray)] ⊃ ∿Ta √   1, UI

208

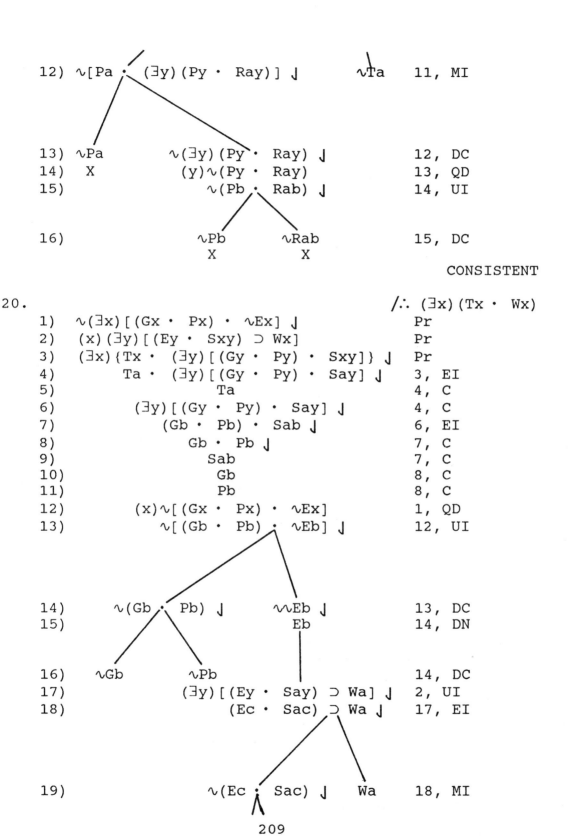

12) ∿[Pa • (∃y)(Py • Ray)] ⌡   ∿Ta   11, MI

13) ∿Pa   ∿(∃y)(Py • Ray) ⌡   12, DC
14) X   (y)∿(Py • Ray)   13, QD
15)   ∿(Pb • Rab) ⌡   14, UI

16)   ∿Pb   ∿Rab   15, DC
             X   X

                                        CONSISTENT

20.   /∴ (∃x)(Tx • Wx)
    1)   ∿(∃x)[(Gx • Px) • ∿Ex] ⌡   Pr
    2)   (x)(∃y)[(Ey • Sxy) ⊃ Wx]   Pr
    3)   (∃x){Tx • (∃y)[(Gy • Py) • Sxy]} ⌡ Pr
    4)   Ta • (∃y)[(Gy • Py) • Say] ⌡   3, EI
    5)   Ta   4, C
    6)   (∃y)[(Gy • Py) • Say] ⌡   4, C
    7)   (Gb • Pb) • Sab ⌡   6, EI
    8)   Gb • Pb ⌡   7, C
    9)   Sab   7, C
   10)   Gb   8, C
   11)   Pb   8, C
   12)   (x)∿[(Gx • Px) • ∿Ex]   1, QD
   13)   ∿[(Gb • Pb) • ∿Eb] ⌡   12, UI

   14) ∿(Gb • Pb) ⌡   ∿∿Eb ⌡   13, DC
   15)   Eb   14, DN

   16) ∿Gb   ∿Pb   14, DC
   17)   (∃y)[(Ey • Say) ⊃ Wa] ⌡   2, UI
   18)   (Ec • Sac) ⊃ Wa ⌡   17, EI

   19)   ∿(Ec • Sac) ⌡   Wa   18, MI

209

∿Ec   ∿Sac   19, DC
                           CONNSISTENT

11.2.B.

2.   /∴   Mb · Pb
   1) Gb · Pb ⌡   Pr
   2) (x)(Gx ⊃ Mx)   Pr
   3) ∿(Mb · Pb) ⌡   AP
   4)   Gb   1, C
   5)   Pb   1, C
   6)   Gb ⊃ Mb ⌡   2, UI

   8) ∿Gb   Mb   6, MI
        X
   9)   ∿Mb   ∿Pb   3, DC
          X   X   VALID

4.   /∴ (x)(Cx ⊃ Hx)
   1) ∿(∃x)(Cx · ∿Hx) ⌡   Pr
   2) (x)(Hx ⊃ ∿Sx)   Pr
   3) ∿(x)(Cx ⊃ Hx) ⌡   AP
   4) (∃x)∿(Cx ⊃ Hx) ⌡   3, QD
   5) (x)∿(Cx · ∿Hx)   1, QD
   6) ∿(Ca ⊃ Ha) ⌡   4, EI
   7)   Ca   6, DMI
   8)   ∿Ha   6, DMI
   9) ∿(Ca · ∿Ha) ⌡   5, UI

  10) ∿Ca   ∿∿Ha ⌡   9, DC
  11)   X   Ha   10, DN
                X   VALID

8.   /∴ (∃x)(Dx • ∿Hx)
1)   (x)[(Dx ⊃ (∿Ux ⊃ Hx)]   Pr
2)   (∃x)(Dx • ∿Ux) ✓   Pr
3)   ∿(∃x)(Dx • ∿Hx) ✓   AP
4)   (x)∿(Dx • ∿Hx)   3, QD
5)   Da • ∿Ua ✓   2 EI
6)   Da   5 C
7)   ∿Ua   5 C
8)   Da ⊃ (∿Ua ⊃ Ha) ✓   1 UI

9)   ∿Da   ∿Ua ⊃ Ha ✓   8 MI

10)   ∿∿Ua ✓   Ha   9 MI
11)   Ua   10 DN
12)   X   ∿(Da • ∿Ha) ✓ 4 UI

13)   ∿Da   ∿∿Ha ✓   12 DC
14)   X   Ha   13 DN
                                          INVALID

16.   /∴ (∃y)[Vy • (x)(Sx ⊃ Cyx)]
1)   (∃x)Sx ✓   Pr
2)   (x){Sx ⊃ [Ex ⊃ (∃y)(Vy • Cyx)]}   Pr
3)   (x)(Sx ⊃ Ex)   Pr
4)   ∿(∃y)[Vy • (x)(Sx ⊃ Cyx)] ✓   SP
5)   (y)∿[Vy • (x)(Sx ⊃ Cyx)]   4 QD
6)   Sa   1, EI
7)   Sa ⊃ Ea ✓   3, UI

8)   ∿Sa   Ea   7, MI
9)   X   Sa ⊃ [Ea ⊃ (∃y)(Vy • Cya)] ✓   2, UI

10)   ∿Sa   Ea ⊃ (∃y)(Vy • Cya) ✓   9, MI
       X

11)   ∿Ea   (∃y)(Vy • Cya) ✓   10, MI
12)   X   Vb • Cba ✓   11, EI

211

13)   Vb   12, C
14)   Cba   12, C
15)   ∿[Vb • (x)(Sx ⊃ Cbx)] ↲   5, UI

16)   ∿Vb   ∿(x)(Sx ⊃ Cbx) ↲   15, DC
17)   X   (∃x)∿(Sx ⊃ Cbx) ↲   16, QD
18)   ∿(Sc ⊃ Cbc) ↲   17, EI
19)   Sc   18, DMI
20)   ∿Cbc   18, DMI
21)   Sc ⊃ [Ec ⊃ (∃y)(Vy • Cyc)]   2, UI

        Since #16 is nonterminating, it is INVALID

20.   /∴ (∃x)(Tx • Wx)
    1)   ∿(∃x)[(Gx • Px) • ∿Ex] ↲   Pr
    2)   (x)(∃y)[(Ey • Sxy) ⊃ Wx]   Pr
    3)   (∃x){Tx • (∃y)[(Gy • Py) • Sxy]} ↲ Pr
    4)   ∿(∃x)(Tx • Wx) ↲   AP
    5)   Ta • (∃y)[(Gy • Py) • Say] ↲   3, EI
    6)   Ta   5, C
    7)   (∃y)[(Gy • Py) • Say] ↲   5, C
    8)   (Gb • Pb) • Sab ↲   7, EI
    9)   Gb • Pb ↲   8, C
   10)   Sab   8, C
   11)   Gb   9, C
   12)   Pb   9, C
   13)   (x)∿(Tx • Wx)   4, QD
   14)   ∿(Ta • Wa) ↲   13, UI

   15)   ∿Ta   ∿Wa   14, DC
   16)   X   (∃y)[(Ey • Say) ⊃ Wa] ↲ 2, UI
   17)   (Ec • Sac) ⊃ Wa ↲   16, EI

   18)   ∿(Ec • Sac) ↲   Wa   17. MI
                                X

   19)   ∿Ec   ∿Sac   18, DC

                          212

20) (x)∿[(Gx • Px) • ∿Ex] (x)∿[(Gx • Px) • ∿Ex] 1, QD
21)   ∿[(Gb • Pb) • ∿Eb] ✓   ∿[(Gb • Pb) • ∿Eb] ✓ 20, UI

22) ∿(Gb • Pb) ✓   ∿∿Eb ✓   ∿(Gb • Pb) ✓   ∿∿Eb ✓   21, DC
23)   Eb   Eb   22, DN

24)   ∿Gb   ∿Pb   ∿Gb   ∿Pb   22, DC
       X   X   X   X

                                              VALID

11.3.

2.

    (x)(Ex ⊃ ∿Cx)

a)
  1)   (x)(Ex ⊃ ∿Cx)   ——
  2)   Ea ⊃ ∿Ca ✓   1, UI

  3)   ∿Ea   ∿Ca   2, MI

b)
  1)   ∿(x)(Ex ⊃ ∿Cx) ✓   ——
  2)   (∃x)∿(Ex ⊃ ∿Cx) ✓   1, QD
  3)   ∿(Ea ⊃ ∿Ca) ✓   2, EI
  4)   Ea   3, DMI
  5)   ∿∿Ca ✓   3, DMI
  6)   Ca   5, DN

    Since #2 is neither a contradiction nor logically
    true, it is CONTINGENT.

4.

    (x)(y)(Px ⊃ Lxy) ⊃ (x)(∃y)(Px ⊃ Lxy)

  1) ∿[(x)(y)(Px ⊃ Lxy) ⊃ (x)(∃y)(Px ⊃ Lxy)] ✓   ——
  2)   (x)(y)(Px ⊃ Lxy)   1, DMI
  3)   ∿(x)(∃y)(Px ⊃ Lxy) ✓   1, DMI

4)	$(\exists x)\backsim(\exists y)(Px \supset Lxy)$ ✓	3, QD
5)	$(\exists x)(y)\backsim(Px \supset Lxy)$ ✓	4, QD
6)	$(y)\backsim(Pa \supset Lay)$	5, EI
7)	$\backsim(Pa \supset Lab)$ ✓	6, UI
8)	Pa	7, DMI
9)	$\backsim$Lab	7, DMI
10)	$(y)(Pa \supset Lay)$	2, UI
11)	$Pa \supset Lab$ ✓	10, UI

$$\backsim Pa \qquad Lab$$
$$X \qquad\quad X$$

LOGICALLY TRUE

6.

$(x)(Dx \supset Ux) \cdot (\exists x)(\backsim Dx \cdot Ux)$

a)

1)	$(x)(Dx \supset Ux) \cdot (\exists x)(\backsim Dx \cdot Ux)$ ✓	——
2)	$(x)(Dx \supset Ux)$	1, C
3)	$(\exists x)(\backsim Dx \cdot Ux)$ ✓	1, C
4)	$\backsim Da \cdot Ua$ ✓	3, EI
5)	$\backsim Da$	4, C
6)	Ua	4, C
7)	$Da \supset Ua$ ✓	2, UI

$$\backsim Da \qquad Ua$$

8)		7, MI

b)

1. $\backsim[(x)(Dx \supset Ux) \cdot (\exists x)(\backsim Dx \cdot Ux)]$ ✓ ——

2)	$\backsim(x)(Dx \supset Ux)$ ✓	$\backsim(\exists x)(\backsim Dx \cdot Ux)$ ✓	1, DC
3)	$(\exists x)\backsim(Dx \supset Ux)$ ✓		2, QD
4)	$\backsim(Da \supset Ua)$ ✓		3, EI
5)	Da		4, DMI
6)	$\backsim Ua$		4, DMI
7)		$(x)\backsim(\backsim Dx \cdot Ux)$	2, QD
8)		$\backsim(\backsim Da \cdot Ua)$ ✓	7, UI

214

```
9)              ∿∿Da ↓    ∿Ua   8, DC
10)               Da            9, DN
```

Since #6 is neither a contradiction nor logically true, it is CONTINGENT.

8.

   (∃x)Hx • ∿(x)(Dx ⊃ Hx)

a)
```
1)    (∃x)Hx • ∿(x)(Dx ⊃ Hx) ↓    ──────
2)            (∃x)Hx ↓            1, C
3)         ∿(x)(Dx ⊃ Hx) ↓       1, C
4)         (∃x)∿(Dx ⊃ Hx) ↓      3, QD
5)              Ha               2, EI
6)          ∿(Db ⊃ Hb) ↓         4, EI
7)              Db               6, DMI
8)              ∿Hb              6, DMI
```

b)
```
1)   ∿[(∃x)Hx • ∿(x)(Dx ⊃ Hx)] ↓    ──────
```

```
2) ∿(∃x)Hx ↓     ∿∿(x)(Dx ⊃ Hx) ↓   1, DC
3) (x)∿Hx                            2, QD
4)      ∿Ha                          3, UI
5)                 (x)(Dx ⊃ Hx)      2, DN
6)                 Da ⊃ Ha ↓         5, UI

7)                  ∿Da    Ha        6, MI
```

Since #8 is neither a contradiction nor logically true, it is CONTINGENT.

10.

   ∿(x)[Dx ⊃ (Px ∨ Bx)] ⊃ (∃x)[(Px • Dx) • ∿Bx]

215

a)

1) ∿(x)[Dx ⊃ (Px ∨ Bx)] ⊃ (∃x)[(Px · Dx) · ∿Bx] √   ——

2) ∿∿(x)[Dx ⊃ (Px ∨ Bx)] √   (∃x)[(Px · Dx) · ∿Bx] √   1, MI
3) (x)[Dx ⊃ (Px ∨ Bx)   2, DN
4)   Da ⊃ (Pa ∨ Ba)   3, UI

5)   ∿Da   Pa ∨ Ba √   4, MI

6)   Pa   Ba   5, ID
7)   (Pa · Da) · ∿Ba √   2, EI
8)   Pa · Da √   7, C
9)   ∿Ba   7, C
10)   Pa   8, C
11)   Da   8, C

b)

1) ∿{∿(x)[Dx ⊃ (Px ∨ Bx)] ⊃ (∃x)[(Px · Dx) · ∿Bx]} √ ——
2)   ∿(x)[Dx ⊃ (Px ∨ Bx)] √   1, DMI
3)   ∿(∃x)[(Px · Dx) · ∿Bx] √   1, DMI
4)   (∃x)∿[Dx ⊃ (Px ∨ Bx)] √   2, QD
5)   (x)∿[(Px · Dx) · ∿Bx]   3, QD
6)   ∿[Da ⊃ (Pa ∨ Ba)] √   4, EI
7)   ∿[(Pa · Da) · ∿Ba] √   5, UI
8)   Da   6, DMI
9)   ∿(Pa ∨ Ba) √   6, DMI
10)   ∿Pa   9, DID
11)   ∿Ba   9, DID

12)   ∿(Pa · Da) √   ∿∿Ba √   7, DC
13)   Ba   12, DN
                                     X
14)   ∿Pa   ∿Da   12, DC
              X

Since #10 is neither a contradiction nor logically
true, it is CONTINGENT.

216

12.

$(\exists x)[(Px \cdot Dx) \cdot \lor Bx] \cdot (x)(Dx \supset Bx)$

```
1)   (∃x)[(Px · Dx) · ∿Bx] · (x)(Dx ⊃ Bx) √    ─────
2)              (∃x)[(Px · Dx) · ∿Bx] √          1, C
3)                  (x)(Dx ⊃ Bx)                 1, C
4)                (Pa · Da) · ∿Ba √              2, EI
5)                   Pa · Da √                    4, C
6)                     ∿Ba                        4, C
7)                      Pa                         5, C
8)                      Da                         5, C
9)                  Da ⊃ Ba √                     3, UI
```

```
                        /   \
10)              ∿Da        Ba                    9, MI
                  X          X
```

CONTRADICTION

14.

$(\exists x)[Sx \cdot (y)(Cy \supset \lor Axy)]$

a)
```
1)   (∃x)[Sx · (y)(Cy ⊃ ∿Axy)] √    ─────
2)      Sa · (y)(Cy ⊃ ∿Aay) √        1, EI
3)              Sa                    2, C
4)       (y)(Cy ⊃ ∿Aay)              2, C
5)         Cb ⊃ ∿Aab                 4, UI
```
```
              /    \
6)       ∿Cb        ∿Aab             5, MI
```

b)
```
1)   ∿(∃x)[Sx · (y)(Cy ⊃ ∿Axy)] √    ─────
2)    (x)∿[Sx · (y)(Cy ⊃ ∿Axy)]      1, QD
3)       ∿[Sa · (y)(Cy ⊃ ∿Aay)] √    2, UI
```
```
               /        \
4)    ∿Sa        ∿(y)(Cy ⊃ ∿Aay) √    3, DC
5)               (∃y)∿(Cy ⊃ ∿Aay) √   4, QD
6)                ∿(Cb ⊃ ∿Aab) √       5, EI
7)                      Cb              6, DMI
8)                   ∿∿Aab √            6, DMI
9)                     Aab              8, DN
```

217

Since #14 is neither a contradiction nor logically true, it is CONTINGENT.

16.

$\sim$(x)[Sx $\supset$ ($\exists$y)(Gy $\cdot$ Mxy)] $\cdot$ ($\exists$x)[Sx $\cdot$ ($\exists$y)(Gy $\cdot$ Mxy)]

a)
```
1)  ∿(x)[Sx ⊃ (∃y)(Gy· Mxy)] · (∃x)[Sx · (∃y)(Gy· Mxy)] ↓ ---
2)              ∿(x)[Sx ⊃ (∃y)(Gy · Mxy)] ↓              1, C
3)              (∃x)[Sx · (∃y)(Gy · Mxy) ↓               1, C
4)              (∃x)∿[Sx ⊃ (∃y)(Gy · Mxy)] ↓             2, QD
5)              ∿[Sa ⊃ (∃y)(Gy · May)] ↓                 4, EI
6)              Sb · (∃y)(Gy · Mby) ↓                     3, EI
7)                      Sb                                6, C
8)              (∃y)(Gy · Mby) ↓                          6, C
9)                  Gc · Mbc ↓                            8, EI
10)                    Gc                                 9, C
11)                    Mbc                                9, C
12)                    ∿Sb                                5, DMI
13)             ∿(∃y)(Gy · May) ↓                         5, DMI
14)             (y)∿(Gy · May)                            13, QD
15)                 ∿(Gc · Mac) ↓                         14, UI


16)            ∿Gc        ∿Mac                            15, DC
                X
```

b)
```
1)∿{∿(x)[Sx ⊃ (∃y)(Gy· Mxy)] · (∃x)[Sx · (∃y)(Gy· Mxy)]}↓—


2)∿∿(x)[Sx ⊃ (∃y)(Gy· Mxy)] ↓    ∿(∃x)[Sx · (∃y)(Gy· Mxy)]↓
                                                     1, DC
3) (x)[Sx ⊃ (∃y)(Gy · Mxy)]                          2, DN
4)     Sa ⊃ (∃y)(Gy · May) ↓                         3, UI



5)   ∿Sa      (∃y)(Gy · May) ↓                        4, MI
```

218

6)	Gb • Mab ↲		5, EI
7)	Gb		6, C
8)	Mab		6, C
9)	(x)∿[Sx • (∃y)(Gy • Mxy)]		2, QD
10)	∿[Sa • (∃y)(Gy • May)] ↲		9, UI

```
11)          ∿Sa        ∿(∃y)(Gy • May) ↲ 10, DC
12)                     (y)∿(Gy • May)     11, QD
13)                        ∿(Gb • Mab) ↲   12, UI

14)                        ∿Gb    ∿Mab      13, DC
```

Since #16 is neither a contradiction nor logically true, it is CONTINGENT.

18.

$$(\exists x)[(Lx • Sx) • \sim Ax] \equiv (x)[(Lx • Sx) \supset Ax]$$

```
1)   (∃x)[(Lx • Sx) • ∿Ax] ≡ (x)[(Lx • Sx) ⊃ Ax] ↲  ——

2)  (∃x)[(Lx • Sx) • ∿Ax] ↲   ∿(∃x)[(Lx • Sx) • ∿Ax] ↲  1, ME
3)  (x)[(Lx • Sx) ⊃ Ax]       ∿(x)[(Lx • Sx) ⊃ Ax] ↲    1, ME
4)    (La • Sa) • ∿Aa ↲                                 2, EI
5)       La • Sa ↲                                      4, C
6)         ∿Aa                                          4, C
7)         La                                           5, C
8)         Sa                                           5, C
9)    (La • Sa) ⊃ Aa ↲                                  3, UI


10) ∿(La • Sa) ↲   Aa                                   9, MI
                   X

11)∿La      ∿Sa                                         10, DC
12) X        X      (x)∿[(Lx • Sx) • ∿Ax]   2, QD
13)                 (∃x)∿[(Lx • Sx) ⊃ Ax] ↲  3, QD
14)                  ∿[(La • Sa) ⊃ Aa] ↲   13, EI
15)                      La • Sa ↲          14, DMI
```

219

```
16)                                    ∿Aa              14, DMI
17)                                     La              15, C
18)                                     Sa              15, C
19)                      ∿[(La · Sa) · ∿Aa] ↲           12, UI


20)            ∿(La · Sa) ↲              ∿∿Aa ↲         19, DC
21)                                       Aa            20, DN
                                           X
22)        ∿La           ∿Sa                            20, DC
            X             X             CONTRADICTION
```

20.

$$(\exists x)\{Px \cdot (y)[(Ny \cdot Iy) \supset Cxy]\} \supset (y)[(Ny \cdot Iy) \supset (\exists x)(Px \cdot Cxy)]$$

```
1)   ∿((∃x){Px · (y)[(Ny · Iy) ⊃ Cxy]} ⊃
                  (y)[(Ny · Iy) ⊃ (∃x)(Px · Cxy)]) ↲  ───
2)          (∃x){Px · (y)[(Ny · Iy) ⊃ Cxy]} ↲          1, DMI
3)          ∿(y)[(Ny · Iy) ⊃ (∃x)(Px · Cxy)] ↲         1, DMI
4)          (∃y)∿[(Ny · Iy) ⊃ (∃x)(Px · Cxy)] ↲        3, QD
5)          ∿[(Na · Ia) ⊃ (∃x)(Px · Cxa)] ↲            4, EI
6)                    Na · Ia ↲                         5, DMI
7)              ∿(∃x)(Px · Cxa) ↲                       5, DMI
8)                (x)∿(Px · Cxa)                        7, QD
9)                      Na                              6, C
10)                     Ia                              6, C
11)        Pb · (y)[(Ny · Iy) ⊃ Cby] ↲                  2, EI
12)                     Pb                              11, C
13)         (y)[(Ny · Iy) ⊃ Cby]                        11, C
14)              ∿(Pb · Cba) ↲                          8, UI
15)            (Na · Ia) ⊃ Cba ↲                        13, UI



16)      ∿Pb                      ∿Cba                  14, DC
          X

17)              ∿(Na · Ia) ↲              Cba          15, MI
                                            X

18)      ∿Na           ∿Ia                              17, DC
          X             X
                                        LOGICALLY TRUE
```

220

11.4.

2.
   a)   (x)(Fx ∨ ∿Cx)
   b)   (∃x)(∿Cx • Fx)

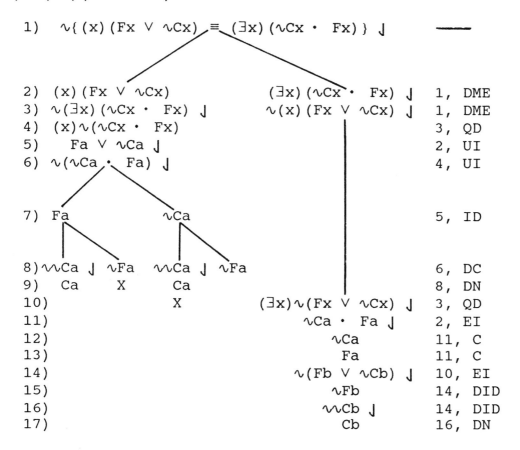

   1)   ∿{(x)(Fx ∨ ∿Cx) ≡ (∃x)(∿Cx • Fx)} ⌡   ——

   2) (x)(Fx ∨ ∿Cx)   (∃x)(∿Cx • Fx) ⌡   1, DME
   3) ∿(∃x)(∿Cx • Fx) ⌡   ∿(x)(Fx ∨ ∿Cx) ⌡   1, DME
   4) (x)∿(∿Cx • Fx)   3, QD
   5)   Fa ∨ ∿Ca ⌡   2, UI
   6) ∿(∿Ca • Fa) ⌡   4, UI

   7) Fa   ∿Ca   5, ID

   8)∿∿Ca ⌡ ∿Fa   ∿∿Ca ⌡ ∿Fa   6, DC
   9) Ca   X   Ca   8, DN
   10)   X   (∃x)∿(Fx ∨ ∿Cx) ⌡   3, QD
   11)   ∿Ca • Fa ⌡   2, EI
   12)   ∿Ca   11, C
   13)   Fa   11, C
   14)   ∿(Fb ∨ ∿Cb) ⌡   10, EI
   15)   ∿Fb   14, DID
   16)   ∿∿Cb ⌡   14, DID
   17)   Cb   16, DN

                          NOT LOGICALLY EQUIVALENT

4.
   a)   ∿(∃x)(Ix • Hx)
   b)   (x)(Ix ⊃ ∿Hx)

   1)   ∿[∿(∃x)(Ix • Hx) ≡ (x)(Ix ⊃ ∿Hx)] ⌡   ——

   2) ∿(∃x)(Ix • Hx) ⌡   (x)(Ix ⊃ ∿Hx)   1, DME

```
 3)  ~(x)(Ix ⊃ ~Hx) J    ~~(∃x)(Ix • Hx) J    1, DME
 4)  (x)~(Ix • Hx)                             2, QD
 5)  (∃x)~(Ix ⊃ ~Hx) J                         3, QD
 6)    ~(Ia ⊃ ~Ha) J                           5, EI
 7)         Ia                                 6, DMI
 8)       ~~Ha J                               6, DMI
 9)         Ha                                 8, DN
10)  ~(Ia • Ha) J                              4, UI


11)  ~Ia      ~Ha                              10, DC
12)   X        X         (∃x)(Ix • Hx) J       3, DN
13)                        Ia • Ha J           12, EI
14)                           Ia               13, C
15)                           Ha               13, C
16)                       Ia ⊃ ~Ha J           2, UI


17)                    ~Ia        ~Ha J  16, MI
                        X          X
                        LOGICALLY EQUIVALENT
```

6.

  a) ~(x)(Ix ⊃ Dx)
  b) (∃x)(Ix • ~Dx)

```
 1)  ~[~(x)(Ix ⊃ Dx) ≡ (∃x)(Ix • ~Dx)] J    ──


 2)  ~(x)(Ix ⊃ Dx) J     (∃x)(Ix • ~Dx) J     1, DME
 3)  ~(∃x)(Ix • ~Dx) J   ~~(x)(Ix ⊃ Dx) J     1, DME
 4)  (∃x)~(Ix ⊃ Dx) J                         2, QD
 5)  (x)~(Ix • ~Dx)                           3, QD
 6)    ~(Ia ⊃ Da) J                           4, EI
 7)         Ia                                6, DMI
 8)       ~Da                                 6, DMI
 9)  ~(Ia • ~Da) J                            5, UI


10)  ~Ia      ~~Da J                          9, DC
11)   X        Da                             0, DN
12)             X       (x)(Ix ⊃ Dx)          3, DN
13)                     Ia • ~Da J            2, EI
```

222

14)	Ia	13, C	
15)	∿Da	13, C	
16)	Ia ⊃ Da ⌡	12, UI	

```
                        Ia            13, C
                       ∿Da            13, C
                    Ia ⊃ Da ⌡         12, UI
                       /
                      /
        17)     ∿Ia        ∿Da        16, MI
                 X          X
                    LOGICALLY EQUIVALENT
```

8.

   a)   (x)(Tx · Sx)

   b)   (x)Tx · (x)Sx

   1) ∿{(x)(Tx · Sx) ≡ [(x)Tx · (x)Sx]} ⌡ ——

```
2) (x)(Tx · Sx)        (x)Tx · (x)Sx ⌡      1, DME
3) ∿[(x)Tx · (x)Sx] ⌡   ∿(x)(Tx · Sx) ⌡    1, DME
4)  ∿(x)Tx ∨ ∿(x)Sx ⌡                        3, DC
          /    \
         /      \
5) ∿(x)Tx ⌡    ∿(x)Sx ⌡                      4, ID
6) (∃x)∿Tx ⌡   (∃x)∿Sx ⌡                     5, QD
7)    ∿Ta         ∿Sa                        6, EI
8) Ta · Sa ⌡   Ta · Sa ⌡                     2, UI
9)    Ta          Ta                         8, C
10)   Sa          Sa                         8, C
11)    X           X        (∃x)∿(Tx · Sx) ⌡  3, QD
12)                           ∿(Ta · Sa) ⌡   11, EI
                                /
                               /
13)                        ∿Ta    ∿Sa        12, DC
14)                       (x)Tx  (x)Tx       2, C
15)                       (x)Sx  (x)Sx       2, C
16)                         Ta     Ta        14, UI
17)                         Sa     Sa        15, UI
                             X      X
                    LOGICALLY EQUIVALENT
```

10.

   a)   (x)(Sx ∨ Tx)

   b)   (x)Sx ∨ (x)Tx

1)   ~{(x)(Sx ∨ Tx) ≡ [(x)Sx ∨ (x)Tx]} ✓ ——

2) (x)(Sx ∨ Tx)   (x)Sx ∨ (x)Tx ✓   1, DME
3) ~[(x)Sx ∨ (x)Tx] ✓   ~(x)(Sx ∨ Tx) ✓   1, DME
4)   ~(x)Sx ✓   3, DID
5)   ~(x)Tx ✓   3, DID
6)   (∃x)~Sx ✓   4, QD
7)   (∃x)~Tx ✓   5, QD
8)   ~Sa   6, EI
9)   ~Tb   7, EI
10)   Sa ∨ Ta ✓   2, UI

11) Sa   Ta   10, ID
12) X   Sb ∨ Tb ✓   2, UI

13)   Sb   Tb   12, ID
14)   X   (∃x)~(Sx ∨ Tx) ✓   3, QD
15)   ~(Sa ∨ Ta) ✓   14, EI
16)   ~Sa   15, DID
17)   ~Ta   15, DID

18)   (x)Sx   (x)Tx   2, ID
19)   Sa   Ta   18, UI
                              X   X
                    NOT LOGICALLY EQUIVALENT

12.
   a)   (x)[Px ⊃ (∃y)(Py · Lxy)]
   b)   (∃x)[Px · (y)(Py ⊃ Lxy)]

1)   ~{(x)[Px ⊃ (∃y)(Py · Lxy)] ≡
                    (∃x)[Px · (y)(Py ⊃ Lxy)]} ✓ ——

2) (x)[Px ⊃ (∃y)(Py· Lxy)]   (∃x)[Px · (y)(Py⊃Lxy)] ✓ 1,DME
3)~(∃x)[Px · (y)(Py⊃Lxy)] ✓ ~(x)[Px ⊃ (∃y)(Py· Lxy)] ✓ 1,DME
4) (x)~[Px · (y)(Py ⊃ Lxy)]   3, QD
5)   ~[Pa · (y)(Py ⊃ Lay)] ✓   4, UI

224

6)   Px ⊃ (∃y)(Py · Lxy) ↲   2, UI

7)   ∿Pa   ∿(y)(Py ⊃ Lay) ↲   5, DC
8)   (∃y)∿(Py ⊃ Lay) ↲   7, QD
9)   ∿(Pb ⊃ Lab) ↲   8, EI
10)   Pb   9, DMI
11)   ∿Lab   9, DMI

12) ∿Pa (∃y)(Py · Lay) ↲   ∿Pa   (∃y)(Py · Lay) ↲   6, MI
13)   Pc · Lac ↲   Pc · Lac ↲   12, EI
14)   Pc   Pc   13, C
15)   Lac   Lac   13, C

16)   (∃x)∿[Px ⊃ (∃y)(Py · Lxy)] ↲ 3, QD
17)   ∿[Pa ⊃ (∃y)(Py · Lay)] ↲16, EI
18)   Pa   17, DMI
19)   ∿(∃y)(Py · Lay) ↲17, DMI
20)   (y)∿(Py · Lay) 19, QD
21)   Pa · Laa ↲ 20, UI
22)   Pa   21, C
23)   Laa   21, C
24)   Pb · (y)(Py ⊃ Lby) ↲ 2, EI
25)   Pb   25, C
26)   (y)(Py ⊃ Lby) 25, C
27)   Pa ⊃ Lba   26, UI

28)   ∿Pa   Lba 27, MI
              X

                NOT LOGICALLY EQUIVALENT

14.
   a) (x)[(Px · Dxx) ⊃ (∃y)(Py · Dyx)]
   b) (x){[Px · (∃y)(Py · Dyx)] ⊃ Dxx}

                        225

1) $\sim((x)[(Px \cdot Dxx) \supset (\exists y)(Py \cdot Dyx)] \equiv$
$(x)\{[Px \cdot (\exists y)(Py \cdot Dyx)] \supset Dxx\})$ ╛ ----

2) $(x)[(Px \cdot Dxx) \supset (\exists y)(Py \cdot Dyx)]$ $(x)\{[Px \cdot (\exists y)(Py \cdot$
$Dyx)] \supset Dxx\}$ 1, DME

3) $\sim(x)\{[Px \cdot (\exists y)(Py \cdot Dyx)] \supset Dxx\}$ ╛ $\sim(x)[(Px \cdot Dxx) \supset$
$(\exists y)(Py \cdot Dyx)]$ ╛   1, DME

4) $(\exists x)\sim\{[Px \cdot (\exists y)(Py \cdot Dyx)] \supset Dxx\}$ ╛   3, QD

5) $\sim\{[Pa \cdot (\exists y)(Py \cdot Dya)] \supset Daa\}$ ╛   4, EI

6) $Pa \cdot (\exists y)(Py \cdot Dya)$ ╛   5, DMI

7) $\sim Daa$ 5, DMI

8) Pa 6, C

9) $(\exists y)(Py \cdot Dya)$ ╛   6, C

10) $Pb \cdot Dba$ ╛   9, EI

11) Pb 10, C

12) Dba 10, C

13) $(Pa \cdot Daa) \supset (\exists y)(Py \cdot Dya)$ ╛   2, UI

14) $\sim(Pa \cdot Daa)$ ╛ $(\exists y)(Py \cdot Dya)$ ╛   13, MI

15) $Pc \cdot Dca$ ╛   14, EI

16) Pc 15, C

17) Dca 15, C

18) $\sim Pa$ $\sim Daa$ 14, DC

19) X $(\exists x)\sim[(Px \cdot Dxx) \supset (\exists y)(Py \cdot Dyx)]$ ╛ 3, QD

20) $\sim[(Pa \cdot Daa) \supset (\exists y)(Py \cdot Dya)]$ ╛ 19, EI

21) $Pa \cdot Daa$ ╛   20, DMI

22) $\sim(\exists y)(Py \cdot Dya)$ ╛   20, DMI

23) Pa 21, C

24) Daa 21, C

25) $(y)\sim(Py \cdot Dya)$ 22, QD

26) $\sim(Pa \cdot Daa)$ ╛   25, UI

27) $\sim Pa$ $\sim Daa$ 26, DC
         X   X

NOT LOGICALLY EQUIVALENT

12.2.A.

2.
```
1)  Pr
2)  Pr
3)  2, UI
4)  3, Com
5)  /∴ 4, 1, DS
```

4.
```
1)  Pr
2)  Pr
3)  2, UI
4)  3, UI
5)  3, 4, HS
6)  /∴ 5, UG
```

6.
```
1)  Pr
2)  Pr
3)  2, Com
4)  3, Simp
5)  1, 4, MP
6)  5, UI
7)  2, Simp
8)  /∴ 6, 7, MP
```

8.
```
1)  Pr
2)  Pr
3)  1, UI
4)  2, UI
5)  3, DN
6)  5, Impl
7)  6, Exp
8)  7, 4, HS
9)  8, Exp
10) 9, Trans
11) 10, Exp
12) /∴ 11, UG
```

10.

```
1)  Pr
2)  1, Simp
3)  1, Com
4)  3, Simp
5)  2, UI
6)  4, UI
7)  5, 6, HS
8)  7, Impl
9)  8, Add
10) 9, Com
11) 10, Assoc
12) 11, DeM
13) 12, Impl
14) 13, Com
15) 14, Exp
16) /∴ 15, UG
```

12.2.B.

2.   ⋏Aa ∨ ⋏Ba

```
1)  (x)[(Ax • Bx) ⊃ ⋏Cx]     Pr
2)  Ca                        Pr
3)  (Aa • Ba) ⊃ ⋏Ca           1, UI
4)  ⋏⋏Ca                      2, DN
5)  ⋏(Aa • Ba)                3, 4, MT
6)  /∴ ⋏Aa ∨ ⋏Ba              5, DeM
```

4.   /∴ (x)[(Ax • Bx) ∨ Cx]

```
1)  (x)(Ax ∨ Cx) • (x)(Bx ∨ Cx)     Pr
2)  (x)(Ax ∨ Cx)                     1, Simp
3)  (x)(Bx ∨ Cx) • (x)(Ax ∨ Cx)     1, Com
4)  (x)(Bx ∨ Cx)                     3, Simp
5)  Ax ∨ Cx                          2, UI
6)  Bx ∨ Cx                          4, UI
7)  Cx ∨ Ax                          5, Com
8)  Cx ∨ Bx                          6, Com
9)  (Cx ∨ Ax) • (Cx ∨ Bx)           7, 8, Conj
10) Cx ∨ (Ax • Bx)                   9, Dist
11) (Ax • Bx) ∨ Cx                   10, Com
12) /∴ (x)[(Ax • Bx) ∨ Cx]          11, UG
```

228

6.   /∴ ~(Aa • Ba)
1) (x)[(Ax ⊃ Bx) ⊃ ~Cx]   Pr
2) Ca   Pr
3) (Aa ⊃ Ba) ⊃ ~Ca   1, UI
4) ~~Ca   2, DN
5) ~(Aa ⊃ Ba)   3, 4 MT
6) ~(~Aa ∨ Ba)   5, Impl
7) ~~Aa • ~Ba   6, DeM
8) ~Ba • ~~Aa   7, Com
9) ~Ba   8, Simp
10) ~Ba ∨ ~Aa   9, Add
11) ~Aa ∨ ~Ba   10, Com
12) /∴ ~(Aa • Ba)   11, DeM

8.   /∴ ~Aa • Ca
1) (x){[Ax • (Bx ∨ Cx)] ⊃ ~Dx}   Pr
2) (x)(~Dx ⊃ ~Ax)   Pr
3) Ca   Pr
4) [Aa • (Ba ∨ Ca)] ⊃ ~Da   1, UI
5) ~Da ⊃ ~Aa   2, UI
6) [(Ba ∨ Ca) • Aa] ⊃ ~Da   4, Com
7) (Ba ∨ Ca) ⊃ (Aa ⊃ ~Da)   6, Exp
8) Ca ∨ Ba   3, Add
9) Ba ∨ Ca   8, Com
10) Aa ⊃ ~Da   7, 9, MP
11) Aa ⊃ ~Aa   10, 5, HS
12) ~Aa ∨ ~Aa   11, Impl
13) ~Aa   12, Taut
14) /∴ ~Aa • Ca   13, 3, Conj

10.   /∴ (x)[(Cx ∨ Ax) ⊃ Dx]
1)(x)[Ax ⊃ (Bx • Cx)]   Pr
2) (x)(Cx ⊃ Dx)   Pr
3) Ax ⊃ (Bx • Cx)   1, UI
4) Cx ⊃ Dx   2, UI
5) ~Ax ∨ (Bx • Cx)   3, Impl
6) ~Ax ∨ (Cx • Bx)   5, Com
7) (~Ax ∨ Cx) • (~Ax ∨ Bx) 6, Dist
8) ~Ax ∨ Cx   7, Simp
9) Ax ⊃ Cx   8, Impl
10) Ax ⊃ Dx   9, 4, HS
11) ~Cx ∨ Dx   4, Impl
12) ~Ax ∨ Dx   10, Impl

229

13) Dx V ∿Cx   11, Com
14) Dx V ∿Ax   12, Com
15) (Dx V ∿Cx) · (Dx V ∿Ax) 13, 14, Conj
16) Dx V (∿Cx · ∿Ax)   15, Dist
17) Dx V ∿(Cx V Ax)   16, DeM
18) ∿(Cx V Ax) V Dx   17, Com
19) (Cx V Ax) ⊃ Dx   18, Impl
20) /∴ (x)[(Cx V Ax) ⊃ Dx] 19, UG

12.2.C.

2.   /∴ (x)(Mx V ∿Lx)
    1)   (x)(Ex V ∿Ex)   Pr
    2)   (x)(Ex ⊃ Mx)   Pr
    3)   (x)(∿Ex ⊃ ∿Lx)   Pr
    4)   Ex V ∿Ex   1, UI
    5)   Ex ⊃ Mx   2, UI
    6)   ∿Ex ⊃ ∿Lx   3, UI
    7)   Mx V ∿Lx   5, 6, 4, CD
    8)   /∴ (x)(Mx V ∿Lx)   7, UG

4.   /∴ (x)(Cx ⊃ Ex)
    1)   (x)(Sx ⊃ Ex) · (x)(Cx ⊃ Ex)   Pr
    2)   (x)(Cx ⊃ Ex) · (Sx ⊃ Ex)   1, Com
    3)   /∴ (x)(Cx ⊃ Ex)   2, Simp

                    ...OR...

                                    /∴ (x)(Cx ⊃ Ex)
    1)   (x)[(Ex V Cx) ⊃ Ex]   Pr
    2)   (Sx ⊃ Cx) ⊃ Ex   1, UI
    3)   ∿(Sx V Cx) V Ex   2, Impl
    4)   (∿Sx · ∿Cx) V Ex   3, DeM
    5)   Ex V (∿Sx · ∿Cx)   4, Com
    6)   Ex V (∿Cx · ∿Sx)   5, Com
    7)   (Ex V ∿Cx) · (Ex V Sx) 6, Dist
    8)   Ex V ∿Cx   7, Simp
    9)   ∿Cx V Ex   8, Com
    10) Cx ⊃ Ex   9, Impl
    12) /∴ (x)(Cx ⊃ Ex)   11, UG

230

6.   /∴ ~Sk
   1)   (x){[Sx • (Mx ⊃ Lx) ⊃ ~Bx}   Pr
   2)   Bk • Lk   Pr
   3)   [Sk • (Mk ⊃ Lk)] ⊃ ~Bk   1, UI
   4)   Bk   2, Simp
   5)   ~~Bk   4, DN
   6)   ~[Sk • (Mk ⊃ Lk)]   3, 5, MT
   7)   ~Sk ∨ ~(Mk ⊃ Lk)   6, DeM
   8)   Lk • Bk   2, Com
   9)   Lk   8, SImp
   10) Lk ∨ ~Mk   9, Add
   11) ~Mk ∨ Lk   10, Com
   12) Mk ⊃ Lk   11, Impl
   13) ~~(Mk ⊃ Lk)   12, DN
   14) ~(Mk ⊃ Lk) ∨ ~Sk   7, Com
   15) /∴ ~Sk   14, 13, DS

8.   /∴ (x){(~Ax • Mx) ⊃ [(Px • Ox) ⊃ ~Ex]}
   1)   (x){(Px • Ox) ⊃ [(Mx • ~Ax) ⊃ Rx]}   Pr
   2)   (x)[(Px • Rx) ⊃ (Ox ⊃ ~Ex)]   Pr
   3)   (Px • Ox) ⊃ [(Mx • ~Ax) ⊃ Rx]   1, UI
   4)   (Px • Rx) ⊃ (Ox ⊃ ~Ex)   2, UI
   5)   [(Px • Ox) • (Mx • ~Ax)] ⊃ Rx   3, Exp
   6)   (Rx • Px) ⊃ (Ox ⊃ ~Ex)   4, Com
   7)   Rx ⊃ [Px ⊃ (Ox ⊃ ~Ex)]   6, Exp
   8)   [(Px • Ox) • (Mx • ~Ax)] ⊃ [Px ⊃ (Ox ⊃ ~Ex)] 6,7, HS
   9)   [(Px • Ox) • (Mx • ~Ax)] ⊃ [(Px • Ox) ⊃ ~Ex] 8, Exp
   10) {[(Px • Ox) • (Mx • ~Ax)] • (Px • Ox)} ⊃ ~Ex 9, Exp
   11) {(Px • Ox) • [(Px • Ox) • (Mx • ~Ax)]} ⊃ ~Ex 10, Com
   12){[(Px • Ox) • (Px • Ox)] • (Mx • ~Ax)} ⊃ ~Ex 11,Assoc
   13) [(Px • Ox) • (Mx • ~Ax)] ⊃ x   12, Taut
   14) [(Mx • ~Ax) • (Px • Ox)] ⊃ ~Ex   13, Com
   15) [(~Ax • Mx) • (Px • Ox)] ⊃ ~Ex   14, Com
   16) (~Ax • Mx) ⊃ [(Px • Ox)] ⊃ ~Ex]   15, Exp
   17) /∴ (x){(~Ax • Mx) ⊃ [(Px • Ox)] ⊃ ~Ex]}   16, UG

10.   /∴ (x)[(Px • Cx) ⊃ (Qx ⊃ Tx)]
   1)   (x){(Px • ~Tx) ⊃ [(Ax ∨ Cx) ⊃ ~(Sx ∨ Qx)]}   Pr
   2)   (Px • ~Tx) ⊃ [(Ax ∨ Cx) ⊃ ~(Sx ∨ Qx)]   1, UI
   3)   ~(Px • ~Tx) ∨ [(Ax ∨ Cx) ⊃ ~(Sx ∨ Qx)   2, Impl
   4)   ~(Px • ~Tx) ∨ [~(Ax ∨ Cx) ∨ ~(Sx ∨ Qx)   3, Impl
   5)   [~(Px • ~Tx) ∨ ~(Ax ∨ Cx)] ∨ ~(Sx ∨ Qx)   4, Assoc
   6)   [~(Px • ~Tx) ∨ ~(Ax ∨ Cx)] ∨ (~Sx • ~Qx)   5, DeM

231

7) [~(Px · ~Tx) ∨ ~(Ax ∨ Cx)] ∨ (~Qx · ~Sx)   6, Com
8) {[~(Px · ~Tx) ∨ ~(Ax ∨ Cx)] ∨ ~Qx} ·
                    {[~(Px · ~Tx) ∨ ~(Ax ∨ Cx)] ∨ ~Sx} 7, Dist
9) [~(Px · ~Tx) ∨ ~(Ax ∨ Cx)] ∨ ~Qx   8, Simp
10) ~(Px · ~Tx) ∨ [~(Ax ∨ Cx) ∨ ~Qx]   9, Assoc
11) ~(Px · ~Tx) ∨ [~Qx ∨ ~(Ax ∨ Cx)]   10, Com
12) [~(Px · ~Tx) ∨ ~Qx] ∨ ~(Ax ∨ Cx)   11, Assoc
13) [~(Px · ~Tx) ∨ ~Qx] ∨ (~Ax · ~Cx)   12, DeM
14) [~(Px · ~Tx) ∨ ~Qx] ∨ (~Cx · ~Ax)   13, Com
15) {[~(Px · ~Tx) ∨ ~Qx] ∨ ~Cx} ·
                    {[~(Px · ~Tx) ∨ ~Qx] ∨ ~Ax}   14, Dist
16) [~(Px · ~Tx) ∨ ~Qx] ∨ ~Cx   15, Simp
17) [(~Px ∨ ~~Tx) ∨ ~Qx] ∨ ~Cx   16, DeM
18) [(~Px ∨ Tx) ∨ ~Qx] ∨ ~Cx   17, DN
19) [~Px ∨ (Tx ∨ ~Qx)] ∨ ~Cx   18, Assoc
20) ~Cx ∨ [~Px ∨ (Tx ∨ ~Qx)]   19, Com
21) (~Cx ∨ ~Px) ∨ (Tx ∨ ~Qx)   20, Assoc
22) (~Px ∨ ~Cx) ∨ (Tx ∨ ~Qx)   21, Com
23) (~Px ∨ ~Cx) ∨ (~Qx ∨ Tx)   22, Com
24) ~(Px · Cx) ∨ (~Qx ∨ Tx)   23, DeM
25) (Px · Cx) ⊃ (~Qx ∨ Tx)   24, Impl
26) (Px · Cx) ⊃ (Qx ⊃ Tx)   25, Impl
27) /∴ (x)[(Px · Cx) ⊃ (Qx ⊃ Tx)]   26, UG

12.3.A.

2.
    1) Pr
    2) Pr
    3) Pr
    4) 2, EI
    5) 1, UI
    6) 3, UI
    7) 6, Trans
    8) 5, 7, HS
    9) 8, 4, MP
    10) /∴ 9, EG

4.
```
1)  Pr
2)  Pr
3)  2, EI
4)  1, UI
5)  3, Simp
6)  3, Com
7)  6, Simp
8)  4, 7, MT
9)  8, DeM
10) 9, Com
11) 5, Add
12) 11, Com
13) 12, DN
14) 10, 13, DS
15) /∴ 14, EG
```

6.
```
1)  Pr
2)  Pr
3)  1, EI
4)  2, UI
5)  3, Simp
6)  3, Com
7)  6, Simp
8)  4, 7, MT
9)  8, DeM
10) 9, DN
11) 10, Impl
12) 11, 5, MP
13) 5, Add
14) 13, Com
15) 12, 13, Conj
16) 15, Dist
17) /∴ 16, EG
```

8.
```
1)  Pr
2)  Pr
3)  1, EI
4)  2, UI
5)  3, Simp
6)  3, Com
7)  6, Simp
8)  7, DeM
9)  2, Equiv
10) 9, Simp
```

11) 10, Exp
12) 11, 5, MP
13) 8, Simp
14) 12, 13, MT
15) 14, add
16) 15, DeM
17) 5, 16, Conj
18) 17, EG

10.
1) Pr
2) Pr
3) Pr
4) Pr
5) 3, EI
6) 1, UI
7) 2, UI
8) 4, UI
9) 5, Simp
10) 5, Com
11) 10, Simp
12) 11, DeM
13) 9, Add
14) 6, 13, MP
15) 14, Add
16) 7, 15, MP
17) 8, 16, MP
18) 17, Com
19) 18, Simp
20) 12, Simp
21) 19, Add
22) /∴ 21, 20, DS

Notice that this proof shows that #10 has an inconsistent premise set and, thus, is valid.

12.3.B.

2.   /∴ (∃x)(Ax · Cx)
1) (∃x)(Ax · Bx)   Pr
2) (x)(Bx ⊃ Cx)   Pr

```
3)  Ax · Bx            1, EI
4)  Bx ⊃ Cx            2, UI
5)  Ax                 3, Simp
6)  Bx · Ax            3, Com
7)  Bx                 6, Simp
8)  Cx                 4, 7, MP
9)  Ax · Cx            5, 8, Conj
10) /∴ (∃x)(Ax · Cx) 9, EG
```

4.
```
                                              /∴ (∃x)[Bx ∨ (Cx · Dx)]
1)  (x)[Ax ⊃ (Bx ∨ Cx)] · (x)[Ax ⊃ (Bx ∨ Dx)]      Pr
2)  (∃x)Ax                                               Pr
3)  (x)[Ax ⊃ (Bx ∨ Cx)]                            1, Simp
4)  (x)[Ax ⊃ (Bx ∨ Dx)] · (x)[Ax ⊃ (Bx ∨ Cx)] 1, Com
5)  (x)[Ax ⊃ (Bx ∨ Dx)]                            4, Simp
6)  Ax                                                 2, EI
7)  Ax ⊃ (Bx ∨ Cx)                                  3, UI
8)  Ax ⊃ (Bx ∨ Dx)                                  5, UI
9)  Bx ∨ Cx                                         7, 6, MP
10) Bx ∨ Dx                                         8, 6, MP
11) (Bx ∨ Cx) · (Bx ∨ Dx)                        9, 10, Conj
12) Bx ∨ (Cx · Dx)                                  11, Dist
13) /∴ (∃x)[Bx ∨ (Cx · Dx)]                       12, EG
```

6.
```
                                            /∴ (∃x)[Ax · (Bx △ Cx)]
1)  (x){Ax ⊃ [Bx ∨ (Cx · Dx)]}      Pr
2)  (∃x)(Ax · ∿Cx)                      Pr
3)  Ax · ∿Cx                            2, EI
4)  Ax ⊃ [Bx ∨ (Cx · Dx)]           1, UI
5)  Ax                                  3, Simp
6)  ∿Cx · Ax                            3, Com
7)  ∿Cx                                 6, Simp
8)  Bx ∨ (Cx · Dx)                      4, 5, MP
9)  (Bx ∨ Cx) · (Bx ∨ Dx)            8, Dist
10) Bx ∨ Cx                             9, Simp
11) ∿Cx ∨ ∿Bx                           7, Add
12) ∿Bx ∨ ∿Cx                           11, Com
13) (Bx ∨ Cx) · (∿Bx ∨ ∿Cx)          10, 12, Conj
14) Bx △ Cx                             13, Equiv
15) Ax · (Bx △ Cx)                      5, 14, Conj
16) /∴(∃x)[Ax · (Bx △ Cx)]            15, EG
```

8. $/\therefore (\exists x)(\sim Cx \lor \sim Ax)$

1)	$(x)(Ax \supset Bx)$	Pr
2)	$(x)[(Bx \cdot Cx) \supset Dx]$	Pr
3)	$(x)[(Ax \cdot Dx) \supset Ex]$	Pr
4)	$(\exists x)\sim Ex$	Pr
5)	$\sim Ex$	4, EI
6)	$Ax \supset Bx$	1, UI
7)	$(Bx \cdot Cx) \supset Dx$	2, UI
8)	$(Ax \cdot Dx) \supset Ex$	3, UI
9)	$Bx \supset (Cx \supset Dx)$	7, Exp
10)	$Ax \supset (Cx \supset Dx)$	6, 9, HS
11)	$(Ax \cdot Cx) \supset Dx$	10, Exp
12)	$(Dx \cdot Ax) \supset Ex$	8, Com
13)	$Dx \supset (Ax \supset Ex)$	12, Exp
14)	$(Ax \cdot Cx) \supset (Ax \supset Ex)$	11, 13, HS
15)	$[(Ax \cdot Cx) \cdot Ax] \supset Ex$	14, Exp
16)	$[Ax \cdot (Ax \cdot Cx)] \supset Ex$	15, Com
17)	$[(Ax \cdot Ax) \cdot Cx)] \supset Ex$	16, Assoc
18)	$(Ax \cdot Cx) \supset Ex$	17, Taut
19)	$\sim(Ax \cdot Cx)$	18, 5, MT
20)	$\sim Ax \lor \sim Cx$	19, DeM
21)	$\sim Cx \lor \sim Ax$	20, Com
22)	$/\therefore (\exists x)(\sim Cx \lor \sim Ax)$	21, EG

10. $/\therefore (\exists x)(Ex \vartriangle Dx)$

1)	$(\exists x)[(Ax \supset Cx) \cdot \sim Bx]$	Pr
2)	$(x)(Cx \supset Dx) \cdot (x)(\sim Ex \supset Ax)$	Pr
3)	$(x)[Dx \supset (Ex \supset Bx)]$	Pr
4)	$(Ax \supset Cx) \cdot \sim Bx$	1, EI
5)	$(x)(Cx \supset Dx)$	2, Simp
6)	$(x)(\sim Ex \supset Ax) \cdot (x)(Cx \supset Dx)$	2, Com
7)	$(x)(\sim Ex \supset Ax)$	6, Simp
8)	$Cx \supset Dx$	5, UI
9)	$\sim Ex \supset Ax$	7, UI
10)	$Dx \supset (Ex \supset Bx)$	3, UI
11)	$Ax \supset Cx$	4, Simp
12)	$\sim Bx \cdot (Ax \supset Cx)$	4, Com
13)	$\sim Bx$	12, Simp
14)	$\sim Ex \supset Cx$	9, 11, HS
15)	$\sim Ex \supset Dx$	14, 8, HS
16)	$\sim\sim Ex \lor Dx$	15, Impl
17)	$Ex \lor Dx$	16, DN
18)	$\sim\sim(Ex \lor Dx)$	17, DN

```
19)  ∿(∿Ex • ∿Dx)              18, DeM
20)  (Dx • Ex) ⊃ Bx            10, Exp
21)  ∿(Dx • Ex)               20, 13, MT
22)  ∿(Ex • Dx)               21, Com
23)  ∿(Ex • Dx) • ∿(∿Ex • ∿Dx)  22, 19, Conj
24)  Ex Δ Dx                   23, Equiv
25)  /∴ (∃x)(Ex Δ Dx)          24, EG
```

12.3.C.

```
2.                                    /∴ (∃x)(Ax • ∿Ix)
     1)   (x)(Sx ⊃ Ax) • (∃x)(Sx • ∿Ix)   Pr
     2)   (x)(Sx ⊃ Ax)                     1, Simp
     3)   (∃x)(Sx • ∿Ix) • (x)(Sx ⊃ Ax)   1, Com
     4)   (∃x)(Sx • ∿Ix)                   3, Simp
     5)   Sx • ∿Ix                         4, EI
     6)   Sx ⊃ Ax                          2, UI
     7)   Sx                               5, Simp
     8)   Ax                               6, 7, MP
     9)   ∿Ix • Sx                         5, Com
     10)  ∿Ix                              9, Simp
     11)  Ax • ∿Ix                         8, 10, Conj
     12)  /∴ (∃x)(Ax • ∿Ix)                11, EG

4.                                    /∴ (∃x)(Nx • Cx)
     1)   (x)[Nx ⊃ (Px ∨ Cx)]         Pr
     2)   (x)(Px ⊃ Rx)                Pr
     3)   (∃x)(Nx • ∿Rx)              Pr
     4)   Nx • ∿Rx                    3, EI
     5)   Nx ⊃ (Px ∨ Cx)              1, UI
     6)   Px ⊃ Rx                     2, UI
     7)   Nx                          4, Simp
     8)   ∿Rx • Nx                    4, Com
     9)   ∿Rx                         8, Simp
     10)  Px ∨ Cx                     5, 7, MP
     11)  ∿Px                         6, 9, MT
     12)  Cx                          10, 11, DS
     13)  Nx • Cx                     7, 12, Conj
     14)  /∴ (∃x)(Nx • Cx)            13, EG
```

6.

		$\therefore$ $(\exists x)(Px \cdot Lx)$
1)	$(x)[(Px \cdot {\sim}Lx) \supset (Ix \supset Sx)]$	Pr
2)	$(\exists x)(Px \cdot {\sim}Sx)$	Pr
3)	$(x)(Px \supset Ix)$	Pr
4)	$Px \cdot {\sim}Sx$	2, EI
5)	$(Px \cdot {\sim}Lx) \supset (Ix \supset Sx)$	1, UI
6)	$Px \supset Ix$	3, UI
7)	Px	4, Simp
8)	${\sim}Sx \cdot Px$	4, Com
9)	${\sim}Sx$	8, Simp
10)	Ix	6, 7, MP
11)	$Ix \cdot {\sim}Sx$	10, 9, Conj
12)	${\sim}{\sim}(Ix \cdot {\sim}Sx)$	11, DN
13)	${\sim}({\sim}Ix \lor {\sim}{\sim}Sx)$	12, DeM
14)	${\sim}({\sim}Ix \lor Sx)$	13, DN
15)	${\sim}(Ix \supset Sx)$	14, Impl
16)	${\sim}(Px \cdot {\sim}Lx)$	5, 15, MT
17)	${\sim}Px \lor {\sim}{\sim}Lx$	16, DeM
18)	${\sim}{\sim}Px$	7, DN
19)	${\sim}{\sim}Lx$	17, 18, DS
20)	Lx	19, DN
21)	$Px \cdot Lx$	7, 20, Conj
22)	$\therefore$ $(\exists x)(Px \cdot Lx)$	21, EG

8.

		$\therefore$ $(x)(Tx \supset Vx)$
1)	$(\exists x)[Cx \cdot (Mx \lor Rx)] \supset (x)(Tx \supset Rx)$	Pr
2)	$(\exists x)[Cx \cdot (Mx \lor Vx)] \supset (x)(Rx \supset Vx)$	Pr
3)	$(\exists x)(Cx \cdot Mx)$	Pr
4)	$Cx \cdot Mx$	3, EI
5)	Cx	4, Simp
6)	$Mx \cdot Cx$	4, Com
7)	Mx	6, Simp
8)	$Mx \lor Rx$	7, Add
9)	$Cx \cdot (Mx \lor Rx)$	5, 8, Conj
10)	$(\exists x)[Cx \cdot (Mx \lor Rx)]$	9, EG
11)	$(x)(Tx \supset Rx)$	1, 10, MP
12)	$Mx \lor Vx$	7, Add
13)	$Cx \cdot (Mx \lor Vx)$	5, 12, Conj
14)	$(\exists x)[Cx \cdot (Mx \lor Vx)]$	13, EG
15)	$(x)(Rx \supset Vx)$	2, 14, MP
16)	$Tx \supset Rx$	11, UI

17) Rx ⊃ Vx   15, UI
18) Tx ⊃ Vx   16, 17, HS
19) /∴ (x)(Tx ⊃ Vx)   18, UG

10.
                                             /∴ (∃x)(Dx • Sx)
1)   (x){Sx ⊃ [(Gx ∨ Bx) ∨ Dx]}   Pr
2)   (x)[Sx ⊃ (Vx • Lx)]   Pr
3)   (x)[(Lx • ∿Dx) ⊃ Fx]   Pr
4)   (x)(Gx ⊃ ∿Fx) • (x)(Bx ⊃ ∿Vx)   Pr
5)   (∃x)Sx   Pr
6)   (x)(Gx ⊃ ∿Fx)   4, Simp
7)   (x)(Bx ⊃ ∿Vx) • (x)(Gx ⊃ ∿Fx)   4, Com
8)   (x)(Bx ⊃ ∿Vx)   7, Simp
9)   Sx   5, EI
10) Sx ⊃ [(Gx ∨ Bx) ∨ Dx]   1, UI
11) Sx ⊃ (Vx • Lx)   2, UI
12) (Lx • ∿Dx) ⊃ Fx   3, UI
13) Gx ⊃ ∿Fx   6, UI
14) Bx ⊃ ∿Vx   8, UI
15) (Gx ∨ Bx) ∨ Dx   10, 9, MP
16) Vx • Lx   11, 9, MP
17) Vx   16, Simp
18) Lx • Vx   16, Com
19) Lx   18, Simp
20) ∿∿Vx   17, DN
21) ∿Bx   14, 20, MT
22) (Bx ∨ Gx) ∨ Dx   15, Com
23) Bx ∨ (Gx ∨ Dx)   22, Assoc
24) Gx ∨ Dx   23, 21, DS
25) Lx ⊃ (∿Dx ⊃ Fx)   12, Exp
26) ∿Dx ⊃ Fx   25, 19, MP
27) ∿∿Fx ⊃ ∿Gx   13, Trans
28) Fx ⊃ ∿Gx   27, DN
29) ∿Dx ⊃ ∿Gx   26, 28, HS
30) ∿∿Gx ∨ Dx   24, DN
31) ∿Gx ⊃ Dx   30, Impl
32) ∿Dx ⊃ Dx   29, 31, HS
33) ∿∿Dx ∨ Dx   32, Impl
34) Dx ∨ Dx   33, DN
35) Dx   34, Taut
36) Dx • Sx   35, 9, Conj
37) /∴ (∃x)(Dx • Sx)   36, EG

239

12.4.A.

2.

    1)   Pr
    2)   Pr
    3)   1, QD
    4)   2, UI
    5)   3, UI
    6)   5, DeM
    7)   6, DN
    8)   7, Impl
    9)   8, 4, HS
   10)   9, UG

4.

    1)   Pr
    2)   1, Simp
    3)   1, Com
    4)   3, Simp
    5)   2, QD
    6)   4, QD
    7)   5, UI
    8)   6, UI
    9)   7, DeM
   10)   9, DN
   11)   10, Impl
   12)   8, DeM
   13)   12, DN
   14)   13, Impl
   15)   11, 14, HS
   16)   15, UG

6.

    1)   Pr
    2)   Pr
    3)   1, QD
    4)   2, UI
    5)   3, UI
    6)   5, Com
    7)   6, Impl
    8)   4, Impl
    9)   8, DeM
   10)   9, Com
   11)   10, Dist
   12)   11, Simp

```
13)    12, Com
14)    13, Impl
15)    7, 15, HS
16)    15, UG
```

8.

```
1)     Pr
2)     Pr
3)     2, QD
4)     1, UI
5)     3, UI
6)     5, DeM
7)     6, DeM
8)     7, DN
9)     8, Dist
10)    9, Simp
11)    10, Impl
12)    4, Impl
13)    12, Com
14)    13, Dist
15)    14, Simp
16)    15, Impl
17)    16, 11, HS
18)    17, Impl
19)    10, Com
20)    18, Com
21)    19, 20, Conj
22)    21, Dist
23)    22, Com
24)    23, DeM
25)    24, Impl
26)    25, UG
```

10.

```
1)     Pr
2)     Pr
3)     2, Simp
4)     2, Com
5)     4, Simp
6)     1, QD
7)     3, QD
8)     5, QD
9)     6, UI
10)    7, UI
11)    8, UI
12)    9, DeM
13)    12, DN
```

```
14)    13, Impl
15)    10, DeM
16)    15, DN
17)    16, Impl
18)    11, DeM
19)    18, DN
20)    19, Impl
21)    20, 14, HS
22)    21, Exp
23)    17, Trans
24)    23, DN
25)    22, 24, HS
26)    25, UG
27)    26, QD
28)    27, Impl
29)    28, DeM
30)    29, DN
```

12.4.B.

2.
                                      /∴ (x)(Bx ⊃ Cx)

```
1)  ∿(∃x)[(Ax ⊃ Bx) • ∿Cx]        Pr
2)  (x)∿[(Ax ⊃ Bx) • ∿Cx]         1, QD
3)  ∿[(Ax ⊃ Bx) • ∿Cx]            2, UI
4)  ∿(Ax ⊃ Bx) ∨ ∿∿Cx             3, DeM
5)  ∿(Ax ⊃ Bx) ∨ Cx               4, DN
6)  ∿(∿Ax ∨ Bx) ∨ Cx              5, Impl
7)  (∿∿Ax • ∿Bx) ∨ Cx             6, DeM
8)  (Ax • ∿Bx) ∨ Cx               7, DN
9)  Cx ∨ (Ax • ∿Bx)               8, Com
10) Cx ∨ (∿Bx • Ax)               9, Com
11) (Cx ∨ ∿Bx) • (Cx ∨ Ax)        10, Dist
12) Cx ∨ ∿Bx                      11, Simp
13) ∿Bx ∨ Cx                      12, Com
14) Bx ⊃ Cx                       13, Impl
15) /∴ (x)(Bx ⊃ Cx)               14, UG
```

4.
                                  /∴ (x)[Ax ⊃ (Dx ⊃ Bx)]

```
1)  ∿(∃x)[(Ax • Bx) • (Cx ∨ Dx)]     Pr
2)  (x)∿[(Ax • Bx) • (Cx ∨ Dx)]      1. QD
3)  ∿[(Ax • Bx) • (Cx ∨ Dx)]         2, UI
```

242

4) ∼(Ax • Bx) ∨ ∼(Cx ∨ Dx)   3, DeM
5) ∼(Ax • Bx) ∨ (∼Cx • ∼Dx)   4, DeM
6) (∼Ax ∨ ∼Bx) ∨ (∼Cx • ∼Dx)   5, DeM
7) (∼Ax ∨ ∼Bx) ∨ (∼Dx • ∼Cx)   5, Com
8) [(∼Ax ∨ ∼Bx) ∨ ∼Dx] •
                  [(∼Ax ∨ ∼Bx) ∨ ∼Cx]   7, Dist
9) (∼Ax ∨ ∼Bx) ∨ ∼Dx   8, Simp
10) ∼Ax ∨ (∼Bx ∨ ∼Dx)   9, Assoc
11) ∼Ax ∨ (∼Dx ∨ ∼Bx)   10, Com
12) Ax ⊃ (∼Dx ∨ ∼Bx)   11, Impl
13) Ax ⊃ (Dx ⊃ ∼Bx)   12, Impl
14) /∴ (x)[Ax ⊃ (Dx ⊃ ∼Bx)]   13, UG

6.   /∴ ∼(x)[(Cx ∨ Dx) ⊃ Bx]

1) ∼(x)∼Ax   Pr
2) ∼(∃x)(Ax • Bx)   Pr
3) (x)(Bx △ Cx)   Pr
4) (∃x)Ax   1, QD
5) (x)∼(Ax • Bx)   2, QD
6) Ax   4, EI
7) Bx △ Cx   3, UI
8) ∼(Ax • Bx)   5, UI
9) ∼Ax ∨ ∼Bx   8, DeM
10) ∼∼Ax   6, DN
11) ∼Bx   9, 10, DS
12) (Bx ∨ Cx) • (∼Bx ∨ ∼Cx)   7, Equiv
13) Bx ∨ Cx   12, Simp
14) Cx   13, 11, DS
15) Cx ∨ Dx   14, Add
16) (Cx ∨ Dx) • ∼Bx   15, 11, Conj
17) (∃x)[(Cx ∨ Dx) • ∼Bx]   16, EG
18) ∼(x)∼[(Cx ∨ Dx) • ∼Bx]   17, QD
19) ∼(x)[∼(Cx ∨ Dx) ∨ ∼∼Bx]   18, DeM
20) ∼(x)[∼(Cx ∨ Dx) ∨ Bx]   19, DN
21) /∴ ∼(x)[(Cx ∨ Dx) ⊃ Bx]   20, Impl

8.   /∴ (∃x)[Ax • (Cx • Dx)]

1) ∼(x)(Ax ⊃ Bx)   Pr
2) (x)(Ax ⊃ Cx)   Pr
3) ∼(∃x)[(∼Bx • ∼Ex) • (Dx ∨ Cx)]   Pr
4) (∃x)∼(Ax ⊃ Bx)   1, QD
5) (x)∼[(∼Bx • ∼Ex) • (Dx ∨ Cx)]   3, QD
6) ∼(Ax ⊃ Bx)   4, EI

243

7)	Ax ⊃ Cx	2,. UI
8)	~[(~Bx · ~Ex) · (Dx ∨ Cx)]	5, UI
9)	~(~Ax ∨ Bx)	6, Impl
10)	~~Ax · ~Bx	9, DeM
11)	Ax · ~Bx	10, DN
12)	~[(Dx ∨ Cx) · (~Bx · ~Ex)]	8, Com
13)	~(Dx ∨ Cx) ∨ ~(~Bx · ~Ex)	12, DeM
14)	~(Dx ∨ Cx) ∨ ~~(Bx ∨ Ex)	13, DeM
15)	~(Dx ∨ Cx) ∨ (Bx ∨ Ex)	14, DN
16)	Ax	11, Simp
17)	Cx	7, 16, MP
18)	Cx ∨ Dx	17, Add
19)	Dx ∨ Cx	18, Com
20)	~~(Dx ∨ Cx)	19, DN
21)	Bx ∨ Ex	15, 20, DS
22)	~Bx · Ax	11, Com
23)	~Bx	22, Simp
24)	Ex	21, 23, DS
25)	Cx · Ex	17, 24, Conj
26)	Ax · (Cx · Ex)	16, 25, Conj
27)	/∴ (∃x)[Ax · (Cx · Dx)]	26, EG

10.

1)	~(∃x)[(Ax · Bx) · ~Cx]	Pr
2)	(x)[Dx ⊃ (~Bx ≡ Ex)]	Pr
3)	~(∃x)[(Dx · Ex) · ~Fx]	Pr
4)	~(x)(Dx ⊃ ~Ax)	Pr
5)	(x)~[(Ax · Bx) · ~Cx]	1, QD
6)	(x)~[(Dx · Ex) · ~Fx]	3, QD
7)	(∃x)~(Dx ⊃ ~Ax)	4, QD
8)	~(Dx ⊃ ~Ax)	7, EI
9)	Dx ⊃ (~Bx ≡ Ex)	2, UI
10)	~[(Ax · Bx) · ~Cx]	5, UI
11)	~[(Dx · Ex) · ~Fx]	6, UI
12)	~(~Dx ∨ ~Ax)	8, Impl
13)	~~(Dx · Ax)	12, DeM
14)	Dx · Ax	13, DN
15)	Dx	14, Simp
16)	Ax · Dx	14, Com
17)	Ax	16, Simp
18)	~(Ax · Bx) ∨ ~~Cx	10, DeM
19)	~(Ax · Bx) ∨ Cx	18, DN
20)	(Ax · Bx) ⊃ Cx	19, Impl

21)	Ax ⊃ (Bx ⊃ Cx)	20, Exp
22)	Bx ⊃ Cx	21, 17, MP
23)	~(Dx • Ex) ∨ ~~Fx	11, DeM
24)	~(Dx • Ex) ∨ Fx	23, DN
25)	(Dx • Ex) ⊃ Fx	24, Impl
26)	Dx ⊃ (Ex ⊃ Fx)	25, Exp
27)	Ex ⊃ Fx	26, 15, MP
28)	~Bx ≡ Ex	9, 15, MP
29)	(~Bx ⊃ Ex) • (Ex ⊃ ~Bx)	28. Equiv
30)	~Bx ⊃ Ex	29, Simp
31)	~~Bx ∨ Ex	30, Impl
32)	Bx ∨ Ex	31, DN
33)	Cx ∨ Fx	22, 27, 32, CD
34)	~~Cx ∨ Fx	33, DN
35)	~Cx ⊃ Fx	34, Impl
36)	/∴ (x)(~Cx ⊃ Fx)	35, UG

12.4.C.

2.

/∴ ~(∃x)(Nx • ~Ex)

1)	~(∃x)(Ax • ~Ex) • ~(∃x)(~Ax • Nx)	Pr
2)	~(∃x)(Ax • ~Ex)	1, Simp
3)	~(∃x)(~Ax • Nx) • ~(∃x)(Ax • ~Ex)	1, Com
4)	~(∃x)(~Ax • Nx)	3, Simp
5)	(x)~(Ax • ~Ex)	2, QD
6)	(x)~(~Ax • Nx)	4, QD
7)	~(Ax • ~Ex)	5, UI
8)	~(~Ax • Nx)	6, UI
9)	~Ax ∨ ~~Ex	7, DeM
10)	~Ax ∨ Ex	9, DN
11)	Ax ⊃ Ex	10, Impl
12)	~~Ax ∨ ~Nx	8, DeM
13)	Ax ∨ ~Nx	12, DN
14)	~Nx ∨ Ax	13, Com
15)	Nx ⊃ Ax	14, Impl
16)	Nx ⊃ Ex	15, 11, HS
17)	~Nx ∨ Ex	16, Impl
18)	~Nx ∨ ~~Ex	17, DN
19)	~(Nx • ~Ex)	18, DeM

20) (x)∿(Nx • ∿Ex)   19, UG
21) /∴ ∿(∃x)(Nx • ∿Ex)   20, QD

4.   /∴ ∿(∃x)[Ax • ∿(Sx ≡ Hx)]
  1)   ∿(∃x)[(Hx • Ax) • ∿Sx]   Pr
  2)   (x){Ax ⊃ [Sx ⊃ (Hx • Mx)]}   Pr
  3)   (x)∿[(Hx • Ax) • ∿Sx]   1, QD
  4)   Ax ⊃ [Sx ⊃ (Hx • Mx)]   2, UI
  5)   ∿[(Hx • Ax) •∿Sx]   3, UI
  6)   ∿(Hx • Ax) ∨ ∿∿Sx   5, DeM
  7)   (Hx • Ax) ⊃ Sx   6, Impl
  8)   (Ax • Sx) ⊃ (Hx • Mx)   4, Exp
  9)   ∿(Ax • Sx) ∨ (Hx • Mx)   8, Impl
  10) [• (Ax • Sx) ∨ Hx] • [∿(Ax • Sx) ∨ Mx]. 9, Dist
  11) ∿(Ax • Sx) ∨ Hx   10, Simp
  12) (Ax • Sx) ⊃ Hx   11, Impl
  13) Ax ⊃ (Sx ⊃ Hx)   12, Exp
  14) (Ax • Hx) ⊃ Sx   7, Com
  15) Ax ⊃ (Hx ⊃ Sx)   14, Exp
  16) ∿Ax ∨ (Sx ⊃ Hx)   13, Impl
  17) ∿Ax ∨ (Hx ⊃ Sx)   15, Impl
  18) [∿Ax ∨ (Sx ⊃ Hx)] • [∿Ax ∨ (Hx ⊃ Sx)] 16, 17 Conj
  19) ∿Ax ∨ [(Sx ⊃ Hx) • (Hx ⊃ Sx)]   18, Dist
  20) ∿Ax ∨ (Sx ≡ Hx)   19, Equiv
  21) ∿Ax ∨ ∿∿(Sx ≡ Hx)   20, DN
  22) ∿[Ax • ∿(Sx ≡ Hx)]   21, DeM
  23) (x)∿[Ax • ∿(Sx ≡ Hx)]   22, UI
  24) ∿(∃x)[Ax • ∿(Sx ≡ Hx)]   23, QD

6.   /∴(∃x)[Px • (∿Rx • ∿Lx)]
  1)   (x)[(Px • Rx) ⊃ (Mx ⊃ Sx)]   Pr
  2)   ∿(x)[(Px • Mx) ⊃ Sx]   Pr
  3)   (x)[Lx ⊃ (Rx ∨ Sx)]   Pr
  4)   (∃x)∿[(Px • Mx) ⊃ Sx]   2, QD
  5)   ∿[(Px • Mx) ⊃ Sx]   4, EI
  6)   (Px • Rx) ⊃ (Mx ⊃ Sx)   1, UI
  7)   Lx ⊃ (Rx ∨ Sx)   3, UI
  8)   ∿[∿(Px • Mx) ∨ Sx]   5, Impl
  9)   ∿∿(Px • Mx) • ∿Sx   8, DeM
  10) (Px • Mx) • ∿Sx   9, DN
  11) Px • Mx   10, Simp

246

```
12) Px                                      11, Simp
13) Mx • Px                                  11, Com
14) Mx                                       13, Simp
15) ∿Sx • (Px • Mx)                          10, Com
16) ∿Sx                                      15, sIMP
17) Mx • ∿Sx                                 14, 16, Conj
18) ∿∿(Mx • ∿Sx)                             17, DN
19) ∿(∿Mx ∨ ∿∿Sx)                            18, DeM
20) ∿(∿Mx ∨ Sx)                              19, DN
21) ∿(Mx ⊃ Sx)                               20, Impl
22) ∿(Px • Rx)                               6, 21, MT
23) ∿Px ∨ ∿Rx                                22, DeM
24) ∿∿Px                                     12, DN
25) ∿Rx                                      23, 24, DS
26) ∿Rx • ∿Sx                                25, 16, Conj
27) ∿(Rx ∨ Sx)                               26, DeM
28) ∿Lx                                      7, 27, MT
29) ∿Rx • ∿Lx                                25, 28, Conj
30) Px • (∿Rx • ∿Lx)                         12, 29, Conj
31) /∴ (∃x)[Px • (∿Rx • ∿Lx)]                30, EG
```

8.   /∴ ∿(x)[(Px • Tx) ⊃ Cx]

```
1)  ∿(x){[Px • (Ux ∨ Tx)] ⊃ Cx}             Pr
2)  ∿(∃x)[(Px • Ux) • (∿Vx ∨ ∿Cx)]          Pr
3)  (∃x)∿{[Px • (Ux ∨ Tx)] ⊃ Cx}            1, QD
4)  (x)∿[(Px • Ux) • (∿Vx ∨ ∿Cx)]           2, QD
5)  ∿{[Px • (Ux ∨ Tx)] ⊃ Cx}                3, EI
6)  ∿[(Px • Ux) • (∿Vx ∨ ∿Cx)]              4, UI
7)  ∿{∿[Px • (Ux ∨ Tx)] ∨ Cx}               5, Impl
8)  ∿∿[Px • (Ux ∨ Tx)] • ∿Cx                7, DeM
9)  [Px • (Ux ∨ Tx)] • ∿Cx                  8, DN
10) Px • (Ux ∨ Tx)                          9, Simp
11) Px                                      10, Simp
12) (Ux ∨ Tx) • Px                          10, Com
13) Ux ∨ Tx                                 12, Simp
14) ∿(Px • Ux) ∨ ∿(∿Vx ∨ ∿Cx)               6, DeM
15) ∿(Px • Ux) ∨ ∿∿(Vx • Cx)                14, DeM
16) ∿(Px • Ux) ∨ (Vx • Cx)                  15, DN
17) ∿(Px • Ux) ∨ (Cx • Vx)                  16, Com
18) [(Px • ∿Ux) ∨ Cx] • [(Px • ∿Ux) ∨ Vx]   17, Dist
19) (Px • Ux) ∨ Cx                          18, Simp
20) (∿Px ∨ ∿Ux) ∨ Cx                        19, DeM
21) ∿Px ∨ (∿Ux ∨ Cx)                        20, Assoc
```

247

22)	∿Px	11, DN
23)	∿Ux ∨ Cx	21, 22, DS
24)	Cx ∨ ∿Ux	32, Com
25)	∿Cx · [Px · (Ux ∨ Tx)]	9, Com
26)	∿Cx	25, Simp
27)	∿Ux	24, 26, DS
28)	Tx	13, 27, DS
29)	Px · Tx	11, 28, Conj
30)	(Px · Tx) · ∿Cx	29, 26, Conj
31)	(∃x)[(Px · Tx) · ∿Cx]	30, EG
28)	∿(x)∿[(Px · Tx) · ∿Cx]	27, QD
29)	∿(x)[∿(Px · Tx) ∨ ∿∿Cx]	28, DeM
30)	∿(x)[∿(Px · Tx) ∨ Cx]	29, DN
31)	/∴ ∿(x)[(Px · Tx) ⊃ Cx]	30, Impl

10.   /∴ ∿(x)[Px ⊃ (∿Vx · ∿Tx)]

1)	∿(∃x)[(Px · Lx) · ∿(Ux △ Gx)]	Pr
2)	∿(x)[(Px · Lx) ⊃ ∿Cx]	Pr
3)	∿(∃x)[(Px · Cx) · ∿(Ux ≡ Vx)]	Pr
4)	(x){[Px · (Gx · ∿Tx)] ⊃ ∿Cx}	Pr
5)	(x)∿[(Px · Lx) · ∿(Ux △ Gx)]	1, QD
6)	(∃x)∿[(Px · Lx) ⊃ ∿Cx]	2, QD
7)	(x)∿[(Px · Cx) · ∿(Ux ≡ Vx)]	3, QD
8)	∿[(Px · Lx) ⊃ ∿Cx]	6, EI
9)	∿[(Px · Lx) · ∿(Ux △ Gx)]	5, UI
10)	∿[(Px · Cx) · ∿(Ux ≡ Vx)]	7, UI
11)	[Px · (Gx · ∿Tx)] ⊃ ∿Cx	4, UI
12)	∿[∿(Px · Lx) ∨ ∿Cx]	8, Impl
13)	∿∿[(Px · Lx) · Cx]	12, DeM
14)	(Px · Lx) · Cx	13, DN
15)	∿(Px · Lx) ∨ ∿∿(Ux △ Gx)	9, DeM
16)	∿(Px · Lx) ∨ (Ux △ Gx)	15, DN
17)	∿(Px · Cx) ∨ ∿∿(Ux ≡ Vx)	10, DeM
18)	∿(Px · Cx) ∨ (Ux ≡ Vx)	17, DN
19)	Px · Lx	14, Simp
20)	∿∿(Px · Lx)	19, DN
21)	Ux △ Gx	16, 20, DS
22)	Px · (Lx · Cx)	14, Assoc
23)	Px · (Cx · Lx)	22, Com
24)	(Px · Cx) · Lx	23, Assoc
25)	Px · Cx	24, Simp

26)	∿∿(Px · Cx)	25, DN
27)	Ux ≡ Vx	18, 26, DS
28)	Cx · Px	25, Com
29)	Cx	28, Simp
30)	∿∿Cx	29, DN
31)	∿[Px · (Gx · ∿Tx)]	11, 30, MT
32)	∿Px ∨ ∿(Gx · ∿Tx)	31, DeM
33)	Px	25, Simp
34)	∿∿Px	33, DN
35)	∿(Gx · ∿Tx)	32, 34, DS
36)	∿Gx ∨ ∿∿Tx	35, DeM
37)	∿Gx ∨ Tx	36, DN
38)	Gx ⊃ Tx	37, Impl
39)	(Ux ∨ Gx) · (∿Ux ∨ ∿Gx)	21, Equiv
40)	Ux ∨ Gx	39, Simp
41)	∿∿Ux ∨ Gx	40, DN
42)	∿Ux ⊃ Gx	41, Impl
43)	∿Ux ⊃ Tx	42, 38, HS
44)	(Ux ⊃ Vx) · (Vx ⊃ Ux)	27, Equiv
45)	Ux ⊃ Vx	44, Simp
46)	∿Vx ⊃ ∿Ux	45, Trans
47)	∿Vx ⊃ Tx	46, 43, HS
48)	∿∿Vx ∨ Tx	47, Impl
49)	Vx ∨ Tx	48, DN
50)	Px · (Vx ∨ Tx)	33, 49, Conj
51)	∿∿[Px · (Vx ∨ Tx)]	50, DN
52)	∿[∿Px ∨ ∿(Vx ∨ Tx)]	51, DeM
53)	∿[Px ⊃ ∿(Vx ∨ Tx)]	52, Impl
54)	∿[Px ⊃ (∿Vx · ∿Tx)]	53, DeM
55)	(∃x)∿[Px ⊃ (∿Vx · ∿Tx)]	54, EG
56)	/∴ ∿(x)[Px ⊃ (∿Vx · ∿Tx)]	55, QD

12.5.A.

2.   /∴ (x)(Bx ⊃ Cx)

1)	(x)[(Ax ∨ Bx) ⊃ Cx]	Pr
→ 2)	∿(x)(Bx ⊃ Cx)	IP
3)	(∃x)∿(Bx ⊃ Cx)	2, QD
4)	∿(Bx ⊃ Cx)	3, EI

```
  5)  (Ax ∨ Bx) ⊃ Cx              1, UI
  6)  ∿(∿Bx ∨ Cx)                 4, Impl
  7)  ∿∿Bx • ∿Cx                  6, DeM
  8)  Bx • ∿Cx                    7, DN
  9)  ∿Cx • Bx                    8, Com
 10)  ∿Cx                         9, Simp
 11)  ∿(Ax ∨ Bx)                  5, 10, MT
 12)  ∿Ax • ∿Bx                   11, DeM
 13)  ∿Bx • ∿Ax                   12, Com
 14)  Bx                          8, Simp
 15)  ∿Bx                         13, Simp
 16)  Bx • ∿Bx                    14, 15, Conj

 17)  /∴ (x)(Bx ⊃ Cx)            2-16, IP
```

4.   /∴ ·(x)(Bx ⊃ Cx)

```
  1)  (x)(Ax ⊃ Bx) ⊃ (x)(Bx ⊃ Cx)   Pr
  2)  (x)(Ax ⊃ Cx) • (x)(Cx ⊃ Bx)   Pr
  3)  ∿(x)(Bx ⊃ Cx)                  IP
  4)  (∃x)∿(Bx ⊃ Cx)                 2, QD
  5)  ∿(Bx ⊃ Cx)                     4, EI
  6)  (x)(Ax ⊃ Cx)                   2, Simp
  7)  Ax ⊃ Cx                        6, UI
  8)  (x)(Cx ⊃ Bx) • (x)(Ax ⊃ Cx)   2, Com
  9)  (x)(Cx ⊃ Bx)                   8, Simp
 10)  Cx ⊃ Bx                        9, UI
 11)  Ax ⊃ Bx                        7, 10, HS
 12)  (x)(Ax ⊃ Bx)                   11, UG
 13)  (x)(Bx ⊃ Cx)                   1, 12, MP
 14)  Bx ⊃ Cx                        13, UI
 15)  (Bx ⊃ Cx) • ∿(Bx ⊃ Cx)        14, 5, Conj

 16)  /∴ (x)(Bx ⊃ Cx)               3-15, IP
```

6.   /∴ ∿(Ba ∨ Da)

```
  1)  (x){[Ax • (Bx ∨ Cx)] ≡ Dx}    Pr
  2)  ∿(Da ∨ ∿Aa)                   Pr
  3)  ∿Da • ∿∿Aa                    2, DeM
  4)  [Aa • (Ba ∨ Ca)] ≡ Da         1, UI
  5)  {[Aa • (Ba ∨ Ca)] ⊃ Da} •
           {Da ⊃ [Aa • (Ba ∨ Ca)]}  4, Equiv
  6)  [Aa • (Ba ∨ Ca)] ⊃ Da         5, Simp
  7)  ∿Da                           3, Simp
```

250

```
       8)  ∿[Aa · (Ba ∨ Ca)]              6, 7, MT
       9)  ∿Aa ∨ ∿(Ba ∨ Ca)               8, DeM
      10)  ∿∿Aa · ∿Da                      3, Com
      11)  ∿∿Aa                            10, Simp
      12)  ∿(Ba ∨ Ca)                      9, 11, DS
      13)  ∿Ba · ∿Ca                       12, DeM
      14)  ∿Ba                             13, Simp
 ┌─→  15)  ∿∿(Ba ∨ Da)                     IP
 │    16)  Ba ∨ Da                         15, DN
 │    17)  Da ∨ Ba                         16, Com
 │    18)  Ba                              17, 7, DS
 │    19)  Ba · ∿Ba                        18, 14, Conj
 └──────────────────────────────────────────────────
      20)  /∴ ∿(Ba ∨ Da)                   15-19, IP

8.                                    /∴ (∃x)(Ax · Cx)
       1)  (x)[Ax ⊃ (Bx ∨ Cx)]             Pr
       2)  (x)(Bx ⊃ Dx)                    Pr
       3)  (∃x)(Ax · ∿Dx)                  Pr
       4)  Ax · ∿Dx                        3, EI
       5)  Ax ⊃ (Bx ∨ Cx)                  1, UI
       6)  Bx ⊃ Dx                         2, UI
       7)  Ax                              4, Simp
       8)  Bx ∨ Cx                         5, 7, MP
       9)  ∿Dx · Ax                        4, Com
      10)  ∿Dx                             9, Simp
      11)  ∿Bx                             6, 10, MT
      12)  Cx                              8, 11, DS
 ┌─→  13)  ∿(∃x)(Ax · Cx)                  IP
 │    14)  (x)∿(Ax · Cx)                   13, QD
 │    15)  ∿(Ax · Cx)                      14, UI
 │    16)  ∿Ax ∨ ∿Cx                       15, DeM
 │    17)  ∿∿Ax                            7, DN
 │    18)  ∿Cx                             16, 17, DS
 │    19)  Cx · ∿Cx                        12, 18, Conj
 └──────────────────────────────────────────────────
      20)  /∴ (∃x)(Ax · Cx)                13-19, IP

10.                                   /∴ (x)[Cx ⊃ (Ex ⊃ Ax)]
       1)  (x){∿Ax ⊃ [(Bx ∨ Cx) ⊃ ∿(Dx ∨ Ex)]}    Pr
 ┌─→   2)  ∿(x)[Cx ⊃ (Ex ⊃ Ax)]           IP
 │     3)  (∃x)∿[Cx ⊃ (Ex ⊃ Ax)]          2, QD
 │     4)  ∿[Cx ⊃ (Ex ⊃ Ax)]              3, EI
```

251

5)	$\sim$Ax $\supset$ [(Bx $\lor$ Cx) $\supset$ $\sim$(Dx $\lor$ Ex)]	1, UI
6)	$\sim$[$\sim$Cx $\lor$ (Ex $\supset$ Ax)]	4, Impl
7)	$\sim\sim\sim$Cx $\cdot$ $\sim$(Ex $\supset$ Ax)	6, DeM
8)	Cx $\cdot$ $\sim$(Ex $\supset$ Ax)	7, DN
9)	Cx $\cdot$ $\sim$($\sim$Ex $\lor$ Ax)	8, Impl
10)	Cx $\cdot$ ($\sim\sim$Ex $\cdot$ $\sim$Ax)	9, DeM
11)	Cx $\cdot$ (Ex $\cdot$ $\sim$Ax)	10, DN
12)	Cx	11, Simp
13)	Cx $\lor$ Bx	12, Add
14)	Bx $\lor$ Cx	13, Com
15)	(Ex $\cdot$ $\sim$Ax) $\cdot$ Cx	11, Com
16)	Ex $\cdot$ $\sim$Ax	15, Simp
17)	Ex	16, Simp
18)	Ex $\lor$ Dx	17, Add
19)	Dx $\lor$ Ex	18, Add
20)	(Bx $\lor$ Cx) $\cdot$ (Dx $\lor$ Ex)	14, 19, Conj
21)	$\sim\sim$[(Bx $\lor$ Cx) $\cdot$ (Dx $\lor$ Ex)]	20, DN
22)	$\sim$[$\sim$(Bx $\lor$ Cx) $\lor$ $\sim$(Dx $\lor$ Ex)]	21, DeM
23)	$\sim$[(Bx $\lor$ Cx) $\supset$ $\sim$(Dx $\lor$ Ex)]	22, Impl
24)	$\sim\sim$Ax	5, 23, MT
25)	$\sim$Ax $\cdot$ Ex	16, Com
26)	$\sim$Ax	25, Simp
27)	$\sim$Ax $\cdot$ $\sim\sim$Ax	26, 24, Conj

28)	/$\therefore$ (x)[Cx $\supset$ (Ex $\supset$ Ax)]	2-27, IP

12.5.B.

2.   /$\therefore$ (x)(Tx $\lor$ $\sim$Bx)

1)	(x)[$\sim$Sx $\supset$ ($\sim$Hx $\cdot$ $\sim$Bx)]	Pr
2)	(x)(Sx $\supset$ Tx)	Pr
3)	$\sim$Sx $\supset$ ($\sim$Hx $\cdot$ $\sim$Bx)	1, UI
4)	Sx $\supset$ Tx	2, UI
5)	$\sim$Tx	CP, /$\therefore$ $\sim$Bx
6)	$\sim$Sx	4, 5, MT
7)	$\sim$Hx $\cdot$ $\sim$Bx	3, 6, MP
8)	$\sim$Bx $\cdot$ $\sim$Hx	7, Com
9)	$\sim$Bx	8, Simp

10)	∿Tx ⊃ ∿Bx	5-9, CP
11)	∿∿Tx ∨ ∿Bx	10, Impl
12)	Tx ∨ ∿Bx	11, DN
13)	/∴ (x)(Tx ∨ ∿Bx)	12, UG

4.   /∴ (x)(Ex ⊃ Ox)

1)	(x)[(Kx ∨ Ux) ⊃ Ox]	Pr
2)	(x)[Ux ∨ (∿Ex • ∿Dx)]	Pr
3)	(Kx ∨ Ux) ⊃ Ox	1, UI
4)	Ux ∨ (∿Ex • ∿Dx)	2, UI
5)	(∿Ex • ∿Dx) ∨ Ux	4, Com
→ 6)	Ex	CP, /∴ Ox
7)	Ex ∨ Dx	6, Add
8)	∿∿(Ex ∨ Dx)	7, DN
9)	∿(∿Ex • ∿Dx)	8, DeM
10)	Ux	5, 9, DS
11)	Ux ∨ Kx	10, Add
12)	Kx ∨ Ux	11, Com
13)	Ox	3, 12, MP

14)	Ex ⊃ Ox	6-13, CP
15)	/∴ (x)(Ex ⊃ Ox)	14, UG

6.   /∴ (x){(Ax • Cx) ⊃ [Rx ⊃ (Dx ⊃ Sx)]}

1)	(x){[Ax • (Cx • Rx)] ⊃ [Dx ⊃ (Gx • Sx)]}	Pr
2)	[Ax • (Cx • Rx)] ⊃ [Dx ⊃ (Gx • Sx)]	1, UI
→3)	Ax • Cx	CP, /∴ Rx ⊃ (Dx ⊃ Sx)
→4)	Rx	CP, /∴ Dx ⊃ Sx
→5)	Dx	CP, /∴ Sx
6)	(Ax • Cx) • Rx	3, 4, Conj
7)	Ax • (Cx • Rx)	6, Assoc
8)	Dx ⊃ (Gx • Sx)	2, 7, MP
9)	Gx • Sx	8, 5, MP
10)	Sx • Gx	9, Com
11)	Sx	10, Simp

12)	Dx ⊃ Sx	5-11, CP

13)	Rx ⊃ (Dx ⊃ Sx)	4-12, CP

14)	(Ax • Cx) ⊃ [Rx ⊃ (Dx ⊃ Sx)]	3-13. CP
15)	/∴ (x){(Ax • Cx) ⊃ [Rx ⊃ (Dx ⊃ Sx)]}	14, UG

8.   /∴ (x)[Tx ⊃ (Sx ⊃ Ox)]
```
    1)   (x)[(Cx · Sx) ⊃ ∿Vx]       Pr
    2)   (x)(∿Ox ⊃ Vx)              Pr
    3)   (x)(Tx ⊃ Cx)               Pr
    4)   (Cx · Sx) ⊃ ∿Vx           1, UI
    5)   ∿Ox ⊃ Vx                  2, UI
    6)   Tx ⊃ Cx                   3, UI
→7)   Tx                        CP, /∴ Sx ⊃ Ox
 →8)   Sx                        CP, /∴ Ox
  9)   Cx                        6, 7, MP
  10)  Cx · Sx                   9, 8, Conj
  11)  ∿Vx                       4, 10, MP
  12)  ∿∿Ox                      5, 11, MT
  13)  Ox                        12, DN

  14)  Sx ⊃ Ox                   8-13, CP

  15)  Tx ⊃ (Sx ⊃ Ox)            7-14, CP
  16)  /∴ (x)[Tx ⊃ (Sx ⊃ Ox)]    15, UG
```

10.   /∴ (x)[(Nx · Cx) ⊃ ∿Mx]
```
    1)   (x){[Cx · (∿Ox ∨ Mx)] ⊃ ∿(Nx ∨ Jx)}   Pr
    2)   [Cx · (∿Ox ∨ Mx)] ⊃ ∿(Nx ∨ Jx)        1, UI
→3)   Nx · Cx                              CP, /∴ ∿Mx
  4)   Nx                                   3, Simp
  5)   Cx · Nx                              3, Com
  6)   Cx                                   5, Simp
  7)   Nx ∨ Jx                              4, Add
  8)   ∿∿(Nx ∨ Jx)                          7, DN
  9)   ∿[Cx · (∿Ox ∨ Mx)]                   2, 8, MT
  10)  ∿Cx ∨ ∿(∿Ox ∨ Mx)                    9, DeM
  11)  ∿∿Cx                                 6, DN
  12)  ∿(∿Ox ∨ Mx)                          10, 11, DS
  13)  ∿∿Ox · ∿Mx                           12, DeM
  14)  ∿Mx · ∿∿Ox                           13, Com
  15)  ∿Mx                                  14, Simp

  16)  (Nx · Cx) ⊃ ∿Mx                      3-15, CP
  17)  /∴ (x)[(Nx · Cx) ⊃ ∿Mx]              16, UG
```

12.6.A.

2.   /∴(∃z)Bzz

    1)   (x)[(∃y)Ayx ⊃ Bxx]   Pr
    2)   (∃x)[(∃y)Ayx · Bxy]   Pr
    3)   (∃y)Ayw · Bwy   2, EI
    4)   (∃y)Ayw ⊃ Bww   1, UI
    5)   (∃y)Ayw   3, Simp
    6)   Bww   4, 5, MP
    7)   /∴ (∃z)Bzz   6, EG

4.   /∴(z)(Dz ⊃ ∿Bz)

    1)   (x)[Ax ⊃ (y)(By ⊃ Cxy)]   Pr
    2)   Aa   Pr
    3)   (x)[Ax ⊃ (w)(Dw ⊃ ∿Cxw)] Pr
    4)   Aa ⊃ (y)(By ⊃ Cay)   1, UI
    5)   Aa ⊃ (w)(Dw ⊃ ∿Caw)   3, UI
    6)   (y)(By ⊃ Cay)   4, 2, MP
    7)   (w)(Dw ⊃ ∿Caw)   5, 2, MP
    8)   By ⊃ Cay   6, UI
    9)   Dy ⊃ ∿Cay   7, UI
  → 10) Dy   CP, /∴ ∿By
    11) ∿Cay   9, 10, MP
    12) ∿By   8, 11, MT

    13) Dy ⊃ ∿By   10-12, CP
    14) /∴ (z)(Dz ⊃ ∿Bz)   13, UG

6.   /∴ (w)[Cw ⊃ (z)(Bz ⊃ Awz)]

    1)   (x)(y)(Axy ⊃ Ayx)   Pr
    2)   (x)[Bx ⊃ (y)(Cy ⊃ Axy)] Pr
    3)   Bz ⊃ (y)(Cy ⊃ Azy)   2, UI
    4)   (y)(Azy ⊃ Ayz)   1, UI
    5)   Azw ⊃ Awz   4, UI
  →6)   Cw   CP, /∴ (z)(Bz ⊃ Awz)
  →7)   Bz   CP, /∴ Awz
    8)   (y)(Cy ⊃ Azy)   3, 7, MP
    9)   Cw ⊃ Azw   8, UI
    10) Azw   9, 6, MP
    11) Awz   5, 10, MP

```
         12)  Bz ⊃ Awz                              7-11, CP
         13)  (z)(Bz ⊃ Awz)                         12, UG
    _____

         14)  Cw ⊃ (z)(Bz ⊃ Awz)                    6-13, CP
         15)  /∴ (w)[Cw ⊃ (z)(Bz ⊃ Awz)] 14, UG

8.                                             /∴ (∃y)(By · ∿Dy)
         1)   (x)[Ax ⊃ (∃y)(By · Cxy)]         Pr
         2)   Aa                                Pr
         3)   (x)[Ax ⊃ (y)(Dy ⊃ ∿Cxy)]         Pr
         4)   Aa ⊃ (∃y)(By · Cay)              1, UI
         5)   Aa ⊃ (y)(Dy ⊃ ∿Cay)             3, UI
         6)   (∃y)(By · Cay)                   4, 2, MP
         7)   (y)(Dy ⊃ ∿Cay)                  5, 2, MP
         8)   By · Cay                          6, EI
         9)   By                                8, Simp
         10)  Cay · By                          8, Com
         11)  Cay                               10, Simp
         12)  Dy ⊃ ∿Cay                        7, UI
         13)  ∿∿Cay                            11, DN
         14)  ∿Dy                              12, 13, MT
         15)  By · ∿Dy                         9, 14, Conj
         16)  /∴ (∃y)(By · ∿Dy)               15, EG

10.                      /∴ (y){(By · Dy) ⊃ (x)[Ax · Dx) ⊃ Cyx]}
         1)   (x)(y)[(Ax ∨ By) ⊃ (Cxy ≡ Cyx)]            Pr
         2)   (x){(Ax · Dx) ⊃ (y)[(By · Dy) ⊃ Cxy]}     Pr
         3)   (∃x)Ax · (∃y)By                            Pr
         4)   (∃x)Ax                                     3, Simp
         5)   (∃y)By · (∃x)Ax                            3, Com
         6)   (∃y)By                                     5, Simp
         7)   Ax                                         4, EI
         8)   By                                         6, EI
         9)   (y)[(Ax ∨ By) ⊃ (Cxy ≡ Cyx)]              1, UI
         10)  (Ax ∨ By) ⊃ (Cxy ≡ Cyx)                   9, UI
         11)  Ax ∨ By                                    7, Add
         12)  Cxy ≡ Cyx                                  10, 11, MP
    →13)  By · Dy              CP, /∴ (x)[(Ax · Dx) ⊃ Cyx]
    →14)  Ax · Dx                                 CP, /∴ Cyx
         15)  (Ax · Dx) ⊃ (y)[(By · Dy) ⊃ Cxy]          2, UI
         16)  (y)[(By · Dy) ⊃ Cxy]                      15, 14, MP
         17)  (By · Dy) ⊃ Cxy                           16, UI
         18)  Cxy                                       17, 13, MP
```

256

```
19) (Cxy ⊃ Cyx) · (Cyx ⊃ Cxy)           12, Equiv
20) Cxy ⊃ Cyx                           19, Simp
21) Cyx                               20, 18, MP

22) (Ax · Dx) ⊃ Cyx                     14-21, CP
23) (x)[(Ax · Dx) ⊃ Cyx]                  22, UG

24) (By · Dy) ⊃ (x)[(Ax · Dx) ⊃ Cyx]      13-23, CP
25) /∴ (y){(By · Dy) ⊃ (x)[Ax · Dx) ⊃ Cyx]}  24, UG
```

12.6.B.

2.
```
                                    /∴ (y)(∃x)(Px · Axy)
1)  (∃x)[Px · (y)Axy]    Pr
2)  Px · (y)Axy          1, EI
3)  Px                   2, Simp
4)  (y)Axy · Px          2, Com
5)  (y)Axy               4, Simp
6)  Axy                  5, UI
7)  Px · Axy             3, 6, Conj
8)  (∃x)(Px · Axy)       7, EG
9)  /∴ (y)(∃x)(Px · Axy) 8, UG
```

4.
```
                                    /∴ (∃x)(Px · Axx)
1)  (∃x)[Px · (y)(Py ⊃ Ayx)]   Pr
2)  Pw · (y)(Py ⊃ Ayw)         1, EI
3)  Pw                         2, Simp
4)  (y)(Py ⊃ Ayw) · Pw         2, Com
5)  (y)(Py ⊃ Ayw)              4, Simp
6)  Pw ⊃ Aww                   5, UI
7)  Aww                        6, 3, MP
8)  Pw · Aww                   3, 7, Conj
9)  /∴ (∃x)(Px · Axx)          8, EG
```

6.
```
                                    /∴(∃x)Wtx
1)  (x)[Sx ⊃ (∃y)(Cy · Exy)]   Pr
2)  St · (x)(Etx ⊃ Wtx)        Pr
3)  St                         2, Simp
4)  (x)(Etx ⊃ Wtx) · Sl        2, Com
5)  (x)(Etx ⊃ Wtx)             4, Simp
```

257

6)	Sl ⊃ (∃y)(Cy • Ety)	1, UI
7)	Etx ⊃ Wtx	5, UI
8)	(∃y)(Cy • Ety)	6, 3, MP
9)	Cy • Ety	8, EI
10)	Ety • Cy	9, Com
11)	Ety	10, Simp
12)	Wtx	7, 11, MP
13)	/∴(∃x)Wtx	12, EG

8.   /∴ (x){(∃y)[Px • (Ly • Txy)] ⊃ (∃y)[Px • (Fy • Txy)]}

1)	(x)(Lx ⊃ Fx)	Pr
→2)	(∃y)[Px • (Ly • Txy)]	CP, /∴ (∃y)(Fy • Txy)
3)	Px • (Ly • Txy)	2, EI
4)	Ly ⊃ Fy	1, UI
5)	(Ly • Txy) • Px	3, Com
6)	Ly • Txy	5, Simp
7)	Ly	6, Simp
8)	Fy	4, 7, MP
9)	Txy • Ly	6, Com
10)	Txy	9, Simp
11)	Fy • Txy	8, 10 Conj
12)	Px	3, Simp
13)	Px • (Fy Txy)	12, 11, Conj
14)	(∃y)[Px • (Fy • Txy)]	13, EG

15)	(∃y)[Px • (Ly • Txy)] ⊃ (∃y)[Px • (Fy • Txy)]	
		2-14, CP

12)	/∴ (x){(∃y)[Px • (Ly • Txy)] ⊃	
	(∃y)[Px • (Fy • Txy)]}	11, UG

10.   /∴ (∃x)(Lx • Fmx)

1)	(∃x)[(Px • Sxm) • Hxm] ⊃ (∃y)(By • Rmy)	Pr
2)	(∃y)(By • Rmy) ⊃ (∃x)(Lx • Fmx)	Pr
3)	(Pr • Srm) • Trm	Pr
4)	(x)[(Px • Txm) ⊃ Hxm]	Pr
5)	(Pr • Trm) ⊃ Hrm	4, UI
6)	Pr • Srm	5, Simp
7)	Pr	6, Simp
8)	Trm • (Pr • Srm)	3, Com
9)	Trm	8, Simp
10)	Pr • Trm	7, 9, Conj
11)	Hrm	5, 10, MP

```
12) (Pr · Sxm) · Hxm                          6, 11, Conj
13) (∃x)[(Px · Srm) · Hrm]                         12, EG
14) (∃y)(By · Rmy)                              1, 13, MP
15) /∴ (∃x)(Lx · Fmx)                           2, 14, MP
```

CHAPTER 13

13.1.A.

Students are to supply their own views here.

13.1.B.

Encourage the students to use their imaginations, even in a wild way, to complete this exercise. Have the students share their examples in class. This exercise can be useful in showing students how the meaning of a sentence is influenced by its context.

13.2.A.

2. Following 'The', 'wimble' is likely to be a noun acting as the singular subject of the sentence. That the string, 'wasps', is the verb is suggested by its following 'wimble' and also ending with an 's' indicating agreement with the singular subject, 'wimble'. That 'wasps' is a transitive verb is suggested by the 'the' following 'wasps'. 'Waddled wips' appears to be the object of the verb 'wasps'. In this case 'wips' is a noun modified by an adjective, waddled'. Both 'wite' and 'wate' seem to be nouns functioning as the objects of the preposition, 'from'.

4. This sentence has two independent clauses one of which follows 'While' ['a sak sot the smearth'] and the other ['a jammer jots the jees'] follows the comma. In both clases 'a' indicated the subject of the clause. In the first independent clause the subject is suggested by 'sak' and in the second by 'jammer'. In the first clause 'sot' appears to be a transitive verb followed by the article, 'the', and the direct object, 'smearth'. The same structure is found in the second clause where 'jees' indicates the direct object of the verb.

13.2.B.

Once again encourage the students to use their imaginations in a wild way to complete this exercise. This will help them to see how many interpretations they can find within one grammatical structure.

13.2.C.

2. hydrogen, molecule, atom, substance

4. cottage, house, building, edifice

13.2.D.

See the answers in the back of the text.

13.2.E.

2. 'Ballet' means an artistic dancing using conventional posses and steps coupled with figures and movements, and often portraying a story or incorporated into a story.

   The Three-Cornered Hat, Giselle, Petrushka, Swan Lake

4. 'Nation' means a community of people possessing more or less definite territory and government independent of any other governments.

   Andora, Germany, Liechtenstein, Spain

6. 'Wine' means a fermented grape juice containing varying percentages of alcohol coupled with ethers and esters.

Chardonnay, Dubonnet, Gattinara, Freisa

8. 'Opera' means an theatrical performance in which music is an essential part, consisting of arias, recitatives and choruses with orchestral accompaniment, interludes and introductions.

<u>Aida</u>, <u>Boris Godunov</u>, <u>Don Giovanni</u>, <u>Tristan and Isolde</u>

10. 'University' means an institution of higher learning maintaining facilities for teaching and research and authorized to grant academic degrees.

Cambridge, Harvard, University of Michigan, Oxford

13.2.F.

2. Steve owns a vehicle.
    Steve owns a sports car.
    Steve owns a Ferrari.

4. Any wimble-wop is an animal.
    Any wimble-wop is a mammal.
    Any wimble-wop is a marsupial.

13.2.G.

Students are to develop their own answers here, but within the context of the five assumptions suggested on page 451 of Section 2, and whatever discussion might have been introduced in class.

13.2.H.

Students are to develop their own answers here, following suggestions introduced in the textbook and whatever further discussion might have been introduced in class.

13.3.A.

2. Contextual

4. Synonymous

6. Lexical

8. Reforming

10. Precising

12. Ostensive

14. Lexical

16. Contextual

18. Synonymous

20. Genus are species

22. Synonymous

24. Enumeration - partial

13.3.B.

Here the students are to supply their own answers, but more importantly, <u>reasons</u> <u>in</u> <u>support</u> of their answers.

13.4.A.

2. Obscure

4. Circular

6. Metaphorical

8. Emotional

10. Circular

12. Circular

14. Obscure

13.4.B.

2. Anyone who has a score of more than 130 on a standard-
   ize intelligence test.

4. Anyone who can perform a task in a manner using the
   minimal amount of effort, materials, and time to
   achieve the desired results.

13.4.C.

2. A heavy piece of fabric generally woven or knotted and
   usually placed on the floor of a dwelling.

4. An electronic devise having the ability to make calcu-
   lations in accordance with a pre-written program of
   instructions.

13.4.D.

2. The weight of an object is the number of marks indicated on a scale when that object is placed on that scale.

4. The temperature of an object is the number of marks indicatedcated on a standard thermometer when that thermometer is appropriately attached to that object.

13.4.E.

2. Washington, Idaho, Montana, North Dakota, Minnesota, Wisconsin, Michigan, Ohio, New York, Vermont, New Hampshire, Maine

4. Democratic Party, Republican Party

13.4.F.

2. 'Printed material' means books, journals, magazines, pamphlets

4. 'Tree' means elms, oaks, palms, pines

CHAPTER 14

14.1.A.

The purpose of this exercise is to help students think about the cogency of statements in terms of logical relations, relevance, and rationality. The exercise also provides an opportunity for the instructor to emphasis the importance of good judgment in grasping and appraising arguments. Often an argument is not flawed in only one way, or is it even clear-cut just why an argument is flawed. But students often want "exact answers." When such "answers" are not forthcoming, students are prone to say that it is all a matter of opinion and that any opinion is as good as any other. Here, the instructor can again emphasis the importance of logical relation, relevance, and rationality, pointing out that while it might be the case that no "exact answer" is possible, nonetheless good judgments can still be made concerning the cogency of an argument.

14.1.B.

This can be a difficult exercise. Students, on the whole, have not given much thought to what they mean by 'rationally acceptable'. But by reflecting on their own criteria, or lack of it, for rational acceptability they can come better to appreciate the "Three Rs" introduced in this section.

14.1.C.

Hopefully, working through this exercise, students will come to see and appreciate the need for mastering the material in this and the next chapter.

AMBIGUITY, EQUIVOCATION, VAGUENESS, and RELATIVE WORDS

2. **Ambiguity (semantic):** The context of the argument does not make clear which of two possible meanings of 'public health' is meant. 'Public health' might be interpreted as either the proper mental and physical functioning of a person or as the optimal balance of social relations in a community. Hence, the premises do not support the conclusion that 'Federal action is required is necessary in dealing with pornography'.

4. **Ambiguity (semantic):** It is not clear whether 'caring' means to provide the means for another's survival such as food, housing, or medical treatment, or to hold a strong interest in the overall welfare of another. Caring for another in the first sense might entail never aiding or allowing the other's death, whereas in the second sense of 'caring' the most caring response sometimes might be to hasten the other's death.

6. **Vagueness:** 'Weapons' is a vague word in that it can refer to a range of things that are very dangerous, moderately dangerous, or to things that are less dangerous. It can also refer to a range of things that are designed and manufactured as instruments of violence to a person's fists. The degree of the potential for violence in schools depends on just what kind of weapons students possess.

8. **Equivocation:** The meaning of 'freedom' changes between its application to whales and to humans. The freedom granted the whales involved the removal of physical impediments to their movements, whereas the freedom that the arguer suggests for humans involves changing social, political, and economic structures.

10. This does not appear to be an argument, but rather a **plea** for anti-abortion.

12. **Equivocation:** The premise states that Turkey is a member of 'various European democratic institutions', while the conclusion states that Turkey is a democracy. 'Democracy' is being used in two different ways. First, Turkey participates as a voting member of various European institutions; second, the national government of Turkey allows

its own citizens freely to participate in governing the country. The truth of the first claim (the premise) in no

way indicates that the second claim (the conclusion) is also true, or even probably true.

14. **Relative words**: It is true that the poverty in America is nothing compared to that of Third World countries. This does not mean, however, that there is no need to fight poverty in the U.S.

Group B.

In all of the groups of exercises remaining in this chapter and the next, Group B asks the students to construct both fallacious and cogent arguments for the same claim. These exercises will show the student how to use fallacies in a persuasive manner and, therefore, hopefully, how to be on guard against some else using them.

Group C.

In all of the groups of exercises remaining in this chapter and the next, Group C asks the students to discover various fallacies in newspapers, magazines, textbooks, etc. Groups A exercises can serve as paradigms for the student in looking for fallacies. These exercises can impress upon the student how fallacies can appear in print and often go unnoticed as fallacies but, nonetheless,; serve to persuade the reader of some position.

APPEAL TO IRRELEVANT AUTHORITY, APPEAL TO PITY, APPEAL TO THE MASSES, and APPEAL TO SPECIAL INTERESTS

2. There appears to be no argument here, but rather a description of what the writer believes to be needed for gun control legislation to be stopped.

4. **Appeal to irrelevant authority**: No reasons are presented supporting why parents should more closely examine the impact of rock music other than the opinion of Mrs. Gore. But being the wife of a U.S. Senator does not make a person an expert in matters of artistic acceptability, moral correctness, or adolescent psychology.

6. **Appeal to the masses**: 'As any American motorist will tell you ··· ' serves to claim that highways need a facelift merely because 'everybody' thinks they do. But if this is so, it is the case not because the average American--who knows little about highway capacity and safety--believes it to be so, but because of evidence such as traffic delay situations and accident statistics. Note that one might view the claim that 'the nation's truckers strongly agree' as an appeal to authority. But they are closer to being a relevant authority since they are professional drivers who spend a great deal of their time on the nation's highways.

8. This is not an argument, but of a **description** of the Assemblies of God punishment of Mr. Swaggart. There is also a suggestion of an **explanation** of why the Assemblies of God acted in the way it did; that is, '··· was controlled by Swaggart's close associates and relatives'.

10. **Appeal to irrelevant authority**: As Deputy Secretary of Defense for Technology Security, Dr. Bryen might not in fact be a security expert. He is more likely to be an administrator. Of course, insofar as Dr. Bryen is citing information given to him by those who are authoritative in topics of security, his views are based on those authorities. But that is another matter.

12. This is not an argument, but merely presents Dr. Mark's proposal.

14. **Appeal to special interests**: In effect, the woman is saying that although 'phone sex' is wrong, it should not be banned because she and others make their living in this practice. She offers these special interests as reasons for continuing 'phone sex.'

APPEAL TO IGNORANCE, FAKE PRECISION, HASTY CONCLUSION, and NEGLECT OF RELEVANT EVIDENCE

2. **Hasty conclusion**: Although Quayle knew Tower for a relatively long period of time, he only indicates interacting with him on the Senate floor and in the Senate Armed Services committee. This limited experience with Tower is not representative of Tower's entire life. There might be times when Tower would drink to excess (for example, while at home or travelling) that Quayle was in no position to observe.

4. **Hasty conclusion**: That none of the three leaders in the party's history has been a woman does not provide evidence that the party systematically discriminates. Three is simply too small a number of leaders from which to draw such a conclusion.

6. **Fake precision**: To support the conclusion that repetitive TV violence is harmful to the future of society, it is claimed that a child is entertained by 10,000 acts of depicted violence before reaching maturity. Surely no one can accurately say how many acts of violence a child sees on TV before reaching maturity.

8. **Fake precision**: How can the arguer know that it will take 20 years--or 30, 40, or 50 for that matter--for machines to control the game? There is no way to measure this, and the comment is at best a phrase used to impress and persuade.

10. **Neglect of relevant evidence**: There are nations around the world that are no more Christian than the U.S. but that have governments that more properly reflect Christian ideals such as charity and compassion. One might cite, for example, both Canada and Sweden. The arguer ignores this

fact in urging that the American people must turn back to [the Christian] God to have a godly government.

12. **Hasty conclusion**: Robertson's political success in one small, relatively conservative state provides little evidence as to his fortunes in other, often very different, states.

14.   This is not an argument but rather an attempt to establish a **causal explanation** as to why inner-city schoolchildren do poorly in testing situations.

CHAPTER 15

AD HOMINEM, TU QUOQUE,
RED HERRING, and STRAW MAN

2. **Ad hominem (abusive)**: The author attacks those he does not like by using such words as 'misfits', 'schlepping', and 'punks'. The ethical, legal, and political issues raised by flag burning are not addressed.

4. **Ad hominem (abusive)**: Dukakis and Simon are portrayed as being out of touch with present reality. It is further insinuated that this is normal for Democrats. But no evidence is given as to the ways in which the views or policies of the Democrats fail.

6. **Tu quoque**: Bush is saying that Rather was also involved in one incident that might indicate weakness in his own professional judgement and integrity, and that, therefore, Bush ought to be excused. But why? Perhaps both should be faulted. Such two wrongs are not relevant to support a conclusion.

8. **Ad hominem (abusive)**: It is claimed that the position of liberals supporting Planned Parenthood are allied with the views of Nazism. All of the negative emotions connected with the Nazi movement are used to discredit the work of these liberals and Planned Parenthood without discussing the actual arguments put forth by either.

10. **Straw man**: The physicians mentioned in this example simply state their medical opinion concerning anencephalic infants. However, the arguer attempts to show that the physicians are inciting moral anarchy.

12. **Tu quoque**: Marcos' claim that the corruption in his regime was less than that of the current regime would, even if true, fail to absolve him of his guilt. It might well be the case that both regimes are culpable.

14. **Tu quoque**: Here is an attempt to exonerate hockey based on nothing more that the claim that it is not the most dangerous of sports. Using this kind of reasoning would lead to only the very worst sport being subject to criticism when in reality all risky sports should be criticized. Moreover, the arguer makes an unfair comparison.

Even though one NHL player has died since 1917, the NHL is
a professional league. The statistics cited for the other
sports more than likely involve play at both the professional and amateur levels, because extremely few professional football players and relatively few professional
boxers have died. Professional leagues tend to have the
lowest death rates because of the training and proficiency
of the participants.

IS-OUGHT FALLACY, DECEPTIVE ALTERNATIVES, WISHFUL THINKING, and NOVELTY

2. **Wishful thinking**: Part of the arguer's reasons for con-
cluding that the shooting was not racially motivated is her
confidence that a jury will agree.

4. **Is-ought**: That abortions have always been commonplace
does not provide any reason to claim that the ought to be
commonplace. This is merely an illicit appeal to tradi-
tion.

6. **Deceptive alternatives**: Freedom and communism do not
exhaust the political alternatives for Central America.
There are other forms of government such as socialism and
fascism. Further, it is not clear that freedom and communism are completely opposed. There are various types of
freedoms that come in various degrees, such as economic,
cultural, political, work, and the like. It is possible to
have a communist system that is more "free" than a democracy.

8. **Wishful thinking**: The arguer's belief is the only "evidence" given for the continued success of the partnership
of the two countries.

10. **Is-ought**: Although the arguer does not explicitly say
so, he strongly suggests that things ought to be the way
they are. After all, 'That's the way it is in the real
world'. This argument can also be seen as containing an
appeal to the masses in referring to what 'anybody believes'.

12. This is not an argument, but a **description** of one person's use of steroids.

14. **Novelty**: This passage explains the Civic's success by Honda's predilection for updating designs, and strongly suggests that new designs are better designs--"fresher" designs. It is in suggesting this that the fallacy of novelty is found. Some new car designs are better than old ones, but they are better because they are more functional, cheaper, aesthetically more pleasing, and the like, and not simply because they are new.

CONFUSING SUFFICIENT and NECESSARY CONDITIONS, QUESTIONABLE CAUSES, SLIPPERY SLOPE, and GAMBLER'S FALLACY

2. **Confusion of necessary and sufficient conditions**: Arms control agreements are necessary in the contemporary world if lasting peace is to be achieved. But the arguer also incorrectly thinks that such controls are sufficient for peace. Of course they are not, as the example shows. But, contrary to the argument, this does not mean that one should not negotiate arms treaties, for these are a necessary condition for lasting peace.

4. **Questionable cause**: One has no reason to believe that the large number of attorneys in D.C. causes its high crime rate. To claim this is to commit a **simple correlation fallacy**. Either of two alternatives is more likely. First, there is no connection between the high number of attorneys which is connected to the needs of the federal government and crime which is connected to poverty. Or, second, the large number of defense attorneys is a result of the high crime rate.

6. **Slippery slope**: No reason has been given to suggest that terrorist attacks must spread to America. In fact, there are reasons--for instance, political stability--to believe that they will remain less prevalent in the U.S.

8. **Questionable** **cause**: No evidence, other than a **corre-lation** of evidence gathered on a relatively small scale, is given in support of the conclusion that 'Age 6 would be a good minimum age for entering first graders'.

10. **Questionable** **causes**: No evidence of a causal connection between an increase in the minimum wage and an increase in employment is given except **simple** **correlation**, and even that has not held in every case.

12. **Gambler's** **fallacy**: The argument concludes that because the visiting team has won since 1980 in a series where home and away games alternate, the visiting team (LSU) will win again this year. But the fortunes of the specific home and visiting teams are determined by the quality of those teams and remain independent of how previous home and visiting teams fared. Sometimes home teams have a slight advantage because of fan support, but this cannot explain the success of visiting teams.

14. **Confusion** **of** **necessary** **and** **sufficient** **conditions**: Even granting that long jail terms in miserable prisons and a return to good old-fashion horsewhipping would both be helpful in winning the war on drugs, they cannot be suffi-cient. Better economic conditions, more opportunities for quality education and vocational training, parental concern and influence in the lives of their children, and the like, are also necessary to reverse the tide in the war on drugs.

CIRCULAR ARGUMENT, INCONSISTENCIES, FACTUAL CERTAINTY, and QUESTION BEGGING

2. This is not an argument, but a **description** of pragmatic inconsistency found in U.S. foreign policy.

4. **Inconsistency**: Although the pharmaceutical companies claim publicly that they are not hiding from anti-abortion forces, private admissions indicate the opposite. Thus, these companies are saying two contradictory things without explaining any change in policy.

6. **Circular argument**: 'Qualified leadership' is the same thing as 'Technically and tactically proficient sergeants and creative, demanding unit commanders'.

8. This is not an argument, but a **description** concerning the attitudes and feelings of a person towards having children.

10. **Inconsistency**: The writer espouses morality over money, but then suggests that one uses money to entice people into what he considers morally preferable professions. This represents a change of position in the argument. But no justification is given for this change.

12. This is not an argument, but a **description** of the attitudes of a person concerning a flag amendment.

14. **Inconsistency**: Despite claiming that it is perilous to assess a presidency before it is over, the arguer does exactly that as part of the argument.

```
************
**************

**** PART TWO ****

**************
*************
```

ANSWERS FOR VARIOUS ODD NUMBERED EXERCISES

NOT IN THE BACK OF THE TEXT

11.

R	W	H	W ∨ H	~(W ∨ H)	R ⊃ ~(W ∨ H)
1	1	1	1	0	0
1	1	0	1	0	0
1	0	1	1	0	0
1	0	0	0	1	1
0	1	1	1	0	1
0	1	0	1	0	1
0	0	1	1	0	1
0	0	0	0	1	1

13.

S	C	D	~D	C ⊃ D	~(C ⊃ D)	S · ~(C ⊃ D)	[S · ~(C ⊃ D)] · ~D	~{[S · ~(C ⊃ D)] · ~D}
1	1	1	0	1	0	0	0	1
1	1	0	1	0	1	1	1	0
1	0	1	0	1	0	0	0	1
1	0	0	1	1	0	0	0	1
0	1	1	0	1	0	0	0	1
0	1	0	1	0	1	0	0	1
0	0	1	0	1	0	0	0	1
0	0	0	1	1	0	0	0	1

15.

T	C	D	B	Y	~C	~Y	~D	~ ~D	~C · ~ ~D	B ∨ ~Y	continued →
1	1	1	1	1	0	0	0	1	0	1	
1	1	1	1	0	0	1	0	1	0	1	
1	1	1	0	1	0	0	0	1	0	0	
1	1	1	0	0	0	1	0	1	0	1	
1	1	0	1	1	0	0	1	0	0	1	
1	1	0	1	0	0	1	1	0	0	1	
1	1	0	0	1	0	0	1	0	0	0	
1	1	0	0	0	0	1	1	0	0	1	
1	0	1	1	1	1	0	0	1	1	1	
1	0	1	1	0	1	1	0	1	1	1	
1	0	1	0	1	1	0	0	1	1	0	
1	0	1	0	0	1	1	0	1	1	1	
1	0	0	1	1	1	0	1	0	0	1	
1	0	0	1	0	1	1	1	0	0	1	
1	0	0	0	1	1	0	1	0	0	0	
1	0	0	0	0	1	1	1	0	0	1	
0	1	1	1	1	0	0	0	1	0	1	
0	1	1	1	0	0	1	0	1	0	1	
0	1	1	0	1	0	0	0	1	0	0	
0	1	1	0	0	0	1	0	1	0	1	
0	1	0	1	1	0	0	1	0	0	1	
0	1	0	1	0	0	1	1	0	0	1	
0	1	0	0	1	0	0	1	0	0	0	
0	1	0	0	0	0	1	1	0	0	1	
0	0	1	1	1	1	0	0	1	1	1	
0	0	1	1	0	1	1	0	1	1	1	
0	0	1	0	1	1	0	0	1	1	0	
0	0	1	0	0	1	1	0	1	1	1	
0	0	0	1	1	1	0	1	0	0	1	
0	0	0	1	0	1	1	1	0	0	1	
0	0	0	0	1	1	0	1	0	0	0	
0	0	0	0	0	1	1	1	0	0	1	

continued →

~ (B ∨ ~Y)	(~C · ~ ~D) ∨ ~(B ∨ ~Y)	T ⊃ [(~C · ~~D) ∨ ~(B ∨ ~Y)]
0	0	0
0	0	0
1	1	1
0	0	0
0	0	0
0	0	0
1	1	1
0	0	0
0	0	0
0	0	0
1	1	1
0	0	0
0	1	1
0	1	1
1	1	1
0	1	1
0	1	1
0	1	1
1	1	1
0	1	1
0	1	1
0	1	1
1	1	1
0	1	1
0	1	1
0	1	1
1	1	1
0	1	1
0	1	1
0	1	1
1	1	1
0	1	1

2.9.B.(61)

9.

C	D	L	N	C Δ D	L Δ N	C Δ D) ≡ (L Δ N)
1	1	1	1	0	0	1
1	1	1	0	0	1	0
1	1	0	1	0	1	0
1	1	0	0	0	0	1
1	0	1	1	1	0	0
1	0	1	0	1	1	1
1	0	0	1	1	1	1
0	0	0	0	1	0	0
0	1	1	1	1	0	0
0	1	1	0	1	1	1
0	1	0	1	1	1	1
0	1	0	0	1	0	0
0	0	1	1	0	0	1
0	0	1	0	0	1	0
0	0	0	1	0	1	0
0	0	0	0	0	0	1

13.

M	S	P	E	C	M·S	(M·S)⊃P	E·C	[(M·S)]≡(E·C)
1	1	1	1	1	1	1	1	1
1	1	1	1	0	1	1	0	0
1	1	1	0	1	1	1	0	0
1	1	1	0	0	1	1	0	0
1	1	0	1	1	1	0	1	0
1	1	0	1	0	1	0	0	1
1	1	0	0	1	1	0	0	1
1	1	0	0	0	1	0	0	1
1	0	1	1	1	0	1	1	1
1	0	1	1	0	0	1	0	0
1	0	1	0	1	0	1	0	0
1	0	1	0	0	0	1	0	0
1	0	0	1	1	0	1	1	1
1	0	0	1	0	0	1	0	0
1	0	0	0	1	0	1	0	0
1	0	0	0	0	0	1	0	0
0	1	1	1	0	0	1	1	1
0	1	1	1	0	0	1	0	0
0	1	1	0	1	0	1	0	0
0	1	1	0	0	0	1	0	0
0	1	0	1	1	0	1	1	1
0	1	0	1	0	0	1	0	0
0	1	0	0	1	0	1	0	0
0	1	0	0	0	0	1	0	0
0	0	1	1	1	0	1	1	1
0	0	1	1	0	0	1	0	0
0	0	1	0	1	0	1	0	0
0	0	1	0	0	0	1	0	0
0	0	0	1	1	0	1	1	1
0	0	0	1	0	0	1	0	0
0	0	0	0	1	0	1	0	0
0	0	0	0	0	0	1	0	0

Chapter 3

    3.1 (67-68)

9. $\sim (B \equiv \sim H) \equiv (B \equiv H)$

```
1  1  0  0 1  1  1  1 1
0  1  1  1 0  1  1  0 0
0  0  1  0 1  1  0  0 1
1  0  0  1 0  1  0  1 0
              ⇑
```

15. [(Q ⊃ K) · (A ⊃ T)] · [G ≡ ~ (K ∨ T)]

```
1 1 1  1  1 1 1   0  1 0 0 1 1 1
1 1 1  1  1 1 1   1  0 1 0 1 1 1
1 1 1  0  1 0 0   0  1 0 0 1 1 0
1 1 1  0  1 0 0   0  0 1 0 1 1 0
1 1 1  1  0 1 1   0  1 0 0 1 1 1
1 1 1  1  0 1 1   1  0 1 0 1 1 1
1 1 1  1  0 1 0   0  1 0 0 1 1 0
1 1 1  1  0 1 0   1  0 1 0 1 1 0
1 0 0  0  1 1 1   0  1 0 0 0 1 1
1 0 0  0  1 1 1   0  0 1 0 0 1 1
1 0 0  0  1 0 0   0  1 1 1 0 0 0
1 0 0  0  1 0 0   0  0 0 1 0 0 0
1 0 0  0  0 1 1   0  1 0 0 0 1 1
1 0 0  0  0 1 1   0  0 1 0 0 1 1
1 0 0  0  0 1 0   0  1 1 1 0 0 0
1 0 0  0  0 1 0   0  0 0 1 0 0 0
0 1 1  1  1 1 1   0  1 0 0 1 1 1
0 1 1  1  1 1 1   1  0 1 0 1 1 1
0 1 1  0  1 0 0   0  1 0 0 1 1 0
0 1 1  0  1 0 0   0  0 1 0 1 1 0
0 1 1  1  0 1 1   0  1 0 0 1 1 1
0 1 1  1  0 1 1   1  0 1 0 1 1 1
0 1 1  1  0 1 0   0  1 0 0 1 1 0
0 1 1  1  0 1 0   1  0 1 0 1 1 0
0 1 0  1  1 1 1   0  1 0 0 0 1 1
0 1 0  1  1 1 1   1  0 1 0 0 1 1
0 1 0  0  1 1 1   0  1 1 1 0 0 0
0 1 0  0  1 0 0   0  0 0 1 0 0 0
0 1 0  1  0 1 1   0  1 0 0 0 1 1
0 1 0  1  0 1 1   1  0 1 0 0 1 1
0 1 0  1  0 1 0   1  1 1 1 0 0 0
0 1 0  1  0 1 0   0  0 0 1 0 0 0
                  ⇑
```

3.2.(70-71)

11. [(S ⊃ M) · (W ⊃ L)] · ~ (S ⊃ L)

```
1 1 1  1  1 1 1   0 0  1 1 1
1 1 1  0  1 0 0   0 1  1 0 0
1 1 1  1  0 1 1   0 0  1 1 1
1 1 1  1  0 1 0   1 1  1 0 0
1 0 0  0  1 1 1   0 0  1 1 1
1 0 0  0  1 0 0   0 1  1 0 0
1 0 0  0  0 1 1   0 0  1 1 1
1 0 0  0  0 1 0   0 1  1 0 0
0 1 1  1  1 1 1   0 0  0 1 1
0 1 1  0  1 0 0   0 0  0 1 0
0 1 1  1  0 1 1   0 0  0 1 1
0 1 1  1  0 1 0   0 0  0 1 0
0 1 0  1  1 1 1   0 0  0 1 1
0 1 0  0  1 0 0   0 0  0 1 0
0 1 0  1  0 1 1   0 0  0 1 1
0 1 0  1  0 1 0   0 0  0 1 0
                ⇑
           CONTINGENT
```

II-5

15. ~ (~ [(K · N) ∨ ~ (T · A)] ∨ [(T · A) ⊃ (N · K)]}

```
0 0  1 1 1  1 0  1 1 1  1  1 1 1  1  1 1 1
0 0  1 1 1  1 1  1 0 0  1  1 0 0  1  1 1 1
0 0  1 1 1  1 1  0 0 1  1  0 0 1  1  1 1 1
0 0  1 1 1  1 1  0 0 0  1  0 0 0  1  1 1 1
0 1  1 0 0  0 0  1 1 1  1  1 1 1  0  0 0 1
0 0  1 0 0  1 1  1 0 0  1  1 0 0  1  0 0 1
0 0  1 0 0  1 1  0 0 1  1  0 0 1  1  0 0 1
0 0  1 0 0  1 1  0 0 0  1  0 0 0  1  0 0 1
0 1  0 0 1  0 0  1 1 1  1  1 1 1  0  1 0 0
0 0  0 0 1  1 1  1 0 0  1  1 0 0  1  1 0 0
0 0  0 0 1  1 1  0 0 1  1  0 0 1  1  1 0 0
0 0  0 0 1  1 1  0 0 0  1  0 0 0  1  1 0 0
0 1  0 0 0  0 0  1 1 1  1  1 1 1  0  0 0 0
0 0  0 0 0  1 1  1 0 0  1  1 0 0  1  0 0 0
0 0  0 0 0  1 1  0 0 1  1  0 0 1  1  0 0 0
0 0  0 0 0  1 1  0 0 0  1  0 0 0  1  0 0 0
⇑
```
CONTRADICTION

3.3(76-77)

13.   /∴ ~ (A ∨ C)
  1) S Δ A   Pr
  2) S   Pr
  3) ~ A ⊃ ~ C   Pr

{[(S Δ A) · S] · (~ A ⊃ ~ C)} ⊃ ~ (A ∨ C)

```
1 0 1 0 1 0 0 1 1 0 1   1 0 1 1 1
1 0 1 0 1 0 0 1 1 1 0   1 0 1 1 0
1 1 0 1 1 0 1 0 0 0 1   1 0 0 1 1
1 1 0 1 1 1 1 0 1 1 0   1 1 0 0 0
0 1 1 0 0 0 0 1 1 0 1   1 0 1 1 1
0 1 1 0 0 0 0 1 1 1 0   1 0 1 1 0
0 0 0 0 0 0 1 0 0 0 1   1 0 0 1 1
0 0 0 0 0 0 1 0 1 1 0   1 1 0 0 0
                       ⇑
```
TAUTOLOGY/VALID

15.   /∴ A ⊃ ~ M
  1) (A · ~ M) ⊃ S   Pr
  2) ~ S ∨ A   Pr
  3) ~ A   Pr

({[(A · ~ M) ⊃ S] · (~ S ∨ A)} · ~ A) ⊃ (A ⊃ ~ M)

```
1 0 0 1  1 1 1  0 1 1 1  0 0 1  1  1 0 0 1
1 0 0 1  1 0 1  1 0 1 1  0 0 1  1  1 0 0 1
1 1 1 0  1 1 1  0 1 1 1  0 0 1  1  1 1 1 0
1 1 1 0  0 0 0  1 0 1 1  0 0 1  1  1 1 1 0
0 0 0 1  1 1 0  0 1 0 0  0 1 0  1  0 1 0 1
0 0 0 1  1 0 1  1 0 1 0  1 1 0  1  0 1 0 1
0 0 1 0  1 1 0  0 1 0 0  0 1 0  1  0 1 0 1
0 0 1 0  1 0 1  1 0 1 0  1 1.0  1  0 1 1 0
                                 ⇑
```
TAUTOLOGY/VALID

II-6

19.   /∴ R

1) ~ (A • ~ M)   Pr
2) ~ (M • ~ A)   Pr
3) C ⊃ (A ≡ M)   Pr
4) R ∨ C   Pr

({[~ (A • ~ M) • ~ (M • ~ A)] • [C ⊃ (A ≡ M)]} • (R ∨ C)) ⊃ R

```
1 1 0 0 1   1 1 1 0 0 1   1 1 1 1 1 1   1 1 1 1   1 1
1 1 0 0 1   1 1 1 0 0 1   1 1 1 1 1 1   1 0 1 1   0 0
1 1 0 0 1   1 1 1 0 0 1   1 0 1 1 1 1   1 1 1 0   1 1
1 1 0 0 1   1 1 1 0 0 1   1 0 1 1 1 1   0 0 0 0   1 0
0 1 1 1 0   0 1 0 0 0 1   0 1 0 1 0 0   0 1 1 1   1 1
0 1 1 1 0   0 1 0 0 0 1   0 1 0 1 0 0   0 0 1 1   1 0
0 1 1 1 0   0 1 0 0 0 1   0 0 1 1 0 0   0 1 1 0   1 1
0 1 1 1 0   0 1 0 0 0 1   0 0 1 1 0 0   0 0 0 0   1 0
1 0 0 0 1   0 0 1 1 1 0   0 1 0 0 0 1   0 1 1 1   1 1
1 0 0 0 1   0 0 1 1 1 0   0 1 0 0 0 1   0 0 1 1   1 0
1 0 0 0 1   0 0 1 1 1 0   0 0 1 0 0 1   0 1 1 0   1 1
1 0 0 0 1   0 0 1 1 1 0   0 0 1 0 0 1   0 0 0 0   1 0
1 0 0 1 0   1 1 0 0 1 0   1 1 1 0 1 0   1 1 1 1   1 1
1 0 0 1 0   1 1 0 0 1 0   1 1 1 0 1 0   1 0 1 1   1 1
1 0 0 1 0   1 1 0 0 1 0   1 0 1 0 1 0   1 1 1 0   1 1
1 0 0 1 0   1 1 0 0 1 0   1 0 1 0 1 0   0 0 0 0   1 0
```
                                                        ⇑

                                             CONTINGENT/INVALID

3.4. (80-81)

9.   /∴ ~ J ⊃ ~ I

1) I ⊃ (~ E Δ T)   Pr
2) ~ E   Pr

{[I ⊃ (~ E Δ J)] • ~ E} • ~ (~ J ⊃ ~ I)

```
1 1   0 1 1 1   0 0 1 0 0   0 1 1 0 1
1 0   0 1 0 0   0 0 1 0 1   1 0 0 0 1
1 0   1 0 0 1   0 1 0 0 0   0 1 1 0 1
1 1   1 0 1 0   1 1 0 1 1   1 0 0 0 1
0 1   0 1 1 1   0 0 1 0 0   0 1 1 1 0
0 1   0 1 0 0   0 0 1 0 0   1 0 1 1 0
0 1   1 0 0 1   1 1 0 0 0   0 1 1 1 0
0 1   1 0 1 0   1 1 0 0 0   1 0 1 1 0
```
                               ⇑

                    CONTINGENT/INVALID

13.   /∴ S

1) S ≡ H   Pr
2) I Δ ~ H   Pr
3) ~ I   Pr

{[(S ≡ H) • (I Δ ~ H)] • ~ I} • ~ S

```
1 1 1   1 1 1   0 1   0 0 1 0 0 1
1 1 1   0 0 0   0 1   0 0 1 0 0 1
1 0 0   0 1 0   1 0   0 0 1 0 0 1
1 0 0   0 0 1   1 0   0 1 0 0 0 1
0 0 1   0 1 1   0 1   0 0 1 0 1 0
0 0 1   0 0 0   0 1   0 1 0 0 1 0
0 1 0   0 1 0   1 0   0 0 1 0 1 0
0 1 0   1 0 1   1 0   1 1 0 1 1 0
```
                           ⇑

                 CONTINGENT/INVALID

17. $/\therefore \ G \supset D$

1) $(H \cdot G) \supset \sim M$ Pr
2) $\sim M \equiv D$ Pr
3) H   Pr

```
({[(H · G) ⊃ ~M] · (~M ≡ D)} · H) · ~(G ⊃ D)
  1 1 1   0 0 1   0   0 1 0 1   0 1   0 0   1 1 1
  1 1 1   0 0 1   0   0 1 1 0   0 1   0 1   1 0 0
  1 1 1   1 1 0   1   1 0 1 1   1 1   0 0   1 1 1
  1 1 1   1 1 0   0   1 0 0 0   0 1   0 1   1 0 0
  1 0 0   1 0 1   0   0 1 0 1   0 1   0 0   0 1 1
  1 0 0   1 0 1   1   0 1 1 0   1 1   0 0   0 1 0
  1 0 0   1 1 0   1   1 0 1 1   1 1   0 0   0 1 1
  1 0 0   1 1 0   0   1 0 0 0   0 1   0 0   0 1 0
  0 0 1   1 0 1   0   0 1 0 1   0 0   0 0   1 1 1
  0 0 1   1 0 1   1   0 1 1 0   0 0   0 1   1 0 0
  0 0 1   1 1 0   0   1 0 0 1   0 0   0 0   1 1 1
  0 0 1   1 1 0   0   1 0 0 0   0 0   0 1   1 0 0
  0 0 0   1 0 1   0   0 1 0 1   0 0   0 0   0 1 1
  0 0 0   1 0 1   1   0 1 1 0   0 0   0 0   0 1 0
  0 0 0   1 1 0   1   1 0 1 1   0 0   0 0   0 1 1
  0 0 0   1 1 0   0   1 0 0 0   0 0   0 0   0 1 0
                                    ⇑
```
CONTRADICTION/INVALID

19. $/\therefore \ \sim C \cdot Q$

1) $(D \cdot R) \supset C$ Pr
2) $R \bigtriangleup Q$ Pr
3) $\sim R$ Pr

```
({[(D · R) ⊃ C] · (R △ Q)} · ~R) · ~(~C · Q)
  1 1 1   1 1   0 1   0 1   0 0 1   0 1   0 1 0 1
  1 1 1   1 1   1 1   1 0   0 0 1   0 1   0 1 0 0
  1 1 1   0 0   0 1   0 1   0 0 1   0 0   1 0 1 1
  1 1 1   0 0   0 1   1 0   0 0 1   0 1   1 0 0 0
  1 0 0   1 1   1 0   1 1   1 1 0   1 1   0 1 0 1
  1 0 0   1 1   0 0   0 0   0 1 0   0 1   0 1 0 0
  1 0 0   1 0   1 0   1 1   1 1 0   0 0   1 0 1 1
  1 0 0   1 0   0 0   0 0   0 1 0   0 1   1 0 0 0
  0 0 1   1 1   0 1   0 1   0 0 1   0 1   0 1 0 1
  0 0 1   1 1   1 1   1 0   0 0 1   0 1   0 1 0 0
  0 0 1   1 0   0 1   0 1   0 0 1   0 0   1 0 1 1
  0 0 1   1 0   1 1   1 0   0 0 1   0 1   1 0 0 0
  0 0 0   1 1   1 0   1 1   1 1 0   1 1   0 1 0 1
  0 0 0   1 1   0 0   0 0   0 1 0   0 1   0 1 0 0
  0 0 0   1 0   1 0   1 1   1 1 0   0 0   1 0 1 1
  0 0 0   1 0   1 0   1 0   1 1 0   1 1   1 0 0 0
                                  ⇑
```
CONTINGENT/INVALID

11. $/\therefore$ A • (C • B) $/\therefore$ 1 • (0 • 0)   = 0
    1) (D ∨ B) ⊃ C   (0 ∨ 0) ⊃ 0   = 1
    2) A ∆ D   1 ∆ 0   = 1
    3) (C ∨ B) ⊃ D   (0 ∨ 0) ⊃ 0   = 1
    4) D ⊃ (B • ~D)   0 ⊃ (0 • ~0)   = 1

Interpretation

A = 1
B = 0
C = 0
D = 0

INVALID

13. $/\therefore$ (C ⊃ B) ∨ ~(B ∨ C)   (1 ⊃ 0) ∨ ~(0 ∨ 1)   = 0
    1) (A ⊃ B) ⊃ (C ⊃ B)   (1 ⊃ 0) ⊃ (1 ⊃ 0)   = 1
    2) (D ⊃ C) ⊃ ~(B ∨ C)   X   (0 ⊃ 1) ⊃ ~(0 ∨ 1)   = 0

Interpretation

A = 1
B = 0
C = 1
D = 0

VALID

19. $/\therefore$ (~ B ∨ D) • (D ∨ ~ A) $/\therefore$ (~ 1 ∨ 0) • (0 ∨ ~ 1)   = 0
    1) A ≡ B   1 ≡ 1   = 1
    2) ~ C ≡ B   ~ 0 ≡ 1   = 1
    3) (A ∨ D) • ~ C   (1 ∨ 0) • ~ 0   = 1

Interpretation

A = 1
B = 1
C = 0
D = 0

INVALID

11.   /∴ ~E ⊃ D
1) (~E·L) ⊃ D   Pr
2) L   Pr
3) ~D·~E   Pr

{[(~E·L) ⊃ D]·L}·(~D·~E)

```
0 1 0 1  1  1  1 1 1  0  0 1  0 0 1
0 1 0 1  1  0  1 1 0  1  0 0  0 0 1
0 1 0 0  1  1  0 0 0  0  1 0  0 0 1
0 1 0 0  1  0  0 0 0  1  0 0  0 0 1
1 0 1 1  1  1  1 1 1  0  0 1  0 1 0
1 0 1 1  0  0  0 1 0  1  0 1  1 1 0
1 0 0 0  1  1  0 0 0  0  1 0  1 1 0
1 0 0 0  1  0  0 0 0  1  0 1  1 1 0
```
                  ⇑
            INCONSISTENT

({[(~E·L) ⊃ D]·L}·(~D·~E)) ⊃ (~E ⊃ D)

```
0 1 0 1  1  1  1 1 1 0  0 1 0 0 1  1  0 1 1  1
0 1 0 1  1  0  1 1 0 1  0 0 0 0 1  1  0 1 1  0
0 1 0 0  1  1  0 0 0 0  1 0 0 0 1  1  0 1 1  1
0 1 0 0  1  0  0 0 0 1  0 0 0 0 1  1  0 1 0  1
1 0 1 1  1  1  1 1 1 0  0 1 0 1 0  1  1 0 1  0
1 0 1 1  0  0  0 1 0 1  0 1 1 0  1  1  0 0 1
1 0 0 0  1  1  0 0 0 0  1 0 1 0 1  1  1 0 1  0
1 0 0 0  1  0  0 0 0 1  0 1 1 0 1  1  1 0 0  1
```
                                 ⇑
                               VALID

13.   /∴ C·~F
1) ~(I·F) ⊃ C   Pr
2) F ⊃ ~C   Pr
3) ~(F·I)   Pr

{[~(I·F) ⊃ C]·(F ⊃ ~C)}·~(F·I)

```
0 1 1 1  1  1  0 1 0 0 1   0 0 1 1 1
0 1 1 1  1  0  1 1 1 1 0   0 0 1 1 1
1 1 0 0  1  1  1 0 1 0 1   1 1 0 0 1
1 1 0 0  0  0  0 0 1 1 0   0 1 0 0 1
1 0 0 1  1  1  0 1 0 0 1   0 1 1 0 0
1 0 0 1  0  0  0 1 1 1 0   0 1 1 0 0
1 0 0 0  1  1  1 0 1 0 1   1 1 0 0 0
1 0 0 0  0  0  0 0 1 1 0   0 1 0 0 0
```
                 ⇑
             CONSISTENT

({[~(I·F) ⊃ C]·(F ⊃ ~C)}·~(F·I)) ⊃ (C·~F)

```
0 1 1 1  1  1  0 1 0  0 1  0 0 1 1 1  1  1 0 0 1
0 1 1 1  1  0  1 1 1  1 0  0 0 1 1 1  1  0 0 0 1
1 1 0 0  1  1  1 0 1  0 1  1 1 0 0 1  1  1 1 1 0
1 1 0 0  0  0  0 0 1  1 0  0 1 0 0 1  1  0 0 1 0
1 0 0 1  1  1  0 1 0  0 1  0 1 1 0 0  1  1 0 0 1
1 0 0 1  0  0  0 1 1  1 0  0 1 1 0 0  1  0 0 0 1
1 0 0 0  1  1  1 0 1  0 1  1 1 0 0 0  1  1 1 1 0
1 0 0 0  0  0  0 0 1  1 0  0 1 0 0 0  1  0 0 1 0
```
                                 ⇑
                               VALID

15.   /∴ D ⊃ (W • P)
   1) (M Δ W) ∨ (P • D)   Pr
   2) (W • M) • ~ D   Pr

```
[(M  Δ  W)  ∨  (P  ·  D)]  ·  [(W  ·  M)  ·  ~ D]
 1  0  1   1  1 1 1   0   1  1 1  0 0 1
 1  0  1   0  1 0 0   0   1  1 1  1 1 0
 1  0  1   0  0 0 1   0   1  1 1  0 0 1
 1  0  1   0  0 0 0   0   1  1 1  1 1 0
 1  1  0   1  1 1 1   0   0  0 1  0 0 1
 1  1  0   1  1 0 0   0   0  0 1  0 1 0
 1  1  0   1  0 0 1   0   0  0 1  0 0 1
 1  1  0   1  0 0 0   0   0  0 1  0 1 0
 0  1  1   1  1 1 1   0   1  0 0  0 0 1
 0  1  1   1  1 0 0   0   1  0 0  0 1 0
 0  1  1   1  0 0 1   0   1  0 0  0 0 1
 0  1  1   1  0 0 0   0   1  0 0  0 1 0
 0  0  0   1  1 1 1   0   0  0 0  0 0 1
 0  0  0   0  1 0 0   0   0  0 0  0 1 0
 0  0  0   0  0 0 1   0   0  0 0  0 0 1
 0  0  0   0  0 0 0   0   0  0 0  0 1 0
                      ⇑
                 INCONSISTENT
```

```
{[(M  Δ  W)  ∨  (P  ·  D)]  ·  [(W  ·  M)  ·  ~ D]}  ⊃  [D  ⊃  (W  ·  P)]
  1  0  1   1  1 1 1   0   1  1 1  0 0 1    1  1  1   1 1 1
  1  0  1   0  1 0 0   0   1  1 1  1 1 0    1  0  1   1 1 1
  1  0  1   0  0 0 1   0   1  1 1  0 0 1    1  1  0   1 0 0
  1  0  1   0  0 0 0   0   1  1 1  1 1 0    1  0  1   1 0 0
  1  1  0   1  1 1 1   0   0  0 1  0 0 1    1  1  0   0 0 1
  1  1  0   1  1 0 0   0   0  0 1  0 1 0    1  0  1   0 0 1
  1  1  0   1  0 0 1   0   0  0 1  0 0 1    1  1  0   0 0 0
  1  1  0   1  0 0 0   0   0  0 1  0 1 0    1  0  1   0 0 0
  0  1  1   1  1 1 1   0   1  0 0  0 0 1    1  1  1   1 1 1
  0  1  1   1  1 0 0   0   1  0 0  0 1 0    1  0  1   1 1 1
  0  1  1   1  0 0 1   0   1  0 0  0 0 1    1  1  0   1 0 0
  0  1  1   1  0 0 0   0   1  0 0  0 1 0    1  0  1   1 0 0
  0  0  0   1  1 1 1   0   0  0 0  0 0 1    1  1  0   0 0 1
  0  0  0   0  1 0 0   0   0  0 0  0 1 0    1  0  1   0 0 1
  0  0  0   0  0 0 1   0   0  0 0  0 0 1    1  1  0   0 0 0
  0  0  0   0  0 0 0   0   0  0 0  0 1 0    1  0  1   0 0 0
                                           ⇑
                                         VALID
```

17. /∴ T

1) (A • ~ U) ⊃ Q   Pr
2) ~ (~ A • U)   Pr
3) ~ (U v Q)   Pr
4) ~ (Q • ~ T)   Pr

({[(A • ~ U) ⊃ Q] • ~ (~ A • U)} • ~ (U v Q)) • ~ (Q • ~ T)

1 0 0 1	1 1	1 1	0 1 0 1	0 0	1 1 1	0 1	1 0 0 1
1 0 0 1	1 1	1 1	0 1 0 1	0 0	1 1 1	0 0	1 1 1 0
1 0 0 1	1 0	1 1	0 1 0 1	0 0	1 1 0	0 1	0 0 0 1
1 0 0 1	1 0	1 1	0 1 0 1	0 0	1 1 0	0 1	0 0 1 0
1 1 1 0	1 1	1 1	0 1 0 0	0 0	0 1 1	0 1	1 0 0 1
1 1 1 0	1 1	1 1	0 1 0 0	0 0	0 1 1	0 0	1 1 1 0
1 1 1 0	0 0	0 1	0 1 0 0	0 1	0 0 0	0 1	0 0 0 1
1 1 1 0	0 0	0 1	0 1 0 0	0 1	0 0 0	0 1	0 0 1 0
0 0 0 1	1 1	0 0	1 0 1 1	0 0	1 1 1	0 1	1 0 0 1
0 0 0 1	1 1	0 0	1 0 1 1	0 0	1 1 1	0 0	1 1 1 0
0 0 0 1	1 0	0 0	1 0 1 1	0 0	1 1 0	0 1	0 0 0 1
0 0 0 1	1 0	0 0	1 0 1 1	0 0	1 1 0	0 1	0 0 1 0
0 0 1 0	1 1	1 1	1 0 0 0	0 0	0 1 1	0 1	1 0 0 1
0 0 1 0	1 1	1 1	1 0 0 0	0 0	0 1 1	0 0	1 1 1 0
0 0 1 0	1 0	1 1	1 0 0 0	1 1	0 0 0	1 1	0 0 0 1
0 0 1 0	1 0	1 1	1 0 0 0	1 1	0 0 0	1 1	0 0 1 0

⇑
CONSISTENT

[({[(A • ~ U) ⊃ Q] • ~ (~ A • U)} • ~ (U v Q)) • ~ (Q • ~ T)] ⊃ T

1 0 0 1	1	1	1 1	0 1 0 1	0 0	1 1 1	0 1	1 0 0 1	1 1
1 0 0 1	1	1	1 1	0 1 0 1	0 0	1 1 1	0 0	1 1 1 0	1 0
1 0 0 1	1	0	1 1	0 1 0 1	0 0	1 1 0	0 1	0 0 0 1	1 1
1 0 0 1	1	0	1 1	0 1 0 1	0 0	1 1 0	0 1	0 0 1 0	1 0
1 1 1 0	1	1	1 1	0 1 0 0	0 0	0 1 1	0 1	1 0 0 1	1 1
1 1 1 0	1	1	1 1	0 1 0 0	0 0	0 1 1	0 0	1 1 1 0	1 0
1 1 1 0	0	0	0 1	0 1 0 0	0 1	0 0 0	0 1	0 0 0 1	1 1
1 1 1 0	0	0	0 1	0 1 0 0	0 1	0 0 0	0 1	0 0 1 0	1 0
0 0 0 1	1	1	0 0	1 0 1 1	0 0	1 1 1	0 1	1 0 0 1	1 1
0 0 0 1	1	1	0 0	1 0 1 1	0 0	1 1 1	0 0	1 1 1 0	1 0
0 0 0 1	1	0	0 0	1 0 1 1	0 0	1 1 0	0 1	0 0 0 1	1 1
0 0 0 1	1	0	0 0	1 0 1 1	0 0	1 1 0	0 1	0 0 1 0	1 0
0 0 1 0	1	1	1 1	1 0 0 0	0 0	0 1 1	0 1	1 0 0 1	1 1
0 0 1 0	1	1	1 1	1 0 0 0	0 0	0 1 1	0 0	1 1 1 0	1 0
0 0 1 0	1	0	1 1	1 0 0 0	1 1	0 0 0	1 1	0 0 0 1	1 1
0 0 1 0	1	0	1 1	1 0 0 0	1 1	0 0 0	1 1	0 0 1 0	0 0

⇑
INVALID

II-12

19.   /∴ ~O·G

1) $(G \supset {\sim}S) \cdot G$ Pr
2) ${\sim}S \supset (G \cdot E)$ Pr
3) $E \equiv (G \lor {\sim}S)$ Pr
4) $G \lor O$ Pr
5) ${\sim}E$ Pr

[({[(G ⊃ ~S) · G] · [~S ⊃ (G · E)]} · [E ≡ (G ∨ ~S)]} · (G ∨ O)] · ~E

```
1 0 0 1 0 1  0 0 1 1  1 1 1   0 1 1  1 1 0 1   0 1 1 1   0 0 1
1 0 0 1 0 1  0 0 1 1  1 1 1   0 1 1  1 1 0 1   0 1 1 0   0 0 1
1 0 0 1 0 1  0 0 1 1  1 0 0   0 0 0  1 1 0 1   0 1 1 1   0 1 0
1 0 0 1 0 1  0 0 1 1  1 0 0   0 0 0  1 1 0 1   0 1 1 0   0 1 0
1 1 1 0 1 1  1 1 0 1  1 1 1   1 1 1  1 1 1 0   1 1 1 1   0 0 1
1 1 1 0 1 1  1 1 0 1  1 1 1   1 1 1  1 1 1 0   1 1 1 0   0 0 1
1 1 1 0 1 1  0 1 0 0  1 0 0   0 0 0  1 1 1 0   0 1 1 1   0 1 0
1 1 1 0 1 1  0 1 0 0  1 0 0   0 0 0  1 1 1 0   0 1 1 0   0 1 0
0 1 0 1 0 0  0 0 1 1  0 0 1   0 1 0  0 0 0 1   0 0 1 1   0 0 1
0 1 0 1 0 0  0 0 1 1  0 0 1   0 1 0  0 0 0 1   0 0 0 0   0 0 1
0 1 0 1 0 0  0 0 1 1  0 0 0   0 0 1  0 0 0 1   0 0 1 1   0 1 0
0 1 0 1 0 0  0 0 1 1  0 0 0   0 0 1  0 0 0 1   0 0 0 0   0 1 0
0 1 1 0 0 0  0 1 0 0  0 0 1   0 1 1  0 1 1 0   0 0 1 1   0 0 1
0 1 1 0 0 0  0 1 0 0  0 0 1   0 1 1  0 1 1 0   0 0 0 0   0 0 1
0 1 1 0 0 0  0 1 0 0  0 0 0   0 0 0  0 1 1 0   0 0 1 1   0 1 0
0 1 1 0 0 0  0 1 0 0  0 0 0   0 0 0  0 1 1 0   0 0 0 0   0 1 0
                                                          ⇑
```
                                                INCONTINGENT

{[({[(G ⊃ ~S)·G] · [~S ⊃ (G · E)]} · [E ≡ (G ∨ ~S)]) · (G ∨ O)] · ~E} ⊃ (~O · G)

```
10 0 101 00 1 111   0 111 101   0 111 001   1 0 101
10 0 101 00 1 111   0 111 101   0 110 001   1 1 011
10 0 101 00 1 100   0 001 101   0 111 010   1 0 101
10 0 101 00 1 100   0 001 101   0 110 010   1 1 011
11 1 010 11 0 1 111   1 111 110   1 111 001   1 0 101
11 1 011 11 0 1 111   1 111 110   1 110 001   1 1 011
11 1 011 01 0 0 100   0 001 110   0 111 010   1 0 101
11 1 011 01 0 0 100   0 001 110   0 110 010   1 1 011
01 0 100 00 1 1 001   0 100 001   0 011 001   1 0 100
01 0 100 00 1 1 001   0 100 001   0 000 001   1 1 000
01 0 100 00 1 1 000   0 010 001   0 011 010   1 0 100
01 0 100 00 1 1 000   0 010 001   0 000 010   1 1 000
01 1 000 10 0 001   0 110 110   0 011 001   1 0 100
01 1 000 10 0 001   0 110 110   0 000 001   1 1 000
01 1 000 10 0 000   0 000 110   0 011 010   1 0 100
01 1 000 10 0 000   0 000 110   0 000 010   1 1 000
                                              ⇑
```
                                          VALID

11. $[U \cdot (R \vee P)] \equiv [(U \cdot R) \vee (P \cdot U)]$

```
1 1  1 1 1   1   1 1 1   1   1 1 1
1 1  1 1 0   1   1 1 1   1   0 0 1
1 1  0 1 1   1   1 0 0   1   1 1 1
1 0  0 0 0   1   1 0 0   0   0 0 1
0 0  1 1 1   1   0 0 1   0   1 0 0
0 0  1 1 0   1   0 0 1   0   0 0 0
0 0  0 1 1   1   0 0 0   0   1 0 0
0 0  0 0 0   1   0 0 0   0   0 0 0
            ⇑
        EQUIVALENT
```

13. $[(R \cdot A) \supset (M \cdot R)] \equiv [R \cdot (A \supset M)]$

```
1 1 1  1   1 1 1   1 1 1 1 1   1
1 1 1  0   0 0 1   1 1 0 1 0   0
1 0 0  1   1 1 1   1 1 1 0 1   1
1 0 0  1   0 0 1   1 1 1 0 1   0
0 0 1  1   1 0 0   0 0 0 1 1   1
0 0 1  1   0 0 0   0 0 0 1 0   0
0 0 0  1   1 0 0   0 0 0 0 1   1
0 0 0  1   0 0 0   0 0 0 1 0
            ⇑
      NOT EQUIVALENT
```

19. $[(T \vee W) \cdot (G \vee S)] \equiv [(S \cdot G) \vee (T \vee W)]$

```
1 1 1  1 1 1 1   1   1 1 1   1   1 1 1
1 1 1  1 1 1 0   1   0 0 1   1   1 1 1
1 1 1  1 0 1 1   1   1 0 0   1   1 1 1
1 1 1  0 0 0 0   0   0 0 0   1   1 1 1
1 1 0  1 1 1 1   1   1 1 1   1   1 1 0
1 1 0  1 1 1 0   1   0 0 1   1   1 1 0
1 1 0  1 0 1 1   1   1 0 0   1   1 1 0
1 1 0  0 0 0 0   0   0 0 0   1   1 1 0
0 1 1  1 1 1 1   1   1 1 1   1   0 1 1
0 1 1  1 1 1 0   1   0 0 1   1   0 1 1
0 1 1  1 0 1 1   1   1 0 0   1   0 1 1
0 1 1  0 0 0 0   0   0 0 0   1   0 1 1
0 0 0  0 1 1 1   0   1 1 1   1   0 0 0
0 0 0  0 1 1 0   1   0 0 1   0   0 0 0
0 0 0  0 0 1 1   1   1 0 0   0   0 0 0
0 0 0  0 0 0 0   1   0 0 0   0   0 0 0
              ⇑
       NOT EQUIVALENT
```

4.1.B.(111-113)

11.   /∴ ~ (M ∨ D) • B

1)   (M ∨ B) • (M ⊃ D) ✓   Pr
2)   ~ D   Pr
3)   ~ [~ (M ∨ D) • B] ✓   AP
4)   M ∨ B ✓   1, C
5)   M ⊃ D ✓   1, C

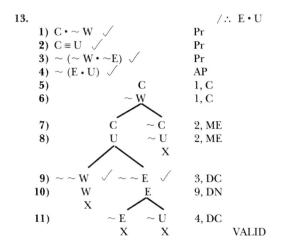

6)   ~ M   D   5, MI
                        X
7)   M   B   4, ID
         X
8) ~ ~ (M ∨ D) ✓   ~ B   3, DC
9)   M ∨ D ✓   X   8, DN

10) M   D   9, ID
      X   X   VALID

13.   /∴ E • U

1) C • ~ W ✓   Pr
2) C ≡ U ✓   Pr
3) ~ (~ W • ~E) ✓   Pr
4) ~ (E • U) ✓   AP
5)   C   1, C
6)   ~ W   1, C

7)   C   ~ C   2, ME
8)   U   ~ U   2, ME
                       X
9) ~ ~ W ✓ ~ ~ E ✓   3, DC
10)   W   E   9, DN
        X
11)   ~ E   ~ U   4, DC
              X   X   VALID

17.   /∴ W Δ H

1) ~ (W ∨ H) ⊃ S ✓   Pr
2) ~ S ⊃ (W ⊃ ~ H) ✓   Pr
3) ~ S   Pr
4)   ~ (W Δ H) ✓   AP

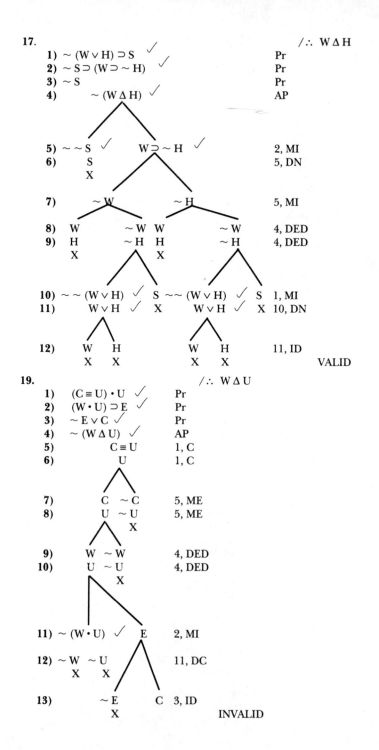

5) ~ ~ S ✓   W ⊃ ~ H ✓   2, MI
6)   S   5, DN
       X

7)   ~ W   ~ H   5, MI

8) W   ~ W W   ~ W   4, DED
9) H   ~ H H   ~ H   4, DED
    X

10) ~ ~ (W ∨ H) ✓ S ~ ~ (W ∨ H) ✓ S   1, MI
11)   W ∨ H ✓   X   W ∨ H ✓   X   10, DN

12)   W   H   W   H   11, ID
       X   X   X   X   VALID

19.   /∴ W Δ U

1)   (C ≡ U) • U ✓   Pr
2)   (W • U) ⊃ E ✓   Pr
3)   ~ E ∨ C ✓   Pr
4)   ~ (W Δ U) ✓   AP
5)   C ≡ U   1, C
6)   U   1, C

7)   C   ~ C   5, ME
8)   U   ~ U   5, ME
                  X

9)   W   ~ W   4, DED
10)   U   ~ U   4, DED
              X

11) ~ (W • U) ✓   E   2, MI

12) ~ W   ~ U   11, DC
     X   X

13)   ~ E   C   3, ID
            X   INVALID

II-16

11.   /∴ D

1) (D ⊃ I) • (D ⊃ R) ✓   Pr
2) ~ (~ R ∨ ~ I) ✓   Pr
3)   ~ ~ R ✓   2, DID
4)   ~ ~ I ✓   2, DID
5)   R   3, DN
6)   I   4, DN
7)   D ⊃ I ✓   1, C
8)   D ⊃ R ✓   1, C

9)   ~ D   I   7, MI

10) ~ D   R ~ D   R   8, MI

                        CONSISTENT

13.   /∴ F ≡ G

1) L ≡ T ✓   Pr
2) (T ⊃ F) • (F ⊃ G) ✓   Pr
3) ~ L ∨ G ✓   Pr
4)   T ⊃ F ✓   2, C
5)   F ⊃ G ✓   2, C

6)   L   ~ L   1, ME
7)   T   ~ T   1, ME

8) ~ L G   ~ L   G   3, ID
     X

9) ~ T F ~ T   F ~ T   F   4, MI
     X

10) ~ F G ~ F G ~ F G ~ F G ~ F G   5, MI
     X   X   X

                        CONSISTENT

17.   /∴ N ≡ L

1)   C ⊃ (L Δ ~ N) ✓   Pr
2)   N ⊃ (C ⊃ L) ✓   Pr
3)   ~ (C ∨ ~ N) ✓   Pr
4)   ~ C   3, DID
5)   ~ ~ N ✓   3, DID
6)   N   5, DN

7) ~ N   C ⊃ L ✓   2, MI
     X

8)   ~ C   L   7, MI

9) ~ C   L Δ ~ N ✓ ~ C L Δ ~ N ✓   1, MI

10)   L   ~ N   L   ~ N   10, ED
12) ~ ~ N ✓ ~ L ~ ~ N ✓ ~ L   10, ED
          X   X
13)   N   N   12, DN

                        CONSISTENT

II-17

19.

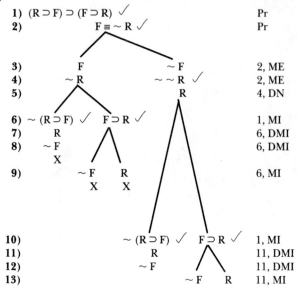

1) (R ⊃ F) ⊃ (F ⊃ R) ✓   Pr
2)   F ≡ ~ R ✓   Pr

3)   F   ~ F   2, ME
4)   ~ R   ~ ~ R ✓   2, ME
5)   R   4, DN

6) ~ (R ⊃ F) ✓   F ⊃ R ✓   1, MI
7)   R   6, DMI
8)   ~ F   6, DMI
    X
9)   ~ F   R   6, MI
       X   X

10)   ~ (R ⊃ F) ✓   F ⊃ R ✓   1, MI
11)   R   11, DMI
12)   ~ F   11, DMI
13)   ~ F   R   11, MI

                                   CONSISTENT

11.

1)	$[\sim A \supset \sim (P \vee C)] \cdot \sim (A \vee \sim P)$ ✓	——
2)	$\sim A \supset \sim (P \vee C)$ ✓	1, C
3)	$\sim (A \vee \sim P)$ ✓	1, C
4)	$\sim A$	3, DID
5)	$\sim \sim P$ ✓	3, DID
6)	P	5, DN

7)	$\sim \sim A$	$\sim (P \vee C)$ ✓	2, MI
8)	A		7, DN
9)	X	$\sim P$	7, DID
10		$\sim C$	7, DID
		X	CONTRADICTORY

13-a.

1) $[(A \cdot C) \vee (C \cdot B)] \supset [C \cdot (B \vee A)]$ ✓ ——

2)	$\sim [(A \cdot C) \vee (C \cdot B)]$ ✓	$C \cdot (B \vee A)$ ✓	1, MI
3)	$\sim (A \cdot C)$ ✓		2, DC
4)	$\sim (C \cdot B)$ ✓		2, DC

5)	$\sim A$	$\sim C$	3, ID

6)	$\sim C$	$\sim B$	$\sim C$	$\sim B$	5, ID

7)		C	2, C
8)		$B \vee A$ ✓	2, C
9)		B A	7, ID

13-b.

1)	$\sim \{[(A \cdot C) \vee (C \cdot B)] \supset [C \cdot (B \vee A)]\}$ ✓	——
2)	$(A \cdot C) \vee (C \cdot B)$ ✓	1, DMI
3)	$\sim [C \cdot (B \vee A)]$ ✓	1, DMI

4)	$\sim C$	$\sim (B \vee A)$ ✓	3, DC
5)		$\sim B$	4, DID
6)		$\sim A$	4, DID

7)	$A \cdot B$ ✓	$C \cdot B$ ✓	$A \cdot B$ ✓	$C \cdot B$ ✓	2, ID
8)	A	C	A	C	7, C
9)	B	B	B	B	7, C
	X	X	X		CONTINGENT

17-a.

  1) $\qquad\qquad (P \equiv F) \equiv (\sim F \,\Delta\, P)$ $\qquad\qquad\qquad$ ——

  2) $\qquad P \equiv F \qquad\qquad \sim (P \equiv F) \qquad\qquad$ 1, ME
  3) $\qquad \sim F \,\Delta\, P \qquad\qquad \sim (\sim F \,\Delta\, P) \qquad$ 1, ME

  4) $\qquad P \qquad\qquad \sim P \qquad\qquad\qquad$ 2, ME
  5) $\qquad F \qquad\qquad \sim F \qquad\qquad\qquad$ 2, ME

  6) $\sim F \qquad P \qquad \sim F \qquad P \qquad\qquad$ 3, ED
  7) $\sim P \sim \sim F \qquad \sim P \sim \sim F \qquad\qquad$ 3, ED
  8) $\quad X \qquad F \qquad\qquad F \qquad\qquad\qquad$ 7, DN
$\qquad\qquad\qquad\qquad\qquad\qquad X$
  9) $\qquad\qquad\qquad\quad P \qquad\qquad\quad F \qquad$ 2, DME
 10) $\qquad\qquad\qquad \sim F \qquad\qquad \sim P \qquad$ 2, DME

 11) $\qquad\qquad \sim F \sim \sim F \qquad \sim F \sim \sim F \qquad$ 3, DED
 12) $\qquad\qquad P \quad \sim P \qquad P \quad \sim P \qquad$ 3, DED
 13) $\qquad\qquad\qquad X \qquad\quad X$
 14) $\qquad\qquad\qquad\qquad\qquad\qquad F \qquad$ 11, DN

17-b.

  1) $\qquad\qquad \sim [(P \equiv F) \equiv (\sim F \,\Delta\, P)]$ $\qquad\qquad$ ——

  2) $\qquad P \equiv F \qquad\qquad\qquad \sim F \,\Delta\, P \qquad$ 1, DME
  3) $\qquad \sim (\sim F \,\Delta\, P) \qquad\qquad \sim (P \equiv F) \qquad$ 1, DME

  4) $\qquad P \qquad\qquad \sim P \qquad\qquad\qquad$ 2, ME
  5) $\qquad F \qquad\qquad \sim F \qquad\qquad\qquad$ 2, ME

  6) $\sim F \sim \sim F \qquad \sim F \sim \sim F \qquad\qquad$ 3, DED
  7) $P \quad \sim P \qquad P \quad \sim P \qquad\qquad$ 3, DED
  8) $\quad X \qquad X \qquad X \qquad F \qquad\qquad$ 6, DN
  9) $\qquad\qquad\qquad\quad X \quad \sim F \qquad\quad P \qquad$ 2, ED
 10) $\qquad\qquad\qquad\qquad \sim P \qquad \sim \sim F \qquad$ 2, ED
 11) $\qquad\qquad\qquad\qquad\qquad\qquad F \qquad$ 10, DN

 12) $\qquad\qquad\qquad\quad P \quad F \quad P \quad\; F \qquad$ 3, DME
 13) $\qquad\qquad\qquad \sim F \; \sim P \sim F \; \sim P \qquad$ 3, DME
$\qquad\qquad\qquad\qquad\quad X \quad\; X \quad\; X \quad\; X \qquad$ TAUTOLOGICAL

19.

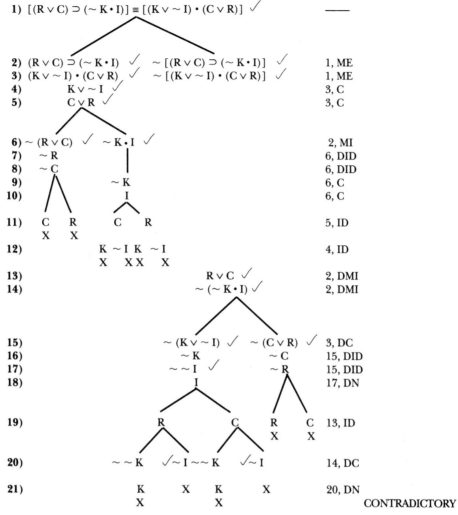

1) $[(R \vee C) \supset (\sim K \cdot I)] \equiv [(K \vee \sim I) \cdot (C \vee R)]$ ✓   ——

2) $(R \vee C) \supset (\sim K \cdot I)$ ✓ $\sim [(R \vee C) \supset (\sim K \cdot I)]$ ✓   1, ME

3) $(K \vee \sim I) \cdot (C \vee R)$ ✓ $\sim [(K \vee \sim I) \cdot (C \vee R)]$ ✓   1, ME

4) $K \vee \sim I$ ✓   3, C

5) $C \vee R$ ✓   3, C

6) $\sim (R \vee C)$ ✓ $\sim K \cdot I$ ✓   2, MI

7) $\sim R$ 6, DID

8) $\sim C$ 6, DID

9) $\sim K$ 6, C

10) I 6, C

11)   C   R   C   R   5, ID
     X   X

12)   K $\sim$I K $\sim$I   4, ID
     X   X X   X

13) $R \vee C$ ✓   2, DMI

14) $\sim (\sim K \cdot I)$ ✓   2, DMI

15) $\sim (K \vee \sim I)$ ✓ $\sim (C \vee R)$ ✓   3, DC

16) $\sim K$ $\sim C$ 15, DID

17) $\sim \sim I$ ✓ $\sim R$ 15, DID

18) I 17, DN

19)   R   C   R   C   13, ID
                    X   X

20) $\sim \sim K$ ✓$\sim$I $\sim \sim K$ ✓$\sim$I   14, DC

21)   K   X   K   X   20, DN
     X   X

                                          CONTRADICTORY

4.4.(125-126)

11.

    a) (P ⊃ L) ⊃ M
    b) M ⊃ (L ⊃ P)

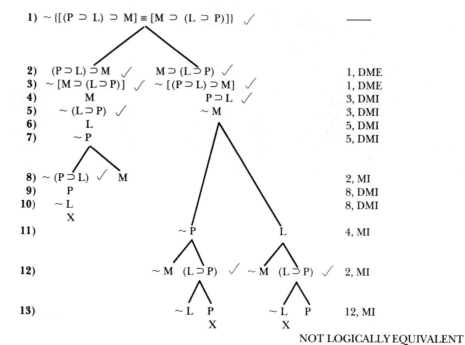

1)   ~{[(P ⊃ L) ⊃ M] ≡ [M ⊃ (L ⊃ P)]} ✓   ——

2)   (P ⊃ L) ⊃ M ✓   M ⊃ (L ⊃ P) ✓   1, DME
3)   ~[M ⊃ (L ⊃ P)] ✓   ~[(P ⊃ L) ⊃ M] ✓   1, DME
4)   M   P ⊃ L ✓   3, DMI
5)   ~(L ⊃ P) ✓   ~M   3, DMI
6)   L   5, DMI
7)   ~P   5, DMI

8) ~(P ⊃ L) ✓   M   2, MI
9)   P   8, DMI
10)   ~L   8, DMI
        X
11)   ~P   L   4, MI

12)   ~M (L ⊃ P) ✓ ~M (L ⊃ P) ✓ 2, MI

13)   ~L P   ~L P   12, MI
            X   X

                              NOT LOGICALLY EQUIVALENT

13.

    a) M ⊃ (F · A)
    b) (M · F) ⊃ A

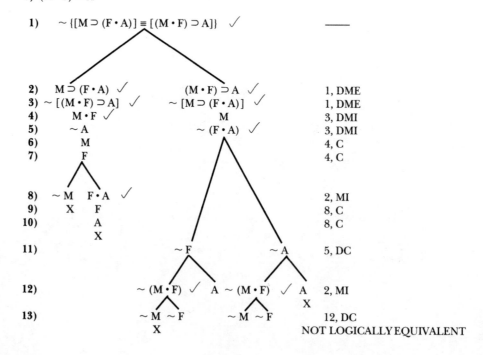

1)   ~{[M ⊃ (F · A)] ≡ [(M · F) ⊃ A]} ✓   ——

2)   M ⊃ (F · A) ✓   (M · F) ⊃ A ✓   1, DME
3) ~[(M · F) ⊃ A] ✓   ~[M ⊃ (F · A)] ✓ 1, DME
4)   M · F ✓   M   3, DMI
5)   ~A   ~(F · A) ✓   3, DMI
6)   M   4, C
7)   F   4, C

8) ~M F · A ✓   2, MI
9)   X   F   8, C
10)   A   8, C
       X
11)   ~F   ~A   5, DC

12)   ~(M · F) ✓ A ~(M · F) ✓ A 2, MI
                          X
13)   ~M ~F   ~M ~F   12, DC
       X

                          NOT LOGICALLY EQUIVALENT

17.

a) $(R \lor H) \cdot \sim R$

b) $(\sim H \supset \sim R) \cdot \sim R$

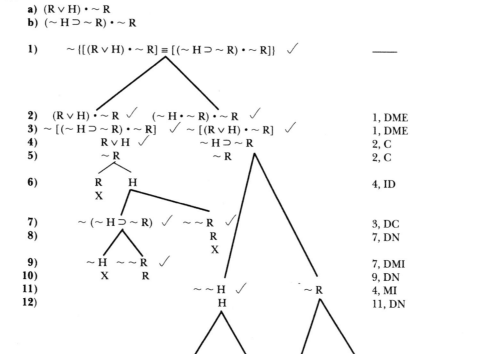

1) $\sim \{[(R \lor H) \cdot \sim R] \equiv [(\sim H \supset \sim R) \cdot \sim R]\}$ ✓ ——

2) $(R \lor H) \cdot \sim R$ ✓ $(\sim H \cdot \sim R) \cdot \sim R$ ✓ 1, DME

3) $\sim [(\sim H \supset \sim R) \cdot \sim R]$ ✓ $\sim [(R \lor H) \cdot \sim R]$ ✓ 1, DME

4) $R \lor H$ ✓ $\sim H \supset \sim R$ 2, C

5) $\sim R$ $\sim R$ 2, C

6) R H 4, ID
X

7) $\sim (\sim H \supset \sim R)$ ✓ $\sim \sim R$ ✓ 3, DC

8) R 7, DN
X

9) $\sim H$ $\sim \sim R$ ✓ 7, DMI

10) X R 9, DN

11) $\sim \sim H$ ✓ $\sim R$ 4, MI

12) H 11, DN

13) $\sim (R \lor H)$ $\sim R$ $\sim (R \lor H)$ ✓ $\sim R$ 3, DC

14) $\sim R$ ✓ $\sim R$ ✓ 13, DID

15) $\sim H$ $\sim H$ 13, DID
X

NOT LOGICALLY EQUIVALENT

19.

a) $(D \cdot C) \vee \sim (F \vee W)$
b) $[F \supset (C \cdot D)] \cdot [W \supset (D \cdot C)]$

1) $\sim ([(D \cdot C) \vee \sim (F \vee W)] \equiv \{[F \supset (C \cdot D)] \cdot [W \supset (D \cdot C)]\}$ ✓ ———

2) $(D \cdot C) \vee \sim (F \vee W)$ ✓ $[F \supset (C \cdot D)] \cdot [W \supset (D \cdot C)]$ ✓   1, DME

3) $\sim \{[F \supset (C \cdot D)] \cdot [W \supset (D \supset C)]\}$ ✓ $\sim [(D \cdot C) \vee \sim (F \vee W)]$ ✓   1, DME

4) $F \supset (C \cdot D)$ ✓   2, C

5) $W \supset (D \cdot C)$ ✓   2, C

6) $\sim (D \cdot C)$ ✓   3, DID

7) $\sim (F \vee W)$ ✓   3, DID

8) $\sim F$ 7, DID

9) $\sim W$ 7, DID

10) $\sim D$ $\sim C$ 6, DC

11) $\sim F \quad C \cdot D$ ✓ $\sim F \quad C \cdot D$ ✓   4, MI

12) $\qquad C$ $\qquad C$ 11, C

13) $\qquad D$ $\qquad D$ 11, C

   $\qquad X$ $\qquad X$

14) $W \quad D \cdot C$ ✓ $W \quad D \cdot C$ ✓   5, MI

15) $X \quad\; D$ $X \quad\; D$ 14, C

16) $\qquad C$ $\qquad C$ 14, C

   $\qquad X$ $\qquad X$

17) $D \cdot C$ ✓ $\sim (F \vee W)$ ✓   2, ID

18) D 17, C

19) C 17, C

20) $\sim [F \supset (C \cdot D)]$ ✓ $\sim [W \supset (D \cdot C)]$ ✓   3, DC

21) $F \quad \sim (C \cdot D)$ ✓ $W \quad \sim (D \cdot C)$ ✓   20, DMI

22) $\sim C \quad \sim D$ $\sim D \quad \sim C$ 21, DC

   $X \qquad X$ $X \qquad\; X$

   $\sim F$ 17, DID

23) $\sim W$ 17, DID

24) $\sim [F \supset (C \cdot D)]$ ✓ $\sim [W \supset (D \cdot C)]$ ✓   3, DC

25) $F \quad \sim (C \cdot D)$ ✓ $W \quad \sim (D \cdot C)$ ✓   24, DMI

   X X

26) $\sim C \quad \sim D$ $\sim D \quad \sim C$ 25, DC

NOT LOGICALLY EQUIVALENT

Chapter 5
5.2.C.(141)

9.   /∴ (S ⊃ M) • (C • L)

1) (S ⊃ M) • C   Pr
2) N • L   Pr
3) S ⊃ M   1, Simp
4) C • (S ⊃ M)   1, Com
5) C   4, Simp
6) L • N   2, Com
7) L   6, Simp
8) C • L   5, 7, Conj
9) /∴ (S ⊃ M) • (C • L) 3, 8, Conj

5.3.A.(147-149)   5.3.B.(150)

9.

1) Pr
2) Pr
3) Pr
4) Pr
5) 1, Simp
6) 1, Com
7) 6, Simp
8) 4, Simp
9) 4, Com
10) 9, Simp
11) 2, 5, DS
12) 11, 8, DS
13) 12, Add
14) 13, Com
15) 3, 10, DS
16) 15, 7, DS
17) 16, Add
18) /∴ 14, 17, Conj

9.   /∴ (B ∨ E) • (C ∨ F)

1) (A ∨ B) • (C ∨ D)   Pr
2) ~ A • ~ D   Pr
3) A ∨ B   1, Simp
4) (C ∨ D) • (A ∨ B)   1, Com
5) C ∨ D   4, Simp
6) ~ A   2, Simp
7) ~ D • ~ A   2, Com
8) ~ D   7, Simp
9) B   3, 6, DS
10) B ∨ E   9, Add
11) D ∨ C   5, Com
12) C   11, 8, DS
13) C ∨ F   12, Add
14) /∴ (B ∨ E) • (C ∨ F) 10, 13, Conj

5.3.C.(150-151)

9.   /∴ (E ⊃ ~ P) ∨ (A • S)

1)	(~ T • C) • (~ E • S)	Pr
2)	~ X ∨ T	Pr
3)	E ∨ (A ∨ X)	Pr
4)	~ T • C	1, Simp
5)	~ T	4, Simp
6)	(~ E • S) • (~ T • C)	1, Com
7)	~ E • S	6, Simp
8)	~ E	7, Simp
9)	S • ~ E	7, Com
10)	S	9, Simp
11)	A ∨ X	3, 8, DS
12)	X ∨ A	11, Com
13)	T ∨ ~ X	2, Com
14)	~ X	13, 5, DS
15)	A	12, 14, DS
16)	A • S	15, 10, Conj
17)	(A • S) ∨ (E ⊃ ~ P)	16, Add
18)	/∴ (E ⊃ ~ P) ∨ (A • S)	17, Com

5.4.B.(156-158)

9.

1)	Pr
2)	Pr
3)	Pr
4)	2, Simp
5)	2, Com
6)	5, Simp
7)	3, Simp
8)	3, Com
9)	8, Simp
10)	1, 4, MP
11)	7, 4, DS
12)	11, 10, DS
13)	6, 12, Conj
14)	9, 13, MP
15)	14, Add
16)	/∴ 15, Com

5.4.C.(158-159)

9.   /∴ ~ G

1)	(A • B) • (C • D)	Pr
2)	[(B • D) ⊃ E] • [(A • C) ⊃ F]	Pr
3)	(E • F) ⊃ ~ G	Pr
4)	A • B	1, Simp
5)	A	4, Simp
6)	B • A	4, Com
7)	B	6, Simp
8)	(C • D) • (A • B)	1, Com
9)	C • D	8, Simp
10)	C	9, Simp
11)	D • C	9, Com
12)	D	11, Simp
13)	(B • D) ⊃ E	2, Simp
14)	[(A • C) ⊃ F] • [(B • D) ⊃ E]	2, Com
15)	(A • C) ⊃ F	14, Simp
16)	B • D	7, 12, Conj
17)	E	13, 16, MP
18)	A • C	5, 10, Conj
19)	F	15, 18, MP
20)	E • F	17, 19, Conj
21)	/∴ ~G	3, 20, MP

5.4.D.(159-161)

9.   / ∴   ~ (G • C) ∨ (C • G)

    1) ~ (~ T ∨ ~ R) ⊃ C   Pr

    2) (~ R ∨ C) ⊃ M   Pr

    3) ~ (~ T ∨ ~ R) ∨ (A ∨ ~ D)   Pr

    4) ~ (A ∨ ~ D)   Pr

    5) (M ∨ ~ A) ⊃ G   Pr

    6) (A ∨ ~ D) ∨ ~ (~ T ∨ ~ R)   3, Com

    7) ~ (~ T ∨ ~ R)   6, 4, DS

    8) C   1, 7, MP

    9) C ∨ ~ R   8, Add

    10) ~ R ∨ C   9, Com

    11) M   2, 10, MP

    12) M ∨ ~ A   11, Add

    13) G   5, 12, MP

    14) C • G   8, 13, Conj

    15) (C • G) ∨ ~ (G • C)   14, Add

    16) / ∴   ~ (G • C) ∨ (C • G)   15, Com

5.5.B.(165-168)

9.

    1) Pr

    2) Pr

    3) Pr

    4) Pr

    5) Pr

    6) Pr

    7) Pr

    8) 7, Simp

    9) 7, Com

    10) 9, Simp

    11) 3, 8, MP

    12) 2, 11, MP

    13) 6, Com

    14) 13, 10, DS

    15) 5, 14, MT

    16) 4, 15, MP

    17) 1, 16, MP

    18) / ∴   17, 12, HS

9. /∴ G ∨ E

1)	[A ∨ (B • ~ C)] • ~ A	Pr
2)	[B ⊃ (D ⊃ E)] • [~ C ⊃ (F ⊃ G)]	Pr
3)	(~ A ∨ F) ⊃ (F ∨ D)	Pr
4)	A ∨ (B • ~ C)	1, Simp
5)	~ A • [A ∨ (B • ~ C)]	1, Com
6)	~ A	5, Simp
7)	B ⊃ (D ⊃ E)	2, Simp
8)	[~ C ⊃ (F ⊃ G)] • [B ⊃ (D ⊃ E)]	2, Com
9)	~ C ⊃ (F ⊃ G)	8, Simp
10)	B • ~ C	4, 6, DS
11)	B	10, Simp
12)	~ C • B	10, Com
13)	~ C	12, Simp
14)	F ⊃ G	9, 13, MP
15)	D ⊃ E	7, 11, MP
16)	~ A ∨ F	6, Add
17)	F ∨ D	3, 16, MP
18)	/∴ G ∨ E	14, 15, 17, CD

5.5.D.(169-170)

9. /∴ (R ∨ U) • (G ∨ B

1)	(C ⊃ R) • (A ⊃ U)
2)	(C ∨ A) • (E ∨ ~ S)
3)	(E ⊃ G) • (~ S ⊃ B)
4)	C ⊃ R
5)	(A ⊃ U) • (C ⊃ R)
6)	A ⊃ U
7)	C ∨ A
8)	(E ∨ ~ S) • (C ∨ A)
9)	E ∨ ~ S
10)	E ⊃ G
11)	(~ S ⊃ B) • (E ⊃ G)
12)	~ S ⊃ B
13)	R ∨ U
14)	G ∨ B
15)	/∴ (R ∨ U) • (G ∨ B)

Chapter 6

6.1.A.(181-183)

9.

1)	Pr
2)	Pr
3)	Pr
4)	Pr
5)	2, Simp
6)	2, Com
7)	6, Simp
8)	4, Simp
9)	4, Com
10)	9, Simp
11)	10, 7, HS
12)	3, 11, MP
13)	12, Com
14)	13, Assoc
15)	1, 14, MP
16)	5, 8, 15, CD
17)	16, Add
18)	17, Assoc
19)	18, Com
20)	/∴ 19, Assoc

6.1.B. (183-184)

9.   /∴ E ⊃ H

  1) ~ (A ≡ B) • ~ (B ≡ C)   Pr
  2) ~ G ⊃ (E ⊃ F)   Pr
  3) G ⊃ (B ≡ A)   Pr
  4) I ⊃ (C ≡ B)   Pr
  5) ~ I ⊃ (F ⊃ H)   Pr
  6) ~ (A ≡ B)   1, Simp
  7) ~ (B ≡ C) • ~ (A ≡ B)   1, Com
  8) ~ (B ≡ C)   7, Simp
  9) ~ (B ≡ A)   6, Com
  10) ~ G   3, 9, MT
  11) E ⊃ F   2, 10, MP
  12) ~ (C ≡ B)   8, Com
  13) ~ I   4, 12, MT
  14) F ⊃ H   5, 13, MP
  15) /∴ E ⊃ H   11, 14, HS

6.1.C. (184-185)

9.   /∴ P ∨ F

  1) (F ∨ T) ∨ (C ∨ D)   Pr
  2) ~ (C ∨ T) • (~ T ⊃ F)   Pr
  3) (F ∨ D) ⊃ (S ⊃ P)   Pr
  4) (~ T ∨ C) ∨ (T ∨ S)   Pr
  5) ~ (C ∨ T)   2, Simp
  6) (~ T ⊃ F) • ~ (C ∨ T)   2, Com
  7) ~ T ⊃ F   6, Simp
  8) F ∨ [T ∨ (C ∨ D)]   1, Assoc
  9) F ∨ [(T ∨ C) ∨ D]   8, Assoc
  10) F ∨ [D ∨ (T ∨ C)]   9, Com
  11) F ∨ [D ∨ (C ∨ T)]   10, Com
  12) (F ∨ D) ∨ (C ∨ T)   11, Assoc
  13) (C ∨ T) ∨ (F ∨ D)   12, Com
  14) F ∨ D   13, 5, DS
  15) S ⊃ P   3, 14, MP
  16) ~ T ∨ [C ∨ (T ∨ S)]   4, Assoc
  17) ~ T ∨ [(C ∨ T) ∨ S]   16, Assoc
  18) [(C ∨ T) ∨ S] ∨ ~ T   17, Com
  19) (C ∨ T) ∨ (S ∨ ~ T)   18, Assoc
  20) S ∨ ~ T   19, 5, DS
  21) /∴ P ∨ F   15, 7, 20, CD

6.2.A. (190-193)

9.

1) Pr

2) Pr

3) Pr

4) 1, Simp

5) 2, Com

6) 5, Simp

7) 4, Trans

8) 7, DN

9) 8, 6, HS

10) 1, Com

11) 10, Simp

12) 11, Trans

13) 12, DN

14) 2, Simp

15) 14, 13, HS

16) 15, 9, 3, CD

17) /∴ 16, Com

6.2.B. (193-194)

9.   /∴ ~ G ∨ D

1) (A ⊃ G) • ~ B   Pr

2) (G ⊃ D) • (~ E ⊃ A)   Pr

3) ~ D ∨ (B ∨ ~ E)   Pr

4) A ⊃ G   1, Simp

5) ~ B • (A ⊃ G)   1, Com

6) ~ B   5, Simp

7) G ⊃ D   2, Simp

8) (~ E ⊃ A) • (G ⊃ D)   2, Com

9) ~ E ⊃ A   8, Simp

10) A ⊃ D   4, 7, HS

11) ~ E ⊃ D   9, 10, HS

12) (B ∨ ~ E) ∨ ~ D   3, Com

13) B ∨ (~ E ∨ ~ D)   12, Com

14) ~ E ∨ ~ D   13, 6, DS

15) ~ D ⊃ ~ G   7, Trans

16) D ∨ ~ G   11, 15, 14, CD

17) /∴ ~ G ∨ D   16, Com

6.2.C.(194-195)

9. $/\therefore\ U \cdot H$

    1) $\sim H \supset \sim (L \supset F)$ Pr
    2) $L \vee B$ Pr
    3) $(\sim B \supset \sim L) \cdot (\sim F \supset \sim B)$ Pr
    4) $F \supset R$ Pr
    5) $(F \vee R) \supset U$ Pr
    6) $\sim B \supset \sim L$ 3, Simp
    7) $(\sim F \supset \sim B) \cdot (\sim B \supset \sim L)$ 3, Com
    8) $\sim F \supset \sim B$ 7, Simp
    9) $\sim F \supset \sim L$ 8, 6, HS
    10) $L \supset F$ 9, Trans
    11) $\sim \sim (L \supset F)$ 10, DN
    12) $\sim \sim H$ 1, 11, MT
    13) H 12, DN
    14) $B \supset F$ 8, Trans
    15) $L \supset R$ 10, 4, HS
    16) $R \vee F$ 15, 14, 2, CD
    17) $F \vee R$ 16, Com
    18) U 5, 17, MP
    19) $/\therefore\ U \cdot H$ 18, 13, Conj

6.3.B.(203-204)

9. $/\therefore\ \sim (C \cdot E)$

    1) $\sim A \vee [\sim D \vee (\sim F \cdot \sim C)]$ Pr
    2) $B \cdot (E \supset A)$ Pr
    3) $(E \cdot D) \vee \sim B$ Pr
    4) B 2, Simp
    5) $(E \supset A) \cdot B$ 2, Com
    6) $E \supset A$ 5, Simp
    7) $\sim B \vee (E \cdot D)$ 3, Com
    8) $\sim \sim B$ 4, DN
    9) $E \cdot D$ 7, 8, DS
    10) E 9, Simp
    11) $D \cdot E$ 9, Com
    12) D 11, Simp
    13) A 6, 10, MP
    14) $\sim \sim A$ 13, DN
    15) $\sim D \vee (\sim F \cdot \sim C)$ 1, 14, DS
    16) $\sim \sim D$ 12, DN
    17) $\sim F \cdot \sim C$ 15, 16, DS
    18) $\sim C \cdot \sim F$ 17, Com
    19) $\sim C$ 18, Simp
    20) $\sim C \vee \sim E$ 19, Add
    21) $/\therefore\ \sim (C \cdot E)$ 20, DeM

6.3.A.(200-203)

9.

    1) Pr
    2) Pr
    3) 1, Com
    4) 3, Dist
    5) 4, Simp
    6) 5, Com
    7) 6, Dist
    8) 7, Simp
    9) 8, Com
    10) 9, DN
    11) 10, DeM
    12) 11, DN
    13) 2, 12, MT
    14) 13, DN
    15) 14, Dist
    16) 15, Simp
    17) 16, Com
    18) 17, Dist
    19) 18, Simp
    20) 19, DN
    21) $/\therefore\ $ 20, DeM

6.3.C. (204-205)

9. /∴ ~ (I • ~ A) • ~ (~ I • A)

1)	S ⊃ ~ (A • ~ I)	Pr
2)	~ [~ (A ∨ P) • I]	Pr
3)	S • ~ P	Pr
4)	S	3, Simp
5)	~ P • S	3, Com
6)	~ P	5, Simp
7)	~ (A • ~ I)	1, 4, MP
8)	~ (~ I • A)	7, Com
9)	~ (~ A ∨ P) ∨ ~ I	2, DeM
10)	(~ ~ A • ~ P) ∨ ~ I	9, DeM
11)	(A • ~ P) ∨ ~ I	10, DN
12)	~ I ∨ (A • ~ P)	11, Com
13)	(~ I ∨ A) • (~ I ∨ ~ P)	12, Dist
14)	~ I ∨ A	13, Simp
15)	~ I ∨ ~ ~ A	14, DN
16)	~ (I • ~ A)	15, DeM
17)	/∴ ~ (I • ~ A) • ~ (~ I • A)	16, 8, Conj

6.4.A. (209-212)

9.

1)	Pr
2)	Pr
3)	1, Simp
4)	1, Com
5)	4, Simp
6)	5, Trans
7)	6, Exp
8)	7, Com
9)	8, Exp
10)	3, Exp
11)	10, 9, HS
12)	11, Exp
13)	12, Com
14)	13, Exp
15)	2, 14, HS
16)	15, Exp
17)	16, Assoc
18)	17, Com

6.4.B.(212)

9.   /∴ ∴ (A • B) ⊃ (C ⊃ D)

  1) C ⊃ (E ⊃ D)   Pr
  2) E ∨ F   Pr
  3) (F • B) ⊃ ~ A   Pr
  4) C ⊃ (~ D ⊃ ~ E)   1, Trans
  5) (C • ~ D) ⊃ ~ E   4, Exp
  6) ~ ~ E ∨ F   2, DN
  7) ~ E ⊃ F   6, Impl
  8) (C • ~ D) ⊃ F   5, 7, HS
  9) F ⊃ (B ⊃ ~ A)   3, Exp
  10) (C • ~ D) ⊃ (B ⊃ ~ A) 8, 9, HS
  11) (C • ~ D) ⊃ (~ ~ A ⊃ ~ B) 10, Trans
  12) (C • ~ D) ⊃ (A ⊃ ~ B) 11, DN
  13) (C • ~ D) ⊃ (~ A ∨ ~ B) 12, Impl
  14) (C • ~ D) ⊃ ~ (A • B) 13, DeM
  15) ~ ~ (A • B) ⊃ ~ (C • ~ D) 14, Trans
  16) (A • B) ⊃ ~ (C • ~ D) 15, DN
  17) (A • B) ⊃ (~ C ∨ ~ ~ D) 16, DeM
  18) (A • B) ⊃ (C ⊃ ~ ~ D) 17, Impl
  19) /∴ (A • B) ⊃ (C ⊃ D) 18, DN

6.4.C.(213-214)

9.   /∴ (K • I) ⊃ F

  1) (K ∨ F) ⊃ (S • F)   Pr
  2) ~ (K ∨ F) ∨ (S • F)   1, Impl
  3) (~ K • ~ F) ∨ (S • F)   2, DeM
  4) (~ K • ~ F) ∨ (F • S)   3, Com
  5) [(~ K • ~ F) ∨ F] • [(~ K • ~ F) ∨ S] 4, Dist
  6) (~ K • ~ F) ∨ F   5, Simp
  7) F ∨ (~ K • ~ F)   6, Com
  8) (F ∨ ~ K) • (F ∨ ~ F)   7, Dist
  9) F ∨ ~ K   8, Simp
  10) ~ K ∨ F   9, Com
  11) (~ K ∨ F) ∨ ~ I   10, Add
  12) ~ K ∨ (F ∨ ~ I)   11, Assoc
  13) ~ K ∨ (~ I ∨ F)   12, Com
  14) K ⊃ (~ I ∨ F)   13, Impl
  15) K ⊃ (I ⊃ F)   14, Impl
  16) /∴ (K • I) ⊃ F   15, Exp

6.5.A. (219-222)

9.

1) Pr

2) Pr

3) 2, Simp

4) 2, Com

5) 4, Simp

6) 5, DeM

7) 6, DN

8) 7, Impl

9) 1, 3, DS

10) 9, Dist

11) 10, Simp

12) 11, Com

13) 12, Dist

14) 13, Simp

15) 14, Com

16) 15, Impl

17) 16, 8, Conj

18) /∴ 17, Equiv

6.5.B. (222)

9.   /∴ B

1) A ≡ B   Pr

2) C Δ ~ B   Pr

3) ~ A ⊃ (~ D ⊃ C)   Pr

4) ~ D   Pr

5) (A ⊃ B) • (B ⊃ A)   1, Equiv

6) (C ∨ ~ B) • (~ C ∨ ~ ~ B)   2, Equiv

7) A ⊃ B   5, Simp

8) (~ C ∨ ~ ~ B) • (C ∨ ~ B)   6, Com

9) ~ C ∨ ~ ~ B   8, Simp

10) ~ C ∨ B   9, DN

11) C ⊃ B   10, Impl

12) (~ A • ~ D) ⊃ C   3, Exp

13) (~ D • ~ A) ⊃ C   12, Com

14) ~ D ⊃ (~ A ⊃ C)   13, Exp

15) ~ A ⊃ C   14, 4, MP

16) ~ ~ A ∨ C   15, Impl

17) A ∨ C   16, DN

18) B ∨ B   7, 11, 17, CD

19) /∴ B   18, Taut

6.5.C. (223-224)

9.   /∴ A ⊃ (E Δ ∼ F)

1) (F • A) ⊃ E   Pr
2) (A • E) ⊃ (D • F)   Pr
3) (A • E) ⊃ (F • D)   2, Com
4) ∼ (A • E) ∨ (F • D)   3, Impl
5) [∼ (A • E) ∨ F] • [∼ (A • E)` ∨ D]   4, Dist
6) ∼ (A • E) ∨ F   5, Simp
7) ∼ (F • A) ∨ E   1, Impl
8) (∼ F ∨ ∼ A) ∨ E   7, DeM
9) (∼ A ∨ ∼ F) ∨ E   8, Com
10) ∼ A ∨ (∼ F ∨ E)   9, Assoc
11) ∼ A ∨ (E ∨ ∼ F)   10, Com
12) (∼ A ∨ ∼ E) ∨ F   6, DeM
13) ∼ A ∨ (∼ E ∨ F)   12, Assoc
14) ∼ A ∨ (∼ E ∨ ∼ ∼ F)   13, DN
15) [∼ A ∨ (E ∨ ∼ F)] • [∼ A ∨ (∼ E ∨ ∼ ∼ F)]   11, 14, Conj
16) ∼ A ∨ [(E ∨ ∼ F) • (∼ E ∨ ∼ ∼ F)]   15, Dist
17) ∼ A ∨ (E Δ ∼ F)   16, Equiv
18) /∴ A ⊃ (E Δ ∼ F)   17, Impl

II-35

7.1.B.(234-235)

9. $/ \therefore \sim (A \cdot \sim E)$

1)	$(\sim A \supset \sim B) \supset (C \cdot D)$	Pr
2)	$D \supset (C \cdot E)$	Pr
3)	A	CP, $/ \therefore$ E
4)	$\sim \sim A$	3, DN
5)	$\sim \sim A \vee \sim B$	4, Add
6)	$\sim A \supset \sim B$	5, Impl
7)	$C \cdot D$	1, 6, MP
8)	$D \cdot C$	7, Com
9)	D	8, Simp
10)	$C \cdot E$	2, 9, MP
11)	$E \cdot C$	10, Com
12)	E	11, Simp
13)	$A \supset E$	3 - 12, CP
14)	$\sim A \vee E$	13, Impl
15)	$\sim A \vee \sim \sim E$	14, DN
16)	$/ \therefore \sim (A \cdot \sim E)$	15, DeM

7.1.C. (235-236)

9. /∴ G ⊃ (D ⊃ F)

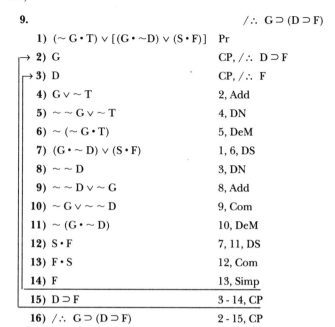

1) (~ G • T) ∨ [(G • ~D) ∨ (S • F)] Pr
2) G CP, /∴ D ⊃ F
3) D CP, /∴ F
4) G ∨ ~ T 2, Add
5) ~ ~ G ∨ ~ T 4, DN
6) ~ (~ G • T) 5, DeM
7) (G • ~ D) ∨ (S • F) 1, 6, DS
8) ~ ~ D 3, DN
9) ~ ~ D ∨ ~ G 8, Add
10) ~ G ∨ ~ ~ D 9, Com
11) ~ (G • ~ D) 10, DeM
12) S • F 7, 11, DS
13) F • S 12, Com
14) F 13, Simp
15) D ⊃ F 3 - 14, CP
16) /∴ G ⊃ (D ⊃ F) 2 - 15, CP

7.2.A. (245)

9. /∴ ~ (~ F • ~ C)

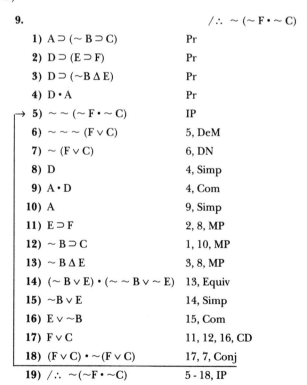

1) A ⊃ (~ B ⊃ C) Pr
2) D ⊃ (E ⊃ F) Pr
3) D ⊃ (~B Δ E) Pr
4) D • A Pr
5) ~ ~ (~ F • ~ C) IP
6) ~ ~ ~ (F ∨ C) 5, DeM
7) ~ (F ∨ C) 6, DN
8) D 4, Simp
9) A • D 4, Com
10) A 9, Simp
11) E ⊃ F 2, 8, MP
12) ~ B ⊃ C 1, 10, MP
13) ~ B Δ E 3, 8, MP
14) (~ B ∨ E) • (~ ~ B ∨ ~ E) 13, Equiv
15) ~B ∨ E 14, Simp
16) E ∨ ~B 15, Com
17) F ∨ C 11, 12, 16, CD
18) (F ∨ C) • ~(F ∨ C) 17, 7, Conj
19) /∴ ~(~F • ~C) 5 - 18, IP

9. /∴ C ⊃ ~ I

1)	(C • D) ⊃ [I ⊃ (L • S)]	Pr
2)	~ (D ⊃ S)	Pr
→ **3)**	~ (C ⊃ ~I)	IP
4)	~ (~ D ∨ S)	2, Impl
5)	~ ~ D • ~ S	4, DeM
6)	D • ~S	5, DN
7)	D	6, Simp
8)	~ S • D	6, Com
9)	~ S	8, Simp
10)	~ (~ C ∨ ~ I)	3, Impl
11)	~ ~ (C • I)	10, DeM
12)	C • I	11, DeM
13)	C	12, Simp
14)	I • C	12, Com
15)	I	14, Simp
16)	C • D	13, 7, Conj
17)	I ⊃ (L • S)	1, 16, MP
18)	L • S	17, 15, MP
19)	S • L	18, Com
20)	S	19, Simp
21	S • ~ S	20, 9, Conj
22)	/∴ C ⊃ ~ I	3 - 21, IP

9. $/\therefore\ B \supset (C \cdot D)$

1)	$(A \cdot B) \supset (A \cdot C)$	Pr
2)	$(A \cdot D) \lor (\sim B \cdot A)$	Pr
3)	$(A \cdot D) \lor (A \cdot \sim B)$	2, Com
4)	$A \cdot (D \lor \sim B)$	3, Dist
5)	A	4, Simp
6)	$(D \lor \sim B) \cdot A$	4, Com
7)	$D \lor \sim B$	6, Simp
8)	$\sim B \lor D$	7, Com
9)	B	CP, $/\therefore\ C \cdot D$
10)	$\sim (C \cdot D)$	IP
11)	$\sim C \lor \sim D$	10, DeM
12)	$A \cdot B$	5, 9, Conj
13)	$A \cdot C$	1, 12, MP
14)	$C \cdot A$	13, Com
15)	C	14, Simp
16)	$\sim \sim C$	15, DN
17)	$\sim D$	11, 16, DS
18)	$\sim \sim B$	9, DN
19)	D	8, 18, DS
20)	$D \cdot \sim D$	19, 17, Conj
21)	$C \cdot D$	10 - 20, IP
22)	$/\therefore\ B \supset (C \cdot D)$	9 - 21, CP

9.   /∴ ~ (~ B • ~ F)

    1) ~ (C • ~ F) • ~ (P • ~ B)   Pr

    2) C ∆ P   Pr

    3) ~ (C • ~ F)   1, Simp

    4) ~ (P • ~ B) • ~ (C • ~ F)   1, Com

    5) ~ (P • ~ B)   4, Simp

    6) (C ∨ P) • (~ C ∨ ~ P)   2, Equiv

    7) C ∨ P   6, Simp

    8) (~ C ∨ ~ P) • (C ∨ P)   6, Com

    9) ~ C ∨ ~ P   8, Simp

  10) ~ C ∨ ~ ~ F   3, DeM

  11) ~ C ∨ F   10, DN

  12) ~ P ∨ ~~B   5, Dem

  13) ~ P ∨ B   12, DN

  14) B ∨ ~ P   13, Com

  15) F ∨ ~ C   11, Com

→ **16)** ~ B   CP, /∴ F

 →**17)** ~ F   IP

  18) ~ C   15, 17, DS

  19) P   7, 18, DS

  20) ~ P   14, 16, DS

  21) P • ~ P   19, 20, Conj

  22) F   17 - 21, IP

  23) ~ B ⊃ F   16 - 22, CP

  24) ~ ~ B ∨ F   23, Impl

  25) ~ ~ B ∨ ~ ~ F   24, DN

  26) /∴ ~ (~ B • ~ F)   25, Dem

9. $/\therefore\ A \equiv C$

1)	$(A \cdot B) \lor (\sim A \cdot \sim B)$	Pr
2)	$(\sim B \supset \sim D) \cdot (\sim A \supset \sim C)$	Pr
3)	$\sim (\sim D \cdot \sim C) \cdot \sim (A \cdot B)$	Pr
4)	$\sim (A \cdot B) \cdot \sim (\sim D \cdot \sim C)$	3, Com
5)	$\sim (A \cdot B)$	4, Simp
6)	$\sim A \cdot \sim B$	1, 5, DS
7)	$(\sim A \supset \sim C) \cdot (\sim B \supset \sim D)$	2, Com
8)	$\sim A \supset \sim C$	7, Simp
9)	$\sim A$	6, Simp
10)	$\sim C$	8, 9, MP
11)	$\sim (\sim D \cdot \sim C)$	3, Simp
12)	$\sim \sim (D \lor C)$	11, DeM
13)	$D \lor C$	12, DN
14)	$C \lor D$	13, Com
15)	D	14, 10, DS
16)	$\sim B \supset \sim D$	2, Simp
17)	$\sim B \cdot \sim A$	6, Com
18)	$\sim B$	17, Simp
19)	$\sim D$	16, 18, MP
20)	$D \cdot \sim D$	15, 19, Conj

9. /∴ F • I

   1) (F • ~ I) ⊃ (I ∨ E)   Pr
   2) E ⊃ ~ (M ∨ V)   Pr
   3) ~ I ∨ ~ (E ∨ V)   Pr
   4) F • V   Pr
   5) V • F   4, Com
   6) V   5, Simp
   7) ~ (E ∨ V) ∨ ~ I   3, Com
   8) V ∨ E   6, Add
   9) E ∨ V   8, Com
   10) ~ ~ (E ∨ V)   9, DN
   11) ~ I   7, 10, DS
   12) V ∨ M   6, Add
   13) M ∨ V   12, Com
   14) ~ ~ (M ∨ V)   13, DN
   15) ~ E   2, 14, MT
   16) ~ I • ~ E   11, 15, Conj
   17) ~ (I ∨ E)   16, DeM
   18) ~ (F • ~ I)   1, 17, MT
   19) ~ F ∨ ~ ~ I   18, DeM
   20) ~ F ∨ I   19, DN
   21) I ∨ ~ F   20, Com
   22) ~ F   21, 11, DS
   23) F • V   4, Com
   24) F   23, Simp
   25) F • ~ F   24, 22, Conj

7.4.A.(256)

9.

→	1) ~{A ≡ [A • (A ∨B)]}	IP
	2) ~ ({A •[A • (A ∨ B)]} ∨ {~ A • ~ [A • (A ∨ B)]})	1, Equiv
	3) ~{A • [A • (A ∨ B)]} • ~ {~ A • ~ [A • (A ∨ B)]}	2, DeM
	4) ~{A • [A • (A ∨ B)]}	3, Simp
	5) ~{~ A • ~ [A • (A ∨ B)]} • ~ {A • [A • (A ∨ B)]}	3, Com
	6) ~{~ A • ~ [A • (A ∨ B)]}	5, Simp
	7) ~ A ∨ ~ [A • (A ∨ B)]	4, DeM
	8) ~ A ∨ [~ A ∨ ~ (A ∨ B)]	7, DeM
	9) ~ A ∨ [~ A ∨ (~ A • ~ B)]	8, DeM
	10) (~ A ∨ ~ A) ∨ (~ A • ~ B)	9, Assoc
	11) ~ A ∨ (~ A • ~ B)	10, Taut
	12) (~ A ∨ ~ A) • (~ A ∨ ~ B)	11, Dist
	13) ~ A • (~ A ∨ ~ B)	12, Taut
	14) ~ ~ {A ∨ [A • (A ∨B)]}	6, DeM
	15) A ∨ [A • (A ∨ B)]	14, DN
	16) (A ∨ A) • [A ∨ (A ∨ B)]	15, Dist
	17) A • [A ∨ (A ∨ B)]	16, Taut
	18) A	17, Simp
	19) ~ A	13, Simp
	20) A • ~ A	18, 19, Conj
	21) A ≡ [A • (A ∨ B)]	1 - 20, IP

7.4.B.(257)

9.

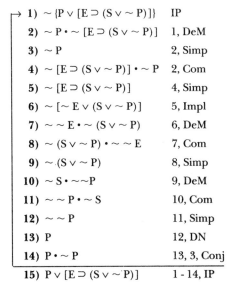

→	1) ~ {P ∨ [E ⊃ (S ∨ ~ P)]}	IP
	2) ~ P • ~ [E ⊃ (S ∨ ~ P)]	1, DeM
	3) ~ P	2, Simp
	4) ~ [E ⊃ (S ∨ ~ P)] • ~ P	2, Com
	5) ~ [E ⊃ (S ∨ ~ P)]	4, Simp
	6) ~ [~ E ∨ (S ∨ ~ P)]	5, Impl
	7) ~ ~ E • ~ (S ∨ ~ P)	6, DeM
	8) ~ (S ∨ ~ P) • ~ ~ E	7, Com
	9) ~ (S ∨ ~ P)	8, Simp
	10) ~ S • ~~P	9, DeM
	11) ~ ~ P • ~ S	10, Com
	12) ~ ~ P	11, Simp
	13) P	12, DN
	14) P • ~ P	13, 3, Conj
	15) P ∨ [E ⊃ (S ∨ ~ P)]	1 - 14, IP

9.   /∴ (S ⊃ G) ⊃ [V ∨ (G • ~ S)]

1) $(S \equiv G) \supset V$ Pr

2) $[(S \supset G) \cdot (G \supset S)] \supset V$ 1, Equiv

3) $(S \supset G) \supset [(G \supset S) \supset V]$ 2, Exp

4) $(S \supset G) \supset [\sim V \supset \sim (G \supset S)]$ 3, Trans

5) $(S \supset G) \supset [\sim \sim V \vee \sim (G \supset S)]$ 4, Impl

6) $(S \supset G) \supset [V \vee \sim (G \supset S)]$ 5, DN

7) $(S \supset G) \supset [V \vee \sim (\sim G \vee S)]$ 6, Impl

8) $(S \supset G) \supset [V \vee (\sim \sim G \cdot \sim S)]$ 7, DeM

9) /∴ $(S \supset G) \supset [V \vee (G \cdot \sim S)]$ 8, DN

                              /∴ (S ≡ G) ⊃ V

1) $(S \supset G) \supset [V \vee (G \cdot \sim S)]$ Pr

2) $(S \supset G) \supset [V \vee \sim \sim (G \cdot \sim S)]$ 1, DN

3) $(S \supset G) \supset [V \vee \sim (\sim G \vee \sim \sim S)]$ 2, DeM

4) $(S \supset G) \supset [V \vee \sim (\sim G \vee S)]$ 3, DN

5) $(S \supset G) \supset [V \vee \sim (G \supset S)]$ 4, Impl

6) $(S \supset G) \supset [\sim \sim V \vee \sim (G \supset S)]$ 5, DN

7) $(S \supset G) \supset [\sim V \supset \sim (G \supset S)]$ 6, Impl

8) $(S \supset G) \supset [(G \supset S) \supset V]$ 7, Trans

9) $[(S \supset G) \cdot (G \supset S)] \supset V$ 8, Exp

10) /∴ $(S \equiv G) \supset V$ 9, Equiv

11. No persons who hate anyone are persons who will be content.
No times during which persons hate anyone are times during which persons are content.

All H are C.

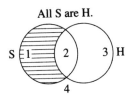

15. All persons who are silent are persons who hear the most.

All S are H.

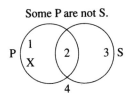

19. Some people who try a great deal are not people who succeed.

Some P are not S.

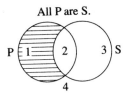

23. All persons who are in the audience are students.

All P are S.

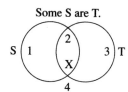

27. Some students are persons who desire good job training.

Some S are T.

9.1.A.(302-303)

11. All baroque musical compositions are non-symphonic pieces.
Some symphonic pieces are not non-atonal works.
_____
So, some atonal works are not baroque musical compositions.

$$\begin{array}{l} \text{All C are non-P} \\ \underline{\text{Some P are not non-W}} \\ \text{Some W are not C} \end{array}$$

This argument has five terms that must be reduced to three:

$$\begin{array}{ll} \text{No C are P} & \text{(obversion)} \\ \underline{\text{Some P are W}} & \text{(obversion)} \\ \text{Some W are not C} \end{array}$$

No baroque musical compositions are symphonic pieces.
Some symphonic pieces are atonal works.
_____
So, some atonal works are not baroque musical compositions.

EIO - 4

15. Some persons who drink beer are alcoholics.
All alcoholics are persons who suffer from a potentially deadly disease.
_____
So, some persons who suffer from a potentially deadly disease are persons who drink beer.

$$\begin{array}{l} \text{Some B are A} \\ \underline{\text{All A are D}} \\ \text{Some D are B} \end{array}$$

IAI - 4

9.2.A.(316)

11. EIO - 4

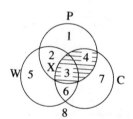

VALID

13. AAA - 3

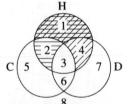

INVALID under both a Boolen and existential
interpretation. No existential assumptions of 'C's.
'D's, or 'H's make 13 valid.

11. All baroque buildings are very ornate buildings.
All baroque buildings are buildings filled with light.

So, all buildings filled with light are very ornate buildings.

All B are O
All B are L

All L are O

AAA - 3

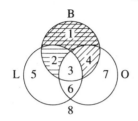

INVALID for Boolean interpretation

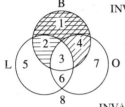

INVALID for any assumption of existence

13. All buildings designed by Christopher Wren are buildings that are non-pre-Palladian architecture.
Some buildings that are pre-Palladian architecture are Gothic structures.

Some Gothic structures are not buildings designed by Christopher Wren.

All B are non-A
Some A are S

Some S are not B

This argument has four terms that must be reduced to three:

No B are A (obversion)
Some A are S

Some S are not B

No building designed by Christopher Wren are buildings that are pre-Palladian architecture.
Some buildings that are pre-Palladian architecture are Gothic structures.

Some Gothic structures are not buildings designed by Christopher Wren.

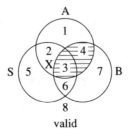

valid

11. All things that are salt are things found widely in nature.
All things that are sodium chloride are things that are salt.

So, some things that are sodium chloride are things found widely in nature.

> All S are F
> All C are S
> _____
> Some C are F

AAI - 1   INVALID under a Boolean interpretation

Rule broken: #5; while having all universal premises, the conclusion is particular. Hence, a fallacy of existential import appears in this argument.

Valid if S's are assumed to exist

13. All high school students are non-college graduates hoping to have a profitable life.
No person with a baccalaureate degree is a person who is a high school student.

So, some persons with a baccalaureate degree are not college graduates hoping to have a profitable life.

> All S are non-G
> No D are S
> _____
> Some D are not G

This argument has four terms that must be reduced to three:

> No S are G (obversion)
> No D are S
> _____
> Some D are not G

No high school students are college graduates hoping to have a profitable life.
No person with a baccalaureate degree is a person who is a high school student.

So, some persons with a baccalaureate degree are not college graduates hoping to have a profitable life.

EE0 - 2   INVALID

Rule broken: #4; all of the premises of this argument are negative. Hence, a fallacy of exclusive premises appears in this argument.

9. Some conservative people are not non-reasonable people.

So, some non-resonable people are not Democrats.

> ...???...
> Some C are non-R
> _____
> Some non-R are not D

> All C are D
> Some C are non-R
> _____
> Some non-R are not D

All conservative people are Democrats.
Some conservative people are not non-reasonable people.

So, some non-reasonable people are not Democrats.

AII - 1   VALID

9. (1)

All persons identical to Mikhail Gorbachev are persons who are liberal politicians.
All non-liberal politicians are non-accepted by Gorbachev.
All persons identical to Mikhail Gorbachev are persons who take a non-traditional approach to internal affairs in the U.S.S.R.
Some traditional approaches to internal affairs in the U.S.S.R. are not approaches likely to survive under Mikhail Gorbachev.

So, some non-accepted politicians are not likely to survive under Mikhail Gorbachev.

(2)

All G are L
All non-l are non-A
All G are non-T
Some T are not S

Some non-A are not S

All non-L are non-A
All G are L
All G are non-T
Some T are not S

Some non-A are not S

(3)

All non-L are non-A
All G are L

All G are A

All A are L (contraposition)
All G are L

All G are A

AAA - 2   INVALID

Rule broken: #1; L is not distributed in either premise. Hence, a fallacy of undistributed middle appears in this argument.

10.1. (336-337)

    13. ~ (x)[(Rx ∨ Px) ⊃ Wx]

    17. (∃x)[(Gx • SX) • ~ Ox] ≡ ~ (x)[Sx ⊃ (Gx ⊃ Ox)]

    21. (x)[Mx ⊃ (Hx ⊃ Ex)] ⊃ (x)[(Cx • Mx) ⊃ (Hx ⊃ Ex)]

    25. ~ (We ∨ Ue) ⊃ (Pe • ~ Ae)

    29. [(Fh • Sh) ∨ (Gh • Ah)] ⊃ ~ (Pw ∨ Dw)

10.2 . (347-348)

    13. (x)[(Vx ∨ ~ Sx) ⊃ ~ Ax]

    17. (∃x)[(Mx • Sx) • ~ Px]

    21. (∃x)[(Mx • Px) • ~ (Cx ∨ Ax)]

    25. (x){[(Tx • Ux) • Px] ⊃ (~ Sx ⊃ Hx)}

    29. (x)({Cx • [Ax) ⊃ [Px ∨ Nx)]} ⊃ ~ (Sx • Hx))

10.3. (353-355)

    13. ~ (x)[(Rx ∨ Px) ⊃ Wx]

    17. (∃x)[(Gx • SX) • ~ Ox] ≡ ~ (x)[Sx ⊃ (Gx ⊃ Ox)]

    21. (x)[Mx ⊃ (Hx ⊃ Ex)] ⊃ (x)[(Cx • Mx) ⊃ (Hx ⊃ Ex)]

    25. ~ (x)[(Px • Ix) ⊃ Fx] • ~ (∃x)[(Px • Ix) • ~ Rx]

    29. Rs ⊃ (x)[(Cx ⊃ Dx) ⊃ (Hx ∨ Sx)]

10.4. (362-364)

    13. (x)[(Lx • Px) ⊃ Fxg]

    17. (x)[Px ⊃ (∃x)(Fy • Nxy)]

    21. (∃x){Sx • (y)[(Py • Pyx) ⊃ Axy]}

    25. (x)({Px • (∃x)[(Py • Nyx) • Lxy]} ⊃ Lxg)

    29. (∃x){(Mx • (∃y)(Iy • Cxy)] • (∃z)(Sz • Uxz)}

11.   /∴ ~ (x)(Ax ⊃ Hx)

    1) (x)[(Ax • Gx) ≡ ~ (Sx ∨ Hx)]   Pr
    2) (∃x)(Ax • Gx) ✓   Pr
    3) ~ ~ (x)(Ax ⊃ Hx) ✓   AP
    4)   (x)(Ax ⊃ Hx)   3, DN
    5)   Aa • Ga ✓   2, EI
    6)   Aa   5, C
    7)   Ga   5, C
    8)   Aa ⊃ Ha ✓   4, UI

    9)   ~ Aa   Ha   8, MI
          X
    10) (Aa • Ga) ≡ ~ (Sa ∨ Ha) ✓   1, UI

    11) Aa • Ga ✓   ~ (Aa • Ga) ✓ 10, ME
    12) ~ (Sa ∨ Ha) ✓ ~ ~ (Sa ∨ Ha)   10, ME
    13)   Aa   11, C
    14)   Ga   11, C
    15) ~ Sa   12, DID
    16) ~ Ha   12, DID
    17)   X   ~ Aa   ~ Ga   11, DC
                   X   X   VALID

13.   /∴ (x)[(Vx • Ax) ⊃ Cx]

    1) ~ (∃x)[Vx • (Ax • ~ Mx)] ✓   Pr
    2) ~ (∃x)[(Ax • Mx) • ~ Cx] ✓   Pr
    3) ~ (x)[(Vx • Ax) ⊃ Cx] ✓   AP
    4) (∃x)~ [(Vx • Ax) ⊃ Cx]   3, QD
    5)   ~ [(Va • Aa) ⊃ Ca] ✓   4, EI
    6)   Va • Aa ✓   5, DMI
    7)   ~ Ca   5, DMI
    8)   Va   6, C
    9)   Aa   6, C
    10) (x)~ [Vx • (Ax • ~ Mx)]   1, QD
    11) (x)~ [(Ax • Mx) • ~ Cx]   2, QD
    12)   ~[Va • (Aa • ~ Ma)] ✓   10, UI

    13) ~ Va   ~ (Aa • ~ Ma) ✓   12, DC
         X
    14)   ~ Aa   ~ ~ Ma ✓   13, DC
    15)   X   Ma   14, DN
    16)   ~ [(Ax • Mx) • ~ Cx] ✓   11, UI

    17) ~ (Ax • Mx) ✓ ~ ~ Ca ✓   16, DC
    18)   Ca   17, DN
                    X
    19)   ~ Aa   ~ Ma   17, DC
            X   X   VALID

17.   / ∴   (∃x) [Px • (y) (Py ⊃ Axy)]

1)   (x) [Px ⊃ (∃y) (Py • Axy)]   Pr
2)   ~ (∃x) [Px • (y) (Py ⊃ Axy)]   ✓   AP
3)   (x) ~ [Px • (y) (Py ⊃ Axy)]   2, QD
4)   Pa ⊃ (∃y) (Py • Aay)   ✓   1, UI
5)   ~ Pa   (∃y) (Py • Aay)   ✓   4, MI

6)   Pb • Aab   ✓   5, EI
7)   Pb   6, C
8)   Aab   6, C
9)   Pb ⊃ (∃y) (Py • Axb)   ✓   1, UI

10) ~ Pb   (∃y) (Py • Aby)   ✓   9, MI
11)   Pc • Abc   ✓   10, EI
12)   Pc   11, C
13)   Abc   11, C

.
.
.

Since this truth tree is nonterminating, exercise 17 is invalid.

11.2.A. (388-389)

11.   / ∴   (∃x) [(Rx • Ix) • ~ Px]

1)   (x) [Ix ⊃ (Sx Δ Rx)]   Pr
2)   (∃x) [(Sx • Ix) • Px]   ✓   Pr
3)   (Sa • Ia) • Pa   ✓   2, EI
4)   Sa • Ia   ✓   3, C
5)   Pa   3, C
6)   Sa   4, C
7)   Ia   4, C
8)   Ia ⊃ (Sa Δ Ra)   ✓   1, UI

9)   ~ Ia   Sa Δ Ra   ✓   8, MI
       X

10)   Sa   Ra   9, ED
11)   ~ Ra   ~ Sa   9, ED
             X   CONSISTENT

13.   / ∴   (∃x) [(Gx • Ex) • Px]

1)   (x) [(Ex ⊃ (Sx ≡ Gx)]   Pr
2)   ~ (x) [Ex ⊃ (Rx ∨ Px)]   ✓   Pr
3)   (∃x) ~ [Ex ⊃ (Rx ∨ Px)]   ✓   2, QD
4)   ~ [Ea ⊃ (Ra ∨ Pa)]   ✓   3, EI
5)   Ea   4, DMI
6)   ~ (Ra ∨ Pa)   ✓   4, DMI
7)   ~ Ra   6, DID
8)   ~ Pa   6, DID
9)   (Ea ⊃ (Sa ≡ Ga)   ✓   1, UI

10)   ~ Ea   Sa ≡ Ga   ✓   9, MI
       X

11)   Sa   ~ Sa   10, ME
12)   Ga   ~ Ga   10, ME

                              CONSISTENT

15.   /∴ (x)[(Hx • Sx) ⊃ Cx]

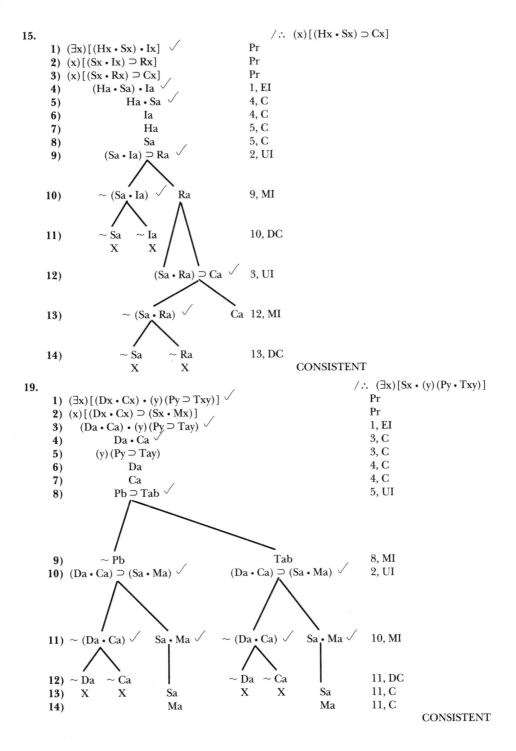

1) (∃x)[(Hx • Sx) • Ix] ✓   Pr
2) (x)[(Sx • Ix) ⊃ Rx]   Pr
3) (x)[(Sx • Rx) ⊃ Cx] ✓   Pr
4)   (Ha • Sa) • Ia ✓   1, EI
5)   Ha • Sa ✓   4, C
6)   Ia   4, C
7)   Ha   5, C
8)   Sa   5, C
9)   (Sa • Ia) ⊃ Ra ✓   2, UI

10)   ~ (Sa • Ia) ✓   Ra   9, MI

11)   ~ Sa   ~ Ia   10, DC
          X   X

12)   (Sa • Ra) ⊃ Ca ✓   3, UI

13)   ~ (Sa • Ra) ✓   Ca   12, MI

14)   ~ Sa   ~ Ra   13, DC
               X   X   CONSISTENT

19.   /∴ (∃x)[Sx • (y)(Py • Txy)]

1) (∃x)[(Dx • Cx) • (y)(Py ⊃ Txy)] ✓   Pr
2) (x)[(Dx • Cx) ⊃ (Sx • Mx)]   Pr
3)   (Da • Ca) • (y)(Py ⊃ Tay) ✓   1, EI
4)   Da • Ca ✓   3, C
5)   (y)(Py ⊃ Tay)   3, C
6)   Da   4, C
7)   Ca   4, C
8)   Pb ⊃ Tab ✓   5, UI

9)   ~ Pb   Tab ✓   8, MI
10) (Da • Ca) ⊃ (Sa • Ma) ✓   (Da • Ca) ⊃ (Sa • Ma) ✓   2, UI

11) ~ (Da • Ca) ✓   Sa • Ma ✓   ~ (Da • Ca) ✓   Sa • Ma ✓   10, MI

12) ~ Da   ~ Ca   ~ Da   ~ Ca   11, DC
13) X   X   Sa   X   X   Sa   11, C
14)   Ma   Ma   11, C

                                                   CONSISTENT

II-53

11. /∴ (∃x)[(Rx • Ix) • ~ Px]

1) (x)[Ix ⊃ (Sx Δ Rx)]   Pr
2) (∃x)[(Sx • Ix) • Px] ✓   Pr
3) ~ (∃x)[(Rx • Ix) • ~ Px] ✓   AP
4) (x)~ [(Rx • Ix) • ~ Px]   3, QD
5) (Sa • Ia) • Pa ✓   2, EI
6)   Sa • Ia ✓   5, C
7)   Pa   5, C
8)   Sa   6, C
9)   Ia   6, C
10)   Ia ⊃ (Sa Δ Ra) ✓   1, UI

11) ~ Ia   Sa Δ Ra ✓   19, MI
     X

12)   Sa   Ra   11, ED
13)   ~ Ra   ~ Sa   11, ED
                  X
14)   ~ [(Ra • Ia) • ~ Pa] ✓   4, UI

15) ~ (Ra • Ia) ✓   ~ ~ Pa ✓   14, DC
16)   Pa   15, DN

17) ~ Ra   ~ Ia   15, DC
        X   **INVALID**

13. /∴ (∃x)[(Gx • Ex) • Px]

1) (x)[(Ex ⊃ (Sx ≡ Gx)]   Pr
2) ~ (x)[Ex ⊃ (Rx ∨ Px)] ✓   Pr
3) ~ (∃x)[(Gx • Ex) • Px] ✓   AP
4) (x)~ [(Gx • Ex) • Px]   3, QD
5) (∃x)~ [Ex ⊃ (Rx ∨ Px)] ✓   2, QD
6)   ~ [Ea ⊃ (Ra ∨ Pa)] ✓   5, EI
7)   Ea   6, DMI
8)   ~ (Ra ∨ Pa) ✓   6, DMI
9)   ~ Ra   8, DID
10)   ~ Pa   8, DID
11)   (Ea ⊃ (Sa ≡ Ga) ✓   1, UI

12)   ~ Ea   Sa ≡ Ga ✓   11, MI
        X

13)   Sa   ~ Sa   12, ME
14)   Ga   ~ Ga   12, ME
15) ~ [(Ga • Ea) • Pa] ✓   ~ [(Ga • Ea) • Pa] ✓   4, UI

16) ~ (Ga • Ea) ✓ ~ Pa   ~ (Ga • Ea) ✓ ~ Pa   15, DC

17) ~ Ga   ~ Ea   ~ Ga   ~ Ea   16, DC
      X   X   X   **INVALID**

19.

1) (∃x)[(Dx • Cx) • (y)(Py ⊃ Txy)] ✓   Pr
2) (x)[(Dx • Cx) ⊃ (Sx • Mx)]   Pr
3) ∼ (∃x)[Sx • (y)(Py • Txy)] ✓   AP
4) (x)∼ [Sx • (y)(Py • Txy)]   3, QD
5) (Da • Ca) • (y)(Py ⊃ Tay) ✓   1, EI
6) Da • Ca ✓   5, C
7) (y)(Py ⊃ Tay)   5, C
8) Da   6, C
9) Ca   6, C
10) Pb ⊃ Tab ✓   7, UI

/∴ (∃x)[Sx • (y)(Py • Txy)]

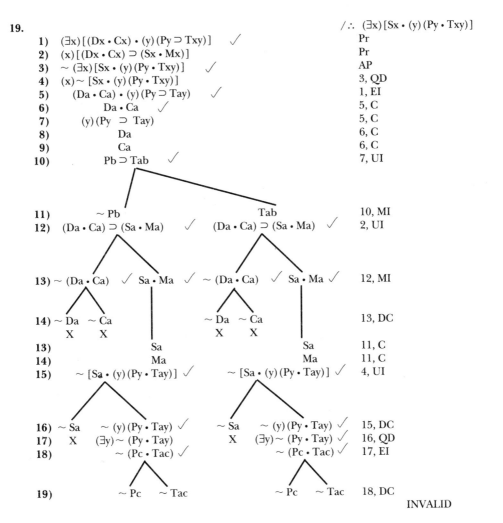

11)   ∼ Pb   Tab   10, MI
12) (Da • Ca) ⊃ (Sa • Ma) ✓   (Da • Ca) ⊃ (Sa • Ma) ✓   2, UI

13) ∼ (Da • Ca) ✓ Sa • Ma ✓   ∼ (Da • Ca) ✓ Sa • Ma ✓   12, MI

14) ∼ Da ∼ Ca   ∼ Da ∼ Ca   13, DC
     X   X   X   X

13)   Sa   Sa   11, C
14)   Ma   Ma   11, C
15) ∼ [Sa • (y)(Py • Tay)] ✓   ∼ [Sa • (y)(Py • Tay)] ✓ 4, UI

16) ∼ Sa   ∼ (y)(Py • Tay) ✓   ∼ Sa   ∼ (y)(Py • Tay) ✓ 15, DC
17) X   (∃y)∼ (Py • Tay)   X   (∃y)∼ (Py • Tay) ✓ 16, QD
18)   ∼ (Pc • Tac) ✓   ∼ (Pc • Tac) ✓   17, EI

19)   ∼ Pc   ∼ Tac   ∼ Pc   ∼ Tac   18, DC

INVALID

11. $(\exists x)[Px \cdot (Bx \cdot Dx)]$

a)

1)	$(\exists x)[Px \cdot (Bx \cdot Dx)]$ ✓	—
2)	$Pa \cdot (Ba \cdot Da)$ ✓	1, EI
3)	Pa	2, C
4)	$Ba \cdot Da$ ✓	2, C
5)	Ba	4, C
6)	Da	4, C

b)

1)	$\sim (\exists x)[Px \cdot (Bx \cdot Dx)]$ ✓	—
2)	$(x) \sim [Px \cdot (Bx \cdot Dx)]$	1, QD
3)	$\sim [Pa \cdot (Ba \cdot Da)]$ ✓	2, UI

4) $\sim Pa$ $\sim (Ba \cdot Da)$ ✓   3, DC

5) $\sim Ba$ $\sim Da$ 4, DC

Since exercise 11 is neither contradictory nor logically true, it is CONTINGENT.

13. $(x)[Sx \supset (\exists y)(Gy \cdot Mxy)]$

a)

1)	$(x)[Sx \supset (\exists y)(Gy \cdot Mxy)]$	—
2)	$Sa \supset (\exists y)(Gy \cdot May)$ ✓	1, UI

3) $\sim Sa$ $(\exists y)(Gy \cdot May)$ ✓   2, MI

4)	$Gb \cdot Mab$ ✓	3, EI
5)	Gb	4, C
6)	Mab	4, C

b)

1)	$\sim (x)[Sx \supset (\exists y)(Gy \cdot Mxy)]$ ✓	—
2)	$(\exists x) \sim [Sx \supset (\exists y)(Gy \cdot Mxy)]$ ✓	1, QD
3)	$\sim [Sa \supset (\exists y)(Gy \cdot May)]$ ✓	2, EI
4)	Sa	3, DMI
5)	$\sim (\exists y)(Gy \cdot May)$	3, DMI
6)	$(y) \sim (Gy \cdot May)$	5, QD
7)	$\sim (Gb \cdot Mab)$ ✓	6, UI

8) $\sim Gb$ $\sim Mab$ 7, DC

Since exercise 13 is neither contradictory nor logically true, it is CONTINGENT.

19. $(x)[Tx \supset (\exists y)(Sy \cdot Exy)] \cdot (x)[Tx \supset (y)(Sy \supset \sim Exy)]$

a)

1)	$(x)[Tx \supset (\exists y)(Sy \cdot Exy)] \cdot (x)[Tx \supset (y)(Sy \supset \sim Exy)]\checkmark$	—
2)	$(x)[Tx \supset (\exists y)(Sy \cdot Exy)]$	1, C
3)	$(x)[Tx \supset (y)(Sy \supset \sim Exy)]$	1, C
4)	$Ta \supset (\exists y)(Sy \cdot Eay)\checkmark$	2, UI
5)	$Ta \supset (y)(Sy \supset \sim Eay)\checkmark$	3, UI

6)	$\sim Ta$	$(\exists y)(Sy \cdot Eay)\checkmark$	4, MI
7)		$Sb \cdot Eab\checkmark$	6, EI
8)		Sb	7, C
9)		Eab	7, C

10)	$\sim Ta$	$(y)(Sy \supset \sim Eay)$	$\sim Ta$	$(y)(Sy \supset \sim Eay)$	5, MI
11)		$Sb \supset \sim Eab$			10, UI
12)	$\sim Sb$	$\sim Eab$			11, MI
13)				$Sb \supset \sim Eab\ \checkmark$	10, UI
14)			$\sim Sb$	$\sim Eab$	13, MI
			X	X	

b)

1)	$\sim \{(x)[Tx \supset (\exists y)(Sy \cdot Exy)] \cdot (x)[Tx \supset (y)(Sy \supset \sim Exy)]\}\ \checkmark$		—

2)	$\sim (x)[Tx \supset (\exists y)(Sy \cdot Exy)]\ \checkmark$	$\sim (x)[Tx \supset (y)(Sy \supset \sim Exy)]\ \checkmark$	1, DC
3)	$(\exists x)\sim [Tx \supset (\exists y)(Sy \cdot Exy)]$		2, QD
4)	$\sim [Ta \supset (\exists y)(Sy \cdot Eay)]\ \checkmark$		3, EI
5)	Ta		4, DMI
6)	$\sim (\exists y)(Sy \cdot Eay)\ \checkmark$		4, DMI
7)	$(y)\sim (Sy \cdot Eay)$		6, QD
8)	$\sim (Sb \cdot Eab)\ \checkmark$		7, UI

9)	$\sim Sb \qquad \sim Eab$		8, DC
10)		$(\exists x)\sim [Tx \supset (y)(Sy \supset \sim Exy)]\ \checkmark$	2, QD
11)		$\sim [Ta \supset (y)(Sy \supset \sim Eay)]\ \checkmark$	10, EI
12)		Ta	11, DMI
13)		$\sim (y)(Sy \supset \sim Eay)\ \checkmark$	11, DMI
14)		$(\exists y)\sim (Sy \supset \sim Eay)\ \checkmark$	13, QD
15)		$\sim (Sb \supset \sim Eab)\ \checkmark$	14, EI
16)		Sb	15, DMI
17)		$\sim \sim Eab\ \checkmark$	15, DMI
18)		Eab	17, DN

Since exercise 19 is neither contradictory nor logically true, it is CONTINGENT.

11.

a) (x)[Px ⊃ (Lx ⊃ Kx)]
b) (x)[(~ Kx • Px) ⊃ ~ Lx]

1) ~ {(x)[Px ⊃ (Lx ⊃ Kx)] ≡ (x)[(~ Kx • Px) ⊃ ~ Lx]} ✓   —

2) (x)[Px ⊃ (Lx ⊃ Kx)]   (x)[(~ Kx • Px) ⊃ ~ Lx]   1, DME
3) ~ (x)[(~ Kx • Px) ⊃ ~ Lx] ✓   ~ (x)[Px ⊃ (Lx ⊃ Kx)] ✓   1, DME
4) (∃x)~ [(~ Kx • Px) ⊃ ~ Lx]   3, QD
5)   ~ [(~ Ka • Pa) ⊃ ~ La] ✓   4, EI
6)   ~ Ka • Pa ✓   5, DMI
7)   ~ ~ La ✓   5, DMI
8)   La   7, DN
9)   ~ Ka   6, C
10)   Pa   6, C
11)   Pa ⊃ (La ⊃ Ka) ✓   2, UI

12)   ~ Pa   La ⊃ Ka ✓   11, MI
         X

13)   ~ La   Ka   12, MI
14)   X   X   (∃x)~ [Px ⊃ (Lx ⊃ Kx)] ✓   3, QD
15)   ~ [Pa ⊃ (La ⊃ Ka)] ✓   14, EI
16)   Pa   15, DMI
17)   ~ (La ⊃ Ka) ✓   15, DMI
18)   La   17, DMI
19)   ~ Ka   17, DMI
20)   (~ Ka • Pa) ⊃ ~ La ✓   2, UI

21)   ~ (~ Ka • Pa) ✓   ~ La   20, MI
                                     X

22)   ~ ~ Ka ✓   ~ Pa   21, DC
23)   Ka   X   22, DN
                X   LOGICALLY EQUIVALENT

13.

a) (x)[Px ⊃ (Kx Δ Hx)]
b) ~ (∃x)[Px • (Hx ≡ Kx)]

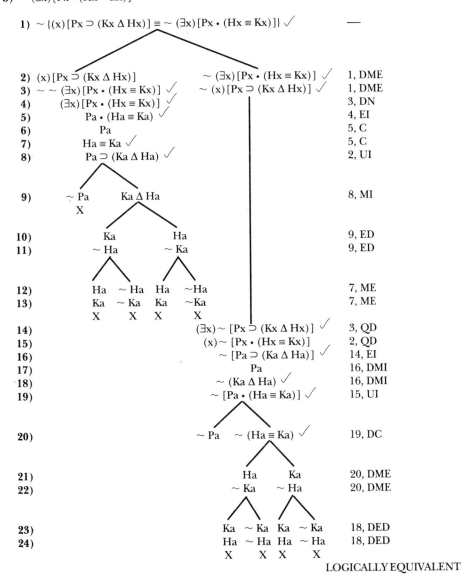

1) ~ {(x)[Px ⊃ (Kx Δ Hx)] ≡ ~ (∃x)[Px • (Hx ≡ Kx)]} ✓   —

2) (x)[Px ⊃ (Kx Δ Hx)]   ~ (∃x)[Px • (Hx ≡ Kx)] ✓   1, DME
3) ~ ~ (∃x)[Px • (Hx ≡ Kx)] ✓   ~ (x)[Px ⊃ (Kx Δ Hx)] ✓   1, DME
4)   (∃x)[Px • (Hx ≡ Kx)] ✓   3, DN
5)   Pa • (Ha ≡ Ka) ✓   4, EI
6)   Pa   5, C
7)   Ha ≡ Ka ✓   5, C
8)   Pa ⊃ (Ka Δ Ha) ✓   2, UI

9)   ~ Pa   Ka Δ Ha   8, MI
        X

10)   Ka   Ha   9, ED
11)   ~ Ha   ~ Ka   9, ED

12)   Ha ~ Ha Ha ~Ha   7, ME
13)   Ka ~ Ka Ka ~Ka   7, ME
        X   X   X   X

14)   (∃x)~ [Px ⊃ (Kx Δ Hx)] ✓   3, QD
15)   (x)~ [Px • (Hx ≡ Kx)]   2, QD
16)   ~ [Pa ⊃ (Ka Δ Ha)] ✓   14, EI
17)   Pa   16, DMI
18)   ~ (Ka Δ Ha) ✓   16, DMI
19)   ~ [Pa • (Ha ≡ Ka)] ✓   15, UI

20)   ~ Pa   ~ (Ha ≡ Ka) ✓   19, DC

21)   Ha   Ka   20, DME
22)   ~ Ka   ~ Ha   20, DME

23)   Ka ~ Ka Ka ~ Ka   18, DED
24)   Ha ~ Ha Ha ~ Ha   18, DED
                        X   X   X   X

                                                        LOGICALLY EQUIVALENT

15.
  a) $(\exists x)\{[Px \cdot (y)(Py \supset \sim Txy)] \cdot \sim Txx\}$
  b) $\sim (x)[(Px \cdot Txx) \supset (y)(Py \supset \sim Txy)]$

1)	$\sim ((\exists x)\{[Px \cdot (y)(Py \supset \sim Txy)] \cdot \sim Txx\} \equiv \sim (x)[(Px \cdot Txx) \supset (y)(Py \supset \sim Txy)]) \checkmark$	—
2)	$(\exists x)\{[Px \cdot (y)(Py \supset \sim Txy)] \cdot \sim Txx\} \checkmark \qquad \sim (x)[(Px \cdot Txx) \supset (y)(Py \supset \sim Txy)] \checkmark$	1, DME
3)	$\sim \sim (x)[(Px \cdot Txx) \supset (y)(Py \supset \sim Txy)] \checkmark \qquad \sim (\exists x)\{[Px \cdot (y)(Py \supset \sim Txy)] \cdot \sim Txx\} \checkmark$	1, DME
4)	$[Pa \cdot (y)(Py \supset \sim Tay)] \cdot \sim Taa \checkmark$	2, EI
5)	$Pa \cdot (y)(Py \supset \sim Tay) \checkmark$	4, C
6)	$\sim Taa$	4, C
7)	Pa	5, C
8)	$(y)(Py \supset \sim Tay)$	5, C
9)	$Pa \supset \sim Taa \checkmark$	8, UI
10)	$\sim Pa \qquad \sim Taa$	9, MI
	X	
11)	$(x)[(Px \cdot Txx) \supset (y)(Py \supset \sim Txy)]$	3, DN
12)	$(Pa \cdot Taa) \supset (y)(Py \supset \sim Tay)$	11, UI
13)	$\sim (Pa \cdot Taa) \qquad (y)(Py \supset \sim Tay)$	12, MI
14)	$\sim Pa \qquad \sim Taa$	13, DC
15)	X $\qquad\qquad\qquad Pa \supset \sim Taa$	13, UI
16)	$\sim Pa \qquad \sim Taa$	15, MI
17)	X $\qquad (\exists x) \sim [(Px \cdot Txx) \supset (y)(Py \supset \sim Txy)] \checkmark$	2, QD
18)	$\sim [(Pa \cdot Taa) \supset (y)(Py \supset \sim Tay)] \checkmark$	17, EI
19)	$Pa \cdot Taa \checkmark$	18, DMI
20)	$\sim (y)(Py \supset \sim Tay) \checkmark$	18, DMI
21)	Pa	19, C
22)	Taa	19, C
23)	$(\exists y) \sim (Py \supset \sim Tay) \checkmark$	20, QD
24)	$\sim (Pb \supset \sim Tab) \checkmark$	23, EI
25)	Pb	24, DMI
26)	$\sim \sim Tab \checkmark$	24, DMI
27)	Tab	26, DN
28)	$(x) \sim \{[Px \cdot (y)(Py \supset \sim Txy)] \cdot \sim Txx\}$	3, QD
29)	$\sim \{[Pa \cdot (y)(Py \supset \sim Tay)] \cdot \sim Taa\} \checkmark$	28, UI
30)	$\sim [Pa \cdot (y)(Py \supset \sim Tay)] \qquad\qquad \sim \sim Taa \checkmark$	29, DC
31)	Taa	30, DN
32)	$\sim Pa \qquad \sim (y)(Py \supset \sim Tay) \checkmark$	30, DC
33)	X $\qquad (\exists y) \sim (Py \supset \sim Tay) \checkmark$	32, QD
34)	$\sim (Pc \supset \sim Tac) \checkmark$	33, EI
35)	Pc	34, DMI
36)	$\sim \sim Tac \checkmark$	34, DMI
37)	Tac	36, DN

NOT LOGICALLY EQUIVALENT

12.2.B.(408)

9.   /∴ (x)[(Ax • Cx) ⊃ ~ Dx]

1) (x){[Ax • (Bx ∨ Cx)] ≡ ~ Dx}   Pr

2) [Ax • (Bx ∨ Cx)] ≡ ~ Dx   1, UI

3) {[Ax • (Bx∨Cx)] ⊃ ~ Dx} • {~ Dx ⊃ [Ax • (Bx∨Cx)]}   1, Equiv

4) [Ax • (Bx ∨ Cx)] ⊃ ~ Dx   3, Simp

5) ~ [Ax • (Bx ∨ Cx)] ∨ ~ Dx   4, Impl

6) [~ Ax ∨ ~ (Bx ∨ Cx)] ∨ ~ Dx   5, DeM

7) [~ Ax ∨ (~ Bx • ~ Cx)] ∨ ~ Dx   6, DeM

8) ~ Dx ∨ [~ Ax ∨ (~ Bx • ~ Cx)]   7, Com

9) (~ Dx ∨ ~ Ax) ∨ (~Bx • ~ Cx)   8, Assoc

10) (~ Dx ∨ ~ Ax) ∨ (~ Cx • ~ Bx)   9, Com

11) [(~ Dx ∨ ~ Ax) ∨ ~ Cx] • [(~ Dx ∨ ~ Ax) ∨ ~ Bx]   10, Dist

12) (~ Dx ∨ ~ Ax) ∨ ~ Cx   11, Simp

13) ~ Dx ∨ (~ Ax ∨ ~ Cx)   12, Assoc

14) Dx ⊃ ~ (Ax • Cx)   13, DeM

15) ~ ~ (Ax • Cx) ⊃ ~ Dx   14, Trans

16) (Ax • Cx) ⊃ ~ Dx   15, DN

17) /∴ (x)[(Ax • Cx) ⊃ ~ Dx]   16, UG

12.2.C.(409)

9.   /∴ (x)[(Px • Cx) ⊃ Fx]

1) (x){Px ⊃ [(~ Cx ⊃ ~ Ux) ⊃ (Hx • Bx)]}   Pr

2) (x)[(Px • Bx) ⊃ (Hx • Fx)]   Pr

3) Px ⊃ (~ Cx ⊃ ~ Ux) ⊃ (Hx • Bx)   1, UI

4) (Px • Bx) ⊃ (Hx • Fx)   2, UI

5) ~ (~ Cx ⊃ ~ Ux) ∨ (Hx • Bx)   3, Impl

6) ~ (~ Cx ⊃ ~ Ux) ∨ (Bx • Hx)   5, Com

7) [~ (~ Cx ⊃ ~ Ux) ∨ Bx] • [~ (~ Cx ⊃ ~ Ux) ∨ Hx]   6, Dist

8) ~ (~ Cx ⊃ ~ Ux) ∨ Bx   7, Simp

9) (~ Cx ⊃ ~ Ux) ⊃ Bx   8, Impl

10) ~ Bx ∨ (Hx • Fx)   4, Impl

11) ~ Bx ∨ (Fx • Hx)   10, Com

12) (~ Bx ∨ Fx) • (~ Bx ∨ Hx)   11, Dist

13) ~ Bx ∨ Fx   12, Simp

14) Bx ⊃ Fx   13, Impl

15) (~ Cx ⊃ ~ Ux) ⊃ Fx   9, 14, HS

16) ~ (~ Cx ⊃ ~ Ux) ∨ Fx   15, Impl

17) ~ (~ ~ Cx ∨ ~ Ux) ∨ Fx   16, Impl

18) ~ ~ (~ Cx • Ux) ∨ Fx   17, DeM

19) (~ Cx • Ux) ∨ Fx   18, DN

20) Fx ∨ (~ Cx • Ux)   19, Com

21) (Fx ∨ ~ Cx) • (Fx ∨ Ux)   20, Dist

22) Fx ∨ ~ Cx   21, Simp

23) ~ Cx Fx ∨   22, Com

24) Cx ⊃ Fx   23, Impl

25) /∴ (x) (Cx ⊃ Fx)   24, UG

12.3.A. (414-417)

9.

1) Pr
2) Pr
3) Pr
4) Pr
5) 1, EI
6) 2, UI
7) 3, UI
8) 4, UI
9) 5, Simp
10) 5, Com
11) 10, Simp
12) 11, Simp
13) 11, Com
14) 13, Simp
15) 6, 9, MP
16) 7, Exp
17) 16, 14, MP
18) 8, 12, MT
19) 18, DeM
20) 19, DN
21) 15, 17, 20, CD
22) 21, EG

12.3.B. (417-418)

9.   /∴ (∃x)[~ Ax • (Bx ∨

1)	(x)[Ax ⊃ ~ (Bx ⊃ Cx)]	Pr
2)	(x)[Bx ⊃ (Cx ∨ Dx)]	Pr
3)	(∃x)[~ Dx • (Bx Δ Ex)]	Pr
4)	~ Dx • (Bx Δ Ex)	3, EI
5)	Ax ⊃ ~ (Bx ⊃ Cx)	1, UI
6)	Bx ⊃ (Cx ∨ Dx)	2, UI
7)	~ Bx ∨ (Cx ∨ Dx)	6, Impl
8)	(~ Bx ∨ Cx) ∨ Dx	7, Assoc
9)	Dx ∨ (~ Bx ∨ Cx)	8, Com
10)	~ Dx	4, Simp
11)	~ Bx ∨ Cx	9, 10, DS
12)	Bx ⊃ Cx	11, Impl
13)	~ ~ (Bx ⊃ Cx)	12, DN
14)	~ Ax	5, 13, MT
15)	(Bx Δ Ex) • ~ Dx	4, Com
16)	Bx Δ Ex	15, Simp
17)	(Bx ∨ Ex) • (~ Bx ∨ ~ Ex)	16, Equiv
18)	Bx ∨ Ex	17, Simp
19)	~ Ax • (Bx ∨ Ex)	14, 18, Conj
20)	/∴ (∃x)[~ Ax • (Bx ∨ Ex)]	19, EG

9. /∴ (∃x)[(Px • Hx) • ~ (Rx ∨ Ux)]

1)	(∃x)[Px • ~ (Ux ∨ Rx)]	Pr
2)	(x)[(Px ∨ Nx) ⊃ ~ Fx]	Pr
3)	(x)[~ (Fx ∨ Rx) ⊃ Hx]	Pr
4)	Px • ~ (Ux ∨ Rx)	1, EI
5)	(Px ∨ Nx) ⊃ ~ Fx	2, UI
6)	~ (Fx ∨ Rx) ⊃ Hx	3, UI
7)	Px	4, Simp
8)	~ (Ux ∨ Rx) • Px	4, Com
9)	~ (Ux ∨ Rx)	8, Simp
10)	~ (Rx ∨ Ux)	9, Com
11)	Px ∨ Nx	7, Add
12)	~ Fx	5, 11, MP
13)	~ Rx • ~ Ux	10, DeM
14)	~ Rx	13, Simp
15)	~ Fx • ~ Rx	12, 14, Conj
16)	~ (Fx ∨ Rx)	15, DeM
17)	Hx	6, 16, MP
18)	Px • Hx	7, 17, Conj
19)	(Px • Hx) • ~ (Rx ∨ Ux)	18, 10, Conj
20)	/∴ (∃x)[(Px • Hx) • ~ (Rx ∨ Ux)]	19, EG

12.4.A. (423-427)

9.

    1) Pr
    2) Pr
    3) 1, QD
    4) 2, QD
    5) 3, UI
    6) 5, DeM
    7) 6, DN
    8) 7, Impl
    9) 2, UI
    10) 9, DeM
    11) 10, DN
    12) 11, Impl
    13) 8, 12, HS
    14) 13, Impl
    15) 14, DeM
    16) 15, Com
    17) 16, 16, Com
    18) 17, Dist
    19) 18, Simp
    20) 19, Com
    21) 20, Impl
    22) 21, UG
    23) 22, QD
    24) 23, Impl
    25) 24, DN
    26) 25, DeM
    27) 26, DN

12.4.B. (427-428)

9. $/ \therefore \sim (\exists x)(\sim Cx \cdot \sim Fx)$

  1) $\sim (\exists x)(Ax \cdot \sim Bx) \cdot \sim (\exists x)(Bx \cdot \sim Cx)$ Pr

  2) $(x)(\sim Ax \equiv Dx)$ Pr

  3) $(x)(Dx \supset Ex) \cdot (x)(Ex \supset Fx)$ Pr

  4) $\sim (\exists x)(Ax \cdot \sim Bx)$ 1, Simp

  5) $\sim (\exists x)(Bx \cdot \sim Cx) \cdot \sim (\exists x)(Ax \cdot \sim Bx)$ 1, Com

  6) $\sim (\exists x)(Bx \cdot \sim Cx)$ 5, Simp

  7) $(x)(Dx \supset Ex)$ 3, Simp

  8) $(x)(Ex \supset Fx) \cdot (x)(Dx \supset Ex)$ 3, Com

  9) $(x)(Ex \supset Fx)$ 8, Simp

  10) $(x)\sim (Ax \cdot \sim Bx)$ 4, QD

  11) $(x)\sim (Bx \cdot \sim Cx)$ 6, QD

  12) $\sim Ax \equiv Dx$ 2, UI

  13) $Dx \supset Ex$ 7, UI

  14) $Ex \supset Fx$ 9, UI

  15) $\sim (Ax \cdot \sim Bx)$ 10, UI

  16) $\sim (Bx \cdot \sim Cx)$ 11, UI

  17) $(\sim Ax \supset Dx) \cdot (Dx \supset \sim Ax)$ 12, Equiv

  18) $\sim Ax \lor \sim \sim Bx$ 15, DeM

  19) $\sim Ax \lor Bx$ 18, DN

  20) $Ax \supset Bx$ 19, Impl

  21) $\sim Bx \lor \sim \sim Cx$ 16, DeM

  22) $\sim Bx \lor Cx$ 21, DN

  23) $Bx \supset Cx$ 22, Impl

  24) $Ax \supset Cx$ 20, 23, HS

  25) $Dx \supset Fx$ 13, 14, HS

  26) $\sim Ax \supset Dx$ 17, Simp

  27) $\sim \sim Ax \lor Dx$ 26, Impl

  28) $Ax \lor Dx$ 27, DN

  29) $Cx \lor Fx$ 24, 25, 28, CD

  30) $\sim \sim (Cx \lor Fx)$ 29, DN

  31) $\sim (\sim Cx \cdot \sim Fx)$ 30, DeM

  32) $(x)\sim (\sim Cx \cdot \sim Fx)$ 31, UG

  33) $/ \therefore \sim (\exists x)(\sim Cx \cdot \sim Fx)$ 32, QD

12.4.C.(428-429)

9.   /∴ (∃x)Sx

   1) ~ (∃x)[Fx • ~ (Ix ≡ ~ Ax)]   Pr

   2) ~ (x)(Fx ⊃ Cx)   Pr

   3) ~ (∃x)(Ax • ~ Cx) • ~ (∃x)(Ix • ~ Sx)   Pr

   4) ~ (∃x)(Ax • ~ Cx)   3, Simp

   5) ~ (∃x)(Ix • ~ Sx) • ~ (∃x)(Ax • ~ Cx)   3, Com

   6) ~ (∃x)(Ix • ~ Sx)   5, Simp

   7) (x)~ [Fx • ~ (Ix ≡ ~ Ax)]   1, QD

   8) (∃x)~ (Fx ⊃ Cx)   2, QD

   9) (x)~ (Ax • ~ Cx)   4, QD

 10) (x)~ (Ix • ~ Sx)   6, QD

 11) ~ (Fx ⊃ Cx)   8, EI

 12) ~ [Fx • ~ (Ix ≡ ~ Ax)]   7, UI

 13) ~ (Ax • ~ Cx)   9, UI

 14) ~ (Ix • ~ Sx)   10, UI

 15) ~ (~ Fx ∨ Cx)   11, Impl

 16) ~ ~ Fx • ~ Cx   15, DeM

 17) Fx • ~ Cx   16, DN

 18) Fx   17, Simp

 19) ~ Cx • Fx   17, Com

 20) ~ Cx   19, Simp

 21) ~ Fx ∨ ~ ~ (Ix ≡ ~ Ax)   12, DeM

 22) ~ Fx ∨ (Ix ≡ ~ Ax)   21, DN

 23) Fx ⊃ (Ix ≡ ~ Ax)   22, Impl

 24) ~ Ax ∨ ~ ~ Cx   13,DeM

 25) ~ Ax ∨ Cx   24, DN

 26) Ax ⊃ Cx   25, Impl

 27) ~ Ix ∨ ~ ~ Sx   14, DeM

 28) ~ Ix ∨ Sx   27, DN

 29) Ix ⊃ Sx   28, Impl

 30) Ix ≡ ~ Ax   23, 18, MP

 31) ~ Ax ≡ Ix   30, Com

 32) (~ Ax ⊃ Ix) • (Ix ⊃ ~ Ax)   31, Equiv

 33) ~ Ax ⊃ Ix   32, Simp

 34) ~ ~ Ax ∨ Ix   33, Impl

 35) Ax ∨ Ix   34, DN

 36) Cx ∨ Sx   26, 29, 35, CD

 37) Sx   36, 20, DS

 38) /∴ (∃x)Sx   37, EG

9.   /∴ (x)(Bx ∨ ~ Cx)

1)	(x)(Ax ∨ ~ Ax)	Pr
2)	(x)(Ax ≡ Bx)	Pr
3)	~ (∃x)(Cx • ~ Ax)	Pr
→ **4)**	~ (x)(Bx ∨ ~ Cx)	IP
5)	(∃x)~ (Bx ∨ ~ Cx)	4, QD
6)	~ (Bx ∨ ~ Cx)	5, EI
7)	~ Bx • ~ ~ Cx	6, DeM
8)	~ Bx	7, Simp
9)	~ ~ Cx • ~ Bx	7, Com
10)	~ ~ Cx	9, Simp
11)	(x)~ (Cx • ~ Ax)	3, QD
12)	Ax ≡ Bx	2, UI
13)	~ (Cx • ~ Ax)	4, UI
14)	(Ax ⊃ Bx) • (Bx ⊃ Ax)	12, Equiv
15)	Ax ⊃ Bx	14, Simp
16)	~ Ax	15, 8, MT
17)	~ Cx ∨ ~ ~ Ax	13, DeM
18)	~ ~ Ax	17, 10, DS
19)	~ Ax • ~ ~ Ax	16, 18, Conj
20)	/∴ (x)(Bx ∨ ~ Cx)	4 - 19, IP

9.   /∴ (x){[Cx • (Sx • Hx)] ⊃ ~ (Px ∨ Nx)}

1)	(x)({Cx • [Ax ⊃ (Px ∨ Nx)]} ⊃ ~ (Sx • Hx))	Pr
2)	{Cx • [Ax ⊃ (Px ∨ Nx)]} ⊃ ~ (Sx • Hx)	1, UI
→ **3)**	Cx • (Sx • Hx)	CP, /∴ ~ (Px ∨ Nx)
4)	Cx	3, Simp
5)	(Sx • Hx) • Cx	3, Com
6)	Sx • Hx	5, Simp
7)	~ ~ (Sx • Hx)	6, DN
8)	~ {Cx • [Ax ⊃ (Px ∨ Nx)]}	2, 7, MT
9)	~ Cx ∨ ~ [Ax ⊃ (Px ∨ Nx)]	8, DeM
10)	~ ~ Cx	4, DN
11)	~ [Ax ⊃ (Px ∨ Nx)]	9, 10, DS
12)	~ [~ Ax ∨ (Px ∨ Nx)]	11, Impl
13)	~ ~ Ax • ~ (Px ∨ Nx)	12, DeM
14)	~ (Px ∨ Nx) • ~ ~ Ax	13, Com
15)	~ (Px ∨ Nx)	14, Simp
16)	[Cx • (Sx • Hx)] ⊃ ~ (Px ∨ Nx)	3 - 15, CP
17)	/∴ (x){[Cx • (Sx • Hx)] ⊃ ~ (Px ∨ Nx)}	16, UG

9. $/\therefore\ (\exists x)[Bx \cdot (y)(Ay \supset Cyx)]$

   1) $(x)[Ax \supset (\exists w)(Bw \cdot Cxw)]$ Pr

   2) $(\exists x)(Bx \cdot (y)\{[Ay \cdot (\exists z)(Bz \cdot Cyz)] \supset Cyx\})$ Pr

   3) $Bx \cdot (y)\{[Ay \cdot (\exists z)(Bz \cdot Czz)] \supset Cyx\}$ 2, EI

   4) $Ay \supset (\exists w)(Bw \cdot Cyw)$ 1, UI

   5) Bx 3, Simp

   6) $(y)\{[Ay \cdot (\exists z)(Bz \cdot Czz)] \supset Cyx\} \cdot Bx$ 3, Com

   7) $(y)\{[Ay \cdot (\exists z)(Bz \cdot Czz)] \supset Cyx\}$ 6, Simp

   8) $[Ay \cdot (\exists z)(Bz \cdot Czz)] \supset Cyx$ 7. UI

$\rightarrow$ **9)** Ay CP, $/\therefore$ Cyx

   10) $(\exists w)(Bw \cdot Cyw)$ 4, 9, MP

   11) $Bz \cdot Cyz$ 10, EI

   12) $(\exists z)(Bz \cdot Czz)$ 11, EG

   13) $Ay \cdot (\exists z)(Bz \cdot Czz)$ 9, 12, Conj

   14) Cyx 8, 13, MP

   15) $Ay \supset Cyx$ 4 - 13, CP

   16) $(y)(Ay \supset Cyx)$ 15, UG

   17) $Bx \cdot (y)(Ay \supset Cyx)$ 5, 16, Conj

   18) $/\therefore\ (\exists x)[Bx \cdot (y)(Ay \supset Cyx)]$ 17, EG

9. $/\therefore\ (y)[(Ny \cdot Iy) \supset \sim (x)(Px \supset \sim Cxy)]$

   1) $(\exists x)\{Px \cdot (y)[(Ny \cdot Iy) \supset Cxy]\}$ Pr

   2) $Px \cdot (y)[(Ny \cdot Iy) \supset Cxy]$ 1, EI

   3) Px 2, Simp

   4) $(y)[(Ny \cdot Iy) \supset Cxy] \cdot Px$ 2, Com

   5) $(y)[(Ny \cdot Iy) \supset Cxy]$ 4, Simp

   6) $(Ny \cdot Iy) \supset Cxy$ 5, UI

$\rightarrow$ **7)** $Ny \cdot Iy$ CP, $/\therefore\ \sim (x)(Px \supset \sim Cxy)$

   8) Cxy 6, 7, MP

   9) $Px \cdot Cxy$ 3, 8, Conj

   10) $(\exists x)(Px \cdot Cxy)$ 9, EG

   11) $\sim (x) \sim (Px \cdot Cxy)$ 10, QD

   12) $\sim (x)(\sim Px \vee \sim Cxy)$ 11, DeM

   13) $\sim (x)(Px \supset \sim Cxy)$ 12, Impl

   14) $(Ny \cdot Iy) \supset \sim (x)(Px \supset \sim Cxy)$ 7 - 13, CP

   15) $/\therefore\ (y)[(Ny \cdot Iy) \supset \sim (x)(Px \supset \sim Cxy)]$ 14, UG

Chapter 13

13.3.A. (465-466)

13. Genus and species

17. Operational

21. Definition by subclass, partial

25. Theoretical

13.4.A. (469-470)

13. Viciously circular if 'war' is defined as the absence of peace.

Chapter 14

Pages 490-491

13. *Ambiguity (semantic):* It is not clear whether 'consent' means to indicate active agreement or to acquiesce (that is, implicitly to accept something by forbearing from opposition). In the se- cond sense of 'consent', it appears that Americans do consent to government power even if they do not vote.

Pages 496-497

9. *Appeal to the masses:* That two million people signed a petition to pardon Col. North is not relevant to his proper legal status. Relevant considerations here involve legal ones concerning punishment, rehabilitation, fairness under the law, and executive privilege.

13. *Appeal to irrelevant authority:* Although any scientist is an authority on some matters, most are not authorities on subatomic physics. It does not make reasonable sense to consider an ento- mologist or industrial chemist to be an authority on particle physics. On the other hand, the opinions of the U.S. particle physicists would be relevant in support of the conclusion of this argument.

Pages 502-503

9. *Hasty conclusion:* The ten most recent fatal accidents provide too small a sample from which to draw general conclusions about age and safe driving. In addition, the receiver is only told that these accidents "involve" drivers under the age of eighteen. No indication is given as to whether these drivers were at fault.

13. *Appeal to ignorance:* Simply because no one has yet detected radio signals from aliens provides no reason to conclude that they do not exist. There are millions of possible frequencies to test, considerable background noise to filter out, long delays between transmission and reception, etc.

Chapter 15

Pages 509-511

11. *Red herring:* The dangers posed by driving automobiles, ingesting commercial compounds, and walking across highways are not relevant to evaluating the danger of steroid uses. Because two things are dangerous, it does not follow that they are dangerous in the same ways or for the same reasons. The argument attempts to divert the focus of the receiver from the danger of steroids to other unrelated risks.

15. *Red herring:* Given the U.S. Constitution and Bill of Rights, the rites and traditions of religious organizations are irrelevant to those of the country as a political entity. What is respectful or disrespectful varies from organization to organization. Thus, the standards of one organization should not be applied to another.

Pages 515-517

9. *Novelty.* Although the example sounds as though there is no choice but to face up to this new and unchangeable reality, this argument also strongly implies that this new reality is good simply because it is new. This new reality is an 'opportunity' calling for 'bold' action.

13. *Wishful thinking.* Given the percentage of Afro-Americans in the U.S., it is purely wishful thinking to believe that a black president can be elected by black votes alone, no matter how much some people desire it. The example also contains an instance of a *tu quoque* in that it is claimed that a black president would be no worse than white presidents have been.

Pages 522-524

11. This is not an argument, but a *description* of a series of events and what two people are attempting to do, based on those events.

15. *Questionable cause:* The sole fact that heroin use is statistically correlated with previous marijuana use should not lead one to suppose a causal relation between them. It might be that some third factor causes both. More study of whatever causal mechanisms are involved is needed in order to settle this issue. Note that only marijuana users who 'graduated' to heroin were interviewed. Those who did not are not represented. So it might well be the case that although most heroin users started with marijuana, most marijuana smokers do not move to heroin. Here is a clear case of a biased survey.

Pages 529-531

11. *Question begging.* The duties of the vice-president are defined as 'standing in the shadow of the president'. This begs the question of Bush's performance in that it requires and commands his blind loyalty to President Reagan. This is not the usual definition of the role of the vice-president.

15. *Factual certainty.* The expressions 'absolute, carved-in-stone, 100% true fact' and 'plain, simple, well-known truth' indicate that the arguer wound accept no evidence that weighs against his thesis.